The Complete Woodworker

Edited by Bernard E. Jones

Ten Speed Press

Cover Design by Brenton Beck,
Fifth Street Design Associates
© 1980
Ten Speed Press
P.O. Box 7123
Berkeley, California 94707

All Rights Reserved
ISBN 0-89815-022-1
Library of Congress Catalog Number LC 80-634

EDITOR'S PREFACE

THIS book aims at supplying practical information on the tools and materials, methods, and processes of handcraft woodworking. Two earlier volumes in "The Handcraft Library" cover furniture construction and the preparation of working drawings, the actual practice of woodworking alone being treated in the present addition to the series.

The instruction given in this book covers the selection and use of tools and appliances; sawing, planing, chiselling, and boring; the making of all kinds of joints; the practice of nailing, screwing, gluing, mitre-cutting, and running of mouldings; the making of curved woodwork; the technique of carcase building, table-making, etc.; the methods employed in veneering and inlaying; and the chief processes of finishing woodwork. The information will be found to be easy to follow and to omit nothing of importance; and it is hoped that craftsmen everywhere in the English speaking world will find this volume a satisfactory workshop guide, textbook, and work of reference. The index contains upwards of fourteen hundred entries.

The one thousand illustrations include practical diagrams, working drawings, and about a hundred photographs, a large proportion of the last mentioned having been especially taken by myself.

Two features of the volume are attempts to make good certain omissions in the general literature of woodworking. For example, one chapter provides detailed and lavishly illustrated instructions on the use of the best pattern of the Stanley universal plane, an American tool which has attained general popularity, and with regard to which there come frequent requests for information as to how it should be used. Aeroplane construction is the subject of a particularly up-to-date chapter which is concerned with a branch of woodworking of tremendous importance and of peculiar craft interest.

This book cannot be said to be "by" any author or authors in particular, but in spite of that, I am happy in being able to make a few acknowledgments. For much of the information on the shapes, selection, and sharpening of tools the book is indebted to Messrs. A. Claydon, C. S. Taylor, and L. J. Warner ; on bench selection and bench making, to Messrs. C. W. D. Boxall and E. W. Cunnington; on processes of shaping wood and the making of joints, to Mr. C. W. D. Boxall; on carcase building and table making, to Mr. John Bovingdon ; on aeroplane construction and propeller making, to Messrs. Sydney Camm and E. Wilson; on the construction of a number of typical examples of woodwork, to Mr. R. S. Bowers; and on a number of further matters, to other writers whose names are too many to be mentioned. To them all I express my deep obligations. I wish, also, to acknowledge the courtesy of the Stanley Rule and Level Company in placing a great deal of special information at my disposal, and also to thank Messrs. R. S. Bowers and E. W. Cunnington for their trouble in preparing some hundreds of the diagram illustrations. The very valuable list of woods towards the end of the book has been abbreviated from a more extensive catalogue especially prepared by Prof. G. S. Boulger, F.L.S. ; it was thought wise to render it of utility to readers all over the world by including in it particulars of American, English, Colonial, and other timbers.

B. E. J.

CONTENTS

Contents

The Complete Woodworker

CHAPTER I

The Woodworker's Tools

Whilst the reader of this book will naturally be interested in producing work of reasonably good quality and finish, he may be reminded that sound although rather rough work in wood can be done with but few tools. Much can be accomplished with saw, hammer, and rule, and the third of these even is not essential. If circumstances were such that a piece of work had to be done with the smallest possible number of tools, it would be better to replace the rule with a chisel, and the hammer with a hatchet. The woodworker—particularly the beginner—often uses the phrase "a set of tools." Now, there is no such thing as a complete set of woodworking tools, because what is complete for some kinds of work is insufficient or unsuitable for others. In most tools there are variations in size to suit them for different work ; some vary in form for the same reason, and beyond a limited number which are useful to any worker in wood, there are a great many which are useful only to a specialist in some particular class of work. Generally, therefore, it is better for a beginner to purchase his tools singly, or two or three at a time as required, rather than a large number at once, some of which he may afterwards find he rarely or never uses and which may become spoiled by rust.

Woodworking tools are classed as marking tools, testing tools, cutting tools, driving tools, and holding or cramping tools, and each class includes a number of special tools for particular purposes. The descriptions of the various tools to be given in this chapter will vary according to

B

their importance ; some tools of an elementary character will be dismissed in a few lines, and the more interesting tools will be treated at greater length. In striving to prevent this chapter from degenerating into a mere catalogue, mention of many special kinds of well-known tools has been intentionally omitted, it being always remembered

Fig. 1.—Marking Gauge   Fig. 4.—Marking Awl

Fig. 2.—Mortise Gauge

Fig. 6.—Boxwood Rule

Fig. 5.—Wing Compasses

Fig. 3.—Marking Awl and Knife

Fig. 6A.—Steel Rule

Fig. 7.—Try-square

Fig. 9.—Spirit Level

Fig. 8.—Bevel

that most readers can obtain copies of illustrated tool lists at no expense and little trouble.

TOOLS FOR MARKING, MEASURING AND TESTING

Pencil and Chalk Line.—Tools for marking out the size and shape of work vary considerably. For rough purposes the pencil is often all that is used, but for good and accurate work the pencil is employed only for marks that indicate measurements that are not to be cut. The pencil is convenient for marking on the rough board with the aid of a straightedge, but on a long plank having a dusty and darkened surface the chalk line is essential.

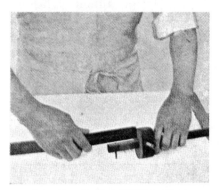

Fig. 10.—Setting Marking Gauge

This is used by the workers in the heavy timber trades as well as by the craftsman, and consists of a fine cord rubbed and filled with chalk and then stretched where required, close to the plank, by the worker and his assistant. It is then lifted and suddenly released (" snapped "), leaving a straight line in chalk on the work. This job can be done single-handed by first making a small saw-cut at the end of the plank in which the cord can be caught, a knot being made at the end of the line to prevent its slipping.

Gauges.—The marking gauge (Fig. 1) is used to make an accurate mark parallel to the planed edge or side of a piece of wood for the purpose of obtaining the width, thickness, or depth of a groove, etc. It is generally made of beechwood, and has a movable stock which, by means of a thumbscrew, is clamped to the stem at the required distance from the sharp spur or point (*see* Fig. 10).

Fig. 11.—Using Marking Gauge

The beginner may experience some difficulty in using this tool, and is advised to practise constantly with it. Generally it is used with the left hand (*see* Fig. 11), this being the more convenient and speedier method when planing, the planed side or edge of the work being invariably next to the craftsman. The division of the fingers should be noticed in the photograph (Fig. 11) ; the thumb is behind the spur, the forefinger on the stock, and the three other fingers on the stem of the tool, the human hand naturally dividing in this manner. The line is obtained by pushing (not pulling) the gauge, probably three strokes being necessary, and care must be taken to keep the stock tightly against the side of the wood. There is a wrist movement

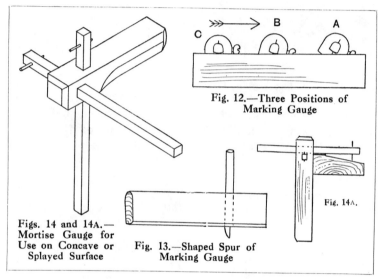

Fig. 12.—Three Positions of Marking Gauge

Fig. 14A.

Figs. 14 and 14A.— Mortise Gauge for Use on Concave or Splayed Surface

Fig. 13.—Shaped Spur of Marking Gauge

necessary whilst gauging, to cause the tooth to enter well into the wood. Fig. 12 shows the positions of the gauge in the first, second, and third strokes, A, B, and C, and it will be noted that the spur is given a dragging movement so that it cannot stick into the wood. The spur should not project farther than $\frac{1}{16}$ in., and if filed to the shape shown in Fig. 13 will assist the worker's endeavours to keep the stock tightly against the side of the wood.

A panel gauge is sometimes required for wide boards, and is generally made by the workman himself, on the same principle as the marking gauge, but with a larger stem. Being a tool for temporary use, it can be made of hard wood with a tight-fitting stock, and will not then require a set-screw.

The ebony mortise gauge (Fig. 2) is used for marking two lines simultaneously as required in mortise and tenon joints, etc. There is one fixed and one movable tooth or spur, the latter being adjusted (*see* Fig. 15, and for detailed explanation p. 154) before the stock is set, being then tightened with a screwdriver. A handy mortise gauge often used by carriage builders is shown in Fig. 14. It should be made of hard wood, the stock being 4 in. or 5 in. long and about 1½ in. square. The stems are ⅝ in. square and made to fit tightly. With this tool the lines are not marked simultaneously, but the narrower stock enables one to use it on a concave surface, and the length of the stock prevents the gauge tilting over out of square.

Fig. 15.—Setting Mortise Gauge to Width of Chisel

With the aid of a longer spur, sometimes a bradawl blade, the tool can be used on a surface that is rebated or bevelled, as shown in Fig. 14A.

When a line is required in any other direction than parallel with the edge of a piece of wood it is marked with a marking knife or marking awl. These can be obtained in combination (as in Fig. 3), with a brass cap to protect the point. The handled marking awl (Fig. 4) is particularly useful for scribing through holes, in recesses, etc.

The compasses most suitable for woodwork are adjusted by means of a wing and thumbscrew, as in Fig. 5. Should the points become blunt they must be ground on the outside to ensure their being in contact when closed.

Rules.—Very little need be said about rules. There are many kinds, of steel, brass and boxwood, and they are marked in various divisions of an inch, also on the metric system of measurement. A rule with $\frac{1}{8}$ in. and $\frac{1}{16}$ in. divisions is necessary for woodwork, and a 2-ft. four-fold boxwood rule (Fig. 6) will be found all-sufficient, though 2-ft. folding steel rules (Fig. 6A) will also be found first-rate for general work; they should be two-fold, with a spring stop joint when unfolded.

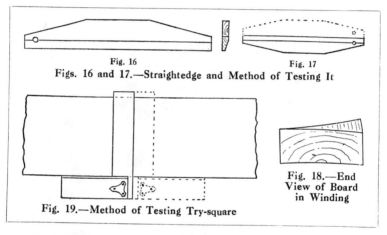

Fig. 16

Fig. 17

Figs. 16 and 17.—Straightedge and Method of Testing It

Fig. 18.—End View of Board in Winding

Fig. 19.—Method of Testing Try-square

Straightedges.—A straightedge (Fig. 16) of convenient size should be made for ordinary use, and almost any kind of well-seasoned wood is suitable, mahogany and walnut being usually favoured; it needs to be about 2 ft. 6 in. long, of 3-in. by $\frac{1}{2}$-in. material, and bevelled on one side to about $\frac{1}{4}$ in. in thickness, as in the section. Fig. 17 shows the method of testing the edge for straightness. Draw a line by its aid, turn over the straightedge (*see* dotted lines), and draw a line over the first one. Then if the two lines coincide, the edge is straight. See that the ends are not reversed, the straightedge being simply folded over as if hinged to the line.

When trueing up the face side of a piece of wood with

a plane, it is often found that the surface is slightly twisted ; the use of a straightedge might not detect the winding or twist, although a skilled worker with a trained eye might be able to discover it on the end view as Fig. 18 (exaggerated). Winding sticks are used to detect the fault, as explained later on p. 90, these sticks being generally about 16 in. long and of $1\frac{3}{4}$-in. by $\frac{1}{2}$-in. material ; sometimes a piece of bone or sycamore is let in near the ends on the upper edges so that any error in the timber can the more readily be seen.

Fig. 20.—Squaring Across a Board

Squares. — The try-square (Fig. 7) has an ebony stock with a steel blade fixed at a right angle. It is used for " trying " or testing the wood for squareness, and is also used to obtain the square line on the wood as shown in the photograph (Fig. 20). The division of the fingers for gripping the tool and the material is the same as with the gauge. Squaring a line round the four sides of a piece of wood cannot be done accurately unless two of the four lines are drawn with the stock kept against the face side or the face edge of the work. The best method of testing the accuracy of the try-square will be gathered from Fig. 19. The board upon which the line is drawn should have a perfectly straight edge. By reversing the try-square the lines should coincide if the angle is 90°. The worker should possess a large and a small try-square, a handy small size being one with a 6-in. blade.

Bevels.—The bevel, as shown in Fig. 8, is used for testing and transferring any angle except a right angle. The blade can be lengthened by means of the slot, and when adjusted to the required angle is tightened with a screw. The angle required is generally struck out geometrically on a board, and the bevel set from the edge of the board and the screw tightened. The bevel can also be set from a protractor. There is a similar tool to the try-square

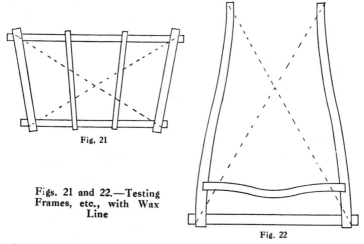

Fig. 21

Figs. 21 and 22.—Testing Frames, etc., with Wax Line

Fig. 22

and bevel which is fixed at 45°, and is useful for mitres of picture frames, moulding, etc., but one is not advised to buy such a tool unless it is especially required, as the ordinary bevel will do what is required.

Spirit Level.—In erecting fittings, a spirit level (Fig. 9) will be useful. It consists of a bent glass tube, mounted in a long, narrow, and true block, almost full of water or spirit. The air bubble occupies a central position when the level is placed on a perfectly horizontal surface.

Wax Line.—The list of testing implements may conclude with a note on the wax line (a cord waxed to prevent stretching), which is generally used by cart or van builders for setting out and testing framing. The principle of its use is that the diagonals of any symmetrical figure are equal. For example, a frame the shape of Fig. 21 or Fig. 22 can be easily tested with the wax line, as can also any pieces that are symmetrically curved. It is often impossible to make long timbers, especially of hard wood, perfectly straight, which means that the shoulders of the joints, if marked

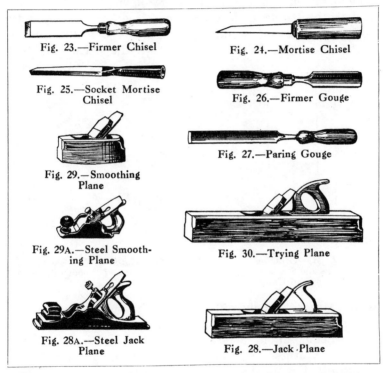

Fig. 23.—Firmer Chisel

Fig. 24.—Mortise Chisel

Fig. 25.—Socket Mortise Chisel

Fig. 26.—Firmer Gouge

Fig. 27.—Paring Gouge

Fig. 29.—Smoothing Plane

Fig. 29A.—Steel Smoothing Plane

Fig. 30.—Trying Plane

Fig. 28A.—Steel Jack Plane

Fig. 28.—Jack Plane

with a try-square, would not give a rectangular frame when jointed together ; hence the use of the wax line for such frames as the bottoms of vans and carts. The worker requires his mate to assist when using the line, and steady adjustment is required until the diagonals are of equal measurement.

PARING TOOLS

Cutting tools may be divided into three divisions, namely, (1) paring tools, which reduce the wood by removing shavings ; (2) rasping tools, which cut the material by means of a number of serrations or teeth, producing small particles of dust ; and (3) boring tools, with cutters so arranged as to remove the material by a circular paring action.

Chisels.—The chisel is the simplest of the paring tools, others being but a modification of it. It is a piece of steel ground off on one side to a wedge of 20° to 25°, an angle sufficiently strong and yet acute enough to penetrate the material. For soft wood the angle may be 20°, and for hard wood 25°. At the extreme edge, the sharpening angle

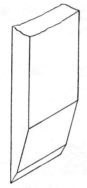

Fig. 31.—Grinding Angle and Sharpening Angle of Chisel

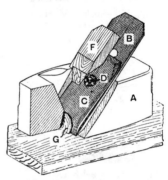

Fig. 32.—Cut-away View showing Construction of Wooden Plane

is 10° larger, namely, 30° to 35°, to give the edge more strength, the two angles—the grinding angle and the setting or sharpening angle—being clearly shown in Fig. 31. Chisels vary in stoutness according to the purpose for which they are required, from the paring chisel with its thin long blade, the firmer chisel, the coachmaker's chisel with its thicker blade, to the very heavy and strong mortise chisel for the harder and rougher wear. The common firmer chisel (Fig. 23) can be obtained in sizes from $\frac{1}{16}$ in. to 2 in. Fig. 24 shows the joiner's mortise chisel, now largely superseded by the socket mortise chisel (Fig. 25), which has a different kind of fixing for the handle ; instead of the blade being shouldered and having a tang that fits into the handle, the blade is made with a strong funnel-shaped ferrule to take a cone-shaped handle. Mortise chisels can be obtained in sizes from $\frac{1}{4}$ in. to $\frac{3}{4}$ in. Other chisels adapted for particular purposes are but modifications of those here mentioned.

The method of using the paring or firmer chisel is dealt with at length in Chapter **VI**. Briefly, in holding it for horizontal paring, the end of the handle butts against the palm of the hand and the fingers are divided as explained before. The left hand covers the blade of the chisel and guides the direction of the cut. In vertical paring, the four fingers grasp the handle, and the thumb is placed on top to prevent the hand slipping ; the left hand holds the work firmly on the bench and also guides the blade with the forefinger. The width of the chisel used should, when possible, be such as to allow of a sliding cut, with which there is less resistance, and the surface obtained is smoother.

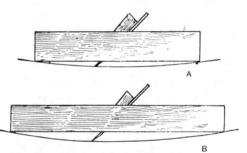

Fig. 33.—Truth of Surface Dependent upon Projection of Cutter and Length of Plane

Gouges.—These are chisels with concave blades. Fig. 26 shows a firmer gouge which is ground or bevelled on the outside. It can be obtained in sizes from $\frac{1}{4}$ in. to $1\frac{1}{2}$ in. wide, and it is used for making hollow cylindrical grooves. In use, the tool is not given a direct forward thrust, but is made to proceed by a series of levering movements, so allowing the worker to keep full control of the gouge and preventing it from drawing in. Fig. 27 shows a paring or scribing gouge, made in sizes from $\frac{1}{8}$ in. to 1 in. in width. It is ground on the inside. One or two of the intermediate sizes, such as $\frac{3}{8}$ in. and $\frac{3}{4}$ in., are sufficient for general work. It is used for paring end grain, and is held in the same way as for vertical chiselling. A kind of gouge used for cutting out curved depressions is bent in its length and ground on the outside like a firmer gouge.

In a later chapter instructions will be found on sharpening chisels and gouges.

Planes.—The plane is a chisel held in a block and so applied as to remove a more or less continuous shaving. A cut-away view, showing the principle of any wooden plane, is presented by Fig. 32, A being the stock, B the cutting iron (the chisel that does the work), C the back iron or break iron, D the screw and nut for fastening the two irons together, and F the wedge that holds the irons in position. A shaving, G, is shown entering the "mouth" of the plane. To obtain a true surface the chisel-like blade has to be made as wide as possible, due consideration being given to the difficulty of pushing it through the material; and it has been found that a plane iron $2\frac{1}{2}$ in. to $2\frac{3}{4}$ in. wide is the limit which will allow full control of the plane.

Planes are used for making surfaces first true and then smooth. The jack plane, which is the essential plane, makes the surface approximately true and moderately smooth. But when smoothness is the chief object, which is the case after other planes have done their work, the plane should be necessarily a small one, and is then known as a smoothing plane. If it is desired to smooth up a rough board and truth is of no consequence, the small plane, which will sink into the hollow places, is again essential, since a large plane merely cuts off the higher portions. From these facts is deduced the principle that the larger the plane the truer is the surface that it makes. This principle would apply as well if the plane could be given breadth as well as length, but the breadth is limited by the width of the cutting iron which a person can work.

The relation between the amount of projection of the cutting iron and the length of the plane is also a factor in producing a true surface. A jack plane set with a cutting iron projecting $\frac{1}{1000}$ in. will make an edge truer than will a trying plane set $\frac{1}{500}$ in.: for example, see A and B (Fig. 33), which show the projections very much exaggerated.

The longest planes made are known as panel planes, and are used for planing the edges of panels; they are about 3 ft. long, but since the advent of woodworking machinery are rarely to be seen in use. The jack plane is shown in Fig. 28, and is made in sizes from 14 in. to 17 in. in length, the cutting irons being from 2 in. to $2\frac{3}{8}$ in. in width. The smoothing plane (Fig. 29) is made in various sizes, a convenient width being one with a 2-in. or $2\frac{1}{8}$-in. iron. The

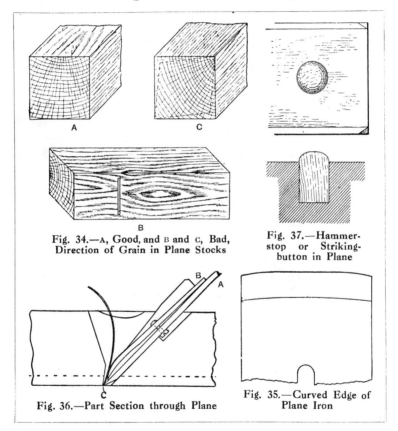

Fig. 34.—A, Good, and B and C, Bad, Direction of Grain in Plane Stocks

Fig. 37.—Hammer-stop or Striking-button in Plane

Fig. 36.—Part Section through Plane

Fig. 35.—Curved Edge of Plane Iron

trying or trueing plane (Fig. 30) can be obtained in lengths from 20 in. to 24 in. and with irons $2\frac{1}{4}$ in. to $2\frac{1}{2}$ in. wide. There are longer trying planes, known as jointers', made up to 30 in. in length and $2\frac{3}{4}$ in. irons, such tools being used only for special work.

The stocks of planes are made of beech wood, which should be cut square with the tree as at A (Fig. 34); the long grain should be as straight as possible, the end of the plane showing the annual layers running nearly parallel with the face, and the medullary rays perpendicular to it ; the layers nearest the heart should be at the top surface of the plane. A plane with the face or sole having heart grain, as illustrated at B, should be avoided, as it indicates that the stock has been cut from a log of crooked growth, this causing the face to wear unevenly, and rendering the stock liable to warp. Plane stocks that have been so cut from the log that the grain on the end appears as illustrated at c become untrue in time, contracting and expanding in the manner indicated by the dotted lines.

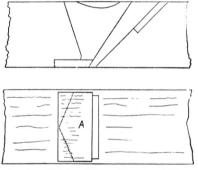

Fig. 38.—Piecing Worn Mouth of Plane

The beech should have been split from the log, and have been properly steamed and seasoned, to prevent warping and twisting, so that the plane may remain true.

It should be said that some of the best and most accurate planes obtainable are made of steel. They are more expensive than wooden planes, and have a number of refinements which make their use very convenient, but they require to be taken great care of and to be kept oiled (and preferably in a close-fitting drawer) to prevent the formation of rust. Typical planes of this type are shown in Figs. 28A and 29A.

The cutting action of the plane will now be considered. The cutting " iron " (the cutting edge is a thin layer of steel) is ground and sharpened at the same angle as a chisel, the two angles being not less than 20° and 30° respectively, but instead of being straight across the width like the chisel, it has the corners very slightly rounded off to prevent their digging into the wood. Fig. 35 shows the shape of the cutting iron when sharpened. The corners are rounded off about $\frac{1}{32}$ in. for a trying and smoothing plane, and $\frac{1}{16}$ in.

Fig. 39.—Striking Jack Plane on Bench to Loosen Wedge

for a jack plane. The bed in which the cutting iron A (Fig. 36) rests is inclined at 45°. The cap iron B, sometimes called a break iron, is attached by screws, and does not quite reach the cutting edge, being $\frac{1}{16}$ in. away from it for trying and smoothing planes and $\frac{1}{8}$ in. away for jack planes. The break iron B deals with the shaving immediately it has been cut, by breaking the fibres, destroying the stiffness of the shaving, and so assisting its passage through the plane and facilitating the working of the tool. The smallness of the mouth c is a check on the splitting action of the plane; the wood in front of the mouth holds down the material until it is cut, thus giving the shaving a gauged thickness.

When the mouth of a plane becomes wide through wear or the retrueing of the face, there is a greater splitting action, and consequently the tool

Fig. 40.—Loosening Wedge of Jack Plane by a Hammer Blow

Fig. 41.—Loosening Wedge of Smoothing Plane by Hammer Blow on Back End

is more difficult to manipulate. After a plane has been in use many years it is shallower and the mouth is wider. Supposing the plane in Fig. 36 to be worn down to the dotted line, it is obvious that the width of the mouth is increased, because of the vee shape of the escapement. An enlarged mouth is remedied by piecing, which can be done as in Fig. 38, and will make the tool work as good as new. Piecing or remouthing consists in letting a piece of wood into the face or sole, as shown in cross section and also in underneath plan by Fig. 38. A is a piece of boxwood, $\frac{1}{2}$ in. thick, of the shape shown by the solid or the dotted lines in plan. It is laid on the face of the plane so as to project over the mouth, marked round with a steel point, and the face recessed to the marks with brace and bits and chisel, making every effort to get a tight fit. The piece is glued in, first scoring it with saw or chisel so that the glue may get a good hold. Cramp up, allow to dry thoroughly for a day or so, and then clean up. Remouthing is frequently necessary in the case of old planes bought second-hand, and will be found to repay all the time and trouble involved.

Fig. 42.—Unscrewing Cutting Iron from Back Iron

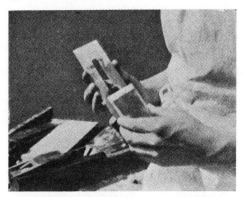

Fig. 43.—Separating Cutting Iron from Back Iron

What is known as a hammer-stop or striking - button is shown in Fig. 37. It is a hardwood plug inserted in the top surface of a jack plane or trying plane between the mouth and the front end; in the case of a smoothing plane it is inserted in the vertical front end. It receives the hammer blows in loosening the iron, and obviates damage to the wood of the plane. A hole the correct diameter and depth is bored, the plug lightly glued and driven in, and its top end rounded off.

The methods of removing the cutting iron, taking apart for sharpening, reassembling and adjusting are of great importance, and will now be explained. The actual sharpening will be left for a later chapter. To remove the iron, hold the back of the stock in the left hand and grasp the wedge and irons with the right, holding them as shown in Fig. 39, the toe of the stock being raised about 9 in. to 1 ft. above the bench. Then strike the bench top (or a hard wood block) with the stock, and if done smartly the wedge and irons will be released from the stock. An easier method is to grasp the stock with the left hand, the fingers reaching to the face of the plane and the left thumb being in-

Fig. 43A.—Adjusting Edges of Cutting Iron and Back Iron

c

Fig. 44.—Inserting Wedge in Jack Plane

serted in the throat and pressing on the iron. Then, with two or three smart blows with the hammer (on the hammer-stop if one has been fitted), the iron and wedge will be gradually released, and the operator can judge when to discontinue striking (*see* Fig. 40).

Smoothing planes are generally treated differently, the plane being held in the left hand as shown in Fig. 41 (p. 16), and being then struck a blow with the hammer on its back end, thus loosening the wedge.

For separating the irons, the screw seldom requires more than a complete turn with a screwdriver (Fig. 42). The cutting iron should be held by its edges between the fingers and thumb of the right hand, and the edges of the back iron or break iron between those of the left hand. The two irons are then, as in Fig. 43, carefully slipped apart.

The cutting iron, having been sharp-

Fig. 45.—Sighting for Projection of Iron

Fig. 46.—Tightening Wedge with Hammer

ened, must be again secured to the back iron. Take the former in the right hand and the back iron in the left hand, slide them together and adjust their edges as in Fig. 43A, so that the edge of the back iron is $\frac{3}{32}$ in. from the edge of the cutting iron, the exact distance varying with the kind of work, type of plane, etc. Hold the irons between the thumb and fingers of the left hand, tighten up the set-screws with the right hand, and finish the work with the screwdriver.

For setting the irons in the stock, hold the stock by the left hand, the four fingers being on the face of the plane whilst the thumb is far into the throat of the plane ready for pressing and holding the irons, the latter being regulated by the right hand, so that the cutting edge projects evenly. This effected, hold the irons firmly in position with the left thumb. With the right hand pick

Fig. 47.—Slightly Adjusting Iron with Hammer

up the wedge, and simultaneously rotate the plane forward
with the left hand, and push the wedge firmly into position,
as shown in Fig. 44. Next rotate back the plane so that
the worker can look down its face (*see* Fig. 45) to see if
any further slight adjustment is necessary, bring it to the
horizontal position, and immediately strike the wedge
smartly once or twice with a hammer (*see* Fig. 46, in which
figure the presence of the wooden bench-hook under the
plane is accidental and has no part in the operation). Again
look down the face, and if there is too much iron projecting, rectify it by tapping the stock on the front or toe,
instantly afterwards tapping the wedge tight. If there is
not enough iron projecting, hold the plane as in Fig. 47,
and tap the iron whilst looking down the face of the plane.

Special Planes.—There are many single-iron planes
smaller in size than the foregoing used by workers for making
recesses, grooves, and mouldings for various purposes, and
two or three of these are of sufficient importance to be
dealt with in detail. Other planes for special purposes
will be referred to in later chapters (see Index).

A rebate plane (Fig. 48) is used for making such recesses
as that shown in Fig. 58. The blade is arranged askew
to facilitate the cutting action, and the tool is used so that
the acute foremost point on the right side cuts into the
corner of the recess. The right side of the recess is therefore planed in the opposite direction. When setting the
plane, the acute corner of the blade should project on the
side of the plane about $\frac{1}{32}$ in., so as to obtain a clean-cut
corner to the recess. The iron is released in the same way
as that of a smoothing plane, and the plane is held as though
edge-planing with a jack plane.

A more complicated tool known as a plough, used for
grooving with the grain of the wood, is shown by Fig. 49.
The stock or body, to which the various cutting irons can
be wedged, is attached to a fence block by means of two
stems, which, when the iron is adjusted, are wedged away
from the fence according to the distance of the groove
from the side of the wood.

A fillister (Fig. 50) somewhat resembles a plough and

is held and adjusted in the same manner. It consists of a rebate plane attached to a fence block, and is used for cutting recesses on the farther edge of a piece of wood, as in sash frames, etc., where the recess is a gauged distance from the front edge, as shown in Fig. 58A. Like the plough,

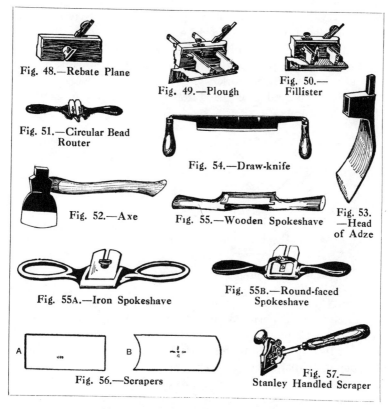

Fig. 48.—Rebate Plane

Fig. 49.—Plough

Fig. 50.—Fillister

Fig. 51.—Circular Bead Router

Fig. 54.—Draw-knife

Fig. 52.—Axe

Fig. 55.—Wooden Spokeshave

Fig. 53.—Head of Adze

Fig. 55A.—Iron Spokeshave

Fig. 55B.—Round-faced Spokeshave

A   B

Fig. 56.—Scrapers

Fig. 57.—Stanley Handled Scraper

it has an adjustable stop which requires to be set to the depth of recess required.

Routers.—These are used for grooving and making recesses for inlaying, and consist of a wooden stock or block in which is wedged a chisel-like blade, whose projection is adjusted according to the depth of groove required. Many routers are made of iron somewhat like, but rather larger than, the spokeshave, and they take cutting irons for beads and mouldings, some of them having adjustable fences, which can be tightened with a screw. The one illustrated (*see* Fig. 51) is a circular bead router, and sufficiently suggests the general shape of this class of tools.

Axes.—Axes vary in size and shape from the heavy, long-handled axe for felling trees to the small hatchet used by firewood choppers. The carpenter's axe (Fig. 52), recommended for general work, weighs $2\frac{1}{2}$ lb. or 3 lb., and is useful not only for splitting up logs and blocks, but for dressing to shape pieces of hard wood such as spokes, fellies, etc., in wheelwright's work.

Adzes.—The adze is used for the trimming of timbers

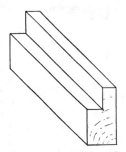

Fig. 58.—Rebate on Near Edge Cut with Rebate Plane

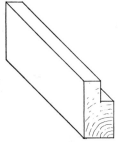

Fig. 58A.—Rebate on Far Edge Cut with Fillister

lying on the ground. Carpenters level floor boards, etc., by its aid, and wheelwrights use it for chopping concave surfaces. The carpenter's adze shown in Fig. 53 has a small hammer-like projection for driving in floor nails should any occur whilst adzing. An expert workman can get a fairly smooth finish with an adze, but it is a tool that is not often required by an amateur woodworker.

Draw-knives.—The draw-knife (Fig. 54) is a very useful tool, especially when dressing curved stuff to shape. The length of blade renders possible the long sliding cut that makes the tool so easy to manipulate. Many craftsmen believe it to be one of the best tools for stop-chamfering. It can be used by pushing away from as well as by drawing toward the worker. The blades are from 8 in. to 12 in. in length, the longer ones being recommended.

Spokeshaves.—These are used for finishing curved surfaces (*see* Fig. 59). The old type of wooden spokeshave made of beech or boxwood, as in Fig. 55, is preferred by some workmen instead of the modern iron ones which are now generally used. With the wooden spokeshaves, the steel blade can be readily reset after sharpening for coarse or fine shavings as required, and the blade is long enough to allow full freedom in varying the fineness of the shaving by using the centre or the outer portions. The improved iron spokeshave (Fig. 55A) has an adjustable mouth for convex surfaces, while the round-faced spokeshave (Fig. 55B) is handy for concave surfaces and for work in general; it has a small break iron which answers the same purpose as the break iron in a plane.

Fig. 59.—Using Spokeshave

Scrapers.—Scrapers (so-called) are actually cutting tools. They are pieces of flat, good quality steel A and B (Fig. 56), having a turned-over edge and in use are held on the slant and pushed away from the worker. They are of great value in clearing up for final surfacing, but require to be sharpened by someone who has grasped the principle on which they work, full instructions being given on pp. 63 to 66, where information on their use is also presented. Special holders for the scrapers are obtainable, these having the advantage that they apply the scraper to the work at the correct angle, one of the best of these holders being the Stanley (Fig. 57). Double-handled scrapers, spokeshave-style, are also made.

RASPING TOOLS

Saws.—A saw is so constructed that while it is strong enough or stiff enough to cut timber without its buckling, it yet produces the minimum amount of waste and requires the minimum of effort to use it. Stiffness is obtained by giving it width in lieu of thickness, and the width increases towards the handle (*see* Fig. 60), where the strain is greatest. With some shorter and narrower saws, the stiffness is obtained by fixing a metal back to the upper edge, as in the tenon

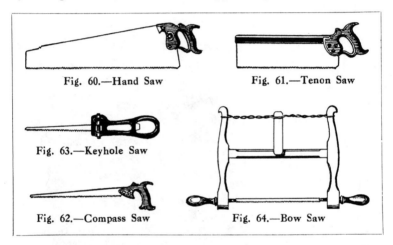

Fig. 60.—Hand Saw   Fig. 61.—Tenon Saw

Fig. 63.—Keyhole Saw

Fig. 62.—Compass Saw   Fig. 64.—Bow Saw

saw (Fig. 61). The back is of brass or iron, and in course of manufacture is folded and closed tightly to the blade. A saw to be used for cutting curves must obviously be narrow ; thus the compass saw (Fig. 62) has a very narrow blade from 10 in. to 18 in. long, a trifle thicker than in other saws, and ground off fairly thin on the back edge. For very sharp curves the blade is used near its point. Keyhole saws (Fig. 63), with adjustable iron handles, have similar blades.

The bow saw is also used for cutting curves ; its construction varies, a usual shape being shown in Fig. 64. The blade being thin and narrow is stiffened by being fixed to a frame which holds it in tension, the two end levers, which pivot at their centres, being pulled together at the top by twisting the cord, thus producing tension on the blade.

Saw teeth have to cut through the maximum length of material with a minimum of resistance; therefore they need to be of strong shape and so arranged that they clear out the waste. For example, Fig. 65 shows teeth that penetrate well but which are not so strong as those in Fig. 66, and would be more liable to be clogged by sawdust than would the second shape shown. The first shape would also draw into the material and, in cutting across the grain,

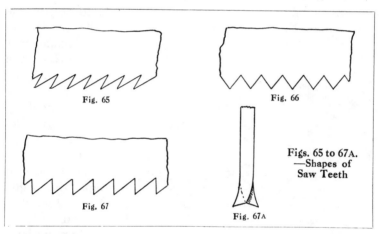

Fig. 65

Fig. 66

Fig. 67

Fig. 67A

Figs. 65 to 67A.
—Shapes of
Saw Teeth

would take too great a bite for the free working of the saw; whereas the second shape would not bite deeply enough without great pressure. Fig. 67 shows a compromise which answers very well; the front of the teeth is about 5° to 10° out of the square, and the point of the tooth, which is the same as the angle between the teeth, is about 65°. Therefore a three-cornered file of 60° fits between the teeth for sharpening.

The teeth of a saw are " set " to give clearance to the blade—that is, alternate teeth are caused to project to the right and left, so giving a double line of cutting points, as illustrated in the section through a saw blade (Fig. 67A). A full-size rip saw for cutting soft wood with the grain has 2½ to 3 teeth to the inch; a half-rip saw about 4 to

the inch; a hand saw for general work about 5 or 6 to the
inch, and a length of not less than 26 in.; a tenon saw
has many more to the inch and a length of from 12 in.
to 16 in.; a smaller but similar-shaped saw, known as a
dovetail saw, has even finer teeth and generally is about
8 in. to 10 in. long. The two sizes of bow saws have blades
8 in. to 12 in. respectively, both sizes being required for
general use.

When using the hand saw and tenon saw, the fingers are
divided as usual—that is, with three fingers on the handle
and the forefinger along the side of handle to steady the
saw. Guide the saw when starting the cut with the thumb
of the left hand just
above the teeth, the
left hand also hold-
ing the wood. The
bow saw is held by
the longer handle,
the fingers divided
as before, and the
left hand partly
overlaps the right
hand (*see* Fig. 68).
Detailed instruc-
tions on using
hand and tenon saws are given in a later chapter.

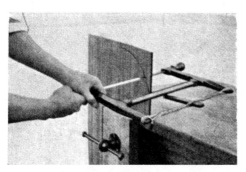

Fig. 68.—Using Bow Saw

Files and Rasps.—Files for wood are generally used on
curved surfaces after the other tools have done their work.
The sliding stroke, forward as well as sideways, ensures
the desired shape in both directions, and any unevenness
is instinctively felt and removed. Two half-round files, one
second-cut and the other smooth, 10 in. and 12 in. long,
will be required; one square and one round bastard-cut
file, both 8 in. long; and a fine-cut flat 6-in. file with a
safe edge. A fine rat's-tail file is useful for sharpening
bits. If saw sharpening is contemplated, one or two 4-in.
three-cornered files should be added.

A rasp is a rough-working tool which does not conduce
to good results, but it is handy at times for rough repairing.

BORING TOOLS

The Brace.—The use of brace and bit, or of a hand-drill and bit, is necessary in boring holes of any size. Even for small holes it is quicker and less fatiguing than the use of a gimlet. The brace is the device by means of which the bits are held and rotated. It may be either a cheap or expensive tool, depending on the type, material and workmanship. It may be a simple thumbscrew brace; almost as simple a tool but with a milled chuck and jaws in place of the tapered hole and thumbscrew; or it may be a device with ball-bearing head and a pawl-and-ratchet gear for convenience in boring holes where there is no room for the full swing of the crank-arm. The reader will get the quality of brace he can afford; in principle they are all alike. That shown in Fig. 69 can be obtained in two or three qualities, with nickel-plate, ball-bearings, etc. A full-size crank of 5 in., making a 10-in. sweep, is desirable. It holds the bits by means of steel spring jaws, which grip when the socket or barrel is screwed up. Ratchet braces are expensive, and an alternative means of boring holes in awkward places is to use a long-arm, sometimes called an extension piece (*see* Fig. 70), which is obtainable in three lengths, 12 in., 18 in., and 24 in., and fits into an ordinary brace.

Hand-drill.—An appliance often possessing advantages over the brace is the hand-drill, which, at any rate for small work, seems likely to oust the more time-honoured device. There is a number of patterns, Fig. 71 being quite typical. The gearing shown allows of the drill or boring bit being rotated at a high speed, and the chuck permits of a variety of bits being employed. Both the amateur and professional woodworker may be well advised to invest in this extremely handy tool. The manner in which it is held is shown in Fig. 85.

Bits.—Sets of bits are generally kept together in cloth or leather rolls, and require special care to ensure the preservation of their cutting qualities. Gedge's twist bits have their cutters in the form of rounded wings or ears (*see* Fig. 72), and are excellent for hard wood; they can be obtained in three lengths, the medium size being generally suitable. The diameters vary from ¼ in. to 1½ in. Jennings' bits (Fig. 73) have winged projecting cutters, and are more suitable for soft wood; they are made in the same sizes as Gedge's bits.

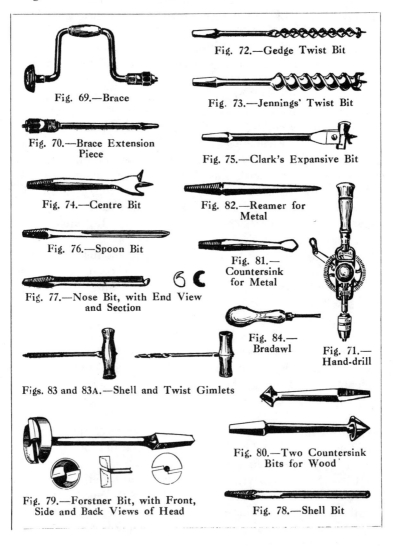

Fig. 69.—Brace

Fig. 72.—Gedge Twist Bit

Fig. 73.—Jennings' Twist Bit

Fig. 70.—Brace Extension Piece

Fig. 75.—Clark's Expansive Bit

Fig. 74.—Centre Bit

Fig. 82.—Reamer for Metal

Fig. 76.—Spoon Bit

Fig. 81.— Countersink for Metal

Fig. 77.—Nose Bit, with End View and Section

Fig. 84.— Bradawl

Fig. 71.— Hand-drill

Figs. 83 and 83A.—Shell and Twist Gimlets

Fig. 80.—Two Countersink Bits for Wood

Fig. 79.—Forstner Bit, with Front, Side and Back Views of Head

Fig. 78.—Shell Bit

Twist bits clear well without having to remove the bit at every few turns, and bore end grain easily. They are largely used for bolt holes, round mortises, etc., and for removing waste of mortises in hard wood. They are rather expensive, and require great care in using, as they are useless if the screwed point is broken off.

Metal gauges for attachment to twist bits are obtainable. They clamp on the bit at any height by means of a wing-nut and bolt, and determine the maximum depth to which a series of holes may be bored. Wooden gauges are easily made by the craftsman himself, as explained in a later chapter.

Centre bits (Fig. 74) are generally used for thinner material, but can be employed on almost any stuff. The projecting vertical cutter (the nicker) enters the wood before the blade (the router), thus giving a clean and smooth hole. It is usual to finish the hole

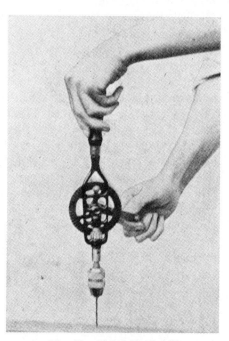

Fig. 85.—Using Hand-drill

from the other side immediately the centre point pierces the wood. These bits are made to cut holes from $\frac{3}{16}$-in. to 2-in. bore. Centre bits are largely used for ornamental work because of their clearness of cut, which leaves a nice clean edge when the hole is bored. They are useful for removing the waste when sinking, or inlaying marquetry work, because they leave a flat surface at the bottom of the hole.

Clark's expansive bits (Fig. 75) are finely made tools;

they have a pointed thread like a twist bit, cut somewhat like a centre bit, and can be adjusted to a nicety for any size of hole. The small size takes two cutters, enabling the worker to bore holes from $\frac{1}{2}$ in. to $1\frac{1}{2}$ in., and the large size takes three or four cutters, boring holes from $\frac{7}{8}$ in. to 4 in. or 5 in.

The three bits known as spoon bits, nose bits, and shell bits are of the same class as one another, and are used for making holes for pins, screws, and sometimes bolts. The spoon bit (Fig. 76) is useful for enlarging holes. The nose bit (Fig. 77), with its small cutter, is suitable for boring end grain, and the shell bit (Fig. 78) is for general use. Spoon and nose bits when damaged or broken can be ground into shell bits. Spoon bits are made in sizes up to $\frac{5}{8}$ in. They are apt to run out of centre when starting ; but the bevelled cutter enables the bit to be worked central if necessary. When using the nose bit it is necessary to start the hole with another bit, as it is difficult to centre.

The Forstner auger bit (Fig. 79) is different from most other bits. It is guided by its circular rim and not by any centre, and is therefore particularly suited when a truly cylindrical hollow or a semi-circular recess is to be produced and finished in one operation. It can be used for boring a groove on the edge or face of work, part of the tool working in air. The hole bored by it is of the same size practically as the bit itself.

Two countersink bits for screw heads in woodwork are shown in Fig. 80 ; a countersink for metal in Fig. 81 ; and a square reamer for enlarging holes in hinges and other fastenings in Fig. 82.

Gimlets.—The gimlet is a true boring tool, and is generally of the shell (Fig. 83) or the twist (Fig. 83A) type, but twist-nose and auger gimlets are in use. It acts well either with or across the grain, but it has a distinct wedge action, and care has to be taken at times to avoid splitting the work.

Bradawls.—The bradawl (Fig. 84) acts by cutting or scraping and partly by wedging the fibres apart, and is not a true boring tool. Its purpose is generally to make a hole for the insertion of a nail (occasionally of a screw), and requires to be used with some amount of thought. If the edge of the bradawl is applied parallel with the grain of the wood, the tool will act as a wedge and possibly split the work (*see* Fig. 86), whereas if the edge of the bradawl lies across the grain the fibres will be cut and splitting obviated, as illustrated. A common method of using a bradawl is to drive it in with the hand, giving the point an oscillating motion; but there is less liability to split the wood if it is driven in by a hammer or mallet with the edge lying across the grain, the work being supported, if necessary, by a piece of waste. A bradawl may be sharpened on a piece of stone.

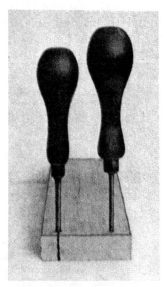

It pays to get a bradawl in which the awl is thoroughly well attached to the handle, the brass-capped variety being, for that reason, the best.

An excellent bradawl for fine holes is a piece of thin knitting needle, sharpened to a wedge point, and fixed in a broach chuck. The chuck can be fixed

Fig. 86.—Bradawls Inserted respectively with and across the Grain

in a bradawl handle, or can be bought complete from tool dealers. Sharpen the needle to an edge, not to a point.

DRIVING TOOLS

Hammers.—Little need be said about these familiar tools. They can be obtained in all sizes and shapes for various purposes, the two patterns generally used by woodworkers being the Warrington (Fig. 87) and the London or Exeter (Fig. 87A). The thin end, known as the pene or pane, is convenient for starting small nails between the

thumb and finger, and also for riveting. Hammer heads
are made of cast steel, and sometimes of iron with a cast-
steel facing. The handles are of ash or beech, and are
fastened on by wedging, the eye of the head being so shaped
as to allow the wedged end to spread. Two different sized
hammers will be required, say a No. 2, weighing about 8 oz.,
and either a No. 5, about 14 oz., or one rather heavier.
For rough outdoor carpentry a much heavier hammer is
found to be desirable.

In fixing a hammer head on a shaft, first shape the shaft

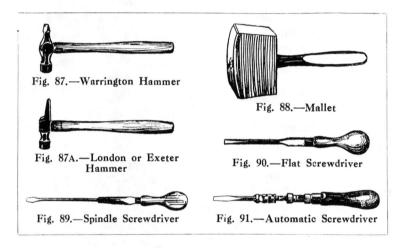

Fig. 87.—Warrington Hammer

Fig. 88.—Mallet

Fig. 87A.—London or Exeter
Hammer

Fig. 90.—Flat Screwdriver

Fig. 89.—Spindle Screwdriver

Fig. 91.—Automatic Screwdriver

to fit the hole, and then make a saw cut in the end, length-
wise of the grain, as long as the head is deep. Drive the
shaft into the hole, and then a wedge of hard wood into the
saw cut. An iron wedge gives a tighter fixing, but it rusts
in time and then works loose ; and a hammer with a loose
head is a dangerous tool.

Mallets.—Wooden hammers (Fig. 88) are used where iron
ones would make bruises or do other damage. Gouge and
chisel handles, wooden pins, etc., should be struck with
mallets, not with hammers. Carpenters' mallets are made
of beech, and the tapered handles are driven in from the
top. The faces are bevelled off so as to give a square blow
to the work, and they form the radial lines of the circular

movement of the tool when swung from the elbow or the shoulder. A medium size, say 5 in., is suitable for most purposes (*see* Fig. 88).

Nail-punch.—The punch or set is used for driving nails below the surface of the work, and is made in two or three sizes, of round or square-section steel, about $4\frac{1}{2}$ in. long, and tapered down to a blunt point, which may be serrated to prevent slipping.

Screwdrivers.—T w o screwdrivers are necessary, one with about a 5-in. blade and the other with a 10-in. The most serviceable patterns are those with spindle blades flattened at the point (*see* Fig. 89), and with flat or oval handles as in Fig. 90. Long screwdrivers with flat blades are not so freely turned when close against a partition or in a crevice. A screwdriver of American design (*see* Fig. 91) has a spiral movement for driving in screws by pressure only, and is

Fig. 92.—Using Automatic Screwdriver

used as shown in Fig. 92. The American mechanic is adept in using this tool, which works on the principle of the Archimedean drill. It answers well with small screws, but most English workers prefer the ordinary screwdriver for stout ones or where there is a great resistance. Another kind has a ratchet, which enables one to turn a screw in or out without releasing the grip of the handle, the turn of the wrist only being required, and such a tool is particularly useful for driving a screw upwards in an inverted

D

position. The combination of a clip with the automatic or ratchet screwdriver (*see* Fig. 93), or screwdriver bit held in a ratchet brace, has advantages at times; in attaching a screw, one hand presses the spring towards the point of the tool, while the fingers of the other hand insert the screw, as illustrated. The tool can be held by one hand only and the screw driven home, the clip generally loosening its hold automatically when the screw is nearly in place; even should it not do so, a slight side pressure on the tool will release the screw.

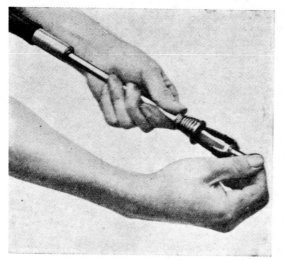

It is often convenient to use a screwdriver bit in a brace. This combination answers well for the removal of stubborn screws, if the screw itself is strong enough to withstand the strain without its head breaking into two.

Fig. 93.—Inserting Screw in Ratchet Screwdriver Clip

Most workers find that a long screwdriver is more easily held in direct line with the axis of the screw than a short one, and is therefore not so liable to come out of the nick, and it is easier to exert the whole of one's strength on a long tool than on a short one. Theoretically, the whole question resolves itself into what is the amount of leverage that can be exerted in turning the screw, and this depends upon the width of the handle in relation to the width of the screw head. But the greater the turning leverage, the greater is the forward pressure required. When a long driver is slightly tilted (as in Fig. 94) in the effort to move a stubborn screw, the top of the handle goes some distance (*see* A) away from an imaginary vertical line running down through the centre of the screw. A short driver could not be safely tilted to a greater angle than a long one ; and therefore the powers of the two tools should be proportionate to the lengths of the lines A and B (Fig. 94).

The shape of the screwdriver point needs consideration. Never sharpen to a rounded shape (Fig. 96), which will slip from the screw head, or to a sharp, thin point, which will break under hard use and damage the screws. Avoid also a point that is wider than the stem, as it is likely to break. The most efficient shape is shown in Fig. 97, but is not often seen in woodworkers' screwdrivers ; there should be no angle on the edge until it is clear of the screw head, so that little

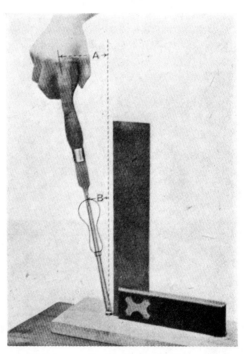

[Fig. 94.—Showing Theoretical Advantage ot Long Screwdriver on Occasion

or no pressure is required to keep the edge of the tool in its place. All the power of the driver is thus available for turning the screw, and this is all the more important when withdrawing a screw that has been in position for some time. The ill-effects of using screwdrivers of poor shape and excessive width are illustrated in Fig. 95. The pointed tool shown at B slips as at C and mutilates the head of the screw, frequently breaking it in two, whereas the square end, as at A, fits snugly and does not slip from the slot. A point of excessive width D tears up the work around the screw head as shown at E, unless tilted as shown at F, when slipping and damage to the screw itself become extremely likely.

HOLDING AND CRAMPING TOOLS

Pincers.—In this tool there is a pair of levers with the pivot or fulcrum so arranged that the force of a hand-grip can be multi-

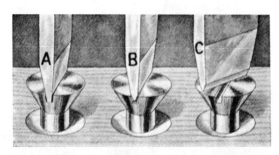
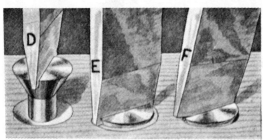

plied enormously, the mechanical advantage obtained being in the same ratio as the lengths of the lever arms measured from the fulcrum. To withdraw a nail another lever is brought into action, the jaws of the pincers acting as a fulcrum, as explained in a later chapter.

Fig. 95.—Effects of Using Screwdrivers of Wrong Shape or Width

The claw on one of the handles is for levering up the head of the nail far enough to obtain a grip with the jaws of the pincers, and can also be used for removing tacks. On the other handle is a cone (*see* Fig. 98) or in some patterns a ball.

Cramps, bench holdfasts, etc., are dealt with in later chapters, and some simple methods of cramping-up work will there be found treated in detail.

SELECTION AND CARE OF TOOLS

Tool Steel.—There are some terms met with, in turning over the pages of a tool catalogue, which convey no information whatever. Such, for example, is the description " silver steel." It had some meaning early in the nineteenth century, when the Sheffield cutlers adopted for their finest razors and instruments a steel which had been alloyed with one five-hundredth part of silver; but such steel is only a curiosity nowadays, and certainly mechanics'

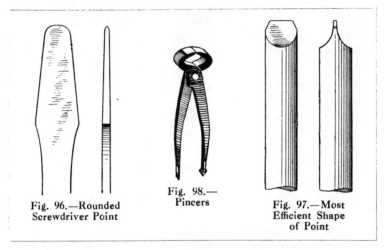

Fig. 96.—Rounded
Screwdriver Point

Fig. 98.—
Pincers

Fig. 97.—Most
Efficient Shape
of Point

tools are not made of it. The trade custom is to apply the term to any tool steel of bright appearance.

In the old days it was necessary to distinguish between crucible steel and a material manufactured by heating Swedish iron in contact with charcoal until the iron was converted, or partly converted, into steel of a somewhat uneven character. Best steel tools are now always made of " crucible cast steel," whatever may be the description stamped on them; while low-quality tools are made of the poorest grades of steel, and the term " warranted cast steel," which the products of third-rate firms often bear, is a trade convention, and does *not* mean that they are guaranteed to be manufactured from high-grade material.

In selecting edged tools, see that the bright parts are of an even colour, free from specks or spots, small holes, or flaws. When sharpening them, very little " wire edge " should appear ; but if none at all is seen, possibly the steel may have been hardened too much, and will then be brittle. Saw blades, also, should be of a bright, even colour, without patches, and free from specks or flaws ; see that the handles are well fitted and firmly fastened with screw rivets to the blades.

Care of Tools.—Chisels, gouges, plane irons, bits, etc., are easily ruined by rust, which, even when removed, leaves a pitted surface. Tools should be kept in the driest place available and wiped with an oily rag occasionally. If in daily use, these precautions may be somewhat neglected, and, ordinarily, rust will not appear ; the bright surfaces may become dark, but they will remain smooth and free from rust. Rust is most serious when it affects cutting edges. A hammer or hatchet may be extremely rusty, and none the worse for it except in appearance. A saw may be rusty and be little the worse after the rust is rubbed off and the surface oiled. Steel squares, compasses, etc., and other non-cutting tools may not be much injured by rust, but precautions should be taken against it unless the tools are in constant use.

Edge tools should not be kept in a bass or basket. It is better to hang up saws and arrange chisels and other tools in racks. All tools should be sufficiently cleaned to maintain them in good order and appearance, and this may be done by occasionally damping a piece of cotton waste or rag with sweet oil (not linseed) or a little vaseline, and rubbing the steel parts. The wooden parts of tools should be occasionally rubbed with cotton waste or rag moistened with linseed oil, taking care not to leave any superfluous oil on the surfaces, as it is liable to become sticky. In the case of new planes it is a good plan to soak them well with linseed oil a short time before using, and then, by well rubbing the surfaces, a dull finish is obtained, and by following this with an occasional rub, the surfaces are kept clean and in good condition. Some people oil a new plane by removing the wedge and irons, stopping up the mouth on the face with putty, and then filling the mouth with linseed oil, leaving it until the oil exudes from the pores at the ends of the stock ; it is allowed to dry, and then polished with friction.

The utility of a tool box-chest is a moot point. To the worker who has room to display his tools in racks in a dry and well-ventilated room, and does not require to move them from place to place, the box offers few advantages. At the same time, however, any expensive tools of iron or steel not likely to be often used are far better kept in a chest or drawer than in an open rack, and it is here that the advantage of a pedestal of somewhat shallow drawers comes in. It is obvious that a mere box or chest with few or no interior fittings is unsuitable for tools that are frequently

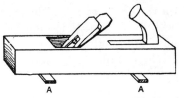

Fig. 99.—Plane Laid on Wooden Strips to Prevent Injury

required, and that if a box is used it should be shallow and provided with trays. A cabinet with drawers is convenient for small tools, and drawers in the bench itself are useful ; indeed, in most cases, ample accommodation can be provided by drawers in the bench, and a simple method of fitting them is to hang them by their upper edges to runners screwed to the under side of the bench top. When planes are laid by on their sides they are liable to have odd tools knocked up against them, to the injury of their faces and cutting edges, and it is safer to lay them on skeleton racks or on strips such as those shown at A in Fig. 99.

CHAPTER II

BENCHES

VERY little serious work can be done in the absence of a bench, the choice of which will depend largely upon the outlay permitted and the space available. Tool dealers' catalogues show many patterns and sizes, to suit all requirements, and in the present chapter three good types will be illustrated—one of them in complete detail—and particulars given also of a bench screw attachment for a kitchen table. It should be pointed out that an ordinary

Fig. 100.—Plain Bench with Instantaneous-grip Vice

kitchen table is not rigid enough for planing on, and, like small benches, is not heavy enough to remain in a fixed position on the floor during planing; it is best to place the front end against a wall and use the plane sufficiently far back to avoid striking the wall with it.

Readers in a position to buy a bench ready made should choose one with a tail vice and spring or cam stops. Good stops are extremely useful for holding pieces of wood in position; in addition, a side vice saves time and trouble.

Some benches are fitted with two boxes for bench screw and runner, so that the same cheek and runner can be used for side vice and tail vice, and the lower part of the bench may be filled in with cupboards and drawers (*see* Fig. 101), there being over the cupboards but below the bench top a well or shelf where a few of the tools may be kept handy, so that their edges do not touch. A plain bench of a kind often favoured by professional workers is shown in Fig. 100; inside rails would increase its rigidity.

Constructing Rigid and Portable Bench.—An excellent

Fig. 101.—Bench with Cupboard and with Fittings for Two Vices

portable bench is shown by Fig. 102, the front and end elevations being given by Figs. 103 and 104. It is quite rigid when in use, and easily erected or taken down in about five minutes. As shown in Figs. 105 and 106, the legs are made in pairs, connected at the bottom by two rails. The top (Fig. 107) is in one piece, with clamping bars across for the legs to fit between, and the vice and peg board are also separate pieces, placed in position after the other parts have been assembled. The dimensions may be varied to suit special requirements, but the general proportions here given should be preserved. The height is important (as drawn, it is 2 ft. 6 in.), and naturally depends on the height of the workman, a good reach over the work being an advantage.

The method of constructing the bench will be here explained ; but the work should not, of course, be attempted until later chapters have been mastered and some amount of skill attained.

Fig. 102.—Portable Bench with Peg Board

The wood used may be red deal, but at least the first board of the top, and the vice cheek, should be of better stuff, such as beech or birch. The legs are 3 in. square, and need to be planed up square and true, and then mortised as in Fig. 108. Each pair is connected together with rails, the top one being $3\frac{1}{2}$ in. wide by 2 in. thick, and the bottom one 3 in. wide by 2 in. thick ; and after gluing up and wedging the bottom rail, they should be further strengthened with a dowel pin or screw through each joint. A good fit is necessary to ensure rigidity. The two pairs of legs are now mortised at the front and back to receive the movable rails, each mortise being $3\frac{1}{2}$ in. long, and 7 in. from the bottom, on the outside of the leg, and $2\frac{3}{4}$ in. long and

$7\frac{1}{2}$ in. from the bottom of the inside of the leg. This mortise allows the rail when in position to be held firm with a wedge, as shown in section by Fig. 109. The front and back rails are finished to $2\frac{3}{4}$ in. wide by $1\frac{1}{2}$ in. thick, and a bare-faced tenon (a tenon having a shoulder on one side

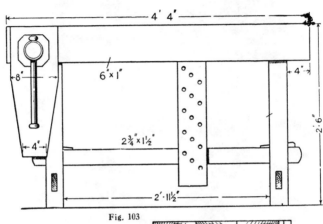

Fig. 103

Figs. 103 and 104.—Front and End Elevations of Portable Bench

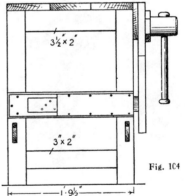

Fig. 104

only) $5\frac{1}{2}$ in. long should be worked on both ends of each; they should then be cut to fit the mortise in the leg, as shown in Fig. 109.

The top of the bench is 1 ft. $9\frac{1}{2}$ in. wide, and is made up of three boards grooved and tongued together, with three 5 in. clamping pieces screwed underneath, as shown in Fig. 107, so that they fit tight against the outside of the legs. Further, to hold the legs in position, four small blocks should be fixed on the inside of the legs. The bench cheek is formed out of a 6-in. by 1-in. board, and is fixed to the edge of the top with stout screws, the holes being previously countersunk.

Fig. 105.—Framework of
Portable Bench

Fig. 106.—Legs at Left End
of Bench, with Screw Block,
Runner, etc., attached

Fig. 107.—Underneath View of Bench Top

The bench screw requires most careful fitting. The
screw should be purchased complete with handle and a
hardwood block or nut. The block needs to be cut to
the shape shown by Fig. 110, and is then fitted to the top
of the leg with two coach screws (*see* Fig. 106); the ½-in.
tenon A in the block is intended to fit in a slot cut on the
underside of the bench top to ensure rigidity. A hole
should next be cut in the bench cheek, to correspond with
that in the block; and, in order to form the vice cheek,

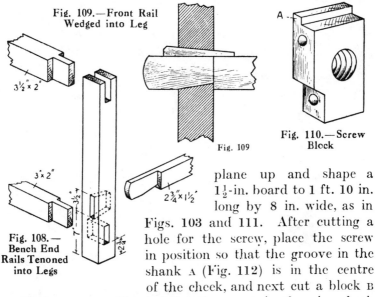

Fig. 109.—Front Rail
Wedged into Leg

Fig. 109

Fig. 110.—Screw
Block

Fig. 108.—
Bench End
Rails Tenoned
into Legs

plane up and shape a
1½-in. board to 1 ft. 10 in.
long by 8 in. wide, as in
Figs. 103 and 111. After cutting a
hole for the screw, place the screw
in position so that the groove in the
shank A (Fig. 112) is in the centre
of the cheek, and next cut a block B
to fill the space. For holding the screw in the vice cheek
and yet to allow of its revolving freely, a piece of hardwood shaped as at C is inserted in a mortise D made in the
side of the cheek. The runner is 2½ in. wide by 1 in. thick,
and should be tenoned into the lower end of the cheek, as
in Fig. 113. The guide box for the runner is clearly shown
in Fig. 105, and should be fixed to the legs after the screw
has been fixed in position on the bench.

The bench lends itself to the fitting of an instantaneous-
grip vice; one is shown in Fig. 100. Catalogues give a few
types to choose from, and they are all good, but much

more expensive than the screw ; they are slid out and
in to accommodate the work in an instant, and the handle
then pushed down to give the grip. An American vice—
the Emmert—is supplied with a number of different-sized
jaws, and can be swung round into various positions to
accommodate work of any width and at such an angle as
best to suit the craftsman.

The peg board, shown clearly in Figs. 102 and 103, is
adjustable, and is of great convenience for supporting
long boards when jointing and planing, as the peg inserted
at the right place
will bear much of
the weight of the
work, thus prevent-
ing leverage of the
jaws of the vice.
The peg board is
5 in. wide and ¾ in.
thick, and is made
to run in grooves
cut in the top edge
of the front rail and
the under edge of
the bench cheek (*see*
Fig. 114). So that
the board may be
easily placed in

[Fig. 111.—Wooden Bench-screw and Cheek

position after the bench has been put together, a small
piece is taken out at the end of the groove in the cheek,
as indicated at A.

A stop on the bench surface is necessary for planing
against, and it must be adjustable for height, as, of course,
it must always be below the surface that is being planed,
so that the plane will pass over it. On a table a stop
can be improvised by inserting an ordinary screw with its
head standing above the surface, and simple hinge stops
are readily obtainable. Sometimes a small clamp can be
used in front of the wood to be planed, and sometimes a
block of wood can be screwed to the surface and small

thin pieces can be raised by putting another piece under them. Variations in the height of the stop are desirable, because if low enough to suit the thinnest wood thicker pieces are liable to jump over.

In the case of the bench here described, the bench stop

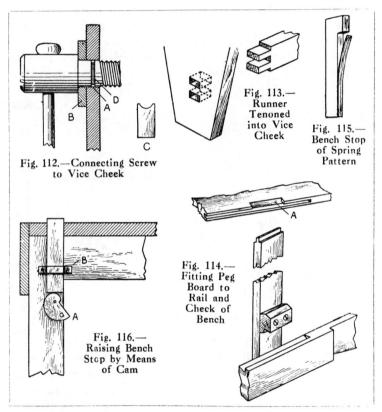

Fig. 112.—Connecting Screw to Vice Cheek

Fig. 113.—Runner Tenoned into Vice Cheek

Fig. 115.—Bench Stop of Spring Pattern

Fig. 114.—Fitting Peg Board to Rail and Check of Bench

Fig. 116.—Raising Bench Stop by Means of Cam

might be of the regulation spring type (*see* Fig. 115) fitting into mortises cut in the bench top, the stop being held at any required height by the spring. This is not the kind recommended, though, in this instance; a superior fitting is of close-grained hard wood, 8 in. long by $1\frac{1}{2}$ in. wide by $1\frac{1}{4}$ in. thick, gradually raised above the bench top by gently turning round the cam A (Fig. 116) clockwise. The cam is fixed to the inside of the front leg by means of a screw, which should be driven in just enough to enable the cam to work easily, a metal washer being inserted between the cam and the leg. The stop should work easily in the mortise made in the bench top, and in order to keep it in a vertical position it is held loosely in a staple, B, made from sheet metal or thick wire.

The cam needs to be shaped in such a way that the outside curve gradually and uniformly increases its distance from the centre. To set out the shape of the cam proceed as follows: From a centre draw sixteen radiating and equi-distant lines, and letter from A to P (*see* Fig. 117).

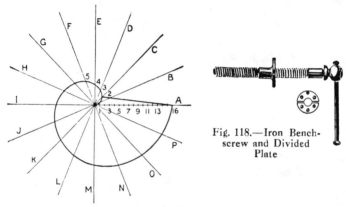

Fig. 118.—Iron Bench-screw and Divided Plate

Fig. 117.—Setting Out Pattern of Cam for Bench Stop

On line A mark off sixteen divisions from the centre, say $\frac{3}{16}$ in. apart, and number each division. Now, starting with the line B, mark off one division on this, and two divisions on C, three divisions on D, four divisions on E, and so on until the sixteenth division is reached on A. Now through these marks the exact curve can be drawn, the centre being the point through which passes the screw on which the cam turns. A knob is screwed in to form a handle for turning the cam.

Kitchen Table Benches.—A makeshift arrangement, possessing one or two obvious faults, is to fit an ordinary table with an iron bench screw (Fig. 118) by boring a hole in the table framework near to a leg, and screwing the nut to the framework at the back of the hole. A piece of stout wood answers as the cheek, and needs a similar hole bored through it. A circular iron plate in two parts, as shown, is supplied with the set, and requires to be screwed on the front of the cheek, so as to fit into the recess formed in the screw spindle. An emergency but faulty bench vice can thus be rigged up in ten minutes. The addition of a runner —so as to make possible the parallel action of the vice-jaw—is a great improvement, and the further provision of a board or block, to serve as the back-jaw, fixed to the table, so as to bring the face of the framework out flush with the edge of the table top, gives a

Fig. 119

Figs. 119 and 120.— Bench Screw Attached to Kitchen Table

good simple vice, but does not overcome the difficulty that the table will probably be too light and not rigid enough for

Fig. 120

heavy planing. Figs. 119 and 120 show an arrangement on the lines of the above. It will be noted that the runner slides in a box attached to the end (tail) of the table.

The screw is not essential to a vice. A wedge-action vice (*see* Fig. 121) is cheaper and can be wholly made, by the worker himself, of hard wood about 2 in. by 1 in. Two pieces (each attached by three screws) project from the underside of the bench top, and to them is dovetailed the front " jaw " (*see* the detail at A) obliquely to the edge of

E

the bench, so as to take the wedges; the " jaw " also projects above the under pieces to the thickness of the bench to which it is fixed. Two or three wedges of different

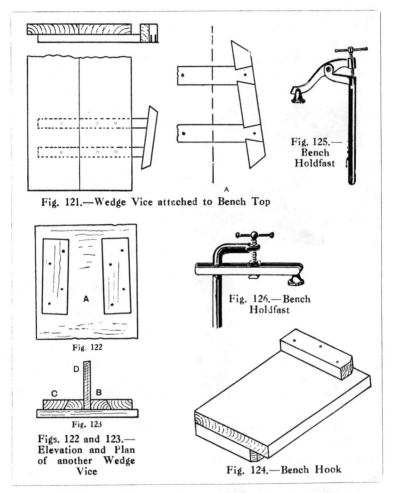

Fig. 121.—Wedge Vice attached to Bench Top

Fig. 125.—Bench Holdfast

Fig. 122

Fig. 126.—Bench Holdfast

Fig. 123

Figs. 122 and 123.—Elevation and Plan of another Wedge Vice

Fig. 124.—Bench Hook

widths will be required, and should be tapered to such an angle as to cause a parallel grip.

Another type of wedge vice (Figs. 122 and 123) may be used for holding wood edgewise for planing. Two pieces c are of hard wood, about $1\frac{1}{2}$ in. thick and 8 in. long, with

Fig. 127.—Sawing-stool

an undercut bevel on the edges that come opposite one another (see the sectional view) when screwed firmly to the plank A or top of the bench ; they occupy a slightly converging position as shown. Two h a r d wood wedges B have one edge bevelled to fit the grooves formed by the two fixed pieces, the other edge being planed up square. When fixing the wood D edgewise, tap the wedges until they are tight. Each stroke of the plane tends to tighten the wedges.

Bench Hook.—This is a block, easily made by the craftsman, in which small work can be held on the bench for tenon-sawing, etc. The left hand holds the work and the right the tool. The hook shown in Fig. 124 is simply three pieces of, possibly odd, stuff screwed together. Let it be of good width, and it will then be convenient for chiselling upon, and will also enable the worker to obtain a better grip of the wood when sawing.

Bench Holdfasts.—It is often a great help to have

Fig. 128   Fig. 129

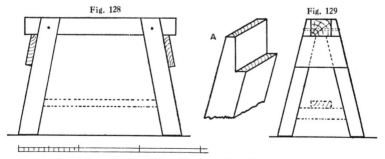

Figs. 128 and 129.—Elevations and Detail of Sawing-stool

some means of holding work tightly down on the bench, leaving both hands free to hold the tool, etc. Workers soon discover for themselves little dodges by which this means may be effected, but the regulation appliance is the holdfast (two patterns of which are shown in Figs. 125 and 126), which may be attached to the end of the bench, but is usually sunk through the top. By means of the screw the arm is caused to grip the work tightly to the bench.

Stools.—One or two sawing stools will be found useful, the ordinary pattern being shown in Fig. 127. One with a broader top will be found convenient for mortising and doing other similar heavy work, and can quite easily be made by the worker himself, to enable him to do which working drawings of a good pattern are presented by Figs. 128 and 129. Such stools are commonly made without the extra side pieces and stretcher shown in dotted lines, but these add rigidity and weight, which are an advantage whenever the stool is used as a substitute for the bench.

CHAPTER III

SHARPENING TOOLS

THE processes of grinding and sharpening tools involve the use of both grindstones and oilstones. A tool is ground to make it thin enough to penetrate the wood and rubbed on an oilstone to make the edge keen. It is sharpened at a more obtuse angle than it is ground, which not only gives a narrower surface for rubbing, thus reducing the labour of sharpening to a minimum, but also strengthens the penetrating edge. The gradual shortening of a tool is caused by the wear and the rubbing on the oilstone ; the grindstone does not shorten, but only makes the tool thinner, as shown in Fig. 130. The edge of the tool shown is one that requires grinding, the old grinding and sharpening surfaces being clearly shown. The dotted line shows the amount of metal to be taken off in grinding.

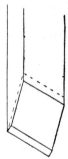

Fig. 130.— Wearing away of Chisel

Grindstones.—The York grindstones known as " Bilston grit " are largely used, and those suitable for woodworkers can be obtained in wooden and iron frames with handles or treadles for turning as wanted (*see* Figs. 131 and 132). A grindstone with an iron frame and trough and treadle with a special apparatus for grinding plane irons, chisels, and gouges can be thoroughly recommended. The levers on to which the tool is fixed can be adjusted for height to obtain the correct grinding angle, and also to make the necessary allowance as the stone wears smaller. The tool can traverse the whole width of the stone by a lateral movement which prevents uneven wear of the stone. The levers swing upwards to allow of the

Fig. 131. — Hand-driven Grindstone

53

tool being inspected when desired. Dealers' catalogues show a number of devices for automatically grinding tools at the correct angles. Water is used on a grindstone to wash away the particles of steel and prevent their filling up the pores of the stone, thus preserving the cutting surface. It is best, if possible, to revolve the grindstone towards the worker, because it ensures a well-ground surface without any burred edge, and the water being thrown on to the tool keeps it cool, so preventing any softening of the steel.

A 2-ft. stone can be fitted to drive by foot power on a strong wooden framing made of $6\frac{1}{2}$-in. by $2\frac{1}{2}$-in. white pine, as in Fig. 132, in which A represents the grindstone running in the bearings B, bolted on the top of the stringers C, bolted to the legs D. The grindstone revolves in the direction of the arrow-head towards the workman, and is driven by the connecting rod E, the top end of which is bored to suit the crank pin keyed on the grindstone spindle. The lower end of the connecting rod is hooked through the eyebolt F, which is fixed with a nut and washer underneath the treadle board G. The treadle board is pivoted by means of an eyebolt and an ordinary bolt fixed into the back leg as indicated at H. There should be a trough underneath to catch the water and refuse. A water drip-can, with adjusting tap to regulate the water drip on the grindstone, should be erected overhead.

A beginner will "burn" his tools if he tries to grind them to a thin edge on a dry stone. The heat resulting from the friction is sufficient to destroy the hardness of the cutting edges, and if, during grinding, the edge of the tool changes to a blue colour, it indicates a change in the temper and the coloured portion must be ground away. Owing to unequal hardness of the grain or careless use, the face of a grindstone may wear untrue, and will then require truing up, which may be done with a piece of iron pipe about $\frac{1}{2}$ in. or so in diameter and of convenient length, a piece of old cycle tube answering very well. A bar of iron or wood will act as a rest if fixed on top of the grindstone frame as at K (Fig. 132). The tube is firmly held on the " rest " as at L, and at the same time rolled across the face of the stone. The grindstone should not be allowed to become so much out of truth as to require much trouble in truing up, but in the case of one being badly out of truth, the stone should be revolved and a true circle line, as large as the uneven diameter of the stone will stand, marked on the side. The high parts can then be roughly chipped off, and the stone turned true.

Of late years small emery wheels turned by hand have been coming on to the market in increasing numbers, and they well replace the big grindstone for home use. Many of them are fitted with adjustable tool-r e s t s, speed gear, etc. Readers who possess a lathe or treadle fretsaw can rig up an emery wheel on that ; tool dealers sell all necessary fittings for the purpose.

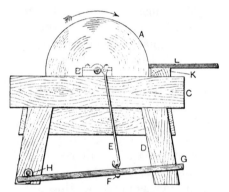

Fig. 132.—Treadle-driven Grindstone in Wooden Frame-work

Oilstones.—There is a large variety of oilstones obtainable, natural and artificial, cheap and expensive, rough cut and fine cut, with many intermediate grades, and also of many shapes for particular purposes. The Charnley Forest stone in past years was largely used by woodworkers ; it was reasonable in price, gave a keen edge to tools, but was slow-cutting. It has been largely superseded by the American Washita stone, which possesses much the same properties. The Canadian stones are fast cutters and produce an edge suited for work in general. Workmen sometimes use a fast-cutting stone and finish on one of a finer cut ; they can obtain artificial oilstones which have opposite faces of different grades, one medium cut and the other coarse cut. The Turkey stones are rather expensive, and wear away quickly, but they cut well. " India " oilstones have remarkable cutting qualities ; they are a composition stone, very strong and durable. There are three grades—fine, medium, and coarse, the medium grade being the most serviceable for general carpentry work. The " India " stone is largely made into slips for sharpening gouges, etc. Arkansas stones are expensive, but are hard, fine cutting, and produce a very keen edge. The small slips for the finer woodcarving tools are generally made of this stone.

Oil (preferably sweet oil) is used for oilstones for the same purpose as water on a grindstone, that is, as a lubricant and to keep the pores of the stone open so as to preserve its full cutting action.

The oilstone should be bought already cased, unless the reader is able to case the stone himself. Stones exhibiting vein marks should be rejected.

One oilstone can be made to serve for both gouges and chisels, but it is best to have two stones, because the gouge wears a stone into ruts in sharpening, and gouges are more easily sharpened in the ruts than on a perfectly flat stone. If there is but one oilstone, one face should be used for gouges only, and the beginner should acquire the habit of sharpening the smaller-size gouges towards the right- or left-hand edge of the stone, reserving the other part for the larger gouges, so that one broad face of the oilstone becomes worn into two or more ruts, lengthwise of the stone, as will suit the curves of various-size gouges. When too badly worn for gouge sharpening a good stone should not be thrown away, but split with a thin-ground cold chisel, and the pieces shaped on the grindstone into slips suitable for sharpening gouges and carving tools.

Wear makes an oilstone uneven, and must be remedied by rubbing the stone on a sheet of emery cloth or glass-paper that has been stretched and tacked down flat, another method being to hold the oilstone on the flat side of a revolving grindstone.

The cover of the oilstone should always be kept on when the oilstone is not in use. Any thickened oil should be rubbed off, and not allowed to form a corrosion with dirt round the edges of the case.

Fig. 133.—Sharpening Plane Iron on Oilstone

Sharpening Chisels and Plane-irons. — Chisels are sharpened in the same way as plane-irons as regards the operations and appliances involved, but whilst chisels should be sharpened straight across the width, plane-irons have a slight convex curvature. Jack-plane irons may have a regular curvature, the curve being a part of a large circle; but trying-plane irons, which are wider, should have the centre portion straight and be rounded down at the ends. When sharpening, these curves can be tested with a straight-edge, or they can be examined from the edge view, which is the practical method.

In grinding chisels and plane-irons on the grindstone take care to make the angle correct (about 20 degrees for soft wood and 25 degrees for hard wood) and to use plenty of water. The sharpening on the oilstone is the operation in which care and skill are particularly necessary. Figs. 133 and 134 show how a

Fig. 134.—Sharpening Chisel: Handle Slightly Too High

plane-iron and a chisel are held on the stone. The right hand has a firm grip of the tool, and the left hand assists in giving the necessary pressure. The tool is held at an angle of 30 degrees to 35 degrees, and care must be taken to see the angle is not altered in the backward and forward strokes, as is very likely to happen in the continual swing of the arms.

Fig. 135 is a photograph showing two tools at incorrect angles, one too acute and the other too obtuse, the correct angle being as shown by the dotted line. The sharpening angle should be straight, as in Fig. 137, and not rounded, as in Fig. 138. As already explained, plane-irons require a lateral motion from side to side of the stone, combined with the usual rubbing motion;

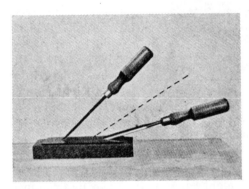

Fig. 135.—Three Sharpening angles—Obtuse, Correct, and Acute

this is shown in Fig. 139, and is necessary to give the corners sufficient rubbing with the object of producing the slight curvature, as explained in the first chapter.

Fig. 136.—Removing Wire Edge

Pressure is required in sharpening, and three or four minutes' work at least is necessary to obtain the keen edge on a plane-iron after grinding. The face of the tool, whether cutter or chisel, is then gently rubbed on the stone, as shown in Fig. 136, to remove the wire edge that invariably turns up, but the tool must be kept perfectly flat, as otherwise the sharpened edge will be seriously damaged.

The operation of sharpening cannot be done well if done

hurriedly. The edge of the tool should be examined occasionally when approaching the finish. Do not feel the edge as a test for sharpness, but see if the shiny edge of bluntness has been removed.

After the oil has been wiped off the tool should be stropped to remove any wire edge that may still exist and make the surfaces of the tool smooth, and therefore give it a keener cutting edge. Some workmen have a knack

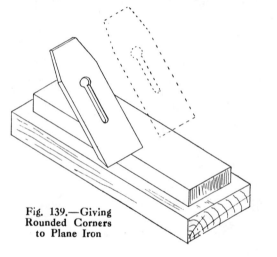

Fig. 139.—Giving Rounded Corners to Plane Iron

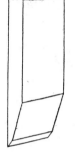

Fig. 137.—Correct Bevel of Chisel

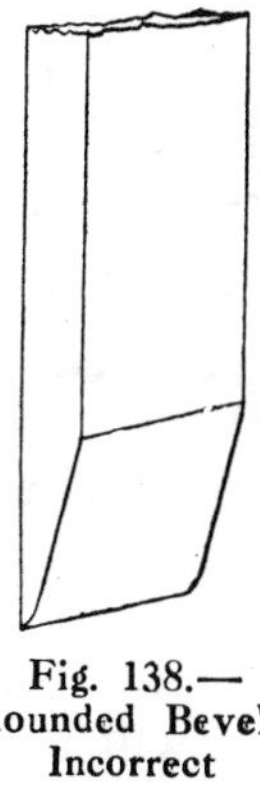

Fig. 138.— Rounded Bevel: Incorrect

of stropping it on the palm of their hand, but beginners are not advised to attempt it. Instead, they should use a strap dressed with crocus powder and tallow.

The chisel is held in the same way as a plane-iron, but it should not be rubbed on the middle of the stone, as this would cause the stone in time to wear hollow in the width and impair its usefulness for sharpening plane-irons. Rub the chisels nearer the edge of the stone, and as the chisel is not like the plane-iron but requires to be perfectly straight on the edge, do not introduce any lateral motion, but keep to the to-and-fro motion only.

Sharpening Gouges.—Firmer gouges having a bevel on the outside present no difficulty in grinding, except that they must not be allowed to remain stationary but kept revolving to and fro to the shape of the curve. The tool handle is held with the right hand, the left hand being merely held loosely on top of the blade to steady it on the grindstone and to regulate the angle of grinding. In Fig. 140 the gouge is shown partly on its right-hand side at B, while, as at C, the rolling motion in grinding has carried the tool farther across the stone, and the tool is shown lying fairly on its back ; the continuation of the motion brings

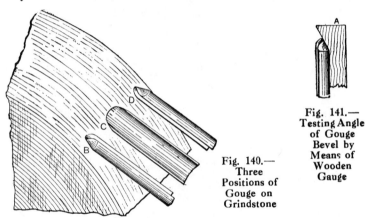

Fig. 140.— Three Positions of Gouge on Grindstone

Fig. 141.— Testing Angle of Gouge Bevel by Means of Wooden Gauge

the grinding round towards the left-hand edge of the tool, as indicated at D. The gouge is not only rolled to and fro, but is kept in motion laterally to and fro, so as not to wear the face of the stone into ruts. If there is any difficulty in judging the grinding angle, a wooden gauge can be made and applied as shown at A (Fig. 141). In grinding gouges that have been sharpened on the oilstone, the sharpening bevel will form a guide to future grindings, the tool being ground at a proper angle until the sharpening bevel appears to the eye as the finest possible line equally round the edge. In the case of new tools, the grinding is continued until the edge is just perceptible.

The sharpening of gouges on the oilstone will now be explained. Fig. 142 shows how to hold the tool. The worker stands at the side of the stone, and a semi-revolving movement is given to the gouge throughout the length of the stroke. An oilstone slip, the shape of the gouge, is then rubbed inside to remove the wire edge (Fig. 143),

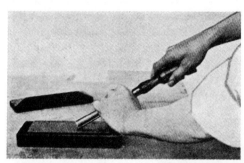

the stone lying close in the hollow of the gouge during the operation. The tool is next finished on the strop.

The grinding of paring gouges having an inside

Fig. 142.—Sharpening Firmer Gouge on Oilstone

bevel is best left in the hands of a competent tool-grinder, but they can be ground by rounding

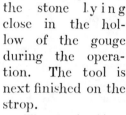

Fig. 144.—Sharpening Paring Gouge on Oilstone Slip

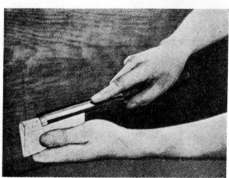

Fig. 143.—Removing Wire Edge from Firmer Gouge

off the corner of the grindstone with a piece of iron to fit the gouge to be ground, or on narrow, shaped emery wheels. First, the end may need to be made square with the stone, so as to act as a guide when grinding the bevelled surfaces, great care being necessary.

To sharpen a paring gouge having an inside bevel requires the use of an oilstone slip, as shown in Fig. 144. The tool should be held quite firmly and a regular stroke given to the slip, the outside of the gouge being afterwards gently rubbed on an oilstone and carefully revolved while so doing. Stropping thoroughly then fits the tool for use.

Sharpening Spokeshaves.—The wooden spokeshave is one of the " sweetest " cutting tools in the carpenter's kit, but owing to the difficulty in sharpening and keeping it in order, many workers have discarded it in favour of the iron spokeshave. The usual way of sharpening the blade of a wooden spokeshave is to knock out the blade, and sharpen it by rubbing the bevel with an oilstone slip (*see* Fig. 145). The flat

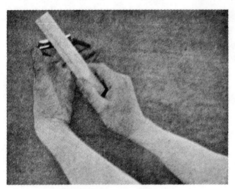

Fig. 145.—Sharpening Spokeshave on Oilstone Slip

face of the blade is then rubbed with the slip or on an oilstone to remove the wire e d g e. A practical man has proved the worth of the following method, which is the reverse of the above ; that is, all the sharpening is done on the flat face, and the bevel is simply rubbed with the slip to remove the wire edge. Knock in the blade flush with the stock, so that it just refuses to take a shaving. Then, grasping the handles, rub the spokeshave backwards and forwards on the oilstone, taking care to prevent it from rocking ; that is, treat it as if it were the flat face of a chisel or plane-iron. Knock out the blade and remove the wire edge with the slip. Then adjust for cutting.

Owing to the wearing of the stock, the mouth will become imperfect, and maybe the face of the blade may become slightly rounded from front to back owing to repeated sharpening. Knock in the blade until the stock projects the slightest fraction of an inch above the blade ; it may be necessary to remove a little of the stock to make room for the shoulders of the blade. Then, grasping the handles, grind the blade and the wood until the front edge of the mouth is restored to a straight line. Then rub on the oilstone as before directed. If a blade becomes loose, a slip of paper $\frac{1}{8}$ in. wide placed in the socket (on the end grain) will help to make it tight.

Fig. 146.—Diagram Illustrating Cutting Action of Scraper

Sharpening Scrapers.—A "scraper" does not scrape if it is properly sharpened; instead, it cuts. Fig. 146 shows the cutting principle, but is not a true section. Properly sharpened and used, each stroke should remove from the work a fine shaving, nearly as wide as the scraper. The tool is held as in Figs. 147 and 148, inclined with gentle pressure until its edge gets a "tooth" in the work, and then pushed away, although very

Fig. 147   Fig. 148
Figs. 147 and 148.—Using the Scraper

occasionally the scraper is used by drawing it towards the worker. It removes the marks and ridges left by a smoothing plane, and its use is followed by that of glass-paper. Occasionally the scraper is used as almost the sole means of dressing up cross-grained surfaces occurring

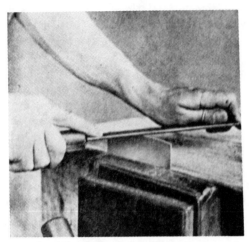

Fig. 149.—Filing Scraper Edge Square

in woods having a decidedly curly grain, on which a smoothing plane can produce no results worth having.

An excellent scraper can be made from the broken-off end of an old saw blade, its corner being rounded for scraping the hollow parts of mouldings, etc. A scraper is sharpened by squaring its edge and then burring it over. Fig. 149 shows it being filed square, after which it is ground smooth on the oilstone, as in Fig. 150, or on the side of the stone, as in Fig. 151. When the edge is quite smooth and square it is ready for setting. Both edges of a scraper should be set, also the round corners, as shown by Fig. 152. For setting the edges, any suitable hard-steel tool may be used ; the back of an old razor blade set rigid in a wood handle makes an excellent tool for the purpose, or a punch, the back of a gouge, or an old chisel the steel of which has been found by experience to be too hard for the use for which it was intended. The scraper is laid flat on the bench, the chisel, etc., laid upon it as

Fig. 150.—Smoothing Scraper Edge on Oilstone

Fig. 151.—Smoothing Scraper Edge on Side of Oilstone

in Fig. 153, and then, with a good even pressure, the chisel is pushed forward to the other corner. This is repeated seven or eight times, and each side of each edge is treated the same. The burred edges have now to be turned in the proper direction for cutting, by stroking along them

several times with considerable force, in one of the ways shown by Figs. 154 and 155, keeping the chisel at right angles with the scraper. Finally, the chisel is held slant, and also at an angle of about

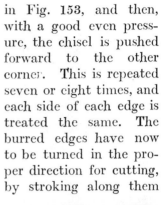

Fig. 152.—Squaring Scraper Corners

65° with the scraper; then, with firm, even, but only moderate pressure, it is drawn along the edge (this time towards the body) about twice only, as shown in Fig. 156. The process of " sharpening " has produced a burr edge and turned it over, approximately as in Fig. 146.

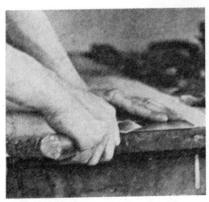

Fig. 153.—Burring the Scraper

F

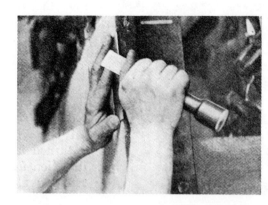

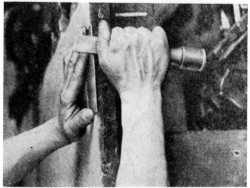

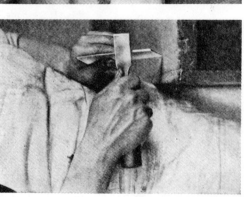

Figs. 154 and 155.—Two Positions for Turning Edge of Scraper

Fig. 156.—Finishing Edge of Scraper

Sharpening Centre-bits.—A centre-bit cannot be properly sharpened or rectified until the duties of its various cutting parts have been understood. Fig. 157 is a front and two side views of a correctly finished centre-bit ready for boring. The centre pin A is the first to enter the surface, and on this being worked deeper in the wood, the cutter or nicker B comes into action and describes a circle

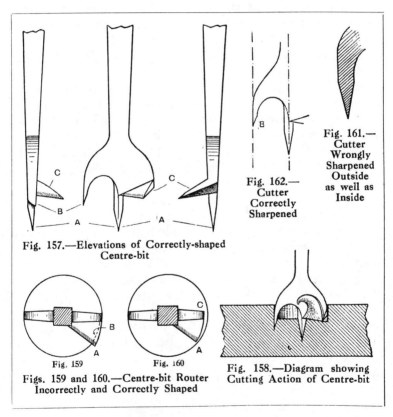

Fig. 161.—Cutter Wrongly Sharpened Outside as well as Inside

Fig. 162.—Cutter Correctly Sharpened

Fig. 157.—Elevations of Correctly-shaped Centre-bit

Fig. 159   Fig. 160

Figs. 159 and 160.—Centre-bit Router Incorrectly and Correctly Shaped

Fig. 158.—Diagram showing Cutting Action of Centre-bit

about $\frac{1}{16}$ in. deep round the pin before the router c tears up all the wood within the circle. In Fig. 158, which is a section through a partly bored hole, is shown the action of the bit in cutting. The pin is not truly central, the circle cut by the bit being therefore of larger diameter than the width of the tool. Thus the bit bores a hole full

$\frac{1}{16}$ in. larger than the size marked on the bit. In all cases it is, therefore, advisable to make a trial boring in a piece of waste wood previous to using any size bit, so that the exact diameter of the hole it cuts may be ascertained.

It often happens with a newly purchased bit that it does not work altogether satisfactorily, and possibly it bores a ragged and uneven hole. This is one of the commonest troubles, and the fault usually lies in the router. At the extreme point A (Fig. 159) the router protrudes beyond the circle made by the cutter, and will need to be slightly filed away, as in the dotted line B. The outer edge of the router should incline slightly to the centre from A to C (Fig. 160), so as to allow a clearance in turning, the extreme point only just, if at all, touching the side of the hole. If the back of the outer edge C is the same distance from the centre pin as the point A, it will cause unnecessary rubbing on the side of the hole, and will tend to add to the labour of the workman, and often give the boring a ragged and unfinished appearance.

In sharpening the router it should always be filed on the upper surface to a chisel edge, inclining slightly upwards from the point, as in the photograph (Fig. 163), and finished off with an oilstone slip to give it a smooth and keen edge.

The nicker or cutter is often at fault or needs sharpening. Frequently it will be found that the extreme point is wrongly sharpened on both sides, similar to Fig. 161, so that in actual boring the diameter of the cutting edge is smaller than the hole it cuts. Thus, after the point enters the surface of the wood, the two outwardly sloping sides are forced wedge-like into the wood, and cause, to a certain extent, the bit to tighten, and labour to be lost on the part of the operator. The correct shape of the cutter should be as shown at B (Fig. 162), the outside edge being perfectly parallel with the centre line of the bit. The sharpening should always be done very carefully on the inside edge with a round file and oilstone slip, and the cutting edge should be tapered off and rounded from front to back, as shown at B (Fig. 157). The centre pin is triangular in section, and if blunted is easily put right with a few strokes of a file.

Sharpening Nose-bits.—The nose-bit is sharpened with a triangular file, a small one with the file teeth cut to the point being most suitable; and in sharpening the bevel is filed from the inside of the nose. A few light strokes of the file should suffice for sharpening; and the filing should cease whenever the wire edge appears, which is unmistakably known by the gripping feel of the edge when touched with the finger.

Sharpening Gimlets.—The gimlet is an awkward tool to sharpen when it gets dull, the amateur generally trying to improve it with a file and seldom succeeding. The best method is to bore, with the tool to be sharpened, a hole through an odd piece of 1-in. hardwood, remove the gimlet, fill the hole with sharp emery, add a drop or two of oil,

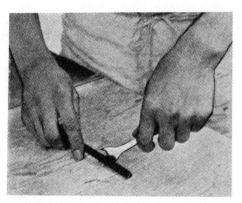

Fig. 163.—Sharpening Centre-bit Router with File

and re-insert the gimlet. Work it to and fro a number of times, and to finish the sharpening bore a second hole with the tool and repeat the process, but using the emery dry. This is also an excellent method of removing rust from a neglected tool.

Sharpening Saws.—The teeth of a saw must not only be sharp, but they need to be " set," as explained on p. 25. Setting may be done by two methods : by hammering or by bending with a saw set.

Bending the teeth over by hammering is the general method pursued by saw sharpeners. The saw is held horizontally on the rounded edge of the steel plate shown in Fig. 164. This plate is 4 in. or 5 in. long, about $\frac{3}{8}$ in. thick, and wide enough to receive two strong pins and to be conveniently gripped in the vice. The pins project a trifle at the sides, and prevent the plate from dropping during the process of hammering. The rounded edge can be made by grinding or filing down to a full $\frac{1}{16}$ in. at each side. A double-paned hammer made on purpose for saw-setting can be obtained, or the cross pane of an ordinary hammer used. Every alternate tooth is struck near the point so as to effect a bending in the tooth itself and not entirely from its root. The teeth are gradually moved over the plate during the process throughout the whole length of the blade. This operation requires only one or two moderately light blows for each tooth, and they should be given evenly. Many workmen set the teeth by hammering over a hardwood block bevelled as shown in Fig. 165.

For setting the teeth by bending, many kinds of saw sets are obtainable. The common type generally used is shown in Fig. 166. A good saw set will take saws of any thickness, and has a sliding gauge which acts as a stop in bending, so that one can ensure each tooth being bent by the same amount throughout the blade. Another kind of saw set has a pair of handles, somewhat like a pair of pliers or forceps, and the teeth are gripped and bent to the right set without difficulty (*see* Fig. 167).

For sharpening, the saw must be gripped tightly in the vice near to the teeth, so as to prevent vibration. Have a pair of battens or clamps, pieces of wood about 3 in. by 1 in., and long enough for the hand-saw (as shown in Fig. 168), screw them together at one end, and chamfer the edges so as to obtain clearance for the file. After the saw is set it is usual to rub a fine flat file lightly along the edge of the teeth to remove any unevenness that may exist, this operation being known as jointing. Then, with a three-cornered file, proceed to sharpen the teeth. Always use the file so as to sharpen the front of the teeth that are bent toward the worker. The file should point upwards at an angle of 15° to the horizontal, and it also should be inclined towards the handle of the saw about 20° from the square filing stroke. Fig. 168 on this page illustrates the filing of the teeth from both sides of the saw. In this way the front of each tooth is filed to an acute angle

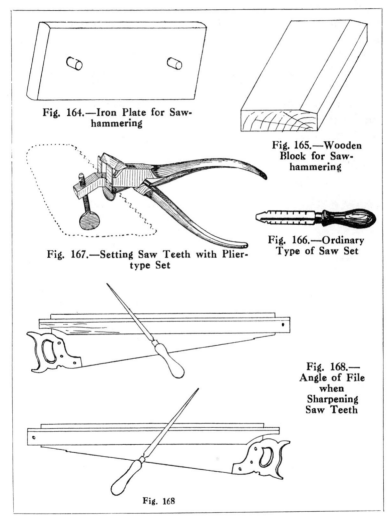

Fig. 164.—Iron Plate for Saw-hammering

Fig. 165.—Wooden Block for Saw-hammering

Fig. 167.—Setting Saw Teeth with Plier-type Set

Fig. 166.—Ordinary Type of Saw Set

Fig. 168.—Angle of File when Sharpening Saw Teeth

Fig. 168

on the outer side ; as the file cuts on the forward stroke, no burr can exist on the acute corner because it is nearer to the worker, and any burr that is caused will be on the inner edge and not the cutting edge of the tooth ; each stroke of the file not only sharpens the front of the tooth but also bevels the back of the tooth that is bent to the opposite side. Upon close inspection it will be seen that, when the saw is finished, each tooth is bevelled off on the inner side, back and front, so that the chisel-pointed edge at the top is lower on the inner side of the tooth. In other words, each tooth forms part of a triangular pyramid of which the outer side is the base. The edges of the teeth then form a valley at their junction, the existence of which can be demonstrated by placing a needle in it.

CHAPTER IV

SAWING

Using the Hand Saw.—The first difficulty that will be encountered in using a saw is that of starting the saw cut, or kerf, as it is called. The larger the saw tooth, the greater is the difficulty. The saw should be held in the right hand as in Figs. 169 and 170, and the work grasped with the left, holding the thumb of the left hand in such a position as to guide the saw blade to the mark. A moment's practice will show what is meant. Some people prefer to hold in the thumb under the forefinger, and guide the saw with the forefinger and knuckle, as in Fig. 171. From the start the saw must be held at right angles to the surface of the work, and there is only one way of automatically ensuring this. Fig. 169 shows the saw blade, centre of the wrist, elbow, shoulder, and right eye as nearly as possible in one vertical plane, the body being properly balanced and the right arm free to work without the elbow touching the side.

Fig. 169.—Rip-sawing : Front View

The beginner often does well to test the squareness of his sawing, by means of a square held as in Fig. 172.

The angle at which the saw is held is of importance, that shown in Fig. 174 being about right. A common mistake is to " lay " the saw ; that is, to bring it too much into the horizontal, and this is especially the case when learning to follow the pencil lines with the saw. It is a habit which the beginner should get out of as soon as he can. The stroke should be wellnigh the full length of the

73

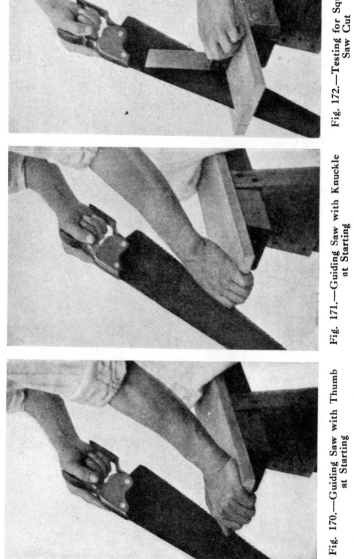

Fig. 170.—Guiding Saw with Thumb
at Starting

Fig. 171.—Guiding Saw with Knuckle
at Starting

Fig. 172.—Testing for Squareness of
Saw Cut

saw, although this must depend somewhat upon the length of the worker's arm; but in any case jerky sawing should be avoided. To lessen the strain on the hand and also to assist the saw in keeping to the line, do not grip the tool very tightly.

Rip-sawing.— In rip-sawing —that is, sawing length-wise or with the grain— the plank requires to be supported at each end, either on sawing stools or boxes (*see* Figs. 169, 173, and 174). When the

Fig. 173

Figs. 173 and 174.— Rip-sawing

work tends to close and pinch the saw, a tendency which is always more evident when the sawing is not true, it will be necessary to hold the cut open, for which purpose the services of

Fig. 174

an assistant should be obtained, or, frequently, a small wedge may be inserted.

In ripping down a short length it is often convenient to hold it in the bench vice; then the right hand grips the saw handle in the usual way, and the left also holds the saw, it being applied at the junction of the blade and the handle about 1 in. in advance of the right thumb.

Cross Cutting.—The cut is started in the same way as before, but if the outer end of the work is unsupported, it soon becomes necessary to hold it with the left hand (*see* Fig. 175), and care must be taken when nearing the end of the cut to saw very gently to avoid breaking the piece off and leaving an ugly splinter.

Fig. 175.—Cross-cut Sawing : Holding End to Prevent Breakage

Using the Tenon Saw. —The tenon saw is generally used with greater exactness than is the hand saw. The teeth are very much finer, and the saw cut is much closer the plane of the finished surface. The cut is started in the way already explained, and the saw requires to be held very accurately. As its name implies, it is largely used for cutting tenons on the ends of rails, etc., which fit into mortises in other parts of the construction. The tenons are almost always put together as they come from the saw, and it follows that very careful sawing is essential. In Fig. 176 A, B, and C indicate the waste wood which is to be removed by two cuts of a tenon saw, one with the grain and the other at right angles. Of course, the work must be set out before the tenon sawing is attempted, and the setting out lines are clearly shown in the illustration. At A the saw kerf has been made *inside* the line, thus making the tenon too thin and causing a loose fit ; at B the kerf is *on* the line,

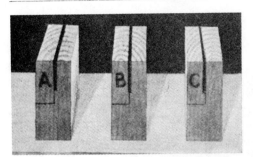

Fig. 176.—Sawing Tenons : Kerfs in End Grain

and the tenon will still be a trifle on the thin side; at c the kerf has been made *outside* the line in its proper place. This illustration, together with Fig. 177 which corresponds in many ways, suggests the obvious rule that saw kerfs must be made in the *waste*.

The position of the tenon saw at starting a cut with the grain is shown in Fig. 178. The start is made by a slight backward stroke. As the cut proceeds the saw is brought more nearly to the horizontal, and its handle is gradually lowered or the work adjusted, so that the line on the side of the work facing the

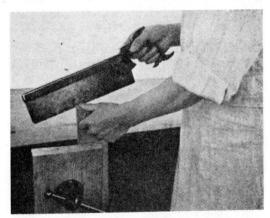

Fig. 178.—Tenon-sawing with the Grain : Starting

craftsman can be followed (*see* Fig. 179), finishing the cut with horizontal strokes. Another method of starting the cut is shown in Fig. 180 (next page), which should be compared with Fig. 178.

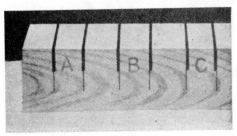

Fig. 177.—Sawing Notches : Kerfs across Grain

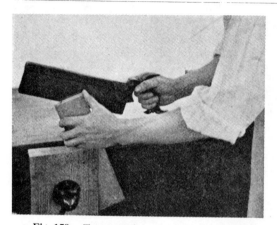

Fig. 179.—Tenon-sawing with the Grain: The Cut continued

In making halved joints, the tenon saw is used across the grain, the start being as in Fig. 181, and the completion of the cut as in Fig. 182. It will be noted that the work is held in the bench hook (*see* page 51). In sawing across the grain it is more than ever necessary that the saw cut be made in the waste (*see* Fig. 177), as the recess which will be formed between the saw cuts in making a halved joint will receive a piece of wood which is already the full width of the stuff that is being used. In other words, the piece of wood that will go into the recess cannot be made wider to make up for any inaccuracy caused by careless sawing, whereas should a tenon be cut a trifle narrower than intended, the mortise can be cut accordingly, or the difficulty can be overcome in other ways which may not be apparent when the work is casually examined.

Small, slender pieces of stuff are sometimes cut in quite a different manner from the above. The tenon saw with fine teeth is held upside down with its end against the side of the bench and its handle

Fig. 180.—Starting Tenon-sawing at Near Edge

against the worker's body; then the piece of wood is held in both hands and lightly worked over the teeth towards the worker.

It must always be remembered that a saw cuts in one direction only—that is, on the outward stroke. On the return stroke it merely scrapes the work, and if habitually pressed into the wood on the return stroke will soon get blunt. It is interesting to note that the craftsmen of the Far East use a saw that cuts on the inward stroke. Huge saws employed in mills sometimes have teeth arranged to cut in either direction.

Fig. 181

Figs. 181 and 182.—Cutting across Grain with Tenon Saw

Lining out for Sawing.—Except for rough work, no saw cut should ever be made unless a guide line has first been drawn. Lines at right angles to the edges of a plank are drawn with the help of a square, as in Fig. 20. Lines parallel with the edges can be drawn with a marking gauge as in Fig. 183, or

Fig. 182

with a rule held in the manner shown in Fig. 184. The second method shown needs some practice, and the first is the more accurate. Set the gauge by measuring with a rule from the back end of the stem to the stock; place the

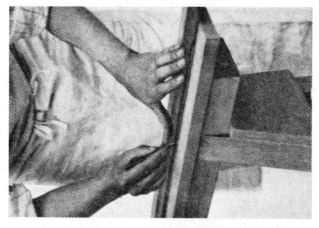

Fig. 184.—Lining-down with Fore-finger, Rule and Pencil

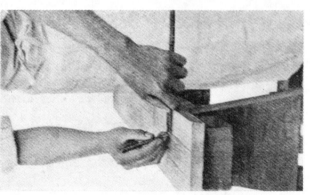

Fig. 185.—Lining-down with Pencil and Straightedge

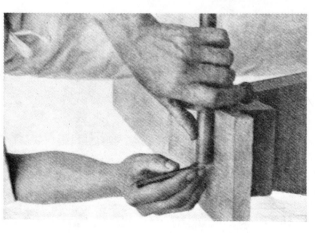

Fig. 183.—Lining-down with Marking Gauge and Pencil

gauge in position, hold the pencil against the end of the stem, and mark the board by a backward movement of the gauge, holding the pencil tightly against it. In using the rule, as in Fig. 184, the right hand holds the pencil tightly against the end, and the rule is slid along the work. Still another method is to mark off at each end of the plank the breadth required, and draw a connecting line by means of a straightedge and pencil as in Fig. 185. In connection with this method, it is helpful to know a quick way of dividing a board into a number of narrow and equal widths. Assume the plank shown in Fig. 186 has a width of 7 in. plus an odd fraction, and it is required to divide it into four strips. The work cannot be done accurately by dividing the width into four and then setting off from the rule. Instead, place the rule across the

Fig. 186.—Quick Method of Dividing Board into a number of Equal Widths

plank on the slant, as shown, with one end flush with one edge, and the 12-in. division over the other edge; divide 12 in. by the number of strips required, this giving 3 in.; therefore mark the board at 3 in., 6 in., and 9 in., repeat the operation at the other end of the work, and connect up with straightedge and pencil as before.

Care must be taken in holding the try square in lining out and marking off that its stock is kept tightly to the edge of the work. First the scribing awl should be placed

G

on the mark that is to be squared across ; then the square slid up until it touches the awl, and the mark then made (*see* Fig. 20). In squaring lines from one surface to another the face or trued-up surface (note the " face mark " in Fig. 187) is first treated, the work turned over, the scribing knife or awl placed in the end of the cut already made, and the square slid up to it as before (*see* Figs. 188 and 189). One point in these illustrations should be particularly noted : the stock of the square is used from the face edge, the truth of the other edges being a doubtful quantity.

Some of the illustrations show pencils, and others of them show marking or scribing awls or knives in use in conjunction with the straightedges and squares. The knife or awl gives more accurate results than the pencil, and this is particularly so when marking off measurements from a rule, as in Fig. 190, when the edge of the tool can be brought in contact with the end of the mark on the rule, holding the knife or awl perfectly upright and looking down upon it vertically and not from one side.

ECONOMY IN CUTTING UP STUFF

Stuff should be cut up with as little waste as possible. Some amount of waste is unavoidable in the form of scraps, but when small bits are wanted they should always be cut from these scraps. Pieces should not be cut to length without the certainty that no mistake in dimensions is being made, and without first considering whether they are being cut from pieces that will leave as little ultimate waste as possible. Cutting to length is a more serious matter than cutting to width, because a piece too short cannot generally be used, while width can often be made up. It is a safe practice to consider well and measure twice before cutting. A further precaution is to avoid direct measurement with a rule as far as possible, and especially in cases where the same dimension has to be marked a number of times, it being then safer and quicker to transfer the measurement direct from the place where the piece of wood has to fit, or to cut a strip to length or make a knife- or pencil-mark

Fig. 189.—Scribing from Face

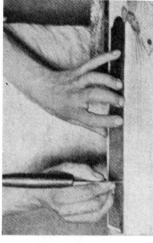

Fig. 190.—Marking off from Rule with Knife

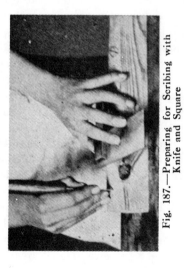

Fig. 187.—Preparing for Scribing with Knife and Square

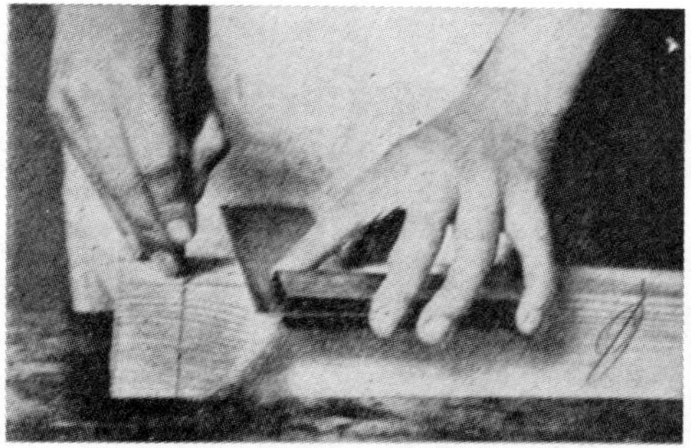

Fig. 188.— Preparing to Scribe from Face

on a strip, and transfer from this to the piece to be cut. As an extra precaution, arrow-heads or ticks may be made, as in Fig. 191, on the strip or on the piece to be cut if other marks are likely to cause confusion, and these reduce possibility of mistake in transferring or cutting. Measurement on the strip or on the piece to be cut should always be taken from the left end, and if the end has to be planed or squared, that work should be done before the length is marked.

In scheming to avoid waste, remember that short scraps are seldom of value, no matter how wide they are, while long narrow strips are frequently useful. It is often convenient to saw right across a board, although the piece cut off has to be reduced in width, leaving a portion which must either be wasted or worked in elsewhere. Three examples of cutting pieces from a board are shown in Fig. 192. The piece at A is so much less in width and length than the entire board that it would be simply cut out. The piece at B is so nearly the full width of the board that there would be little advantage in leaving the narrow piece intact with the wide part, and therefore the board would usually be sawn right across and the piece wanted reduced to width afterwards. The piece at C is so nearly the length of the board that the short bit of full width remaining would be of no value on the board, and it would be found more convenient to rip the full length and cut the short bit off the strip after. These examples show single pieces cut from a board, but in many cases pieces are cut out as required at different times, and the remaining portion will have various widths and lengths. Pieces cut out usually start from the same end, and as far as possible from one side only, leaving the other end and side of the board untouched. Complete boards or large pieces should usually not be cut if the piece or pieces required can be got from scraps. On the other hand, it is a pity to spoil a good piece of scrap by cutting it so that a considerable portion is unlikely to be of use. In such a case it may be more economical to cut from a larger piece or from a board. The object aimed at should be to have as few unworkable pieces as possible left over after the job is done. The wood remaining should be in a few large pieces rather than many small ones, and if the small ones are useless the smaller they are the less will be wasted.

Another point is to mark out the pieces so that defects

Fig. 191.—Arrow-heads indicating Part of Material Required

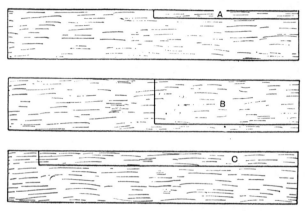

Fig. 192.—Pieces to be Cut from Boards

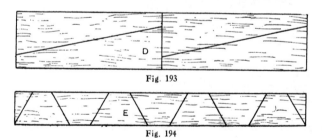

Fig. 193

Fig. 194

Figs. 193 and 194.—Cutting to Avoid Waste of Time and Material

in the wood shall either be cut out or be in places where they will either not be seen or not be a source of weakness. A knot in a narrow strip may seriously weaken it, although it would be of no consequence in a wide piece. A shake or crack may be a serious disadvantage in some places, but not in others.

The ends of a board are generally full of grit and have a great many incipient cracks, and cannot be planed or chiselled without damage to the cutting edge. Therefore, except in rough work, it is usual to saw from $\frac{1}{2}$ in. to 1 in.

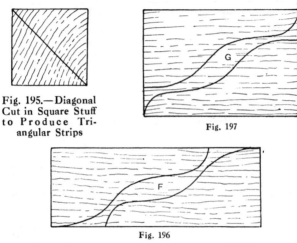

Fig. 195.—Diagonal Cut in Square Stuff to Produce Tri- angular Strips

Fig. 197

Fig. 196

Figs. 196 and 197.—Brackets Set Out for Sawing

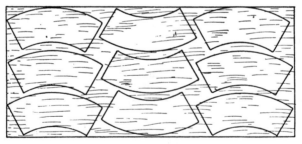

Fig. 198.—Segments Set Out for Sawing

or so off the end as waste, the exact amount depending on the condition of the end.

Examples of cutting to avoid waste and, to some extent, also to reduce the amount of sawing, are presented by Figs. 193 to 198. Wedges are cut as at D (Fig. 193), and blocks with ends not at right angles as at E (Fig. 194). Strips of triangular cross section are cut in pairs from a strip of square section, as in Fig. 195, but this is sometimes inconvenient, and it is often necessary for one half of the strip of square section to be pared and planed away and wasted in chips and shavings. Brackets and other irregular shapes, when more than one is required, can generally be marked out economically as in Figs. 196 and 197, and in such cases it is best to mark out and cut one first and use it as a template from which to mark the others, although it may be more convenient to make a special template of cardboard, thin wood, or paper. The sawing does not necessarily follow the exact outlines. When it has to be done by hand it is usually best to make only a single cut between the lines of adjoining shapes and reduce afterwards with gouge or chisel or spokeshave. It will be noticed that the brackets at F and G (Figs. 196 and 197) are alike, though the stuff is of different proportions. Segments for building rings, a class of work that constantly occurs in patternmaking, are arranged as in Fig. 198 when cut from a large piece of board ; of course, small scraps are used as far as possible in work of this kind.

A worker is often tempted to split small pieces instead of sawing by hand, but this is wasteful because it is unusual for a piece to split exactly as wanted. Still, the saving of time often justifies splitting ; the direction of grain should be noticed first, and if there is any doubt about the direction the split will take it is advisable to saw instead.

CHAPTER V

PLANING

PLANING is a process which naturally follows sawing. It has already been shown that trying and jack planes are used to make the surface of the work flat, the smoothing plane being reserved for the final surfacing. The length of the jack plane is such that it is difficult for even the beginner to make the work hollow; the plane bridges any depressions in the work because of its length, and prevents the cutting iron from coming into contact with the wood. It follows that the beginner need never fear that he will plane his work hollow. He is much more likely to get a convex effect by paying more attention to the margin of the work than to the middle.

Figs. 199 and 200 show how the jack plane or the trying plane should be held, the right hand grasping the toat or handle, the forefinger being extended so that it touches the iron. It will be noted that the fingers of the left hand extend down the far side of the stock, whilst the thumb is on the near side, exactly as illustrated. The worker should adopt such a position that his arms will have free play and allow of the plane being moved in a straightforward direction, not a swinging or circular motion. The proper poise is everything; the left foot should be parallel to the bench with the right foot at right angles to it. The strokes of the plane should be regular and as long as possible consistent with ease; and, at all cost, short, abrupt strokes should be avoided. If the body is held in the correct position, the worker will soon fall into the proper method of applying pressure on the tool. At the beginning of the stroke the left-hand presses down the forepart of the plane, but towards the end of the stroke the pressure is given by the right hand on the back of the plane.

On a flat surface and with a tool in thoroughly good

Fig. 199

Figs. 199 and 200.—Using the Jack Plane

order, it should be possible to take off a thin shaving nearly as wide as the cutting iron and as long as the work; but the beginner will not do this at first. After the first stroke, if the grain of the wood appears to be torn up it will be evidence that the planing has been against the grain and therefore either the plane or the work should be reversed. Sometimes the grain will be torn up in a few places and be smooth at others, indicating a very irregular grain, which, of course, no mere reversal of tool or work will overcome; and the only course then will be to use a tool in perfect condition both as regards keenness and adjustment, a very fine edge being essential; or the work may need to be finished with a scraper if the grain is very irregular.

"Sweet" action of the plane is assisted by applying a little oil to the face of the

Fig. 200

plane, just in advance of the cutter. The whole of the plane block may be oiled occasionally (*see* p. 38).

The principal use of the trying and jack plane is in producing a true surface free from winding, and before planing up it is necessary to test the surface to see if and where it is at fault, the method of doing so being to use winding strips, as shown in Fig. 201. These strips are perfectly parallel pieces of stuff, accurately planed up and tested. They are placed on the plank one at each end and the worker then

Fig. 201

Figs. 201 to 203.—Use of Winding Sticks in Testing a Surface

Fig. 202

Fig. 203

sights from one to the other, when if the board is in winding the top edges of the two strips will at once betray the fault (*see* Fig. 202), whereas if the plank is true the edges of the strips will be parallel, as in Fig. 203. The operation of sighting is often called " boning."

Other methods of testing for winding and squareness are employed on reasonably short and narrow work ; the use of the square, for example, has only to be shown (*see* Fig. 204) for it to be understood. If the blade is applied at intervals of a few inches, inaccuracies will soon be discovered. Another method is to use the blade of

Fig. 204.—Testing Squareness of Planed Work

the square merely as a short straightedge, applying it as in Fig. 205, and noting where no light can be seen between the blade and the work. Diagonal testing with a straightedge, as in Fig. 206, is on the same principle and very useful at times.

Work is held for planing on the flat of the bench, its end bearing against a stop of some kind, or when planing the edge of a strip or board the work is held in the vice, as in Fig. 207, which shows how the fingers of the left hand touch the work and

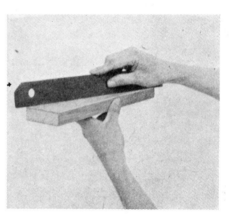

Fig. 206.—Testing Planed Work with Straightedge Diagonally

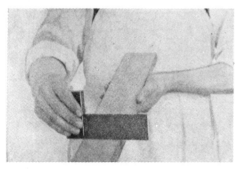

Fig. 205.—Testing Planed Work with Blade of Square

act as a fence, thus steadying the plane and keeping the centre of the cutter applied to the work. Note the position of the thumb, which is shown in the illustration as pressing on a button, the purpose of which is explained on page 17.

In edge planing, the position of the tool in relation to the edge of the work is of importance, owing to the fact that the cutting iron is slightly curved. This is made quite clear in Fig. 208, which suggests that the central position is the only one for obtaining a perfectly square edge.

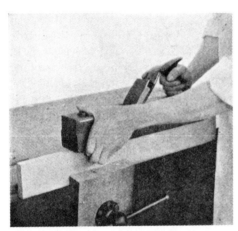

Fig. 207.—Edge Planing

Planing to Breadth and Thickness.—This is done on work that has been gauged—that is, marked with fine lines by the marking gauge —and the method of setting the gauge is as follows: Loosen its screw and take up the gauge in the left hand, holding a rule in the right; then the stock of the gauge can be moved sideways by the thumb or by the rule, so as accurately to adjust the distance between it and the point of the tooth (*see* Fig. 10, p. 3). When set as required, the first finger of the left hand holds the stock while the screw is tight-

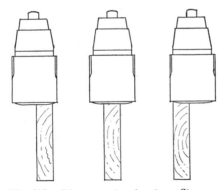

Fig. 208.—Diagrams showing how Shape of Plane Iron affects Edge Planing

ened up, afterwards testing with the rule to see that the stock has not been shifted in the course of tightening up. In use, the gauge is held, as clearly shown in Fig. 11, p. 3, with three fingers on the stem, one on the stock, and the thumb touching the stem as close as possible to the marking point. Press in the stock close to a trued-up face of the work, and push the gauge forward so as to form a light scratch. Lightness is necessary, because if the point is driven far into the work, it will tend to follow the grain and squeeze the stock into the work or push it out of contact. The scratch can be deepened by repeating the stroke, always working away from the body and not towards it.

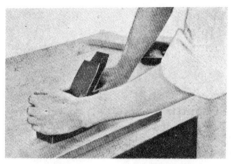

Fig. 209.—Using the Smoothing Plane

Using the Smoothing Plane.— The method of holding the smoothing plane is shown in Fig. 209; it is grasped firmly at front and back by the left and right hands respectively. There is some art in using it, as careless manipulation will leave a tool mark at the end of each stroke. The plane, being held exactly as illustrated, should be applied firmly, but

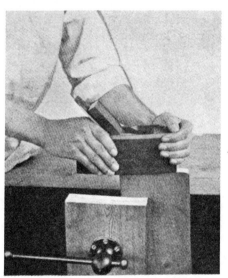

Fig. 210.—Use of Smoothing Plane on End Grain

lifted sharply when the end of the stroke is reached. Its use should result in a perfectly smooth surface, but very much depends upon the adjustment of the iron, and a common mistake is for the cutting iron to project too far, a fault easily corrected by a tap or two with a hammer on the back of the plane, remembering to tighten the wedge immediately afterwards. As the planing progresses, the left hand should be passed occasionally over the surface, and any inequalities will at once be felt. Another method is to incline the work in such a way that it is lighted almost entirely from one side, thus causing the inequalities to be detected by their shadows.

The smoothing plane needs to be used with extreme care on end grain (*see* Fig. 210), otherwise there is the risk of splitting the wood at the far edge. To avoid this accident it is usual not to extend the stroke to the full width of the work, and reverse the latter when required ; and it also assists if the far end can be lightly chamfered off before starting, as in Fig. 210, but circumstances do not always allow of this. Planing end grain is avoided as much as possible, but when it must be done the tool needs to be very keen and closely set. A good plan is to clamp an odd piece of stuff against the edge towards which the cutting is to be done, so that any splintering occurs on the odd piece and not on the actual work. An example of this is given in a later chapter.

CHAPTER VI

PARING, REBATING, AND CHAMFERING

Paring.—A woodworker needs to become expert in the use of the chisel, because so much of his work consists in making joints from which the waste wood is cut away chiefly by means of that tool. It is most important to have correctly ground and keen tools, and to use as large a chisel within reason as the work will permit.

Paring is done both horizontally and vertically, and the formation of a groove or notch required for a halved joint will afford practice in both kinds. The photograph (Fig. 211) shows how the work is held in the bench vice after the cross cuts have been made with tenon or dovetail saw (*see* an earlier chapter). In wood of particularly straight grain

Fig. 211.—Horizontal Paring

it might be possible to take out a thick piece with the mallet and chisel without endangering the work, but the safer and better practice is to remove the waste in the form of parings or thin shavings, the chisel being held horizontally with the right hand and guided with the left. Fig. 212 is a diagram of the action of paring, whilst Fig. 213 shows the effect of clumsily using the chisel entirely from one side and attempting to remove the bulk of the waste by means of a deep cut, this resulting in splitting a piece off the edge of the notch. It is always better to work from each side in turn.

Some workers use the chisel as shown in Fig. 214, making slanting cuts from each side and afterwards paring down

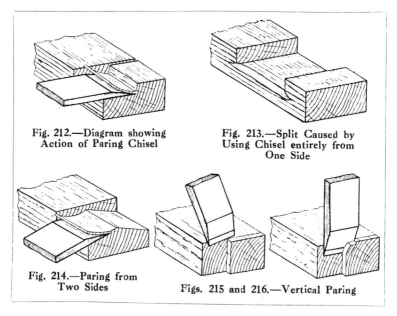

Fig. 212.—Diagram showing Action of Paring Chisel

Fig. 213.—Split Caused by Using Chisel entirely from One Side

Fig. 214.—Paring from Two Sides

Figs. 215 and 216.—Vertical Paring

the high part in the middle ; for the final paring of the bottom of the notch the blade of the chisel is held and guided by the thumb and first finger of the left hand, while the right hand imparts a sweeping motion from left to right, so that the chisel cuts obliquely to the grain.

Should it be necessary to detach the shavings by means of a vertical cut the chisel is held as in Fig. 217, with its flat side against the wall of the cut. Then, slightly inclining it, its edge is drawn along the angle to cut away the chips.

In overhand paring it is possible to exert more power than when the chisel is held horizontally. As shown in

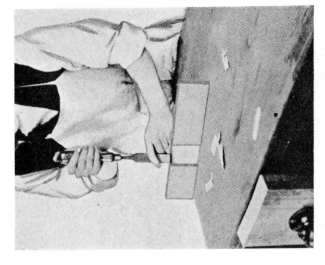

Fig. 218.—Overhand Paring in Making
Halved Joint

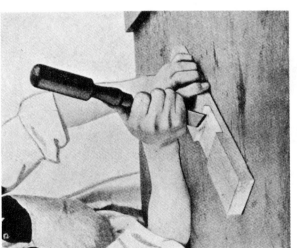

Fig. 217.—Cleaning-out Corners of Halving
with Chisel held Vertically

H

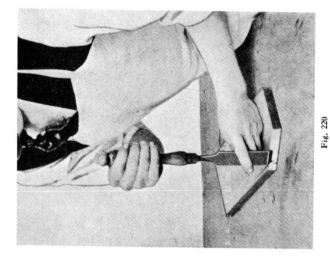

Fig. 220

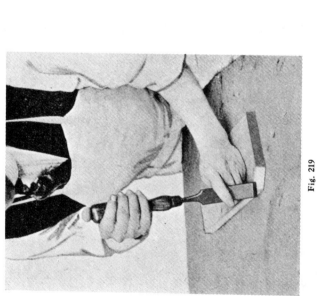

Fig. 219

Figs. 219 and 220.—Overhand Paring of Corner : Working Inwards and Working Outwards respectively

Fig. 218, the left hand rests on the work and guides the chisel, whilst the right one grasps the handle, thumb on top, and applies the effort. It is necessary to advance the right shoulder or there will be a tendency to cut on the slant. The same position is correct when paring end grain, but the tool must be in excellent condition and the parings made will be thinner. It will be found easier to start the cut by slightly inclining the chisel sideways, as in Fig. 215, but of course keeping the face of the chisel in the vertical plane ; having started the cut, the chisel can

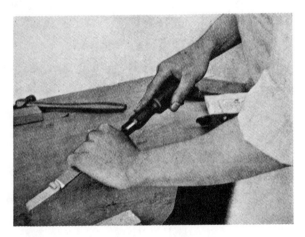

Fig. 221.—Approximately Horizontal Paring of Corner

be brought upright again as in Fig. 216. With this method there is more likelihood of paring the end of a piece of wood true, it being easier to make a second cut in exactly the same plane as the first. Remember that the chief considerations are a reasonably wide chisel, a keen edge, and correct position of the shoulder.

There is a risk, when paring off a corner, of splitting the work, unless the following point is remembered : Start at the edge and work inwards as in Fig. 219, and not at the end, and work towards the edge (*see* Fig. 220). In the latter case, when nearing completion, the chisel will exert a wedge action with possibly the result shown, but the safest of all methods of paring off a corner is to support the work not on the flat of the bench, but vertically in the vice, so that the edge to be pared occupies an approximately horizontal position, as in Fig. 221 ; in using the chisel, the left hand should cause the edge to work from left to right, the effort being applied with the right hand, but the latter should not be relied upon to remove the stuff simply by powerful thrusts.

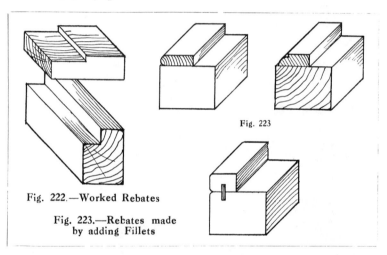

Fig. 223

Fig. 222.—Worked Rebates

Fig. 223.—Rebates made by adding Fillets

REBATING

Rebating with Cutting Gauge.—A rebate is an open-sided groove cut on the edge of work, as in Fig. 222. (Rebates are also made by adding fillets, *see* Fig. 223.) The method of making a rebate varies with the size of the work, very small rebates being cut by means of the cutting gauge, as illustrated in Figs. 224 and 225, the gauge having been set to the proper dimension and worked up and down, every forward stroke taking the knife or cutter deeper into the work. When the cut is as deep as the gauge can make it, the work is turned over, the gauge re-set (if any alteration is necessary), and the cutting done as before until the cutter reaches the first cut, when the waste will fall out. This is not a satisfactory method of doing the work if the wood is not of straight grain or is soft, as then there is a tendency to roughness in the cut and a likelihood of the cutter following the grain.

Rebate Planes.—The execution of a rebate of ordinary size is effected by means of the rebate plane obtainable in a variety of styles from tool dealers (*see* p. 20). A home-made rebate plane is shown in Fig. 226, this being simply a piece of wood 7 in. or 8 in. long, $3\frac{1}{2}$ in. wide, $1\frac{1}{4}$ in. thick,

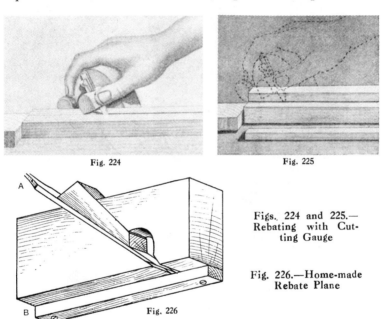

Fig. 224

Fig. 225

Figs. 224 and 225.—Rebating with Cutting Gauge

Fig. 226.—Home-made Rebate Plane

in which has been made a wedge-shaped groove or housing, by means of the tenon saw and chisel. The groove is just deep enough to take a $\frac{3}{4}$-in. chisel A. As shown, a curved piece requires to be removed to form a mouth from which the shavings can get away, and the wedge is made and fixed to hold the chisel firmly in place without chatter. A strip of wood B, screwed on as shown to the under side of the plane, acts as a fence, and its edge comes into contact with the edge of the work.

The shop-bought rebate plane seldom has a fence of

this kind; instead, the fence has to be attached by some means or other to the work that has to be rebated. In Fig. 227, for example, a fence is nailed to the work, but this method unfortunately involves some amount of injury because of the nail holes, and is therefore open to objection. Another method is to use two or more G-cramps in the way shown by Fig. 228; there must, first of all, be a piece of board A, housed to receive the bottoms of the G-cramps B, this being screwed down to the bench C. Upon A is laid the work D, and

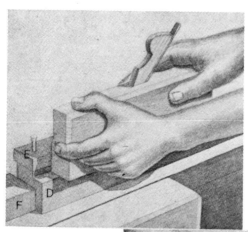

Fig. 227.—Rebating with Fence Nailed to Work

upon this the fence E carefully adjusted to a line already gauged, and then the cramps are screwed up tightly. The plane is worked until the required depth is obtained, it being

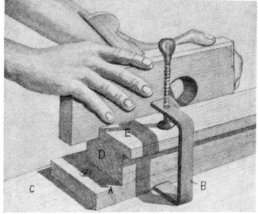

Fig. 228.—Rebating with Fence Clamped to Work

held close to the fence. In Fig. 227, D is a stop.

Guide Used in Rebating or Fielding Small Panels.— An adjustable guide is invaluable for such jobs as fielding (rebating) the margin of small panels. In such work, where the stuff is already cut to size, it is not possible to fix temporarily a guiding fillet with nails without leaving unsightly holes, and the panel board is too thin to allow of starting the rebate with the plough plane. A pair of guides are shown in position on a fielded panel in Fig. 229, A representing the panel.

Using them in pairs keeps the work horizontal to the bench. Little need be said as to the construction, which is shown in the enlarged section, Fig. 230. Four pieces of oak or mahogany, 1 in. by $\frac{3}{4}$ in., and 1 ft. $3\frac{1}{2}$ in. long, give about 1 ft. 2 in. between the bolts—a useful size for small work. If longer guides are made, the size, 1 in. by $\frac{3}{4}$ in., should

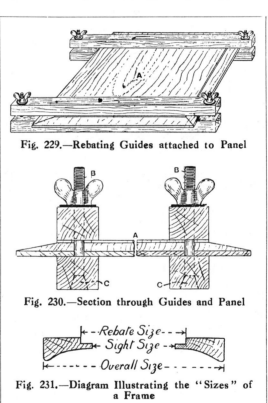

Fig. 229.—Rebating Guides attached to Panel

Fig. 230.—Section through Guides and Panel

Fig. 231.—Diagram Illustrating the "Sizes" of a Frame

be proportionally increased to avoid bending in use. The connecting bolts B are $\frac{1}{4}$ in. in diameter wrought-iron, with a square tapered countersunk head at C, and have a washer and small butterfly nut. They are about 3 in. over all, and the countersunk heads prevent the bolts revolving when screwing up. These bolts can be purchased at most ironmongers. (Fig. 230 might convey the impression that the bolts pass *through* the panel, but, of course, that is not the case, as Fig. 229 makes quite clear.) The slips of wood should be planed up true, and the holes for the bolts carefully bored. The square countersinking should be pared with a chisel, and the bolts should fit tight in the bottom pieces of the wood.

When fielding the margin of a panel, it is well first to fit it to the rebate of the door, or other framing for which it is being prepared, and, having marked the sight size with pencil lines, set off the boundary of the raised portion with further pencil lines parallel to, and at even distance from, the first. Make a slight saw cut on these boundary lines, and then fix the guides. Use a skew rebate plane and get down the full depth required on the square. Then tilt the rebate plane to form the bevel, which with advantage may be glasspapered before the guides are removed.

The term "sight size" is used in the foregoing paragraph. A frame—be it a picture frame or the rebated framework round a panel—has three sizes, both horizontally and vertically—the overall, sight, and rebate—all three of which are explained in Fig. 231.

Stopped Rebates.—These need to be worked at the ends by means of a chisel and saw, as, of course, the plane cutter cannot be taken into the extreme ends. The rebate is set out by means of the marking gauge in the ordinary way, but at each end there is made a saw cut, the saw being held slantwise, so that the saw kerf terminates at the gauge lines respectively at the top and the side of the work. The chisel and mallet are employed to make a number of cuts at each end inwards from the saw cut as in Fig. 232, the waste is then removed (*see* Fig. 233), and this portion of the rebate finished by vertical and horizontal paring (*see* Figs. 234 and 235), the rest of the rebate being worked in the ordinary way—if small, with the cutting gauge, otherwise with a rebate plane. Unfortunately, when a plane is used, more of the rebate has to be cut with a chisel than in the other case. However, there is a type of plane known as a bull-nose (*see* Fig. 236), in which the cutter is very near the front, thus allowing of the planing of the rebate much nearer the end than in the case with the ordinary rebate plane.

Chamfering.—The appearance of woodwork is often much improved by various forms of edge bevelling known

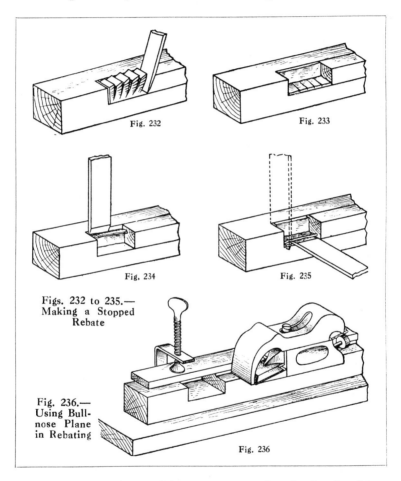

Fig. 232

Fig. 233

Fig. 234

Fig. 235

Figs. 232 to 235.— Making a Stopped Rebate

Fig. 236.— Using Bull- nose Plane in Rebating

Fig. 236

as " chamfering " (*see* Figs. 238 to 241). A simple object to start with for the sake of practice is an octagonal prism, which can be converted afterwards into cylindrical form for use as a blind roller, ruler, etc. In making an octagonal prism from a square piece of wood, first plane up the stuff quite square in section. On one end, draw the diagonals of the square, and set the marking gauge to a distance equal to half of a diagonal, as illustrated in Figs. 242 and 243. Then, with the gauge set to this distance, mark the

eight gauge lines (*see* Fig. 244). Of course, the stock of the gauge will rub against each face of the work twice in order to gauge these eight lines. The extremities of these lines should then be joined on the end

Fig. 237.—American Cornering Tool

of the work, which should then be placed with one of the diagonals vertical, and the chamfer made by planing down to the gauge lines.

A simple form of cradle to hold the piece firmly while planing is shown at Fig. 245, and is made by chamfering two strips of wood along one edge and nailing them together so that they form a V-groove. A piece about 2 in. long is then fitted into the groove and fixed by nails or screws at one end of the cradle as shown, so as to form a stop against which the work may be placed. The octagonal prism may easily be planed into approximately cylindrical

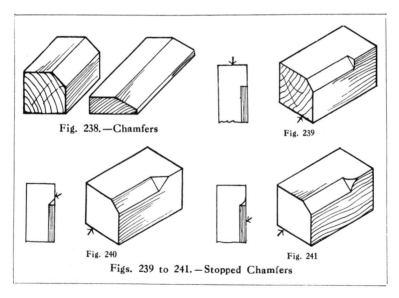

Fig. 238.—Chamfers

Fig. 239

Fig. 240

Fig. 241

Figs. 239 to 241.—Stopped Chamfers

form, using first the jack and then the smoothing plane (Fig. 246), finishing with fine No. 2 or No. 1 glasspaper.

Rounding an Edge.—This has much in common with chamfering. A rounded edge is seldom quite semicircular, being usually not more than a sector of a circle containing

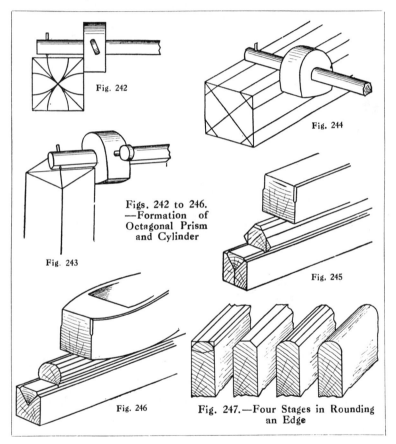

Fig. 242

Fig. 244

Figs. 242 to 246.—Formation of Octagonal Prism and Cylinder

Fig. 243

Fig. 245

Fig. 246

Fig. 247.—Four Stages in Rounding an Edge

an angle of about 150°, as in the first diagram of Fig. 247, in which figure the rounding-off is shown in four stages. A cornering tool used in America is shown by Fig. 237. It is a piece of bent steel, with a hole at each end, the edge of the hole being so sharpened that it acts as the edge of a gouge. It is used only on small work.

Chamfering and Rounding-off End Grain. — When chamfering or rounding-off end grain with a smoothing plane, the precautions mentioned on p. 94, with regard to the planing of end grain, must be observed. The plane should be held as in Fig. 248, and the cutting done obliquely to the grain. Liability to splitting is lessened by cramping a piece of waste A (Fig. 249) to the far edge, and the illus-

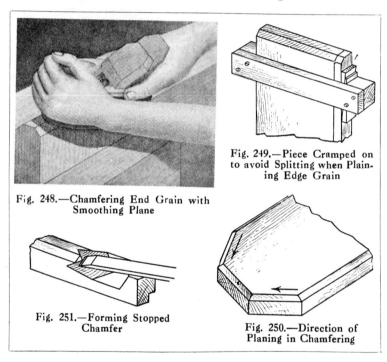

Fig. 249.—Piece Cramped on to avoid Splitting when Plaining Edge Grain

Fig. 248.—Chamfering End Grain with Smoothing Plane

Fig. 251.—Forming Stopped Chamfer

Fig. 250.—Direction of Planing in Chamfering

tration makes this clear. In such a case as that illustrated by Fig. 250, the arrows denote the direction in which the planing should be done.

Stop Chamfering.—Practice in stop chamfering is afforded by the square base or panel shown by Fig. 252. The material is set out as Fig. 253, using a bevel or template for making the splays of the stops. A suitable template (*see* Fig. 251) is a piece of wood rebated on the under side so as to form two surfaces at right angles to each other, one end being

splayed at the desired angle corresponding to the inclination of the
stop. Saw
kerfs are
next made
as indi-
cated, care

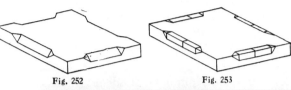

Fig. 252   Fig. 253

being taken that
they do not
quite touch the
lines. The work
should next be
firmly cramped
either directly
to the bench top
or to a block
that has been
securely fast-
ened by some
means to the
bench. Then,
with a keen
chisel held as in
Fig. 254, most
of the superflu-
ous wood can be
removed. Ob-
serve that the
bevel of the
chisel rests upon
the work.

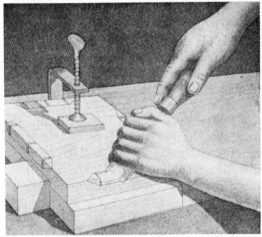

Fig. 254

Generally,
for hard wood,
the chiselling
can be done
best when the
flat face of the
chisel is held
firmly against

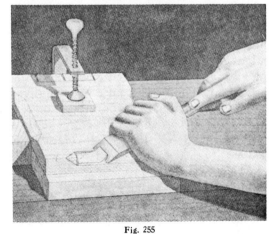

Fig. 255

Figs. 252 to 255.—Setting out and Executing
Stop Chamfers

the surface which is being pared, as in Fig. 255, at the same time sliding the edge up and down and pushing it forward. In repetition work, it saves time to use a template. This is held to the work, the back of the chisel being kept in close contact with its splayed end and pushed forward (*see* Fig. 251).

When making stop chamfers 6 in. or more in length, a short portion should be made at each end by paring with the chisel, and the remainder removed by planing. A very useful plane for this purpose is the bull-nose, one form of which is shown in use in Fig. 256. There is a large variety of iron bull-nose planes now available. A particularly useful tool is a combined rebating and right and left fillister plane. There is a class of Stanley plane (*see* Fig. 257) found very helpful in chamfering, and also for smoothing the surfaces of recesses formed out of the solid; it must be carefully sharpened and set fine. The grain of the wood must also be considered, and the plane made to cut in its direction or obliquely to it, often with a curved-like motion, there being then very little " digging " action.

Details of an Oxford frame ornamented with stop chamfers are given in Figs. 258 to 261. The joint is shown (from the back) together and apart, and the setting out and working of the chamfers are also indicated.

Chamfering with the Drawknife.—The drawknife is an interesting tool which, in the hands of a craftsman thoroughly practised in its use, but not in the hands of a raw beginner, might well be used for chamfering. This tool, actually, is merely a roughing-down tool, and, like the carpenter's hatchet or hand axe, its use is generally limited to removing superfluous material preparatory to the application of the finishing tools, such as plane, spokeshave, etc. The drawknife with a fairly long blade gives an excellent slide cut. Take the case of an ordinary stop chamfer or a curved stop chamfer, as shown in Fig. 262. The drawknife may be used for removing the waste, and possibly for finishing the chamfer. The knife can be used by the sliding cut by drawing to or pushing away. Special chamfering attachments for drawknives (*see* Fig. 263A) can be obtained, those illustrated being of American origin.

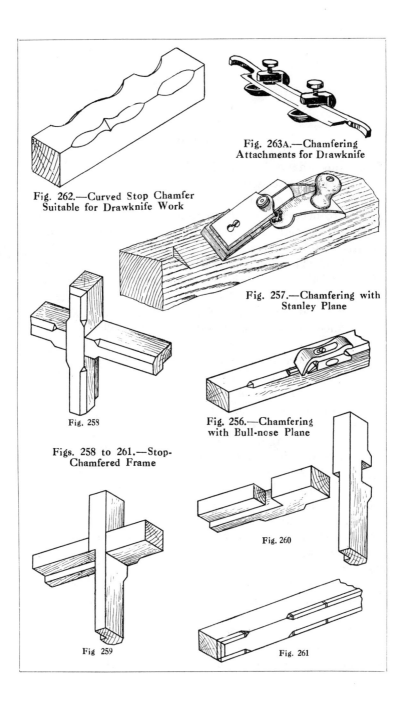

Fig. 263A.—Chamfering
Attachments for Drawknife

Fig. 262.—Curved Stop Chamfer
Suitable for Drawknife Work

Fig. 257.—Chamfering with
Stanley Plane

Fig. 258

Fig. 256.—Chamfering
with Bull-nose Plane

Figs. 258 to 261.—Stop-
Chamfered Frame

Fig. 260

Fig 259

Fig. 261

CHAPTER VII

BORING

THE brace, hand-drill, and principal bits used in boring holes in wood are described on pp. 27 to 31, and for their ordinary use no instructions further than those already given are necessary ; but there are some points of interest and some special matters to which attention may be drawn in this chapter.

Making Through-holes with a Centre-bit.—There is, of course, no difficulty in doing this, but when working on thin stuff it is difficult to avoid breaking away the fibres of the wood at the bottom of the hole and so giving a jagged appearance to the under side, but the following method should prove useful if carefully performed. Support the work on a piece of waste wood, maintain the bit at right angles to the work, and continue boring until the point of the bit can be felt on the under side. Then remove the bit, reverse the work, insert the bit, and rotate so as to make a deep cut with the nicker, but do not necessarily take off any shavings. Again reverse the work, replace the bit in its first position, and continue the cutting, when, if the operation has been carefully performed, a disc of wood will fall out. The cut-away views (Figs. 263 to 265) further explain what is meant.

Boring Semi-circular Groove.—Assume that a semi-circular groove is to be cut across the face of a piece of wood. Square the centre of the groove across the face, and then with a tenon-saw make a slight cut the full width. Treat another piece of stuff—any waste piece—in exactly the same way. Now, if these two pieces are clamped together, saw cuts inwards, and, held in the vice, a bit can then be run down between them. The cuts will act as a lead, and both pieces will, on separation, contain a groove. The Forstner auger bit will bore a semicircular groove.

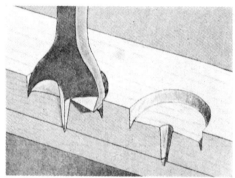

Fig. 263

Boring Out Slots and Long Holes.— Fig. 266 suggests a method of removing the waste in forming in thin stuff a hole long in proportion to its width. The actual work illustrated is the division piece of a

knife-box, and the hand- or lifting-hole is to be cut before the piece is sawn to shape; in the photograph, the outline of the top of the division piece will possibly be recognised. In this case five holes bored with a centre-bit leave the ends of

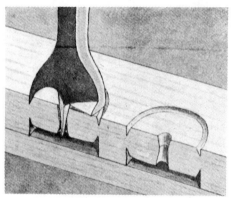

Fig. 264

the slot of the correct shape and remove most of the waste, the final shape being obtained by paring. Of course, where dimensions allow, such a hole would be cut with a tenon-saw or fretsaw, first boring a small hole through which the saw can be passed. In a

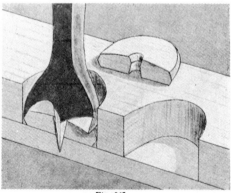

Fig. 265

Figs. 263 to 265.—Boring Through-holes with Centre-bit

I

Fig. 266.—Boring-out Waste of Slot

later chapter reference will be made to the use of the twist bit in removing the bulk of the waste in forming mortises.

A modification of the foregoing is in connection with the use of the very large centre-bits, in rotating which great strain is felt. If a small twist-bit is run into the wood, almost but not quite the full depth of the required hole, a number of times, it will remove so much stuff as to make the work of the centre-bit very much lighter. But take care to leave plenty of wood at the centre of the hole where the point of the centre-bit will come, and to see that the twist-bit holes do not touch the circumference of the hole, as otherwise the centre-bit will not work well.

Boring Taper Holes.—A method of boring holes tapering from $1\frac{3}{8}$ in. or so to 1 in. through hard wood 2 in. square is as follows : Having marked the centres of the hole on

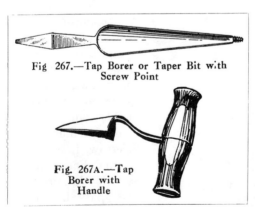

Fig 267.—Tap Borer or Taper Bit with Screw Point

Fig. 267A.—Tap Borer with Handle

opposite sides of the work, bore the hole with a $1\frac{1}{4}$-in. centre-bit about $\frac{1}{8}$ in. deep ; then continue half-way through with a 1-in. centre-bit or twist-bit. Turn the work over and complete the hole, which can then be finished with gouge, file, and glasspaper. But this is not the most practical method. It would be quicker to use a tap borer (*see* Fig. 267) as employed for boring tap holes in barrels, first boring through with a $\frac{7}{8}$-in. or 1-in. bit. The handled tap borer (Fig. 267A) would be useful in this connection.

Boring Wide Boards Edgewise.—Assume that it is required to bore a number of $\frac{3}{8}$-in. holes through boards

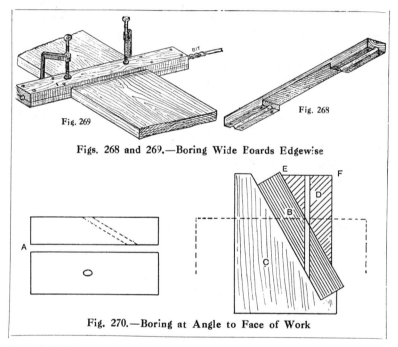

Figs. 268 and 269.—Boring Wide Boards Edgewise

Fig. 270.—Boring at Angle to Face of Work

$\frac{7}{8}$ in. thick and 1 ft. 3 in. wide. At Fig. 268 is shown a piece of wood notched out to half the thickness of the board ; the projecting portion at each end should be hollowed out to form a semi-circular groove so that the bit or auger will just sink into it half-way. Two short pieces of wood should be similarly hollowed out and screwed on at the ends, thus leaving a hole for the bit to work in accurately. This contrivance can be secured to the board with a couple of hand screws, and the boring can be performed as indicated at Fig. 269. With care, there should be no difficulty in boring the holes from each edge so that they will meet.

Boring at Awkward Angle to Face of Work.—There is often difficulty in boring holes in cylindrical objects or at an awkward angle to the edge of a straight object, and it is generally overcome by making a cradle or box to hold the work so that the boring bit may be held upright and yet be applied to the work at the requisite angle. A cylinder may be held in a rough box (put together of waste pieces) that will just receive it, and might be wedged in if thought likely to move. Then the holes can be bored through the cover of the box into the rounded surface, the work having first been carefully set out on the cover of the box. Holes at awkward angles are best made when the work is supported in a cradle or on an inclined plane, a wedge-shaped piece of waste stuff being temporarily secured to the face of the work so that the boring bit will enter at right angles. Thus, A (Fig. 270) is plan and section through a piece in which the hole has been bored by supporting the work shown at B either in a strong vice (dotted lines indicate vice-jaw) or on a block or on two triangular pieces of rough stuff C, temporarily securing a second triangular block D in position on the face of the work, and then boring at right angles to E F. If the work is held in the vice, there should be a piece of waste over the back of the hole, so as to prevent splintering, or the work should be reversed when the point of the bit appears on the under side.

Cutting Large Holes in Thin Stuff.—The tool shown in Fig. 271 has been found useful for cutting holes in ¼-in. three-ply wood, the holes varying from 1 in. to 4 in. in diameter. The illustration shows the tool or bit ready for fixing in the ordinary joiner's brace. The centre point A is made from a broken ¼-in. centre-bit ground to shape, taking the original point as a guide for grinding. The collar B (shown separately on the right) is made from $\frac{5}{8}$-in. by $\frac{1}{8}$-in. wrought-iron bent to shape, drilled and tapped to fit the set-screw C, which is $\frac{3}{4}$ in. by $\frac{3}{16}$ in. in diameter; also, it has two holes drilled and filed to shape to allow the centre point A to fit tight. The cutter D should be made up from $\frac{3}{8}$-in. by $\frac{3}{32}$-in. steel forged and ground to shape, and hardened at the cutting edge ; it can be set to make various sizes by means of the set-screw c. If required to cut discs with square edges, the cutter should be formed as shown in detail E, that is, with the bevel outwards. By using two cutters, one with the bevel inwards D and one with the bevel outwards (as shown dotted), washers can be cut with square edges.

Boring Square Holes.—There is, of course, no mystery at all in mortising out square holes with an ordinary

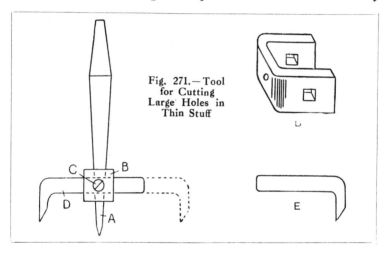

Fig. 271.—Tool for Cutting Large Holes in Thin Stuff

mortising machine ; indeed, it is the common practice of the trade, but that is outside the question of boring square holes in wood for ordinary purposes. As a matter of fact, the boring of square holes in any material is useless practically, but as a trick it can be managed by folding a piece of lead or paper between two pieces of wood, and boring down through the wood and paper to the depth of half the diameter of the boring bit, as shown in Fig. 272, in which the shaded line A represents the folded paper or thin sheet-lead, and B the pieces of wood between which it is held in the vice C. A centre-bit is shown in the sketch for boring purposes ; but a square-ended wood counter-sinking bit would be better. By re-folding the paper, two or more holes may be bored at one operation.

A tool for boring square holes is now fairly well known. It consists of a square steel tube sharpened at one end on the four inner surfaces. Within this tube revolves a screw-auger bit, which has a shoulder bearing on the end of the square tube which encloses it. It is obvious that (1) the square tube must be held at the beginning of the cut; (2) the strain on the screw nose of the bit must be great, as it must advance both bit and hollow chisel; (3) the tool must be removed from the work frequently, or it will be choked by the wood removed; (4) the work must be very arduous unless motive power is supplied by machinery; (5) the square chisel tube must be kept sharp.

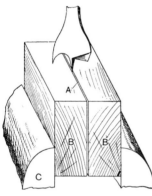

Fig. 272.—Boring a Square Hole

In the "hollow chisel mortiser" made by a Canadian firm, there is a revolving bit within a square chisel, the bit being so placed that its extended lips project slightly in advance of the cutting edges of the chisel. The chisel is fitted in a reciprocating plunger frame, which also carries the bit spindle with its driving pulley. This entire tool carriage is fed to and from the timber, cutting at each stroke a squared and cleaned hole of the desired depth, while a movement of the timber table produces a succession of these holes, and thus forms any length of mortice in any required direction. In operation the chips are all carried out by the revolving bit, and ejected either through the opening in the side of the chisel or from its hollow shank. The chisel has a quick return motion after each stroke, and the work can be laid out by stops on the machine. These particulars are given not because the amateur will find any advantage in investing in such a tool, but because of late years there has been a great deal of curiosity in relation to this subject.

Cutting Screw-threads in Wood.—Screw-threads may be required in holes to receive pins, dowels, etc., and, of course, on those pins, etc., themselves. In holes, the threads are formed by forcing through them a tap (*see* Fig. 273), which is a screwed piece of steel with, say, four flats formed

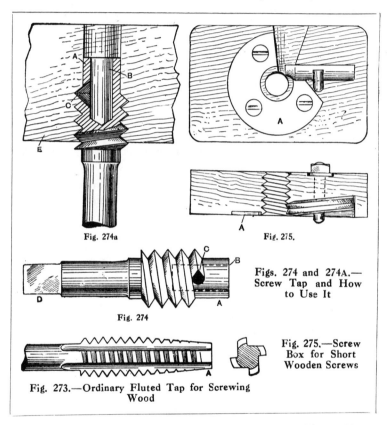

Fig. 274a.

Fig. 275.

Figs. 274 and 274A.—
Screw Tap and How
to Use It

Fig. 274.

Fig. 275.—Screw
Box for Short
Wooden Screws

Fig. 273.—Ordinary Fluted Tap for Screwing
Wood

in it so as to produce scraping or cutting edges. To facilitate its entrance into the hole the first few threads may be tapered off as at A. A better form of tap for wood, and one which could well follow the taper tap and finish the work, is shown in Fig. 274, in which A indicates the front end, B a recess drilled in the tap, and C a hole communicating with the recess and forming also a sharp edge. Fig. 274A shows how this tap is used, the letter references being as before; E is the piece of wood that is being screwed. The tap is gripped in a vice by its square end D, and the work, previously bored, is pushed down on it with a twisting movement. The scrapings pass into the recess and are thus readily disposed of.

For external threads, resort is had to a screw-box, which generally is a block of boxwood or beech with a screwed hole, and at the base of the hole an internally projecting cutter which can be pressed into the work, the box being given a rotating motion. The screw-box shown in Fig. 275 allows of the full thread being cut close up to a shoulder. The box is bored and threaded, and to obviate undue wear a plate or washer A is countersunk and attached with screws. This type of box is used principally in the lathe. Nowadays, steel screw-boxes are coming into more extended use. They have single or double handles according to their size, and are more convenient and efficient than the wooden ones.

CHAPTER VIII

HALVED, LAPPED, NOTCHED AND HOUSED JOINTS

Various Forms of Halved and Notched Joints.—All joints of this class have a strong likeness, and Figs. 276 to 278 and 287 to 290 show the chief kinds. They are of common occurrence in both carpentry and cabinet work, suitable applications of lapped and halved joints being in the divisions of drawers and pigeon-holes, in cabinets, in the cross-rails of occasional tables, and for transverse jointing generally.

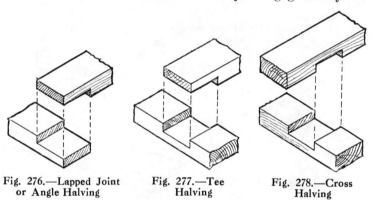

Fig. 276.—Lapped Joint or Angle Halving

Fig. 277.—Tee Halving

Fig. 278.—Cross Halving

Making Halved Joints.—The lapped or halved joint in its various forms is almost so simple as not to require explanation, but the making of the model cross halved joint shown in Fig. 279 may be briefly described, as exemplifying all. To make such a model, a piece of wood as in Fig. 280 would be required. By means of a marking gauge, square and marking knife, this is set out as shown, and the parts that are to be removed are marked with a cross as indicated to minimise risk of error. The depth of each notch is half the thickness of the wood, whilst the width will coincide with that of the stuff. With a tenon-saw, cut down just inside the lines—that is in the waste—starting the cut

121

as in Fig. 181, and continuing it as in Fig. 182. The waste between the two saw kerfs is removed by means of a chisel, which may be used overhand, as in Fig. 218, or horizontally as in Fig. 211; in either case, it may be necessary to clean

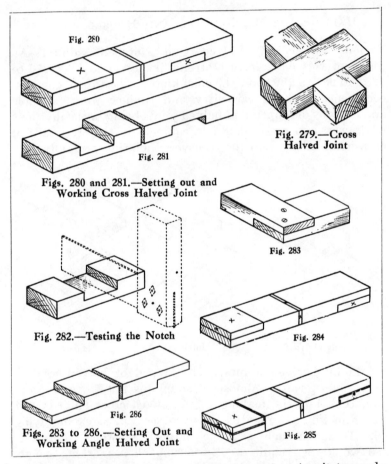

Fig. 280

Fig. 281

Fig. 279.—Cross Halved Joint

Figs. 280 and 281.—Setting out and Working Cross Halved Joint

Fig. 283

Fig. 282.—Testing the Notch

Fig. 284

Fig. 286

Fig. 285

Figs. 283 to 286.—Setting Out and Working Angle Halved Joint

out the angles by inclining the chisel and drawing it towards the worker as shown in Fig. 217. For testing the bottom of the notch, hold the blade of the square as in Fig. 282, between the worker and the light; any unevenness will then show. The work now resembles Fig. 281. The making of an angle lap joint (Figs. 283 to 286) is still more simple, and does not require separate explanation; in this case, of course, the waste is wholly removed with tenon-saw.

For the oblique halved joint shown in Fig. 287, the work is the same as for the ordinary cross lap joint, but the

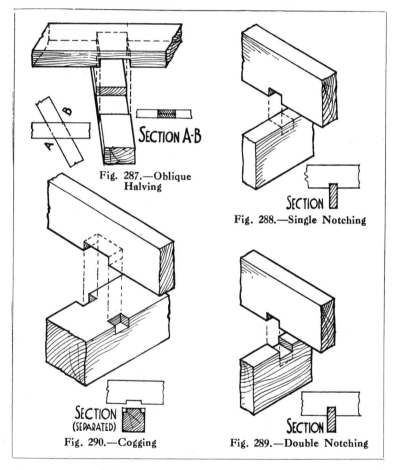

SECTION A-B

Fig. 287.—Oblique
Halving

SECTION

Fig. 288.—Single Notching

SECTION
(SEPARATED)

Fig. 290.—Cogging

SECTION

Fig. 289.—Double Notching

setting out is different. The marking gauge is used as before, but the oblique lines across the face of the stuff are obtained by means of a bevel accurately set to the lines of the marking drawing; sometimes it is convenient to put the one piece of stuff over the other and to mark off from each of them to give the face lines. These lines should be squared down to meet those marked by the gauge.

Where great strain comes upon the halved joint, there is danger of the stuff being split, as indicated in Fig. 291, to obviate which experienced craftsmen often adopt the construction shown in Fig. 292, which has great lateral strength and stability, the latter being largely due to the wedge action produced between the two parts of the joint. It is no longer, however, a simple joint to make. In setting out, square lines on the face and two sides, and with the marking gauge indicate the bottom of the notch. The degree of angle to be employed should be slight, and should be marked with a bevel. The angle should correspond roughly with that

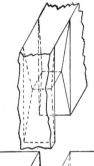

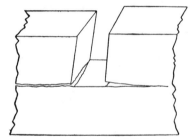

Fig. 291.—Failure of Halved Joint

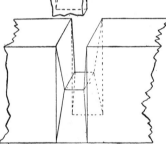

Fig. 292.—Form of Halved Joint to Prevent Splitting

indicated in the illustration—one in six is found to be sufficient. This joint had better not be attempted until the joints described in later chapters have been mastered, as both sawing and chiselling must be very accurately performed, or the joint will be a failure.

Notched Joints.—No special instructions should be necessary for the making of notched joints (see Figs. 288 to 290). Such joints occur occasionally in ordinary woodworking, but their chief application is in constructional carpentry. Similarly, Figs. 293 to 299 illustrate a few joints used principally in building construction, but which

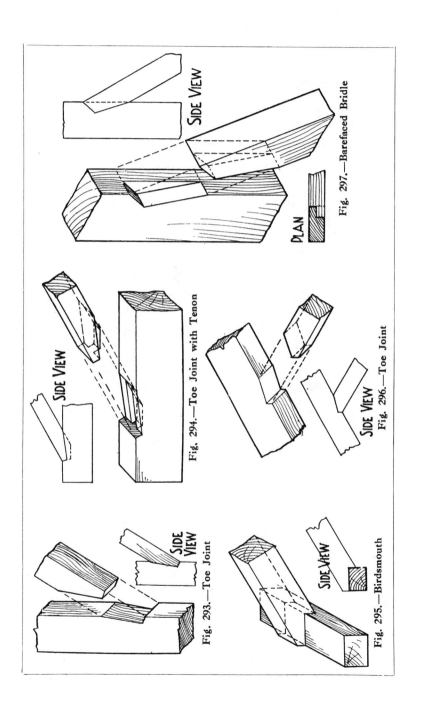

SIDE VIEW

PLAN

Fig. 297.—Barefaced Bridle

SIDE VIEW

Fig. 294.—Toe Joint with Tenon

SIDE VIEW

Fig. 296.—Toe Joint

SIDE VIEW

Fig. 293.—Toe Joint

SIDE VIEW

Fig. 295.—Birdsmouth

may occasionally be required by the woodworker—especially in the erection of a workshop, studio, etc. It is not thought necessary to describe them in detail.

Housed Joints.—Housing consists in sinking the ends of a shelf, etc., into grooves cut for their reception in the upright supports. Simple forms of housing are shown in

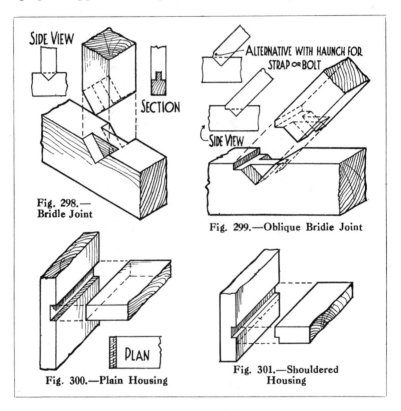

Fig. 298.—Bridle Joint

Fig. 299.—Oblique Bridle Joint

Fig. 300.—Plain Housing

Fig. 301.—Shouldered Housing

Figs. 300 to 302, the last showing what is known as stopped housing, that is, the groove is stopped before reaching the face edge of the upright, this giving a neater finish. The setting out and working of the model housed joint shown in Fig. 303 is explained in Fig. 304. It should be noted that the distance between the lines which determine the width of the groove should be about $\frac{1}{32}$ in. less than the thick-

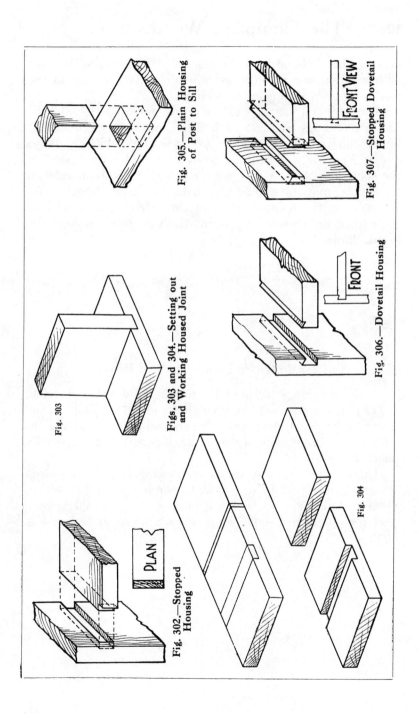

Fig. 305.—Plain Housing of Post to Sill

Front View

Fig. 307.—Stopped Dovetail Housing

Front

Fig. 306.—Dovetail Housing

Fig. 303

Figs. 303 and 304.—Setting out and Working Housed Joint

Fig. 304

Plan

Fig. 302.—Stopped Housing

ness of the shelf, etc., to be housed. The cutting is done
with a tenon-saw as close as possible to the lines, and the
waste removed by means of a chisel.

The stopped housing is obviously not quite so simple.
The grooves are set out as before, and the end line that
limits the length of the groove is marked with a gauge
(*see* A, Fig. 308).   Then the grooves are cut with a saw on
the slant until lines A and B are reached.   The remainder of
the cutting may have to be done with the chisel, though some
workers use the point of the saw, first driving a chisel into
the end of the groove to prevent the saw going beyond the
proper limit.

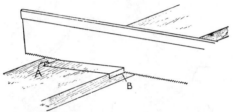

Fig. 308.—Cutting Stopped Groove or Housing

A much stronger form of housing is the dovetail housing,
either plain or stopped (*see* Figs. 306 and 307).   The method
of working this will be readily understood after mastering the
examples of dovetailing given in later pages.   See especially
pages 205 and 206.

One of the simplest forms of housing is that employed
sometimes at the foot of a post to connect it rigidly with a
plate or sill.   The foot of the post is not reduced in size,
and fits snugly in a hole (mortise) cut in the plate (*see* Fig.
305).

CHAPTER IX

BUTTED, TONGUED, AND FEATHER-TONGUED JOINTS

Glued Butt Joints.—These joints (*see* Fig. 309) are often adopted where two or more widths have to be joined edge to edge to form wide panels, table-tops, etc. The strength of a butt joint is merely that of the glue employed, and a thick, uneven streak of glue means an unreliable joint. The surfaces in contact need to be planed as true as it is possible to get them, and to be coated with good glue, the greater part of which must be squeezed out in course of making the joint.

The edges will need to be shot true with a trying plane, and tested with the try-square, and also by bringing the two edges into contact (the boards being supported vertically) between the worker and the light. Inequalities will then betray themselves, should be indicated with a pencil mark on the face side, and then planed off. Rubbing one board on the other will indicate by the feel whether the contact is good. Again place the surfaces in contact, and with a straightedge see that the faces are perfectly flush. It is, of course, possible to get smooth edge surfaces everywhere in contact, but for the joint to be spoilt by the planed edges not being precisely at right angles to the faces. In long joints, say more than 5 ft., some workmen deliberately introduce a slight but even hollowness extending to within a few inches of each end, but the amount of the hollowness must only be such that the pressure of the cramps will obliterate it. However, as cramping should be unnecessary in most cases, and as the adoption of the method might be regarded as an admission that the craftsman cannot produce true edges and is actually choosing the lesser of two evils, it is better to see that the preliminary testing and rubbing demonstrate that there is an end to end contact.

J   129

The services of an assistant are of great advantage during the next stage of the work.

The gluing up is best done in a warm, well ventilated room, and the work should have been gently warmed as well, for should the glue be suddenly chilled in course of application, its strength will suffer. Have the glue of the best quality, fresh, of good and even consistency, and hot. Clamp one board, face outwards, in the bench vice, trued edge upwards; lean the other face inwards against it so that the two surfaces to be jointed are more or less in line, and apply the glue rapidly and copiously to both of them at once, laying it on with a sweeping stroke, and not " working " the brush as though painting. Bring the surfaces immediately into contact, and with as much pressure as possible rub or slide the top board over the lower one to and fro, so as to squeeze out air and superfluous glue.

When, in the course of only a few seconds, the movement becomes less free and the solidity of the joint is assured, bring the top board into its precise position in relation to the bottom one, and, if the job allows, insert a light sprig at each end as shown in Fig. 312, to prevent the work shifting accidentally; these sprigs will be withdrawn after the glue is hard.

Should the top board be shifted by the now possibly sticky hands after the rubbing is completed, the joint will have been destroyed; it will need to be unmade, the glue washed off with hot water, and another attempt made.

Cramping is necessary only in the case of thin wood; a device on the lines of one of those illustrated in Chapter XV. will answer the purpose best.

Butt-jointing Warped Boards.—When both boards are warped in the width, they can often be straightened by wetting the hollow sides with water and placing together, pressing them straight with handscrews and clamps of wood, or placing under weights. Another way—when the board is wanted for immediate use—is to wet the hollow side and heat the round side before a fire. But for boards that are warped in the length, it is well to keep a few ribs of wood about 1 in. square, and quite straight. These may be screwed to the board about 1 in. from the edge to be joined, as shown by Fig. 310. If the board is warped wavy, the position of the screws should be as shown in Fig. 311, and sometimes it is necessary to cramp close with hand-screws before driving in the screws.

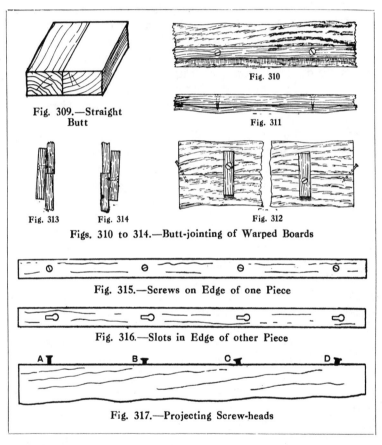

Fig. 309.—Straight Butt

Fig. 310

Fig. 311

Fig. 313

Fig. 314

Fig. 312

Figs. 310 to 314.—Butt-jointing of Warped Boards

Fig. 315.—Screws on Edge of one Piece

Fig. 316.—Slots in Edge of other Piece

Fig. 317.—Projecting Screw-heads

With furniture which has been made with unseasoned timber, what is known as a broken joint often occurs ; this is caused by both boards shrinking and parting where they have been joined. In the case of a table-top which has been polished, and it is necessary to remove and rejoint it, it is desirable to keep the surface as level as possible to avoid having to plane or scrape the polished surface. For this purpose should be kept a few pieces of wood about 5 in. long by 1 in. by ½ in., with a screw through each about 2 in. from one end. When the joint is ready for gluing, a sprig should be partly driven in at each end as shown in Fig. 312, which also shows the pieces screwed across the joint to bring it level. Observation of the joint must decide the position of these. For instance, where the top piece overhangs, the screw must pull it back as Fig. 313 shows, and vice versa (*see* Fig. 314). It is necessary to act quickly in gluing, driving the sprigs and screwing on the pieces, feeling the surface and regulating the screws till quite level.

Slotted Screw Joints.—These are straight-butt joints, generally but not always glued, in which concealed screws are used (*see* Figs. 315 and 316). These screws are driven into the edge of one board, their heads being left well out, while key-hole mortises are made in the edge of the other member. When the two pieces are brought together, the screws enter the wider parts of the mortises, and the joint is tightened up merely by forcibly sliding one member on the other, the joint surfaces having previously been glued if so desired. This joint is not always a success, one reason of failure being that the direction of the grain of the wood is not always allowed for. The slots for the screws should be made in the direction in which the grain runs away from the edge of the wood. The head of the screw will then be drawn in more deeply, and the joint will be tight. If arranged the other way, the grain will so lead the head of the screw as to slacken the joint instead of tightening it. Another cause of failure is in leaving the heads of the screws too far out as at A (Fig. 317). They will then bend instead of passing along the grain as they should do ; and the same fault occurs if the screws used are too slight. Screws of as stout gauge as possible should always be used. Should the grain of the wood be such as to draw the joint together, the screws may be inserted exactly straight as at B ; but otherwise it is best to slope them somewhat as at C, thus giving the head a slight lead.

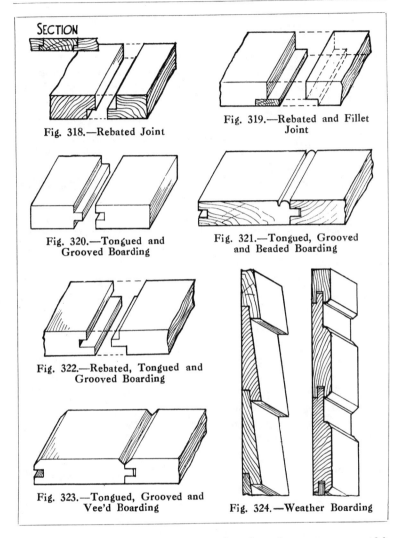

SECTION

Fig. 318.—Rebated Joint

Fig. 319.—Rebated and Fillet Joint

Fig. 320.—Tongued and Grooved Boarding

Fig. 321.—Tongued, Grooved and Beaded Boarding

Fig. 322.—Rebated, Tongued and Grooved Boarding

Fig. 323.—Tongued, Grooved and Vee'd Boarding

Fig. 324.—Weather Boarding

On no account must the screw be sloped as at D, as this will at once force the boards apart.

Take care to make the slots deep enough, and, in driving the joint together, press the top board down firmly. Above all, fit each joint before the glue is put on, taking it apart again for the final gluing up.

Straight Rebated Joints.—These (*see* Fig. 318) require to be made with as much care as is bestowed upon the plain butt joint, and, in addition, there is the rebating to execute (for full instructions, see an earlier chapter, pp. 100 to 104). Sometimes the rebate is made on the back or underside of each piece, but much shallower (*see* Fig. 319), and a fillet to occupy the space of the two rebates is fitted. Machine-rebated stuff is obtainable from timber merchants, and while this is good enough for rough work, it is not suitable for cabinet-makers' purposes.

Tongued and Grooved Joints.—A variety of these joints are in use (*see* Figs. 320 to 323), and matchboarding already worked is obtainable. But it is rare to find in this cheap material a plank having a perfect tongue or a perfect groove throughout, and the careful furniture maker is not likely to use such stuff. In forming joints of the tongue-and-groove class, it is necessary to make a groove in one piece and to form a corresponding tongue on the other. The groove is made with a " plough," and the tongue is formed by the use of a special plane that cuts a rebate on each edge of the stuff.

Weather boarding of the best class affords an example of the tongued, grooved, and chamfered joint ; but simple rebating is also employed for the purpose (*see* Fig. 324).

The Plough.—The woodworker speaks of " ploughing " a groove, and grooves may be necessary for a variety of purposes, the commonest being jointing by ploughing and tonguing. Special forms of planes known as ploughs are made and sold for the purpose, and the " Universal " plane is, of course, an excellent plough, in addition to fulfilling many other functions.

A substitute for a plough may be made something on the lines of the rebating plane already illustrated (*see* p. 101). A piece of wood, about 3 in. thick and any convenient width and length, has a rebate run along its bottom edge as shown at A (Fig. 325). A housing for chisel B and wedge C, and also a recess D to serve as a mouth for the shavings, will need to be made. The projecting part E must be a mere shade narrower than the chisel B, and the latter must have its bevel side downwards. F is a fence, the depth of the rebate in which will determine the distance between the edge of the work and the ploughed groove.

A home-made plough more of the regulation pattern is shown by Fig. 326, its fence being shown separately by

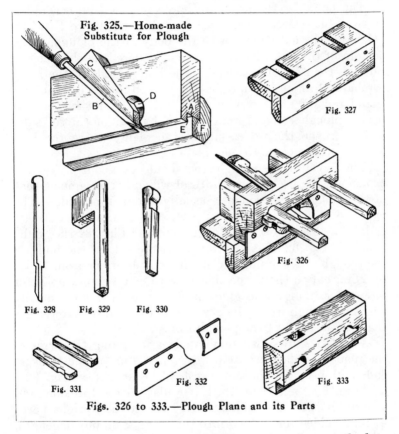

Fig. 325.—Home-made Substitute for Plough

Fig. 327

Fig. 326

Fig. 328   Fig. 329   Fig. 330

Fig. 331   Fig. 332   Fig. 333

Figs. 326 to 333.—Plough Plane and its Parts

Fig. 327. Two pieces of wood, squared and smoothed to the required thickness, $\frac{3}{4}$ in., are required. The horizontal piece is $8\frac{1}{2}$ in. by $2\frac{1}{4}$ in. by $\frac{3}{4}$ in., with two sinkings of $\frac{3}{16}$ in. deep and $\frac{3}{4}$ in. wide, at equal distances from each end, as shown. The distance between these sinkings should be $3\frac{1}{2}$ in. The upright piece is screwed on at each end to the horizontal piece, the space in the centre being for the sinking of a plough stop if required. The body of the plough is $7\frac{1}{2}$ in. by $3\frac{1}{2}$ in. by $1\frac{3}{4}$ in. It is shown by Fig. 333, where the position of the hole for the plough iron and wedge, the two holes for the arms of the plough to slide through, and the position of wedge slots are also given.

The holes for the arms are bored with a $\frac{3}{4}$-in. centre-bit or twist-bit. Great care must be taken to ensure that the holes shall be cut square with the body of the plough. The bottom of the holes having been cut square, the slots at the side are then cut for wedges. The bottom side of the body is rebated 1 in. on the upright and $\frac{3}{4}$ in. on the horizontal, and chamfered off as shown in Fig. 327. The slot in the top for the plough iron and wedge is $\frac{7}{8}$ in. by $\frac{5}{8}$ in. on the top side, and $\frac{11}{16}$ in. on the under-side of the plane, where the iron and the wedge come through.

The bevel of the plough iron should be about 45°. Fig. 330 shows the wedge, the width of which is the same as that of the plough iron, which is usually about $\frac{5}{8}$ in. wide. The wedge is $\frac{7}{8}$ in. at its thickest part, and $\frac{3}{8}$ in. at its thinnest end. Fig. 328 shows the plough iron, and Fig. 332 the guide, which in Fig. 326 is shown fixed on the side of the body of the plough. The guide can be made of brass or iron, $7\frac{1}{2}$ in. by 2 in., cut to the shape shown, with countersunk holes for screws for fixing ; the guide is firmly screwed on centrally with the plough iron. Plenty of room should be allowed for shavings in front of the plough iron.

Fig. 331 shows two small wedges for fixing the arms of the plough. They are $3\frac{1}{2}$ in. by $\frac{3}{8}$ in., $\frac{5}{8}$ in. at the thickest end, and $\frac{3}{8}$ in. at the narrowest. The arms (*see* Fig. 329) are 9 in. long and $\frac{3}{4}$ in. thick (circular on the top side, and square on the under side), and $2\frac{1}{2}$ in. in the upright part ; $\frac{3}{16}$ in. is added for sinking into the fence, 2 in. on the length, and the rest of the length (7 in.), which slides through the body of the plane, should be circular on the top side and square on the under side. The two arms should be glued, screwed, and firmly fixed in the fence.

If the reader can afford a regular plough, he may be recommended to purchase one of the kind shown by Figs. 334 and 335. The stock of the plane is held or released.

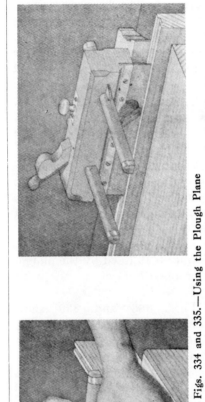

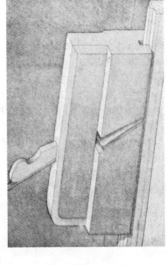

Figs. 334 and 335.—Using the Plough Plane

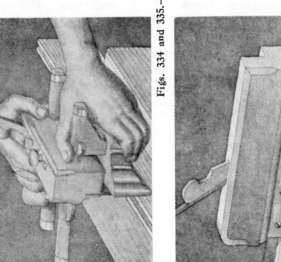

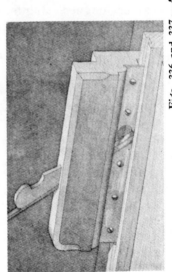

Figs. 336 and 337.—A Pair of Matching Planes

and adjusted to the two stems, by two wedges, thus allowing the plough iron (the cutting iron) to be regulated so that grooves can be made any desired distance from the edge or face of the work against which the fence is pressed. By turning the thumb-screw head at the top, the gauge for depth is regulated. After the plough is set, the work should be fixed in the bench screw or some other arrangement so as to hold it fast; then, holding the plough as in Fig. 334, start working the plough at the far end of the wood to almost the proper depth, then gradually work back, and finally give a push or two for the whole length.

Matching Planes.—What is known as a pair of matching planes might be found useful when much " grooving and tonguing " is to be done—in this form of joint a tongue on the edge of one board fits into a groove on the edge of another. Matching planes comprise a grooving or ploughing plane (Fig. 336) and a tonguing plane (Fig. 337), but, of course, the function of the former is fulfilled by the plough planes already described. These planes closely fit the work shaped by them.

Feather-tongued Joints.—Figs. 338 and 339 show what is known as ploughing and feather-jointing. For this two edges are brought with the trying plane to a state of perfect straightness, so that when they are placed together the two surfaces make complete contact. Then the edges are ploughed to form a groove to receive a strip of wood which must not be too tight, as there must be an allowance for the glue. The width of the strip must be slightly less than the combined depths of the grooves; a combined gauge and planing-board for the tongues is shown by Fig. 340. The grain of the strip is parallel with that of the boards and the joint is completed by gluing up and cramping.

When the grain of the tongue is at right angles to that of the boards, the tongue is known as a " cross feather," and the joint is much stronger than in the other case. Obviously as the tongue is made by cutting strips across a thin board at right angles to the grain, it cannot be prepared in such long lengths as in the other case. Boarding jointed together with wide tongues is shown by Fig. 342.

The strongest tongue or feather is of hoop iron, and nothing more than a saw kerf is required to accommodate it (*see* Fig. 341).

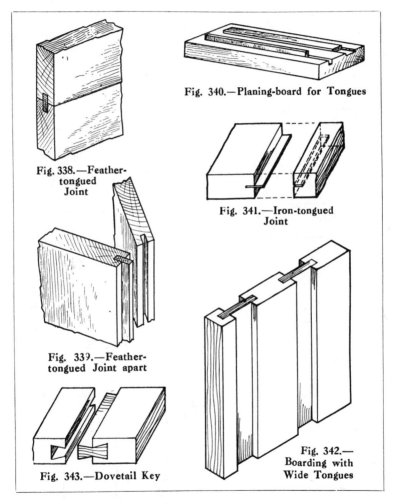

Fig. 340.—Planing-board for Tongues

Fig. 338.—Feather-tongued Joint

Fig. 341.—Iron-tongued Joint

Fig. 339.—Feather-tongued Joint apart

Fig. 343.—Dovetail Key

Fig. 342.— Boarding with Wide Tongues

A key or feather may, on rare occasions, take the form of a double-dovetail (*see* Fig. 343).

Simple Angle Joints.—A few of the simpler forms of angle joints will be dealt with in concluding this chapter, leaving mortising, dowelling, dovetailing, etc., to be described in later chapters. *Angle Butt Joints.*—The simplest of all angle joints is the butt joint (Fig. 344), which may be glued, screwed, or nailed, generally the last-named, as in Fig. 345.   The little object shown in Fig. 346—a soap box of the simplest description—will afford some practice

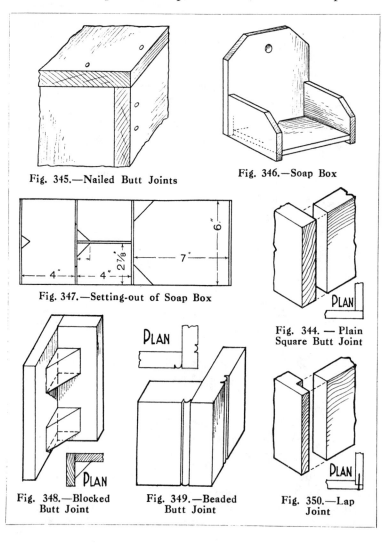

Fig. 345.—Nailed Butt Joints

Fig. 346.—Soap Box

Fig. 347.—Setting-out of Soap Box

Fig. 344. — Plain Square Butt Joint

Fig. 348.—Blocked Butt Joint

Fig. 349.—Beaded Butt Joint

Fig. 350.—Lap Joint

in the making of butt joints, while it also introduces oblique paring. The setting out of the parts of the box on a single piece of board is shown in Fig. 347, the board being planed up to $\frac{1}{2}$ in. thick, 6 in. wide, and about 1 ft. 3 in. long. At the back of the bottom shelf, which is inclined to prevent the soap from sliding out and to allow of the water easily draining off, is a triangular space which is removed with saw or chisel, and serves the purpose of a draining hole. In making the butt joints all that is necessary is that they should be set out accurately and that, in sawing, the blade of the saw should be at right angles to the surface of the work. In a job that is to be properly finished, the sawn

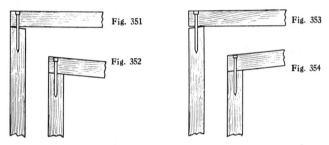

Figs. 351 to 354.—Examples of Imperfectly Nailed Butt Joints

edge must be shot with a plane. Examples of badly-made butt joints are shown in Figs. 351 to 354. Obviously, the butt joint is a feeble one, relying entirely for its resistance to internal pressure on the glue, screws or nails which hold the parts together. When such a joint is used in furniture making or building construction, it is usual to strengthen it by gluing triangular blocks in the angle at the back, as shown in Fig. 348. The beading of a butt joint, as in Fig. 349, relieves the severe plainness. *Lapped Angle Joints.*—In the single lap joint (Fig. 350) one member is rebated to half its thickness and to a width equal to the thickness of the other member. This is a little stronger than the plain butt joint, but not much, although, of course, it resists external pressure much better. Such joints are often nailed. Ornament may be introduced by working an ovolo mould on the rebated member, as in Fig. 355. The double lap joint is of stronger

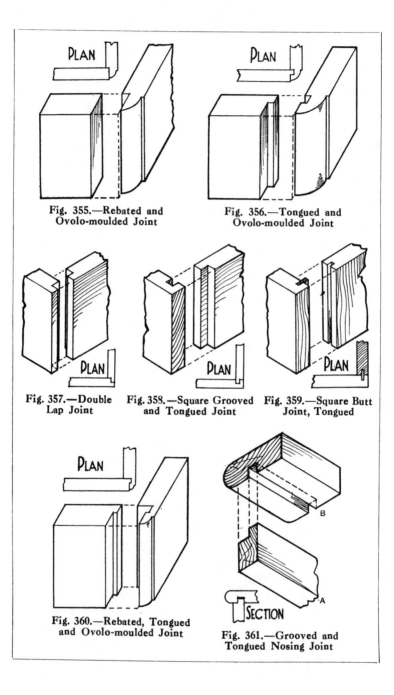

Fig. 355.—Rebated and Ovolo-moulded Joint

Fig. 356.—Tongued and Ovolo-moulded Joint

Fig. 357.—Double Lap Joint

Fig. 358.—Square Grooved and Tongued Joint

Fig. 359.—Square Butt Joint, Tongued

Fig. 360.—Rebated, Tongued and Ovolo-moulded Joint

Fig. 361.—Grooved and Tongued Nosing Joint

form (*see* Fig. 357); each member has a rebate cut in it equal both in depth and width to half the thickness of the stuff. *Grooved and Tongued Angle Joints.*—The simple grooved and tongued joint shown by Fig. 358 is an improvement on any of the joints mentioned earlier in this paragraph. In one member is cut a groove or housing as deep and as wide as half the thickness of the stuff; in the other member is a rebate of the same dimensions as the groove. These proportions are not always observed, as, for example, in the

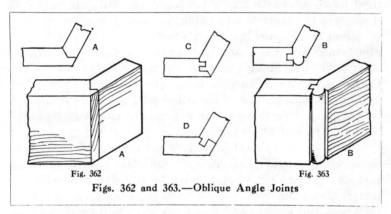

Figs. 362 and 363.—Oblique Angle Joints

ovolo moulded joint (Fig. 356) or the rebated, tongued and ovolo moulded joint (Fig. 360). The grooved and tongued joint is commonly used in stair construction, the riser A (Fig. 361) being tongued and the nosed tread B being grooved. Sometimes the tongue in an angle joint is a cross-grained feather, as illustrated in Fig. 359. It is not necessary to describe the methods of working these simple angle joints. They involve principally rebating and ploughing, which have already been described.

Oblique Angle Joints.—These may be mitred as described in a later chapter, or may take any of the forms shown, A, B, C, D (Figs. 362 and 363).

CHAPTER X

DOWELLED JOINTS

DOWELLING possesses the advantage of making an invisible but strong and quickly executed joint, which may be safely used as an alternative to other forms of joint. It is largely displacing the mortise and tenon, because it can be executed so much more quickly. In a dowel joint, the wooden pin glued into the holes at right angles to the joint surfaces assists the action of the glue on the surfaces themselves. Occasionally, for collapsible work, the dowels are glued into half of the joint only, and the other part is simply positioned by the projecting dowels; an example of this is to be found in the extra leaf of an expanding dining-table.

Dowels.—The dowel joint is a good one, but it needs to be carefully made; the surfaces must be planed well and accurately, the dowel holes must be bored square with the surfaces, and the dowels must be of good material, of correct thickness and length, and free from warp and twist (*see* Figs. 364 to 366). The strongest dowels are made by splitting straight-grained hardwood, first sawing off from the board blocks of proper length and then splitting off the dowels, the size of which will vary from $\frac{1}{4}$ in. to 1 in. square. Perhaps the best plan is to make dowels in length, say two or three times the length of one dowel, it being then more convenient to shape them with a plane A (Fig. 369), first trimming them to hexagonal section B, and finally to circular section C, a device for holding the stuff being shown in Fig. 367. They are tested for size and brought to shape by passing through a hole made in a piece of hardwood, or through a hole made in a piece of wrought-iron by a drill, the hole being left just as the drill leaves it. When the dowelling is to be performed in a hard wood, it is advisable to make a slight V-groove in the dowel, so that the air and superfluous glue may easily exude when the dowel is driven home.

Dowels may be cut to lengths as required, and the square arrises lightly removed with knife or chisel.

There are many other methods of producing dowels, and in some of them the lathe plays its part. Many workers prefer to buy them ready-made, as they do not consider that the labour pays for itself.

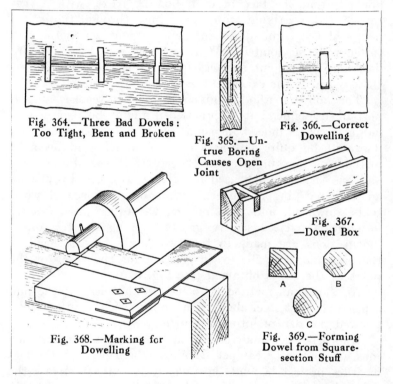

Fig. 364.—Three Bad Dowels: Too Tight, Bent and Broken

Fig. 365.—Un-true Boring Causes Open Joint

Fig. 366.—Correct Dowelling

Fig. 367.—Dowel Box

Fig. 368.—Marking for Dowelling

Fig. 369.—Forming Dowel from Square-section Stuff

Marking for Dowelling.—The edges of the boards that will butt when the joint is complete need to be prepared with the greatest accuracy (*see* p. 129). Then the two boards, on edge, are placed together back to back, so that the two surfaces that will ultimately come into contact are flush with one another, as shown in Fig. 368. There will now be another opportunity of checking the squareness of the planing—a matter of the greatest importance. The boards need to be held together by means of handscrews or in the

K

bench vice, taking care not to bruise the stuff.   The distances apart of the dowels will vary from a few inches to 1 ft., according to the kind of work and to the strength required, and the centres may be set out on one edge only by means of a marking gauge and rule or dividers, first marking the longitudinal centre line on each edge by means of the gauge applied from the face of each board.   Next, with a try-square and a striking knife, draw lines through the centre points at the required distance apart, right across the two surfaces to be jointed.   There is now a series of square lines across the joint surfaces intersecting the gauged lines thereby giving the exact centres of the dowel holes.

The above method is given because it teaches an important principle, but in practice it might be regarded as old-fashioned; indeed, in some cases in furniture making, it would be quite impracticable.   A quick and accurate method of marking the exact centre of the dowel hole, and one that is much used in cabinet shops, is by placing an ordinary pin on the centre line of one piece of wood to be dowelled, and then placing the other piece exactly in position over this.   By gently tapping the top piece, indentations are made in the two pieces by the head of the pin, and thus the exact position for the entry of the point of the bit is obtained (*see* Fig. 370).

An American method is to use, in the place of the pin, a piece of sheet steel about $\frac{1}{2}$ in. square with a tiny double-pointed pin driven into the centre.

Another quick and reliable method of marking for such jobs as a chair or cabinet framing, where perhaps the legs or stiles project beyond the rails, is to cut a template the exact size and shape of the end of the rail in veneer or thin zinc, and prick the centres of the dowels through as shown in Fig. 371.   The template may then be reversed and placed on the end of the rail and the centre pricked through, care being taken to mark from the face edge in each case.

To make a template for marking dowel holes on furniture legs, take a piece of zinc about $3\frac{1}{2}$ in. in diameter, and with a pair of compasses scribe the arcs A B, B C, and C A (*see* Fig. 372).   Draw the three radial lines shown.   At

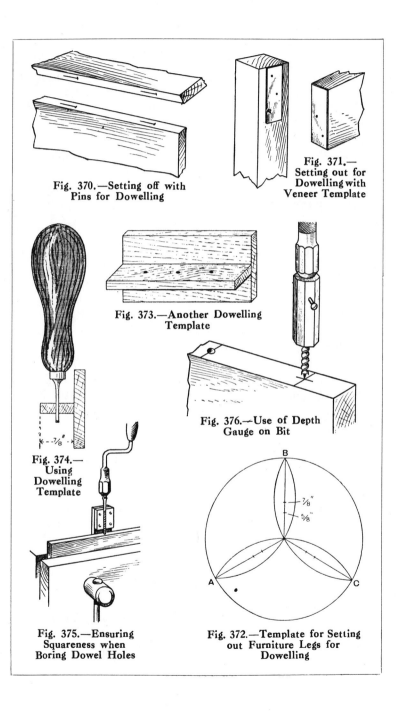

Fig. 370.—Setting off with
Pins for Dowelling

Fig. 371.—
Setting out for
Dowelling with
Veneer Template

Fig. 373.—Another Dowelling
Template

Fig. 374.—
Using
Dowelling
Template

Fig. 376.—Use of Depth
Gauge on Bit

Fig. 375.—Ensuring
Squareness when
Boring Dowel Holes

Fig. 372.—Template for Setting
out for Furniture Legs for
Dowelling

$\frac{5}{8}$ in. and $\frac{7}{8}$ in. from the centre make holes with a fine awl on each line. The outer holes will be suitable for marking on couch legs, and the inner holes for smaller legs.

Figs. 373 and 374 show a template made of hard wood ; it can be in two pieces, or cut out of the solid. It would be useful for marking the centres of dowels for doors that are not mortised together, such as on some sideboards, chiffoniers, etc. It should be as long as the rail is wide. The holes should be the same distance from each end, so that the template can be used both ways. The projecting part should be the same thickness as the rails and stiles of the doors.

Boring for Dowelling.—Taking a twist bit, place its point on the intersections of the lines and bore down to the depth required, using, until experienced in this work, a try-square as a check upon the squareness of the drill with the work. A simple contrivance that will considerably help in boring the holes truly in, say, flat boards is shown by Fig. 375. It consists of a short length of battening with a block screwed to one end. In this block a semicircular groove is made with a gouge to correspond with the diameter of the bit, and in use it is held tightly in the bench screw at right angles to the edge to be bored.

Without a gauge of some sort it will not be easy to bore the holes of proper and uniform depth, and therefore it is recommended to pass over the drill a gauge of the type illustrated in Fig. 376, which is simply a round or hexagonal piece of wood of convenient length, bored right through, and having one or two small set-screws as shown, by means of which the gauge can be secured at the desired height. Any roughness should be removed from the lip of the hole, as otherwise some of the borings might get between the abutting surfaces and spoil the appearance of the joint. In determining the length of the dowels it is a mistake to make them exactly the combined depths of the two holes into which the dowel will fit. There must be slight allowance for glue and for roughness at the bottoms of the holes, and it is therefore safer to make the dowel $\frac{1}{8}$ in. shorter than the combined depths.

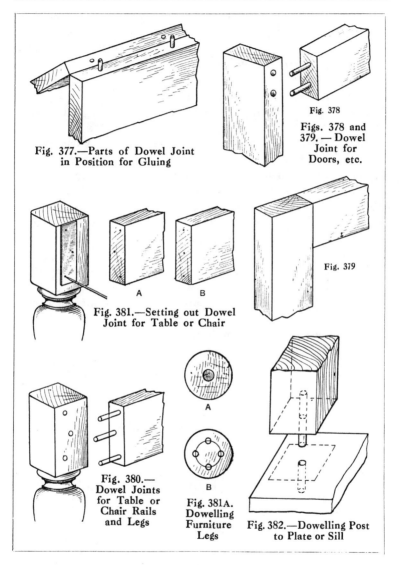

Fig. 377.—Parts of Dowel Joint in Position for Gluing

Fig. 378

Figs. 378 and 379. — Dowel Joint for Doors, etc.

Fig. 379

Fig. 381.—Setting out Dowel Joint for Table or Chair

A   B

Fig. 380.— Dowel Joints for Table or Chair Rails and Legs

Fig. 381A. Dowelling Furniture Legs

Fig. 382.—Dowelling Post to Plate or Sill

Gluing Dowels.—Next comes the gluing. First glue the dowel into one half of the joint, gently tapping it into place. Next, placing the other part exactly in the position shown in Fig. 377, rapidly apply the glue with the brush, allowing a little to flow into the holes, and then immediately bring the joint together and cramp up. In making an ordinary straight butt joint without dowels, the superfluous glue is rubbed out, but in a dowel joint all rubbing is impossible, and the removal of superfluous glue depends entirely upon the pressure applied. For this reason it is desirable to use the glue slightly thinner than in the other case.

Angle Dowel Joints.—There are many varieties of dowel joints besides the straight butt joint just described, as, for example, the dowelled joint used in framing doors (*see* Figs. 378 and 379), or in framing tables or chairs (Figs. 380 and 381). Success depends here upon accurate setting out, an excellent method of effecting this being to use a sheet-metal template as already described. The dowels should be disposed as at A (Fig. 381) and not as at B.

Fig. 381A shows at A and B two methods of dowelling together the broken leg of a chair or table, the single dowel A being suitable for a light table, and the multiple dowel system for chairs or heavy tables.

Dowelling is a convenient method of connecting a post to a plate or sill (*see* Fig. 382).

CHAPTER XI

MORTISE-AND-TENON JOINTS

Variety of Mortise-and-tenon Joints.—There is a great number of mortise-and-tenon joints, those shown by Figs. 383 to 400, and others illustrated throughout this chapter, being merely a selection. As a class, they are of great importance, and are in universal use.

Simple Mortise-and-tenon Joint.—It is proposed to describe the making of a simple type of mortise-and-tenon joint, illustrating its construction by means of a number of line drawings, and the method of making it by a number of photographs especially taken for the purpose. Other mortise-and-tenon joints have been, or will be in due course, fully illustrated, but it will be unnecessary to explain in the case of every one of them the methods of manipulating the saw and chisel. The "closed" type of mortise-and-tenon joint shown in Fig. 402 is one of the simplest. (An "open" tenon is a joint made between the ends of two members, the mortise being a mere slot, as in Fig. 422). The setting out and working are shown in Figs. 403 and 404. It is a rule to make the thickness of the tenon one-third the thickness of the wood, but this is not invariable, as the width of the chisel employed will determine the exact width of the mortise and, of course, the tenon must be a good fit. The length of the tenon finished will be the width of the member in which the mortise is made, but the worker may occasionally prefer to make it a little longer than that, and plane off the excess when the joint is otherwise finished.

The making of the tenon on the end of one member of the joint will first be explained. For marking both tenon and mortise (the mortise, of course, is the slot or opening into which the tongue or tenon fits) it is desirable to use a mortise gauge (Fig. 409, p. 157), this having two marking or scratching pins which can be set at such a distance apart

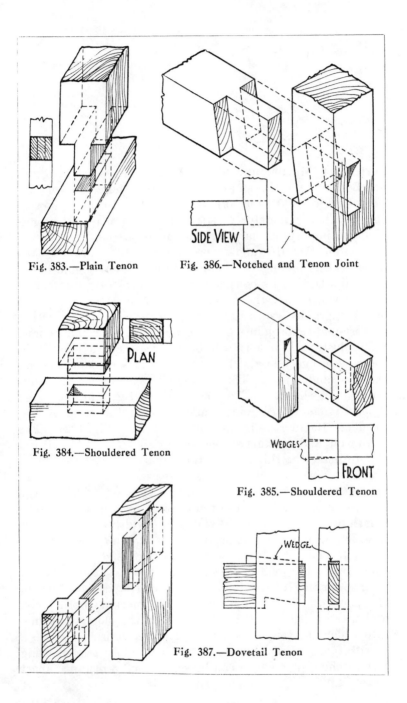

Fig. 383.—Plain Tenon

Fig. 386.—Notched and Tenon Joint

SIDE VIEW

PLAN

Fig. 384.—Shouldered Tenon

WEDGES

FRONT

Fig. 385.—Shouldered Tenon

WEDGE

Fig. 387.—Dovetail Tenon

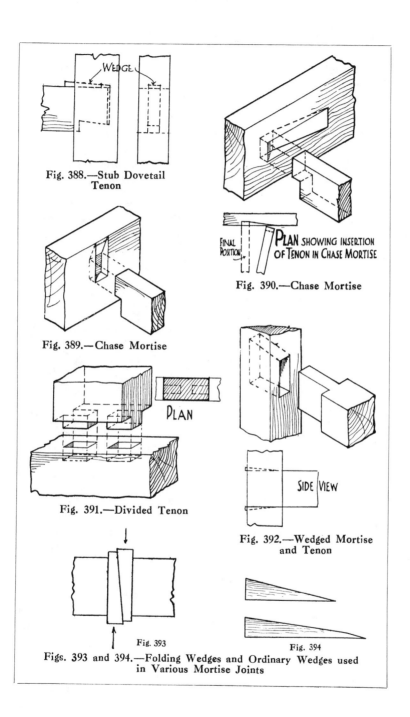

WEDGE

Fig. 388.—Stub Dovetail
Tenon

PLAN SHOWING INSERTION
OF TENON IN CHASE MORTISE

FINAL
POSITION

Fig. 390.—Chase Mortise

Fig. 389.—Chase Mortise

PLAN

Fig. 391.—Divided Tenon

SIDE VIEW

Fig. 392.—Wedged Mortise
and Tenon

Fig. 393

Fig. 394

Figs. 393 and 394.—Folding Wedges and Ordinary Wedges used
in Various Mortise Joints

and at such a distance from the face of the gauge stock that they may be made to scratch two parallel lines which precisely mark out the thickness of tenon or mortise. The method of setting the mortise gauge to the exact width is interesting. Assuming, for example, that stuff $1\frac{1}{2}$ in. thick is being worked upon, the tenon will be $\frac{1}{2}$ in. thick, and there will be $\frac{1}{2}$ in. of waste to be cut away on each side of it. Choosing therefore a $\frac{1}{2}$-in. chisel, use this as a gauge in setting the

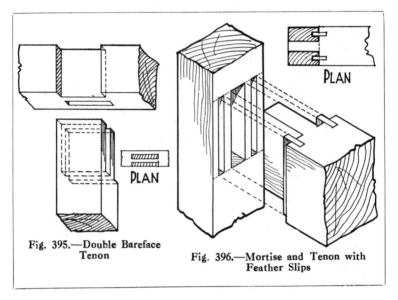

PLAN

PLAN

Fig. 395.—Double Bareface Tenon

Fig. 396.—Mortise and Tenon with Feather Slips

joints of the mortise gauge to the proper distance apart. Loosen the screw in the gauge stock, and turn the nut until the two pins coincide with the width of the chisel, holding this as shown in the drawing and photograph (Figs. 15 and 409), and applying it from the face side of the work. Then slide the stock until it is $\frac{1}{2}$ in. from the innermost pin, and finally tighten the screw. A substitute for a regular mortise gauge can be made of two pieces of wood as shown in Figs. 405 and 406, the marking points consisting of two steel sprigs or panel pins driven in as shown; of course, a new gauge has to be made or the pins altered for each different thickness of work dealt with.

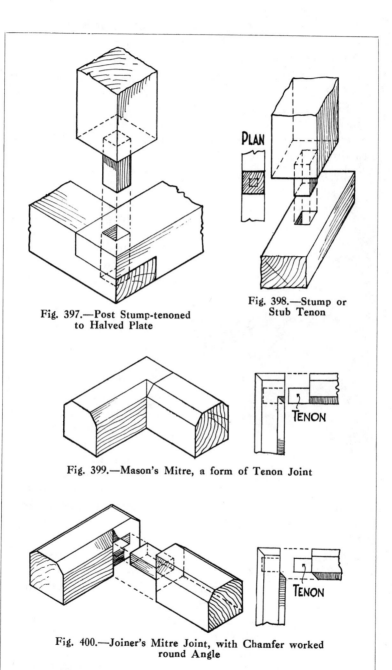

PLAN

Fig. 397.—Post Stump-tenoned
to Halved Plate

Fig. 398.—Stump or
Stub Tenon

TENON

Fig. 399.—Mason's Mitre, a form of Tenon Joint

TENON

Fig. 400.—Joiner's Mitre Joint, with Chamfer worked
round Angle

If the worker does not possess a mortise gauge, he may make shift with an ordinary marking gauge. Drive in the chisel at the correct distance from the face of the work (*see* Fig. 410), remove it, and, from each face of the work in turn, set the gauge to the edge of the chisel cut. Actually, this is inferior to the use of an improvised gauge of the kind already shown.

The gauge lines should run across the end of the work and down each edge as far as the shoulder line, which should be carefully squared on all the four faces of the work. A method of running the lines with pencil and fingers only (*see* Fig. 401) is often employed by experienced craftsmen. Similarly, the mortise should be set out with the gauge on opposite edges (if it is to go through), and likewise squared down on the face.

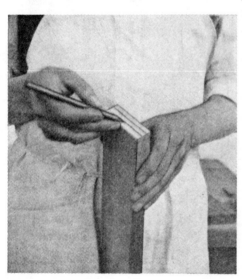

Fig. 401.—Setting Out Tenon with Pencil and Fingers

The tenon is cut by securing the work in the bench screw and sawing down with the grain outside the lines with the tenon saw (Figs. 407 and 408), afterwards placing the work flat on the bench and cutting down on the shoulder lines (also outside the lines, that is, nearer the end) so as to detach the waste. Some amount of practice with a tenon saw will be requisite before proficiency in making a tenon will be gained; and the better the condition of the saw and, within reason, the finer the tooth, the better will be the result and the more easily will it be obtained. Figs. 413 and 413A show photographically the sequence of operations in cutting a tenon.

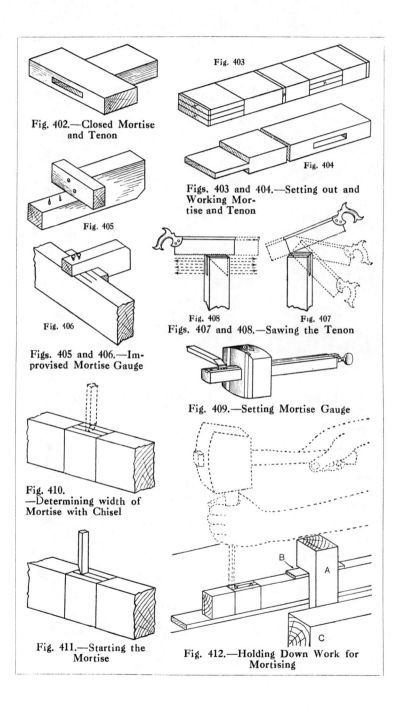

Fig. 402.—Closed Mortise and Tenon

Fig. 403

Fig. 404

Figs. 403 and 404.—Setting out and Working Mortise and Tenon

Fig. 405

Fig. 406

Figs. 405 and 406.—Improvised Mortise Gauge

Fig. 408   Fig. 407
Figs. 407 and 408.—Sawing the Tenon

Fig. 409.—Setting Mortise Gauge

Fig. 410.—Determining width of Mortise with Chisel

Fig. 411.—Starting the Mortise

Fig. 412.—Holding Down Work for Mortising

Fig. 413.—Mortising with Mallet and Chisel

For making the mortise, the worker will use an ordinary chisel and also, if he possesses one, a mortise chisel, the latter being an extra strong and thick tool for forcing the chips out of the mortise. The work requires to be solidly supported, and, in addition, rigidly held down on the bench, for which latter purpose an excellent device is illustrated in Fig. 412, it consisting of a piece of hardwood, 2 or 3 in. square, cut away as shown to leave a head A. Between the work and the head of the clamp is a piece of packing B to prevent injury to the work, and the clamp or grip is held as shown in the bench vice, the cheek of which is indicated by c.

The work having been marked out with a gauge and properly squared up on edges and faces as already directed, the operation of cutting the mortise will

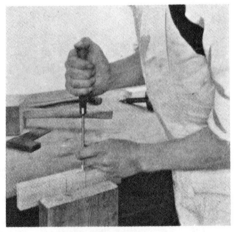

Fig. 413A.—Taking Vertical Cut at End of Mortise

be as shown in the diagrams Figs. 411 and 414 to 417, and
photographs, Figs. 413 and 413A. Drive in the chisel first
with the bevel towards the craftsman, and next with the

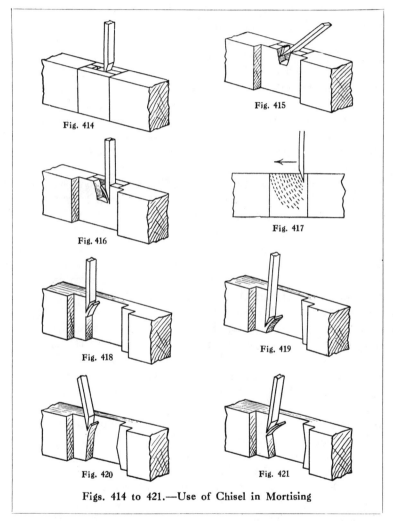

Figs. 414 to 421.—Use of Chisel in Mortising

bevel away from him, there being say $\frac{3}{8}$ in. between the two
cuts. Remove the chip by levering it out with the chisel,
and then proceed to take other cuts until the mortise is

finished from one edge to half its finished depth, taking particular care that the end cuts are vertical, the flat of the
chisel and not the bevelled edge being in contact with the
work.   Then the member can be turned over and the process repeated from the other edge to finish the hole.   Diagrams affording cut-away views of one perfect and three
imperfect mortises are presented by Figs. 418 to 421. Sloping
sides are caused by allowing the chisel to " lead in," and by
attempting to cut the mortise entirely from one side.

Open Mortise-and-tenon Joint at Angle.—This (*see*
Fig. 422) slightly resembles the lap joint, and is used for the
same purpose as that joint; but well-made and properly
glued it is stronger than the lap, and is suitable for such light
framework, etc., as would scarcely permit of an ordinary
mortise-and-tenon being made.   The setting out and construction of the joint are shown in Figs. 423 to 425.   The
mortise gauge and square are used in the manner already
explained.   The saw kerfs are made in the waste.   The
making of the tenon is exactly as already explained in another
example.   To form the mortise in the other piece (Fig. 426),
place the chisel, bevel as shown, about $\frac{3}{16}$ in. away from the
bottom line of the mortise and drive it in for about $\frac{1}{2}$ in. (*see*
Fig. 427); withdraw the chisel, and, without turning it,
make a second cut at, say, $\frac{3}{8}$ in. nearer the outer end, and remove the chip by leverage (Fig. 428).   Holding the chisel as
before, place it just up to the bottom line and drive it in about
half-way, taking great care to keep the chisel vertical.   Repeating these three cuts on the other edge of the work will
leave a piece of waste as shown in Fig. 429, which will fall
out, and the mortise will be complete except, possibly, for
a light paring at the bottom.

Boring out Mortises.—What is known as the coach-
builders' method of cutting a mortise is shown in the photograph (Fig. 431), and is commonly employed by woodworkers
in general.   A number of parallel and truly vertical holes are
made by means of brace and twist bit, and the mortise completed by careful paring with a chisel, taking great care to
avoid enlarging the mortise in so doing.

Open mortises in angle joints can have the waste removed,

after sawing, by boring with the bit, as shown in Fig. 430, finishing with the chisel.

Haunched Mortise-and-tenon Joints.—These are among the most important of this series, and are found useful

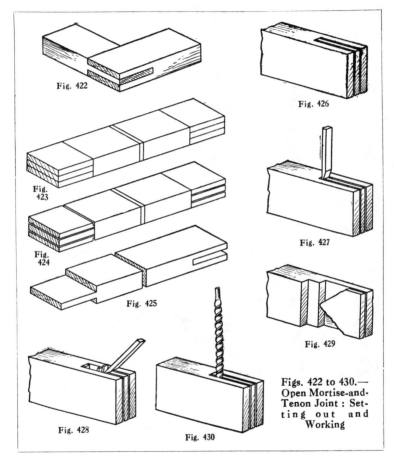

Fig. 422

Fig. 426

Fig. 423

Fig. 424

Fig. 425

Fig. 427

Fig. 429

Fig. 428

Fig. 430

Figs. 422 to 430.—Open Mortise-and-Tenon Joint : Setting out and Working

in many widely different applications, but particularly in panel and sash doors, framings, etc. Figs. 432 to 434 show the joint complete, apart, and set out. Fig. 435 is a cut-away view clearly showing the wedges. It will be noted that only a part of the edge of a haunched tenon shows in an angle joint, in addition to the cross grain on the edge of

L

the work. Careful setting out is essential. Fig. 434 shows the mortise hole as continuing beyond the first squared lines, the space between the two sets of lines indicating the allowance for the wedges, which are a great factor in giving the joint rigidity. In making this joint there are, of course, two haunches to consider—that in the mortise and that on the tenon. The latter will be dealt with first.

Fig. 431.—Boring Out Waste in Forming Mortise

The work having been set out, it may be sawn down and then sawn across the shoulder lines to produce a simple tenon (*see* Figs. 436 and 437). Next, the haunching is set out on the tenon as shown, and the waste removed with a tenon saw. For big, strong work it is easier to adopt the alternative method of setting out the haunch as in Fig. 438, removing the waste as in Fig. 439, setting out the tenon and squaring it down on the newly cut face and edge as clearly illustrated, and then cutting down with the tenon saw as before.

For making the haunched mortise, the work having been carefully set out, first cut a mortise in the ordinary way as at A (Fig. 440), and then form the haunch by sawing down with the end of the tenon saw at B, and paring away the waste with a chisel as in Fig. 441. Of course, the mortise is not straight-ended. The ends slant outwards from the inner edge of the work to allow for the insertion of the wedges.

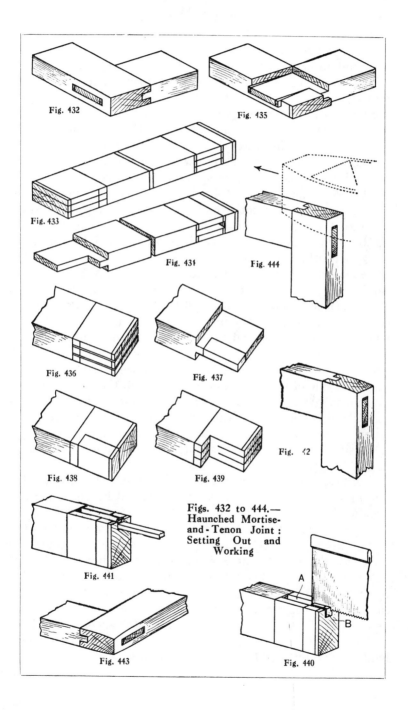

Fig. 432

Fig. 435

Fig. 433

Fig. 434

Fig. 444

Fig. 436

Fig. 437

Fig. 438

Fig. 439

Fig. 442

Fig. 441

Figs. 432 to 444.—
Haunched Mortise-
and - Tenon Joint :
Setting Out and
Working

A

B

Fig. 443

Fig. 440

Some amount of care and skill will be required in finishing the joint after it has been fitted together.   The end of the stile of the door or framing will need to be planed smooth, and it is easy to round the edge as in Fig. 442, or, when truing up the face of the work, to round the face of the stile as in Fig. 443.   Bear in mind, also, that the smoothing plane must be held as indicated by the dotted lines in Fig. 444 ; that is, the planing is done inwards from the outer edge, or otherwise there is the risk of splintering the work.

The rails that connect table legs flush with the underside of the top are frequently haunched-tenoned into mortises cut into the legs.   These mortises run into one another at right angles, and the tenons therefore come into contact with each other, for which purpose they must be mitred at the ends, as in Fig. 445.   In such a case as this, the tenons would be called barefaced (*see* the next paragraph).

Barefaced Tenons.—Figs. 446 to 448 show a barefaced tenon in four stages.   On one side of the tenon is a shoulder, while the other is flush with the face of the rail, and is therefore said to be " barefaced."   This form of tenon is used where one surface of the rail is to be flush with that of a stile, the other side of the rail being set back from that of the stile, as shown.   When the tenon does not pass right through the stile, it is known as a stub tenon.   The use of a barefaced tenon in framing is shown in Fig. 449, the bareface making it possible for the matchboarding to finish flush with the face of the framework.

Oblique Mortise and Tenons.—Joints of this kind (*see* Figs. 450 to 455) are not often required by the general woodworker who, in their place, often uses something of a simpler nature.   The setting out is the most important part of the work.   Three types of this joint are shown, and in each case the setting-out lines are given.   Oblique mortises (*see* Fig. 450) are difficult to cut, but the work is facilitated by using brace and bit prior to the chisel, and adopting the method suggested on p. 116 to ensure boring at the desired angle.   The joints shown by Figs. 450 and 454 may be wedged, glued or pinned, but wedging is not suitable for the joints shown by Fig. 452.

Fox-wedged Mortise-and-tenon Joints.—Figs. 456 and 457 show this joint apart and cut-away. Its advantage is that it gives a really strong joint without the tenon and wedges showing at the end or edge of the work. The mortise is wider at the bottom than at the top (that is, it is dovetailed) by the thickness of the two wedges added together. Perhaps

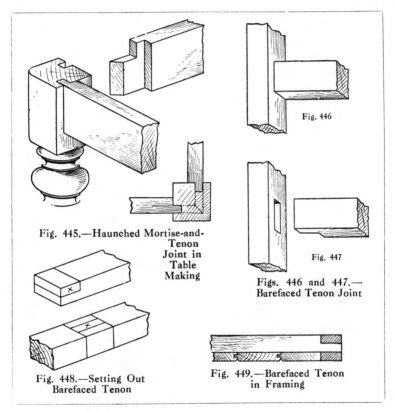

Fig. 445.—Haunched Mortise-and-Tenon Joint in Table Making

Fig. 446

Figs. 446 and 447.—Barefaced Tenon Joint

Fig. 447

Fig. 448.—Setting Out Barefaced Tenon

Fig. 449.—Barefaced Tenon in Framing

the drawings slightly exaggerate (for the purpose of more clearly showing the construction) the thickness of the wedges ; obviously, this must not be such as to involve any risk of splitting the rail. The stub tenon is of ordinary construction, with two saw kerfs run into it as shown. The length of the tenon is slightly less than the depth of the mortise, as clearly shown. The parts should be fitted together first of all with-

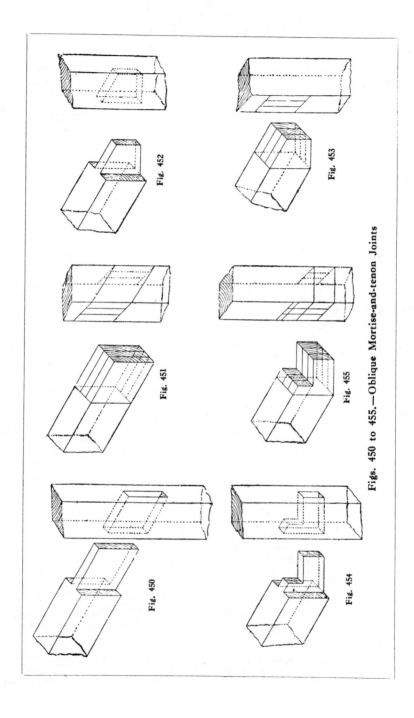

Fig. 450

Fig. 451

Fig. 452

Fig. 453

Fig. 454

Fig. 455

Figs. 450 to 455.—Oblique Mortise-and-tenon Joints

out the wedges ; then, if correct, the parts should be well glued, the wedges slightly inserted into the kerfs, and the joint brought together by means of blows from a hammer or mallet, using a piece of packing to prevent injury to the work.

The fox-wedged secret haunch tenon joint is shown by

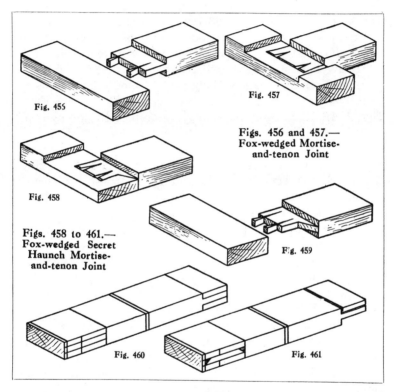

Fig. 455

Fig. 457

Figs. 456 and 457.—
Fox-wedged Mortise-
and-tenon Joint

Fig. 458

Figs. 458 to 461.—
Fox-wedged Secret
Haunch Mortise-
and-tenon Joint

Fig. 459

Fig. 460

Fig. 461

Figs. 458 to 461 cut-away, apart, set-out, and partly worked. The tenon is prepared as for the haunch joint described earlier in this chapter, except that the shoulder is slanting and not square, and the length of the tenon is slightly less than the depth of the mortise. It is saw-kerfed as in the preceding example. The mortise is cut exactly as for the ordinary fox-wedged joint, but is continued to accommodate the haunch of the tenon by carefully sawing down with the end of the tenon saw and then paring away the waste.

Pinned Mortise-and-tenon Joint.—In carpentry work, tenon joints are often secured by means of a wooden pin passing through the tenon and both cheeks of the mortise (*see* Fig. 462). The joint having been prepared in the usual way needs to be well cramped up before pinning. For small work or for making a model joint for practice, a cramp of the kind shown in Fig. 463 may be used. A hole is bored with the twist bit, and a wooden pin, slightly tapering and rather large for the hole, is driven in to make a tight fit.

Draw-boring.—In draw-boring, a wooden pin is passed through both members of the joint to secure one to the other, but chiefly to draw or cramp the tenon into the mortise (*see* Fig. 464). The joint outwardly resembles the pinned joint already described. The mortise and tenon are of ordinary construction, care being taken, in the case of a stub tenon, to see that the tenon is a trifle shorter than the mortise is deep. Disconnect the joint, and run a twist bit through the cheeks of the mortise at the place indicated by the pin in Fig. 464. Put the joint together, and, inserting the same twist bit through the hole in the mortise cheek, make a mark on the tenon, as indicated in the cut-away view (Fig. 465). Next, supporting the tenon on a piece of waste (Fig. 466), place the point of the bit a trifle nearer the shoulder than the mark already made (*see* A and B, Fig. 467), and bore right through. When the joint has again been put together, there will be a hole running through the two cheeks of the mortise and through the tenon, but not in line (*see* Fig. 468). On driving in a suitable steel pin (special pins for the purpose are obtainable from tool merchants) the tenon will be drawn right home into the mortise (Fig. 469). Finally, the steel pin is replaced with a wooden one (Fig. 470). Should the hole in the tenon be too near the shoulder, the pin may fail by being unable to withstand the shearing stress, may split up while being driven into place, or may even break the tenon.

Draw-boring, when properly done, is far better than cramping and pinning. When a cramp is used for a joint, a certain reaction or rebound is sure to take place when the cramp is removed. This reaction, although very small,

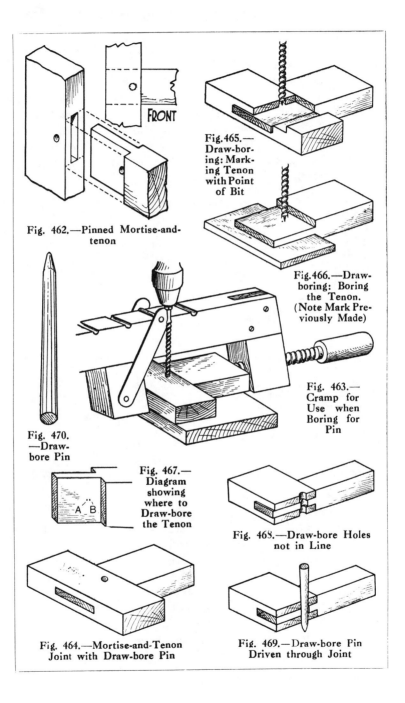

Fig. 462.—Pinned Mortise-and-tenon

FRONT

Fig. 465.—Draw-boring: Marking Tenon with Point of Bit

Fig. 466.—Draw-boring: Boring the Tenon. (Note Mark Previously Made)

Fig. 470.—Draw-bore Pin

Fig. 463.—Cramp for Use when Boring for Pin

Fig. 467.—Diagram showing where to Draw-bore the Tenon

A B

Fig. 468.—Draw-bore Holes not in Line

Fig. 464.—Mortise-and-Tenon Joint with Draw-bore Pin

Fig. 469.—Draw-bore Pin Driven through Joint

causes the pin to give a little. A draw-bored joint allows the pin to cause a constant cramping action on the shoulder, which is far better.

Tusk Tenons.—Figs. 471 and 472 show the tusk tenon joint which is employed chiefly in building construction on the ends of the short joists in the neighbourhood of fireplaces, etc. ; however, it is also used to some extent in general carpentry, especially in the construction of collapsible cottage

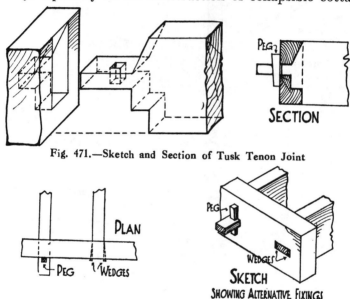

Fig. 471.—Sketch and Section of Tusk Tenon Joint

Fig. 472.—Plan and Sketch showing Pegged Tenon and Wedged Tenon

bookcases, garden frames, etc. ; for example, *see* Fig. 473, which shows the tusk tenon joint securing the end of a collapsible garden frame to the side. It will be noted that this type of tenon is barefaced and has an elongation which projects from the face of the other member of the joint, folding wedges (single ones are inefficient) passing through a hole cut in the tusk and holding everything tight and thereby obviating the use of nails, screws, etc. The tusk tenon used in building construction would not be likely to interest readers, but the kind just referred to will bear explanation, as it will be found generally useful. The front of the frame consists of two widths of $1\frac{1}{4}$ in. boarding, 3 in. and 6 in. respectively, the tusk being made on the wider board; battens, 3 in. by 1 in., nailed on hold the boards together. To set out the tusk, add together the projection of the tusk and the thickness of the side ($2\frac{1}{2}$ in. + $1\frac{1}{4}$ in. = $3\frac{3}{4}$ in.), and square a line across the board at that distance from the end to mark the shoulder. In this particular instance, the tusk is not central, an exception to most joints of this class; it is $2\frac{1}{2}$ in. wide, and a horizontal line drawn at that distance from the bottom edge of the board will determine the top edge of the tusk. At a bare $1\frac{1}{4}$ in. outwards from the shoulder line, square a cross line to mark the inner edge of the hole to receive the wedges. This hole will measure 1 in. by 1 in., and there will thus be $\frac{3}{4}$ in. of stuff above and below it. Set out the hole with the square, and make it

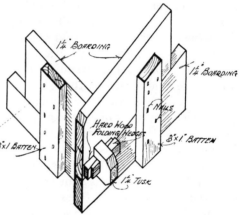

Fig. 473.—Tusk Tenon in Collapsible Garden Frame

by first boring with a twist bit and then paring to shape and size. It is always desirable to make this hole before cutting away the waste to form the tenon, which simple job may now be done. Trim off the corners with a chisel.

The mortises to receive the tusks will be, of course, $2\frac{1}{2}$ in. wide vertically and $1\frac{1}{4}$ in. across, and will need to be set out with care on the side members of the framing, this presenting no difficulty. There should be at least $1\frac{1}{2}$ in. of stuff between the hole and the end of the side, or the wedge action may break out a piece. The hole is made by mortising in any way preferred. The folding wedges should be of 1 in. hardwood, such as oak, elm or teak, 5 in. long, 1 in. wide at the head, and tapering to nothing at the tail.

CHAPTER XII

MITRED AND OTHER JOINTS

Cutting Mitres.—Mitres are cut in mitre blocks and boxes and shot true on mitre-shooting boards or in trimming machines. Instructions on doing the work will be found in a later chapter concerned with mitre cutting and the trimming of squared and mitred edges.

Glued Mitre Joints.—The commonest example of a mitred joint is in a picture frame, but generally this is of a weak description, being simply a butt joint held together with glue and brads, although sometimes keys of various forms are also used. For joinery and cabinet-making purposes, the picture-frame style of joint is rarely strong enough and when butt joints are used they need to be considerably strengthened by means of keys or tongues. The work having been planed true lengthwise is cut in a mitre block or mitre box, and the new edge is shot true in a mitre shooting board, or a trimmer of one of the special kinds may be employed. To make a joint of the picture-frame variety, two pieces would be glued, possibly put in a cramp, and nailed; or one piece could be held vertically in the bench vice, the two surfaces glued, the joint brought together and brads inserted from the top side across the line of the joint. The picture-frame has merely to support its own weight and that of the glass and backing board, whereas a frame used in cabinet-making or joinery may have to withstand twisting stress and possibly very hard usage, and it is therefore necessary to reinforce the joint.

Keyed Mitre Joints.—One of the commonest ways of strengthening a plain mitred joint (Fig. 474) is to hold the two parts of the joint together accurately in the bench vice and make two or more kerfs (Fig. 477) in the thickness of the stuff (*see* Figs. 475 and 476); or the kerfs may be made after the joint has been glued together. The illustrations

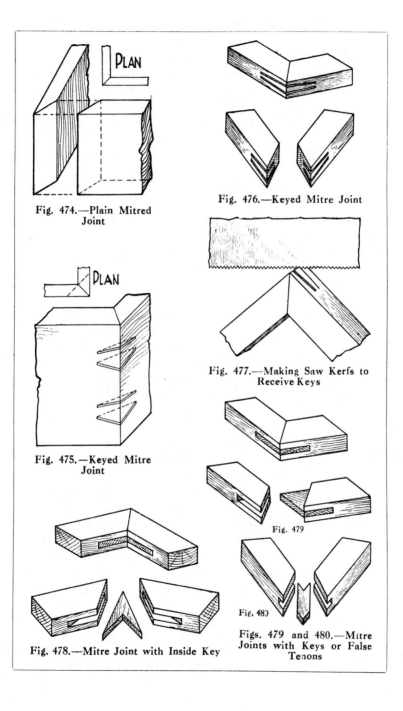

Fig. 474.—Plain Mitred Joint

Fig. 476.—Keyed Mitre Joint

Fig. 477.—Making Saw Kerfs to Receive Keys

Fig. 475.—Keyed Mitre Joint

Fig. 479

Fig. 480

Fig. 478.—Mitre Joint with Inside Key

Figs. 479 and 480.—Mitre Joints with Keys or False Tenons

show that the kerfs should not be parallel with one another, and the effect of this slight dovetailing is to add immensely to the strength of the joint.   The joint having been glued and cramped together, pieces of hardwood veneer are glued and driven into the kerfs.   If there are objections to the kerfs showing on the outer edge of the work, the keys may be inserted into the inside angle, the kerfs having been marked by clamping the members of the joint back to back in the bench vice and scribing for the saw kerfs from each of the faces.   In the case of an internal key it is better to avoid attempting to obtain the dovetail effect, and to insert a single key parallel with the face of the frame.   In all cases, see that the grain of the key is at right angles to the line of joint.

In the case of the two joints shown by Figs. 478 and 479—the former with an inside key and the latter with an outside key or false tenon—it is also necessary to start with a true mitred butt joint.   Measure for the key along both edge and end, and square off cross lines to mark the extremities of the mortise to be cut.   Then preferably, with a mortise gauge or with an improvised gauge similar to Fig. 405 (p. 157), mark on the work the width of the mortise, cut down with tenon saw in the waste, and remove the waste by means of the chisel.   The keys, prepared to thickness, should be carefully fitted, and the joint completed by gluing and cramping.   There is no need to adhere strictly to the form of key shown in Fig. 478, but with this form the mortising is the simplest possible.   Fig. 480 illustrates a possible variation.

Screwed Mitre Joint.—A mitre joint may be strengthened with a screw, the head being well countersunk, and the hole filled up with a suitable stopping.

Dovetail-keyed Mitre Joint.—An excellent method of strengthening a mitre joint made in stout wood is to use a dovetail key let in from the underside, as in Fig. 481.   The butt joint is worked, cramped up, and the hardwood key prepared and laid on the work in its proper position.   Scribing will then give the shape of the recess to be cut out.   The key may be glued in, screwed, or both.

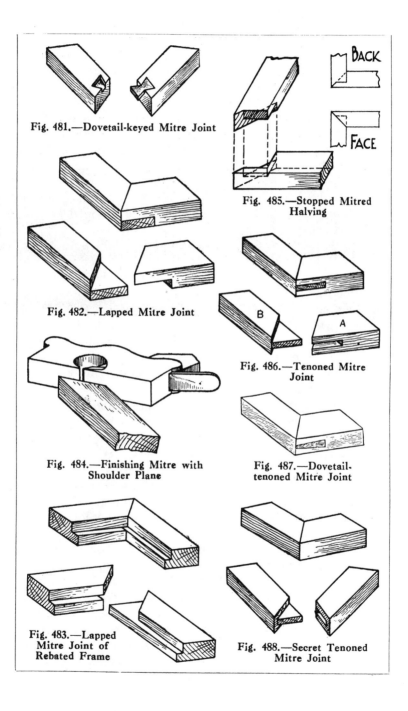

Fig. 481.—Dovetail-keyed Mitre Joint

Fig. 482.—Lapped Mitre Joint

Fig. 484.—Finishing Mitre with Shoulder Plane

Fig. 483.—Lapped Mitre Joint of Rebated Frame

BACK

FACE

Fig. 485.—Stopped Mitred Halving

Fig. 486.—Tenoned Mitre Joint

Fig. 487.—Dovetail-tenoned Mitre Joint

Fig. 488.—Secret Tenoned Mitre Joint

Lapped Mitre Joints.—The key in a mitre joint is not necessarily a false one. It may be actually a part of one member of the joint, in the form, for example, of a lap or tenon. The angle lapped and mitred joint, known also as mitred halving (Figs. 482 and 483), is a strong form and allows of screwing from the back. The presence of a lap or tenon prevents the mitre from being shot in an ordinary mitre shoot and necessitates particularly accurate setting out and working, the mitres being sawn near to the lines and finished with a rebate plane or with a metal shoulder plane (Fig. 484). What is known as the stopped mitred halving is shown in Fig. 485.

Tenoned Mitre Joints.—The open mortise and tenon mitre joint is shown by Fig. 486. One member A of the joint is sawn and shot to a true mitre, and then both members are scribed and the shoulder lines squared on as though for mortising and tenoning. Next the mortise is cut, the bottom of which will be in line with the inner edge of the frame. The same remarks apply with regard to the difficulty of working the tenon B on the other piece, as in the case of the mitred and lapped joint. In the joint shown by Fig. 487, the tenon and mortise are of dovetail form.

The secret, or shouldered, mortise and tenon mitre joint (Fig. 488) may not be so strong as the open joint just mentioned, but its advantage is that the tenon does not show. It is not easy to make, perhaps the best method being to cut the tenon piece as for the open joint (Fig. 486) by making saw kerfs on both mitre lines in the waste, and sawing down the end grain to meet the kerfs. Next cut a strip across grain off the tenon, stopping at the mitred shoulder; then complete the mitre. The length of the front edge of the tenon can be transferred to the gauged mortise piece, the slanting mortise made, and the joint completed.

Lapped Bridle Mitre Joint.—The lapped bridle mitre joint (Fig. 489) is a combination of mitred and tenoned joint, and is very strong, particularly if screwed from the back. First gauge each member of the joint as though for making an open mortise and tenon joint, and square the shoulder line on all four sides of the stuff. Next set out the mitre on the face of each piece. Take the mortise piece A and saw two kerfs in the end grain inside the scribed lines, and remove the waste with the chisel to form the open mortise; next cut the mitre which will remove part

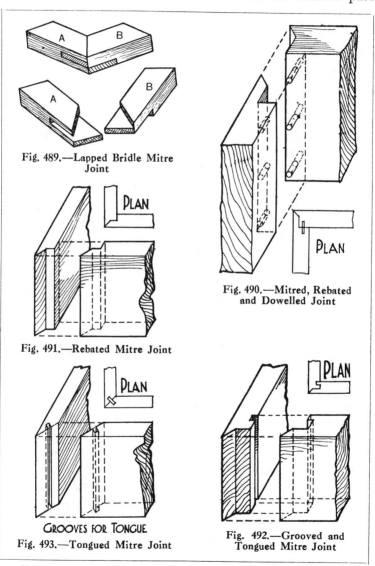

Fig. 489.—Lapped Bridle Mitre Joint

Fig. 491.—Rebated Mitre Joint

Fig. 490.—Mitred, Rebated and Dowelled Joint

GROOVES FOR TONGUE
Fig. 493.—Tongued Mitre Joint

Fig. 492.—Grooved and Tongued Mitre Joint

M

of the front cheek of the mortise. In the tenon piece B,
first cut at the side of the mitre line in the waste and saw
down through the end grain to this kerf, thus producing
in two cuts a mitred shoulder and the front cheek of the
tenon. At the back of this piece, make a kerf at the side
of the squared shoulder line and another in the end grain
of the wood to meet it, thus cutting the rebate into which
the lap of the other member of the joint will fit. It is
obvious that the setting out must be exact and the workmanship perfect.

Dowelled Mitre Joints.—Mitre joints are sometimes
dowelled. The pieces having been mitred, are cramped
together in the bench screw, the face sides being outwards,
and care is taken that the joint surfaces that will abutt
are flush with one another. The squaring and gauging
then proceed as already described for dowelling, and the
boring is done at right angles to the marked surfaces, checking, if necessary, with a try-square. As the dowels will cross
the joint at right angles, a little thought will show that
they must be kept towards the inner angle of the joint, as
otherwise there is no room for long dowels, and careless use
of the bit might cause it to work out on the edge of the stuff.

Rebated Mitre Joints, etc.—A much stronger form
of dowelled joint is shown in Fig. 490 ; often the rebated
mitre joint is employed without dowels (*see* Fig. 491), and
in another variation the joint is tongued (*see* Fig. 492).
The cross-tongued mitre joint is shown by Fig. 493.

Joints for Lengthening Rails, Boards, etc.— Joints
of this type do not much interest the general woodworker,
their chief employment being in building construction.
But here and there, as in the erection of a workshop or
other heavy work of the kind, a knowledge of the proper
joints employed for the purpose will be useful, and a few
of the best of them are therefore here shown, but it is not
proposed to explain in detail how to work them, as in practically every case the method is obvious, especially in the
light of the information given in earlier chapters.

The straight halved joint (Fig. 494) has but little strength ;
the bevel joint (Fig. 495) is better, although not much. A

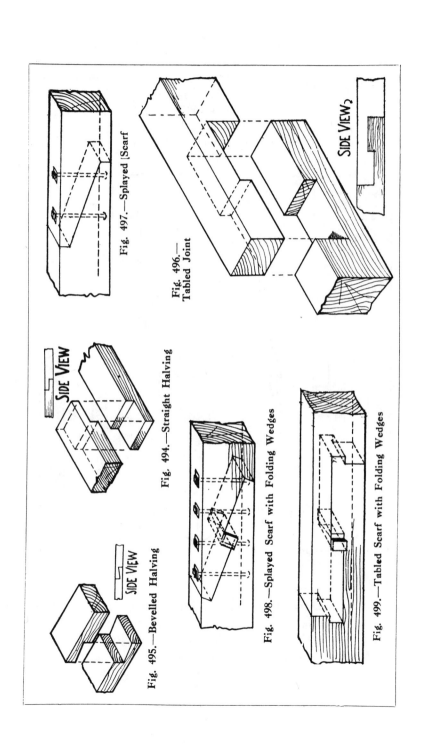

Fig. 497.—Splayed Scarf

Fig. 496.—Tabled Joint

SIDE VIEW₂

SIDE VIEW

Fig. 494.—Straight Halving

SIDE VIEW

Fig. 495.—Bevelled Halving

Fig. 498.—Splayed Scarf with Folding Wedges

Fig. 499.—Tabled Scarf with Folding Wedges

tabled joint (Fig. 496) is far superior and obviously is easily made. An elaboration of this joint has folding wedges, as in Fig. 499. The splayed scarf joint (Fig. 497) is quite simple, and, as shown, is strengthened with a couple of bolts. This joint again has been elaborated, and Fig. 498

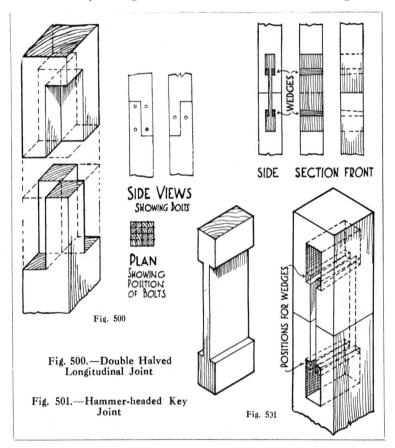

SIDE   SECTION FRONT

SIDE VIEWS
SHOWING BOLTS

PLAN
SHOWING
POSITION
OF BOLTS

Fig. 500

Fig. 500.—Double Halved
Longitudinal Joint

Fig. 501.—Hammer-headed Key
Joint

Fig. 501

shows it adapted to receive folding wedges. It will, of course, be understood that such joints are used in heavy timbers, as well also the double halved joint shown in Fig. 500 ; in this joint each member has what are actually two stopped rebates cut in it, one quarter the area of each member being cut away in each place.

The hammer-headed key joint shown by Fig. 501 is interesting. It will be seen that the joint, when complete, has two rectangular mortises, one in each member, connected together by a narrow slot which crosses the line of joint. Into this I-shaped mortise fits a hammer-headed key, and by means of folding wedges introduced where shown, the joint can be tightened up very effectively.

The lengthening of boards directly interests the maker of furniture and fittings. Fig. 502 shows a method of lengthening boards by the use of round wooden dowels. This method is suitable for light work such as mantelboards, small shelves, etc. Dowelling is fully explained in an earlier chapter. Another method is shown by Fig. 503; this is suitable for larger shelves and places where greater strength is required.

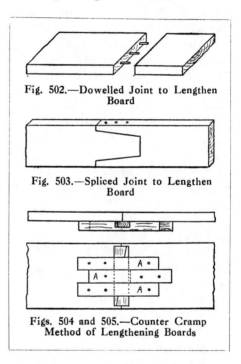

Fig. 502.—Dowelled Joint to Lengthen Board

Fig. 503.—Spliced Joint to Lengthen Board

Figs. 504 and 505.—Counter Cramp Method of Lengthening Boards

Heavier battens or planks could have bolts right through instead of the screws. Figs. 504 and 505 show a method that can be used where a good butt joint is wanted, as in counters, sign- and fascia-boards, where the fillets are not an obstruction. The fillets are cut and fixed at one end so that the wedges can give a cramping action on the joint, and the slots must not be in alignment before wedging. The ends A are screwed after the folding wedges have been driven in.

CHAPTER XIII

Dovetail Joints

Varieties of Dovetail Joints.—Dovetailing is a variety of the mortise and tenon joint, in which the tenons (known as pins) are wider at their outer ends than at their shoulders, the mortises being of corresponding shape. Thus the tenons lock in the mortises, and the strength of the joint—except in one direction only—is largely independent of the glue. The box pin joint (Fig. 506), which can be wholly set out with the dividers and square, is, therefore, not a dovetail joint, although superficially resembling one. In the true dovetail, the pins and mortises widen out in a manner suggestive of the tail of a dove, as shown in the very simplest forms of this class of joint (*see* Figs. 507 to 511). " Dovetailing," as a term, is associated chiefly with box and drawer joints, as illustrated in Figs. 512 to 515.

The Box Pin or Lock Joint.—In this joint (*see* Fig. 506) each member has a number of square-sided pins cut on its end in such a way that they interlock when the joint is fitted together. It is useful for common box construction, but is obviously inferior to dovetailing, to which, in a sense, it serves as a preparatory example. A good proportion is for the pins to be as wide as they are thick, but this is not always adhered to, as the wider the pin the less the amount of work. The joint is of less interest to the craftsman than to the box and packing-case maker, who cuts the joint by machinery. In making the box pin joint, if there is but one or two to do, the marking-gauge is set to the thickness of the stuff and a shoulder line is scribed round on all four sides of each piece. The dividers are also set to the same dimension, and stepped off on the shoulder line on the face of one piece, the square and scriber being then employed to connect up the points with the end. The two pieces are

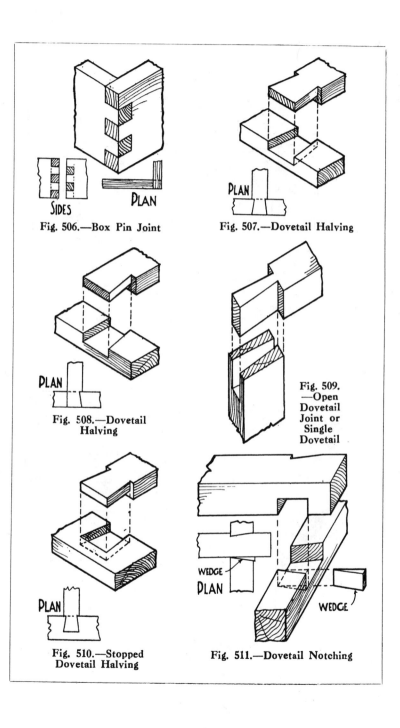

SIDES   PLAN

Fig. 506.—Box Pin Joint

PLAN

Fig. 507.—Dovetail Halving

PLAN

Fig. 508.—Dovetail Halving

Fig. 509.
—Open
Dovetail
Joint or
Single
Dovetail

PLAN

Fig. 510.—Stopped
Dovetail Halving

WEDGE
PLAN
WEDGE

Fig. 511.—Dovetail Notching

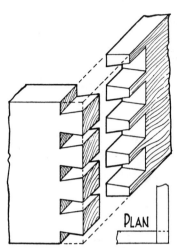

Fig. 512.—Common Dovetailing
or Box Dovetailing

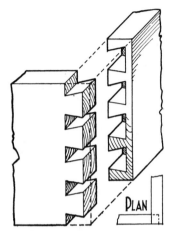

Fig. 513.—Lap Dovetailing
or Drawer Dovetailing

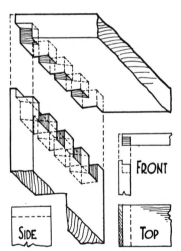

Fig. 514.—Secret Lap Dovetailing

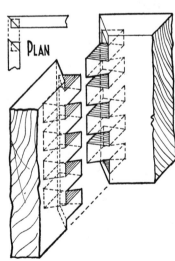

Fig. 515.—Secret Mitre Dovetailing

clamped together in the vice, and the lines squared across their ends and down to the shoulder line on the second piece. Before removing from the vice, mark with crosses the notches or waste on each piece, seeing that pins and notches come

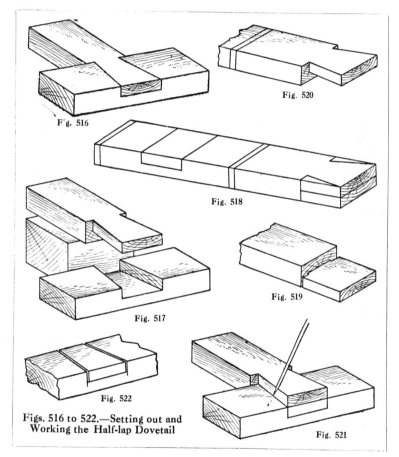

Fig. 520

Fg. 516

Fig. 518

Fig. 517

Fig. 519

Fig. 522

Fig. 521

Figs. 516 to 522.—Setting out and Working the Half-lap Dovetail

opposite to one another. Then remove and saw in the waste close to the lines, cut out the waste with mallet and chisel, and finish by paring.

When many joints of this class have to be made, it may save time to cut first of all a zinc gauge from which to mark the pins.

Half-lap Dovetail.—While there is one particular joint known as the "single dovetail," there is a number of joints known by other names in which a single dovetail is used, as, for example, the half-lap dovetail described below. These very simple forms of dovetailing will serve as an introduction to the various box or drawer dovetail joints on which the amateur furniture maker is often ambitious to make a start.

The half-lap dovetail (Figs. 516 and 517) is an extremely useful form of joint for connecting framing and for other purposes. In Fig. 518 is shown a piece of wood set out for making a simple half-lap dovetail joint for practice purposes only. The dovetail joint is first prepared as part of an ordinary lap joint; then the shoulders

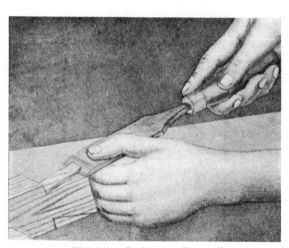

Fig. 523.—Paring the Dovetail

are made by sawing to the lines originally set out (Fig. 519). The pin is finished by careful paring, as in Figs. 520 and 523, and is then placed over the part that is to form the socket, the two pieces held firmly together, and the shape of the pin accurately scribed on the other part (*see* Fig. 521), and lines squared down on the edges. The socket is sawn just inside the lines (Fig. 522), so that the pin is a close fit, and the waste is then removed with a chisel.

Single Dovetail.—The joint specifically known as a single dovetail is that illustrated by Fig. 524, the complete setting out for which is shown in Fig. 525. The two half pins of one member of the joint should be made first.

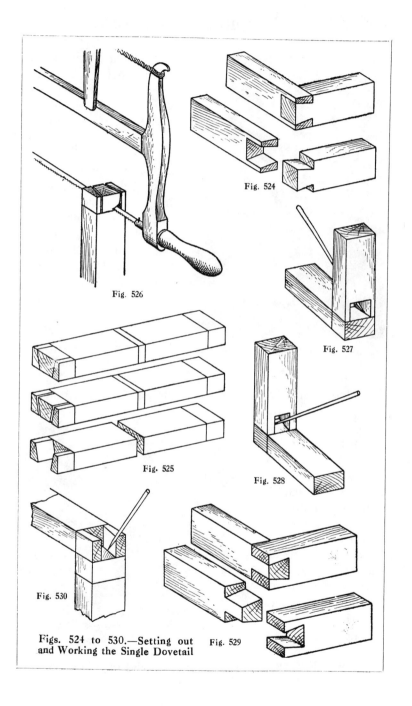

Fig. 524

Fig. 526

Fig. 527

Fig. 525

Fig. 528

Fig. 530

Figs. 524 to 530.—Setting out and Working the Single Dovetail

Fig. 529

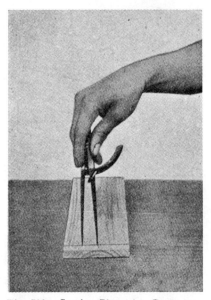

Fig. 531.—Spacing Pins with Compasses

Cut down with a saw after marking out, and then, to remove the waste, use a mallet and chisel, or, if the work is big enough, use a small bow saw (*see* Fig. 526), afterwards paring with a sharp thinly ground chisel from each side. When finishing the socket, hold the chisel with the left hand, the little finger resting on the work, and apply the effort by means of the right hand grasping the handle of the chisel, or by means of light blows with the mallet. When the piece is finished, place it upon the other one (on which the shoulder lines have already been scribed on all four sides) in the position shown by Figs. 527 and 528, it then being an easy matter to scribe the lines of the two half-sockets. Square the lines over the ends, and, by means of a bevel, duplicate on the other face the scribed dovetail. The two half-sockets are then made by sawing. Sometimes the single dovetail resembles Fig. 529,

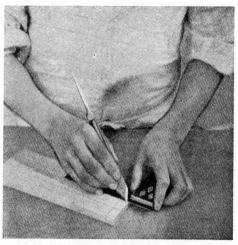

Fig. 532.—Squaring Down the Pins

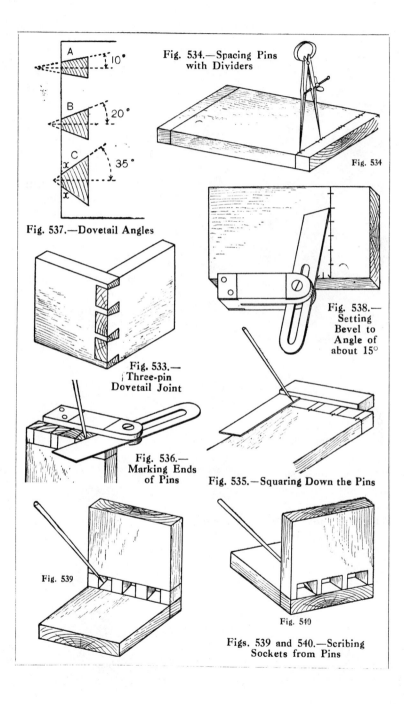

A
10°

B
20°

C
35°
x
x

Fig. 537.—Dovetail Angles

Fig. 534.—Spacing Pins with Dividers

Fig. 534

Fig. 533.—Three-pin Dovetail Joint

Fig. 538.—Setting Bevel to Angle of about 15°

Fig. 536.—Marking Ends of Pins

Fig. 535.—Squaring Down the Pins

Fig. 539

Fig. 540

Figs. 539 and 540.—Scribing Sockets from Pins

Fig. 541.—Marking Ends of Pins with Bevel

this consisting of a full dovetail pin and a complete socket. In this case it is preferable to mark out and cut the socket first, and to get the shape of the pin piece by scribing, as indicated in Fig. 530.

Common or Box Dovetail.—This of all joints is the one that most interests the c r a f t s m a n, either amateur or professional. Having mastered it, he can, by an easy process, proceed to the more elaborate dovetails—lap mitred, etc. Even more than is the case with other joints already described, the marking out is of the first importance and careful workmanship is essential. Running the saw in on the wrong side of a line will make all the difference between a good fitting and a badly fitting joint. A pencil line which has a perceptible thickness is in itself a source of

Fig. 542.—Marking Ends of Pins with Wooden Template

Fig. 543.—Scribing Sockets from Pins

danger, and in setting out it is better to use only the marking knife, preferably one that has a knife edge at one end and an awl point at the other, such as that illustrated in the photograph (Fig. 543) which is here presented. The process of setting out and cutting a box dovetail (*see* Fig. 533) is in itself extremely interesting, and is quite easy providing it be taken patiently step by step. Experienced craftsmen argue between themselves as to the correct order of procedure, some insisting that the pins must be cut first and the sockets marked out from them, and others that the pins should be marked from the sockets. It is a matter which every craftsman must decide for himself.

The "pins first" method.—The members of the joint having been carefully planed and smoothed up, the end should be shot perfectly true in a shooting block, and each member have a line parallel with the end scribed with

Fig. 544.—Scribing with Tenon Saw

a marking gauge on all four sides, the distance from the end being the thickness of the stuff. In the joint illustrated by Fig. 533 there are two complete pins and a half pin at the top and bottom. These pins are thinner at the front than at the back. On the shoulder line mark off at top and bottom half the thickness of the outer side (the thin side) of the pin, and with dividers or compasses (Figs. 531 and 534) accurately divide the intervening distance into three (if there are three pins, into four; for four pins, into five; and so on). From each of the points thus obtained mark off on the shoulder line on both sides of the point half the thickness of the thin side of the pin. Of course, at top and bottom, this last marking off can only be on one side of the point.

The thickness of the pins will depend on the class of work and on the thickness of the stuff; in wood from $\frac{3}{8}$ in. to $\frac{3}{4}$ in. thick it may be $\frac{1}{4}$ in.

The next job is to mark down by means of square and scriber short lines from the end of the work to meet the marks on the shoulder line that determine the thickness of the pins (Figs. 532 and 535). Then fix the work in the vice, and, by means of a bevel or a template, mark off the angles which give the end shape of the pins (Figs. 536 and 541). It is well after this to square down the lines on the other face of the work to meet the shoulder lines, though this is not always done.

The angle to which the bevel is set should not be less than that shown at A (Fig 537), or more than that shown at B. C is too weak, and should on no account be adopted, as pieces are liable to break out at x, and this may happen even in the course of making the joint. An excellent method of obtaining the oblique line to which the bevel may be set is to set out a piece of board in the manner shown by Fig. 538. Square a line across the board and make a mark at every inch. Also mark off the edge of the board 1 in. from the line. The bevel is shown to be set for an inclination of 1 in 5, which represents an angle of slightly more than 15°; 1 in 4 is just over 18°; 1 in 6, nearly 13°; 1 in 7, between 11° and 12°; 1 in 8, about 10°; and 1 in 9, about 9°.

In some figures in this chapter is shown a little template which it is customary for the craftsman to make for himself, after he has decided which bevel or inclination he prefers. Usually it is cut from a solid piece of wood, but doubtless tool merchants could supply it already made, either in wood or metal. When it is desired to cut all the dovetails to a uniform inclination, the template has advantages over the bevel, both as regards accuracy and speed of work (*see* Figs. 542, 549, 557, etc.).

The pins have now been completely set out. With a tenon or dovetail saw cut down beside the lines in the waste so as not to rob the pins by the thickness of the saw teeth. The waste can be removed with a chisel, or, in large work, with a bow saw, finishing with a sharp, thinly ground chisel applied from each side in turn. From the finished pins the sockets can next be marked out.

For marking out the sockets, place the worked member of the joint on the other member exactly as shown in Figs. 539, 540 and 543, and with the point of an awl or knife, used exactly as illustrated, scribe the shapes of the pins on to the other member. Square these lines across the end, as in Fig. 545, and, if thought necessary, duplicate the bevels on the back of the work. The sockets are next cut in exactly the same way as the pins were formed, and the two members of the joint should then be found to fit perfectly.

The " sockets first" method.—The other method of dovetailing—that of cutting the sockets first—will now be described. Take the piece that is to contain the sockets and scribe the shoulder line as before. Along this line at top and bottom mark off one-half the width of a socket. The socket width will vary with the class and thickness of the work, as will be understood from what has already been said. As before, divide the intervening distance into three ; if there were three whole sockets, into four ; for four whole sockets into five ; and so on. Also as before, mark from the centres on each side of them half the width of the socket, and with the bevel or template set out the bevels as in Fig. 546. Then square the lines across the end, and, if desirable, duplicate the bevels on the other face of the work. Make

N

the saw kerfs by the side of the lines in the waste and finish
the sockets as before.   Place the other member of the joint
in the bench screw, pack up the socketed member as shown
in Fig. 547, and with the awl mark the end shapes of the
pins.   Then proceed as already described for the other
method.

Professional workers sometimes mark the pins in a
manner different from the foregoing.   First they saw the
sockets but do not remove the waste.   Then, having placed
the work in the position shown by Figs. 544 and 548, and holding a saw near its end, they insert the saw in the kerfs
and lightly mark the end of the pins in which the piece will
be made.   They square the pins down to the shoulder lines
in the usual way, and then saw down, but it is essential to
remember that the saw kerfs must be made not *on* the light
saw marks already made, but at the side of them in the
waste.   This method is not recommended for adoption by
beginners.

Speed in Setting Out a Number of Dovetails.—Arising
out of the fact that the dovetail marking is on the
end of the stuff for pins and on the face of the stuff for
sockets, it is undoubtedly possible to set out dovetail joints
quicker by the " sockets first " method.   Fig. 549 shows
the method of marking out the pins with a small template,
each board being treated separately ; whereas by the other
method of cutting the sockets first, one setting out will be
sufficient to cut three or four pieces together, as shown in
Fig. 550.

Drawer or Lap Dovetail.—In lap dovetailing the joint
shows only on one side of the work, instead of on both
sides as in the ordinary dovetail (*see* Figs. 551 and 552).
In drawer construction and in other applications where it
is not desirable for the joint to show on the front, the lap dovetail is commonly employed.   The craftsman should examine
a drawer for himself, and he will note that all that shows of
the joint is the end grain on the side.   In a superior form of
lap joint—the secret lap—to be described later, not even
as much as the end grain of the pins shows, and, as far as
external appearances go, the joint is a mere lap joint.

The remarks already made with regard to setting out apply with even more force to the lap dovetail. It will be understood that B (Fig. 552) is the inside view of member A in Fig. 551, and D the inside view of C. The sides of the drawer having been planed up and the ends shot true, both

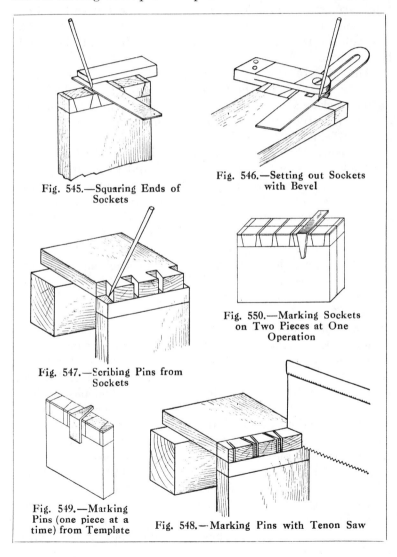

Fig. 545.—Squaring Ends of Sockets

Fig. 546.—Setting out Sockets with Bevel

Fig. 550.—Marking Sockets on Two Pieces at One Operation

Fig. 547.—Scribing Pins from Sockets

Fig. 549.—Marking Pins (one piece at a time) from Template

Fig. 548.—Marking Pins with Tenon Saw

side and front can be marked out for the lap dovetail with one setting of the marking gauge. The drawer side is thinner than the front and laps on to the end of the front to a distance equal to the thickness of the side. Therefore, setting the gauge to this thickness, run the shoulder line on all four surfaces of the side member and along the end and on the inside face of the front member (*see* Figs. 553 to 555). The side of the drawer will carry the pins and the front the sockets.

The pins of the lap dovetail joint will first be made. Fig. 552 presents the best view of them. Their thickness on the back face B will vary from $\frac{3}{8}$ in. to $\frac{3}{4}$ in. according to the stuff employed, a fair proportion being three-quarters of the thickness of the side. Thus, in 1 in. stuff the pins will measure $\frac{3}{4}$ in. on the back face; in $\frac{1}{2}$ in. stuff, $\frac{3}{8}$ in. on the back face; and so on. On the shoulder line at top and bottom, mark off half the thickness of the pins, and with dividers accurately divide the intervening distance into one more space than there will be pins, exactly as already explained for the common dovetail. The points thus given will be the centres of the pins, and from them half the thickness of the pins should be marked off on each side, and by means of square and scriber short lines should be drawn to the end of the work, as shown in Fig. 556. With the help of bevel or template (wood and metal templates are shown in Figs. 557 and 558) bevels are now marked on the end grain of the work as far as the shoulder line already scribed there. With a dovetail saw make kerfs in the waste beside the lines, necessarily holding the saw on the slant, as in Fig. 561, so as not to cut beyond the shoulder lines. The pieces that are to be removed should be marked with a cross to avoid mistake. Holding the work down on the bench by means of some form of grip (an adaptation of that shown by Fig. 412, p. 157, for example), use the chisel vertically and then horizontally, and cut out the waste (*see* Fig. 562), the finishing being executed with a keen and thinly-ground chisel, as shown in Figs. 559 and 560, for which purpose the work should be held in the bench screw.

There is often a tendency to leave the recesses with

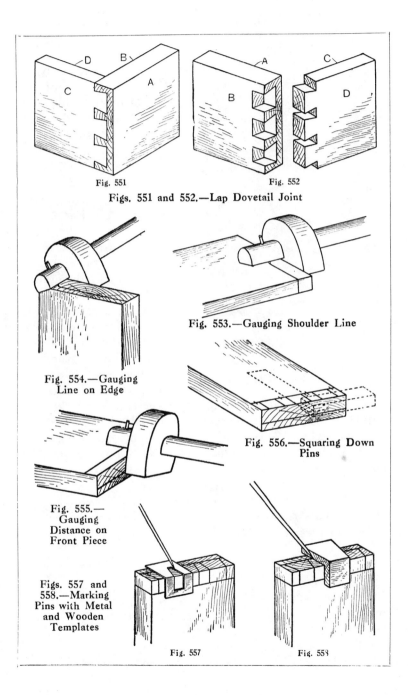

Fig. 551

Fig. 552

Figs. 551 and 552.—Lap Dovetail Joint

Fig. 553.—Gauging Shoulder Line

Fig. 554.—Gauging
Line on Edge

Fig. 556.—Squaring Down
Pins

Fig. 555.—
Gauging
Distance on
Front Piece

Figs. 557 and
558.—Marking
Pins with Metal
and Wooden
Templates

Fig. 557

Fig. 558

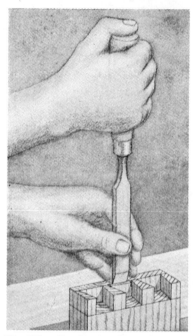

Fig. 559.—Overhand Paring of Socket

sloping backs, as in Fig. 566, the result being badly-fitting and split joints (*see* Figs. 564 and 565), the splitting being caused by excessive pressure against the half pins; and to avoid this it is better to undercut very slightly indeed, this undercutting being shown exaggerated in Fig. 563.

The front of the drawer is marked from the side in exactly the same way as for common dovetailing, except that, as shown in Fig. 567, the end of the front must coincide with the shoulder line scribed on the end of the side. The successive stages are exactly as before described.

If desired, the front of the drawer can be worked first and the pins cut from the sockets, as made clear in Fig. 568.

Secret Lap Dovetail.—In this joint, as already explained, there is no external evidence of dovetailing. The construction will be clear from the three views (Figs. 569 to 571), A being the outer face of the side of the drawer, and B the inner face, while C is the outer face of the front, and D the inner face.

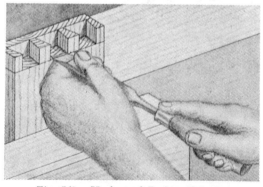

Fig. 560.—Horizontal Paring of Socket

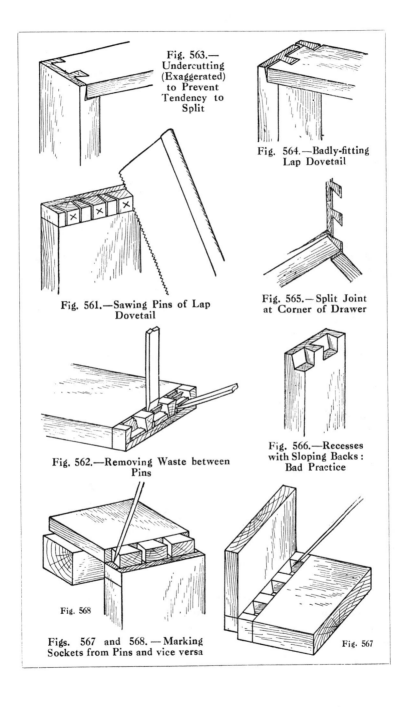

Fig. 563.— Undercutting (Exaggerated) to Prevent Tendency to Split

Fig. 564.—Badly-fitting Lap Dovetail

Fig. 561.—Sawing Pins of Lap Dovetail

Fig. 565.— Split Joint at Corner of Drawer

Fig. 562.—Removing Waste between Pins

Fig. 566.—Recesses with Sloping Backs: Bad Practice

Fig. 568

Figs. 567 and 568. — Marking Sockets from Pins and vice versa

Fig. 567

The front of the drawer has a projecting fillet or lap which conceals the joint and which, in cabinet work, etc., is often finished by rounding off. Much of the work of making this joint will, of course, resemble that already described for other dovetail joints, but attention will be here directed to the necessary differences in working. In the joint already shown the pins are made on the side and the sockets in the front member. Often this arrangement is reversed, as in Figs. 572 and 573, in which it will be seen that the pins have been made in the rebated piece and the sockets in the square-end piece. The front of the drawer is set out as in Fig. 574. Sawing down on the end line and on the first of the face lines will produce a deep narrow rebate, as in Fig. 575, those forming the lap piece; the saw cuts will, of course, be made in the waste and the rebate finished with a rebate plane or shoulder plane. The pins are set out by means of a template (Fig. 576), the use of a bevel being almost, if not quite, inadmissible, and are next cut in the usual way.

To mark the sockets on the side of the drawer, proceed as suggested in Fig. 577, which, after what has already been said on the subject, will be perfectly clear. This method of working will produce a joint of the kind illustrated in Figs. 572 and 573; but there would be no difficulty in cutting the pins in the side members of the drawer and thence marking the sockets on the front.

In making the secret lap dovetail joint it is not convenient to make the sockets first and from them to mark the pins.

As to which is the proper member to carry the pins and which to receive the sockets depends on whether the sides or the front of the drawer will have to stand the greater pressure; the arrangement should be such that the greater the pressure the tighter are the pins squeezed in their sockets. Naturally, when internal pressure is exerted against the socketed member, the pins tend to slide out of the sockets.

Secret Mitred Dovetail Joints.—The top edge of this joint shows a simple mitre line, and there is no external evidence of dovetailing. Fig. 578 is a view of the joint complete, and Fig. 579 shows the members of the joint apart.

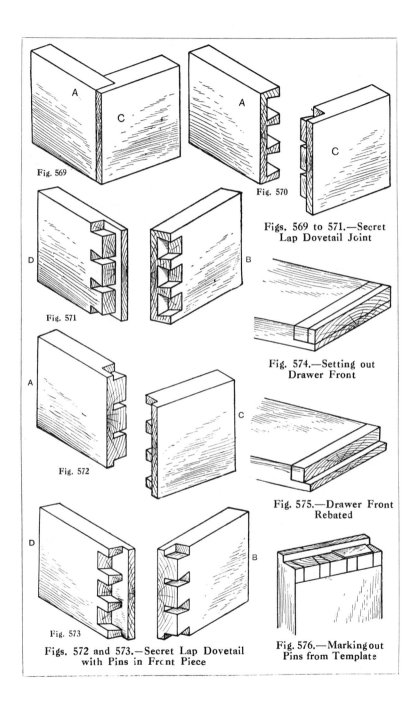

Fig. 569

Fig. 570

Figs. 569 to 571.—Secret Lap Dovetail Joint

Fig. 571

Fig. 574.—Setting out Drawer Front

Fig. 572

Fig. 575.—Drawer Front Rebated

Fig. 573

Figs. 572 and 573.—Secret Lap Dovetail with Pins in Front Piece

Fig. 576.—Marking out Pins from Template

To start with, both pieces of work must be set out and rebated exactly as already shown in Figs. 574 and 575. It will be seen that the mitre is made largely in the lap. On both pieces the mitre is made with a long wide paring chisel. A piece of wood about 1 in. thick is planed at one end to the true angle (45°) required, and adjusted and cramped to the work, as in Fig. 580, the whole being firmly fixed in the bench vice. Then the paring chisel can be used to bring the lap to exactly the same angle as the planed piece. The use of a metal shoulder or rebate plane possesses advantages over the use of a chisel, and Figs. 581 and 583 suggest suitable methods of holding the work for planing. It is desirable to leave on a slight amount to be removed in the final fitting. The pins are set out and made, and the sockets marked out from them and made as described for the secret lap dovetail. Fig. 582 is a variation of this joint, the pins being at some distance from each edge instead of being near each edge; but its advantages are doubtful.

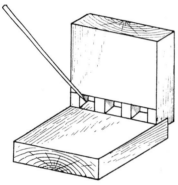

Fig. 577.—Scribing Sockets from Pins

Oblique Dovetail Joints.—Oblique dovetailing, as shown in Fig. 584, requires an elementary knowledge of geometry to find out the various angles. The angle G showing the inclination of piece E, as well as in the elevation of Fig. 585, is a different angle from which the end is cut at H. Again, the other piece of the joint may be a different slope; then it is essential to find out the angles J and K in the piece F. The geometry shown for this joint illustrates a method of turning an oblique surface parallel to view to show its true shape, so it will apply to many other oblique surfaces when the true shape is required.

Fig. 585 gives the plan and elevations of the joint. For the purposes of illustration, the two pieces of wood to be dovetailed are of different slopes, therefore two elevations

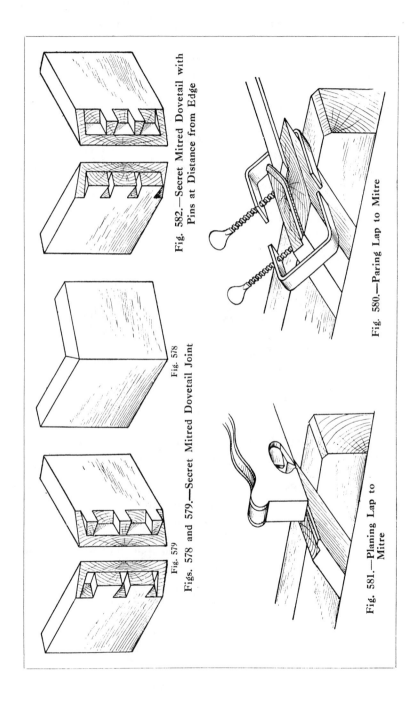

Fig. 582.—Secret Mitred Dovetail with Pins at Distance from Edge

Fig. 578

Figs. 578 and 579.—Secret Mitred Dovetail Joint

Fig. 579

Fig. 580.—Paring Lap to Mitre

Fig. 581.—Planing Lap to Mitre

are required. If they are both the same slope, as is generally the case, of course only one elevation is necessary. This joint forming a part either of a rectangular trough or other rectilinear frame, will show a right angle in the plan, so that if the edges are first bevelled to the required slopes, the ends and shoulder lines on these bevelled edges can be marked out with the try-square.

The elevation on $x^1 y^1$ shows the true inclination of the piece E, therefore the angle can be obtained for the edges with a sliding bevel as shown. The elevation on $x^2 y^2$ shows the inclination and bevelled edge of the piece F. To find out the angle H in piece E, the outside surface is folded

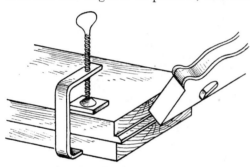

Fig. 583.—Planing Lap to Mitre

down to a horizontal position. In elevation 1 a part of a circle shows how this piece swings down as if the bottom edge was the hinge. The width is then projected on to the plan, which shows the true shape of the piece E with its angle H. The surface of piece F is swung over in the same manner as seen in elevation 2, and the angle K found in the same way.

Fig. 586 shows piece E with the two lines marked round the wood at the angle H on the sides and with a try-square on the edges, that have been previously planed to the angle G (Fig. 585). These lines are the same distance apart as the thickness of piece F measured on the bevelled edge. It is sawn off $\frac{1}{8}$ in. away from the end line, to allow for smoothing off when fixed together. The pins are marked on the end, and arranged so that the centre lines of the pins are parallel to the bevelled edges, as indicated by the dotted lines in Fig. 586. The lines on each side are marked with a gauge down to the shoulder line. Saw down the pins and chisel out the waste.

When the lines have been marked out on piece F at the angle K, and try-squared across the edges, scribe for the sockets as in Fig. 587. Then mark the lines across the ends of piece F as indicated. These lines are parallel to the edges, and are marked with the sliding bevel set as in Fig.

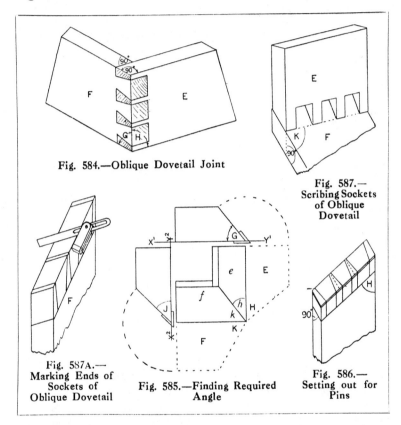

Fig. 584.—Oblique Dovetail Joint

Fig. 587.—Scribing Sockets of Oblique Dovetail

Fig. 587A.—Marking Ends of Sockets of Oblique Dovetail

Fig. 585.—Finding Required Angle

Fig. 586.—Setting out for Pins

587A. Saw down the mortises, and remove the waste pieces with a narrow chisel. The sharp corners of the pins should be trimmed with a chisel before driving together.

Making Dovetail Grooves and Tongues.—Occasionally one meets with a box made of substantial stuff in which each angle consists of a single dovetail, the tongued ends A (Fig. 588) sliding vertically into dovetail grooves in the

front and back B, and the latter sliding into similar grooves
cut in the bottom C. The tongues are made by sawing
their shoulders and then using a rebate plane of which
the face and iron have been altered as in Fig. 588A. So
that it may work down to the right amount, a piece of
stuff should be screwed on as at A. The grooves in the
sides B should be sawn, the waste removed by a chisel,
and finished with router and small iron. The dovetail

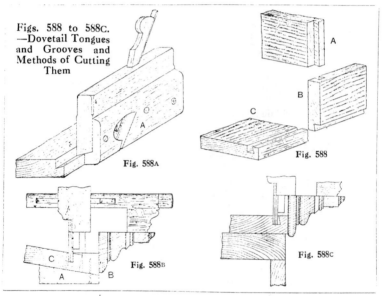

Figs. 588 to 588C.
—Dovetail Tongues
and Grooves and
Methods of Cutting
Them

Fig. 588A

Fig. 588

Fig. 588B

Fig. 588C

grooves in the bottom C can be made in a similar manner,
if it is short, but otherwise they are ploughed as follows :
Prepare a piece of board by splaying it as at A, and also
a strip as at B, which should be nailed on as indicated in
Fig. 588B, having its outer face vertical. Then when the
bottom is placed on as shown at C, a plough plane can
be used, the edge of the iron having been ground and
sharpened to the angle shown. The remainder of the
groove is formed by ploughing with another iron, as shown in
Fig. 588C. When ploughing, as above described, is out of the
question, dovetail grooves should be made first as ordinary
grooves with square edges, and then undercut with a chisel.

CHAPTER XIV

CLAMPED AND LEDGED WORK

Tongued Clamps.—One of the most useful applications of tonguing is in the formation of clamped ends to table tops, paste-boards, drawing-boards, flaps, etc etc. The clamps prevent the work from warping or twisting, and wear much longer than would exposed end grain. Clamping may be done by tonguing, feather-tonguing, dowelling, tenoning, etc. For feather-tonguing, one ploughed groove is in the end grain of the main piece and the other in the longitudinal grain of the clamp, as shown in Figs. 589 and 590. A cross-grained tongue makes, of course, the stronger joint. If desired, the tongue may be a part of the clamp, as in Fig. 591, and in the formation of such a joint as this a pair of matching planes will be useful. After a clamped joint has been carefully fitted, it is taken apart, glued, and cramped together till dry, when the face of the work is carefully planed to truth.

The clamping joint just referred to is the one chiefly in favour for joining lengthwise the boarding employed for backing cupboards, wardrobes, etc., and in this case glue is not used; instead, the outer boards are secured to the framing, and there is then slight accommodation for the small amount of shrinkage or expansion respectively which is sure to occur in a dry or wet atmosphere.

Simpler than but not so good as tongue clamping is the rebated clamp (Fig. 592), for which no instructions are necessary.

Dowel Clamping.—Dowelling (Fig. 593) is an easier method of clamping than by mortising and tenoning. The board and clamp are held in the vice and lines squared across to mark the positions of the dowels. Then the marking gauge can be used to intersect these lines and give the exact dowel centres (*see* also pp. 145 to 147).

The rest of the work will proceed as for ordinary dowelling. In mitre dowelling (Fig. 594) the clamp is first accurately shaped and fitted, and lines squared down the face of the work across the joint. Next these are squared across the edges, and the dowel centres indicated, as before, by means of a gauge; or the dowel centres are set off (p. 146).

Mortise-and-tenon Clamping.—An example of multiple tenons is to be found sometimes in the clamp (part of which is shown in Fig. 595) on the end of a blackboard, etc. Such a board is formed actually of a number of boards joined lengthwise with cross tongues, the heart side of the boards alternating back and front so as to obviate the joints pulling apart when the inevitable shrinkage occurs. Square the two shoulder lines, set out the haunched tenons on the face and back only, and cut them, removing the waste with the chisel, or, instead, do the greater part of the cutting with a bow-saw and finish by paring. Next set out the thickness of the tenons, and, should a circular saw be available, saw on these lines (in the waste) as far as the shoulder lines (Fig. 596), next making saw-kerfs on the latter to detach the waste. In the ordinary way, the tenons will be cut to thickness as far as the shoulder lines of the haunches, the waste removed, and the haunches themselves formed by using a rebate plane or tenon saw and chisel, or a combination of the two methods. The clamping piece will be left a trifle long. In it must be made a series of mortises connected together at their necks by a groove, into which the haunch of the tenons will fit. This groove may be ploughed to the depth of the haunch, and the mortises then cut, partly from the grooved edge and partly from the outer edge, having been first carefully set out. Allowance will need to be made for wedges if these are thought necessary (*see* Fig. 595). The clamps (one at each end of the board), having been fitted, are glued and cramped; they are cut to size when the glue is hard, and the board is finished by shooting the edges and, probably, slightly bevelling the corners.

Mitre Clamping.—In cabinet work, the objection to plain clamping is that the end grain of the clamp shows

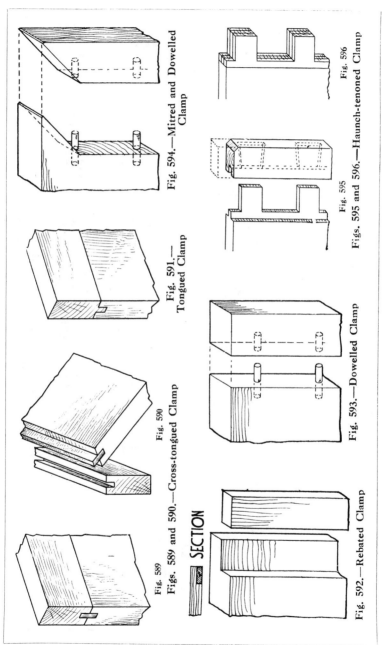

Fig. 594.—Mitred and Dowelled Clamp

Fig. 596

Figs. 595 and 596.—Haunch-tenoned Clamp

Fig. 595

Fig. 591.—Tongued Clamp

Fig. 590

Figs. 589 and 590.—Cross-tongued Clamp

Fig. 589

SECTION

Fig. 593.—Dowelled Clamp

Fig. 592.—Rebated Clamp

O

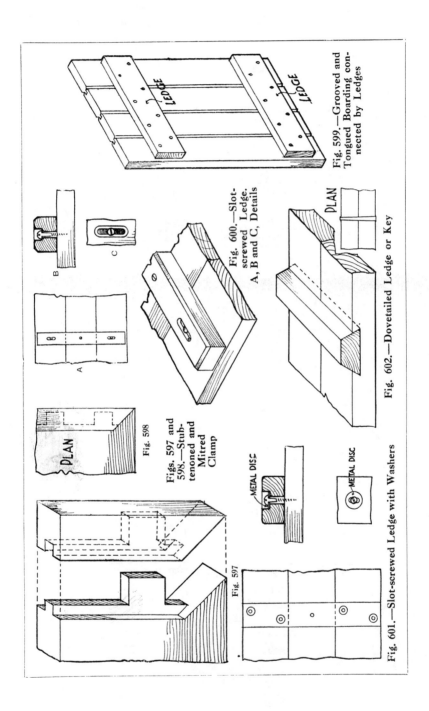

Fig. 599.—Grooved and Tongued Boarding connected by Ledges

Fig. 600.—Slot-screwed Ledge. A, B and C, Details

Fig. 602.—Dovetailed Ledge or Key

PLAN

Figs. 597 and 598.—Stub-tenoned and Mitred Clamp

Fig. 598.

PLAN

Fig. 597.

METAL DISC

METAL DISC

Fig. 601.—Slot-screwed Ledge with Washers

LEDGE

LEDGE

PLAN

A

B

C

on the edges ; to avoid this resort is had to mitre clamping, either dowelled (Fig. 594) or tenoned (Figs. 597 and 598). For the latter the clamp is set out as before explained, and is next mitred at each end. It is very carefully laid in position and its shape scribed on to the board, flap, etc. The mortise will be made in the clamp, but the end of the board carrying the tenons must first be worked. Then the clamp is laid on the tenons and marked for mortising.

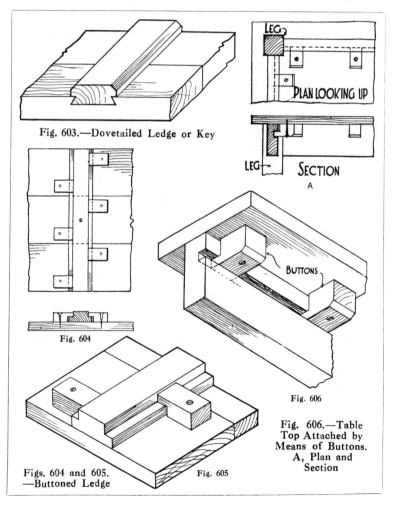

Fig. 603.—Dovetailed Ledge or Key

PLAN LOOKING UP

SECTION
A

BUTTONS

Fig. 604

Fig. 606

Fig. 606.—Table Top Attached by Means of Buttons. A, Plan and Section

Figs. 604 and 605.—Buttoned Ledge

Fig. 605

Ledges.—These serve, to some extent, the same purpose as clamps, that is, they tend to prevent warping, and they are secured to the back—not the ends—of the work. The simplest is the plain nailed or screwed ledge (Fig. 599), of which little need be said. It is used in common door and gate construction.

In the case of screwed ledges there is often some provision for adjustment should shrinkage occur later, this being the approved method in making drawing-boards. Take, for example, a three-board construction, as in Fig. 600. For the middle screw in each brace an ordinary small hole is bored, but for the outer screws there are narrow countersunk slots. Thus, should the joints open in course of time, the outer screws can be eased, the job cramped up, and the screws again tightened. Fig. 601 shows a method in which there is a metal disc under each of the outer screws, this being an improvement.

Dovetail ledges or keys are a far superior method, but involve ever so much more labour, as grooves have to be cut across grain at the back of the work (drawing-board, flap top, etc.), and the ledge slid in from one side. Figs. 602 and 603 show two styles. The method of forming undercut grooves is explained on p. 206.

Buttoned ledges, shown in Figs. 604 and 605, are adjustable should shrinkage lead to warping, since obviously some screws may, if need arise, be eased and others tightened to bring the work back into one plane. Buttons, too, are a very convenient method of attaching table tops to rails, Fig. 606 clearly showing the details of the method. Buttons screwed to the underside of the top have projections which engage in grooves cut on the inside of the rails ; or the effect of the grooves can be obtained by screwing small blocks to the rails inside flush with the top of the framework, the buttons being used as before ; but the grooves are to be preferred.

CHAPTER XV

CRAMPING WORK

SMALL work that has just been glued or that requires to be nailed, screwed, etc., after being tightened up, is held in handscrews or iron cramps. Small iron cramps resemble Fig. 607, the required pressure being applied by means of the screw actuated by wings in the smaller sizes and a lever handle in the larger ones. There is a variety of cramp known as Colt's, manufactured by a New York firm, that has a very quick action and is made in many different patterns. Its feature is the use, instead of a screw, of a cam or eccentric, by means of which pressure can be brought to bear in a moment. Fig. 608 is typical of them all. On raising the handle the cam head operates a plunger carrying at its other end a self-adjusting plate. The opposing jaw can be slid along the malleable-iron bar, the total opening of the 12-in. cramp being 6 in. Large and small cramps are made on this principle.

The ordinary wooden handscrew (Fig. 609) is well known ; an improvement is the Jorgensen, the jaws of which can, in addition to the parallel position, assume a variety of angles with one another (*see* Fig. 609 A).

The joiner's cramp for sashes, etc., etc., is of the kind shown in Fig. 610. Fittings are obtainable (*see* Fig. 610 A) by means of which it is possible to improvise such an appliance. The two parts illustrated can be readily attached to an iron bar or wooden strip.

Work that has been cramped up may be so held by means of dogs (Fig. 611), which, for temporary purposes, are lightly driven in across the joint. In some classes of work the smaller sizes may be wholly driven in and allowed to stay.

Cramping Boards Together.—In the absence of special cramps the craftsman can easily build one or two wholly of wood; indeed, such wooden cramps are used in shops even where iron cramps are also available. It is evident that the glueing of several boards together edge to edge needs considerable pressure, and the purchase of iron cramps sufficiently large for the purpose is generally out of the question. The first alternative is illustrated in Fig. 612, where the boarding is shown glued and put together, and held in position by the cramps. These should be applied if possible at about 1-ft. 3-in. centres right along the boarding. Each one consists of a batten, say 3 in. by 2 in., of

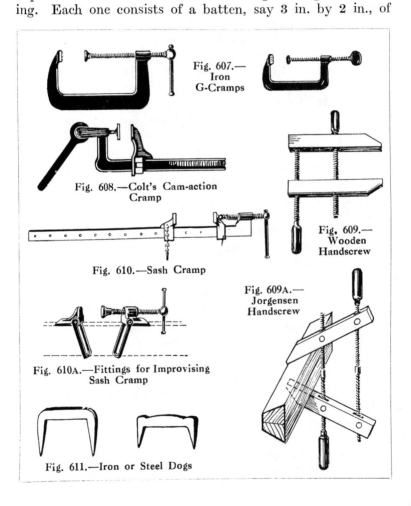

Fig. 607.—Iron G-Cramps

Fig. 608.—Colt's Cam-action Cramp

Fig. 609.—Wooden Handscrew

Fig. 610.—Sash Cramp

Fig. 609A.—Jorgensen Handscrew

Fig. 610A.—Fittings for Improvising Sash Cramp

Fig. 611.—Iron or Steel Dogs

rough piece of wood of about the same size, as at A or B, about 12 in. longer than the width of the boarding, and having blocks of wood about $1\frac{1}{4}$ in. thick very strongly

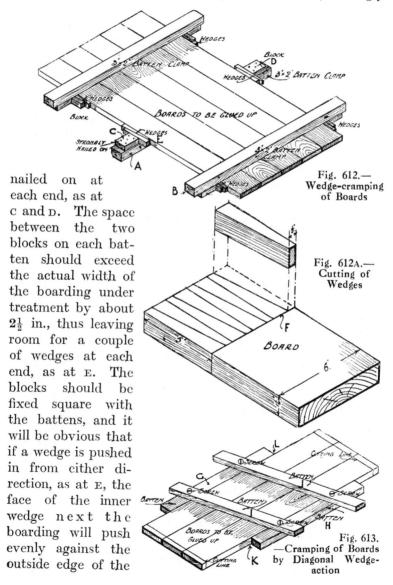

Fig. 612.—Wedge-cramping of Boards

Fig. 612A.—Cutting of Wedges

Fig. 613.—Cramping of Boards by Diagonal Wedge-action

nailed on at each end, as at c and D. The space between the two blocks on each batten should exceed the actual width of the boarding under treatment by about $2\frac{1}{2}$ in., thus leaving room for a couple of wedges at each end, as at E. The blocks should be fixed square with the battens, and it will be obvious that if a wedge is pushed in from either direction, as at E, the face of the inner wedge next the boarding will push evenly against the outside edge of the latter, thus exerting a regular pressure over the whole of its length, this pressure increasing as the wedges are driven farther home. This is the purpose and advantage of using double or " folding " wedges, as they are termed. One used alone would not be nearly so workmanlike and efficient. Having prepared sufficient cramps and wedges, the first set should be put on and lightly fixed at one end, as at B. This will effectually obviate the risk of the boards buckling upwards as the pressure is increased, and to prevent any downward bulge the next cramp should be applied with the batten on the other face, as at A, this alternative arrangement being continued throughout the entire length. Finally, all the wedges should be driven in tight, and the whole put on one side until the glue has thoroughly set, a matter of about twelve hours.

The wedges should be of hard wood, such as oak. Suitable sizes for them are given in Fig. 612 A, which also illustrates how a number of them can be cut quickly and economically. Having set out a piece of board in the manner indicated, it should be sawn along the alternate square and raking lines, next cutting off by sawing across on the line F. In this way there is formed a wedge at each saw-cut entirely without waste. The sawn edges of each wedge should be shot smooth with a plane.

Another method of cramping boards, and one perhaps best suited to the lighter class of joinery work, is explained by Fig. 613. Here the boards are shown just as before, but gripped by a lighter form of cramp made up of a couple of battens as at G and H, connected by mean of two others, arranged as at I and J, with stout screws through their centres where they cross. These screws must hold the parts of the framework thus formed quite securely, but at the same time give them a little play, the result being that when the whole are at right angles, the bars G and H are at their maximum distance apart ; but when they are subjected to a racking movement, the square opening which they frame changes to a rhombus or diamond form, and the bars G and H are brought gradually closer. It is this movement that is turned to account for cramping

purposes, the boarding being
glued and laid on a flat,
even surface, with the cramp
placed in position as in
Fig. 613, and its outer bars
driven with a mallet as far
in a longitudinal direction as
they will go, thus forcing
the boards together. When
the full pressure is attained,
nails at K and L will serve
to prevent its relaxation.

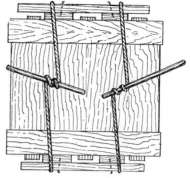

Fig. 614.—Rope Cramp

A rope cramp is shown
in Fig. 614. Strong cord or rope is tied round the work

Fig. 615.—Wedge-cramping of Frame

and twisted with an iron rod, which, when the rope is
sufficiently taut, can
be tied in position.

Fig. 615 shows
some cleats screwed to
a workbench or the
workshop floor, and a
sash frame glued and
cramped up by driven
folding wedges.

The joiner's vice-
screw can also be used

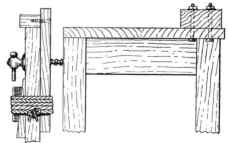

Fig. 616.—Bench Vice Arranged for
Clamping

for the same purpose (*see* Fig. 616). A block is bolted to the back of the bench, and the vice temporarily heightened as shown. The temporary piece is prevented from tilting by securing with five or six turns of stout cord, tightening up the cord with folding wedges, the outer wedge being slightly rounded so as not to chafe the cord ;

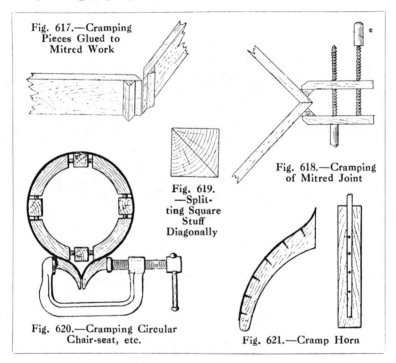

Fig. 617.—Cramping Pieces Glued to Mitred Work

Fig. 618.—Cramping of Mitred Joint

Fig. 619. —Splitting Square Stuff Diagonally

Fig. 620.—Cramping Circular Chair-seat, etc.

Fig. 621.—Cramp Horn

the inner one is the driver. Work placed between the extended vice cheek and the block can be firmly clamped with the bench screw.

Cramping Mitres and Circular Work.—The mitres of the base of a chest, etc., are cramped in the manner shown in Figs. 617 and 618. After the mitres have been shot true two blocks are glued on about 1 in. from the corner. Then, when the mitres are glued, a hand screw can be screwed on, and left until the mitres are dry. Then remove the hand screws, and plane off the blocks. Fig. 618 shows the hand screw on when the mitres are glued up. Fig. 619 shows a method of splitting a piece of 1-in. or 1¼-in. square stuff about as long as the base is deep, to make the blocks.

The foregoing method can also be applied in cramping circular frames, projecting cramping pieces being provided for when setting out ; but the method is not often convenient, and it is better to use, for such work as the frames and rims of chair seats, tables, etc., some form of circular cramp (*see* Fig. 620), for example, a band of steel or of hoop iron screwed or riveted to two horns (Fig. 621), pressure being brought upon the flat ends of the horns by means of any available form of cramp—even the bench vice, if it will open wide enough. Flexible cramps employing steel bands are made in a number of different forms.

CHAPTER XVI

NAILS, SCREWS, BOLTS, AND CLUE

MEANS of holding and fastening together woodwork comprise nails, screws, bolts, and glue, these being used according to the kind, position, strength, and size of the work. For internal work, such as cabinet making and joinery, glue is very largely employed. Its use renders the joint and the adjacent surfaces non-porous, numerous thread-like dowels of glue entering the pores and tying or binding the pieces together. A glued joint, therefore, in many cases should be even stronger than the wood itself, but it is quickly affected by dampness, which softens the glue. Nails are pins or spikes of metal, which, unless their ends are clenched, hold together woodwork simply as a result of the friction caused by the grip of the wood fibres; therefore, should there be any strain tending to separate the pieces or should shrinkage take place, a nailed joint is liable to open. However, nails are good enough for general carpentry purposes and in small work where strain and shrinkage are unlikely.

Fig. 622.—Wood Fibres Holding a "Cut" Nail

The screw is a far superior fastening. The thread of a screw being a circular wedge—a wedge-shaped piece of paper wrapped round a rod will appear as the thread of a screw —really cramps two pieces of wood together. The stiffer the fibres of the wood the greater is the pressure obtained, and the stronger will be the joint. Screwing into end grain is a weaker fixing, but if it is allowable to insert the screw obliquely, a fair amount of strength will be obtained. The bolt is used for making a still more secure fixing; the larger head and the threaded nut, both of which bear on the external surfaces, connected by a tie rod in tension constitute a very strong cramp, and as the thread takes its pull from a metal nut, instead of the fibres of wood as in the screw, a considerable force can be applied with the aid of a spanner.

Nails.—These are made in various shapes and sizes. " Wrought nails " are forged or hammered to shape. " Cut nails " are cut or stamped out from rolled sheet-iron. Nowa-

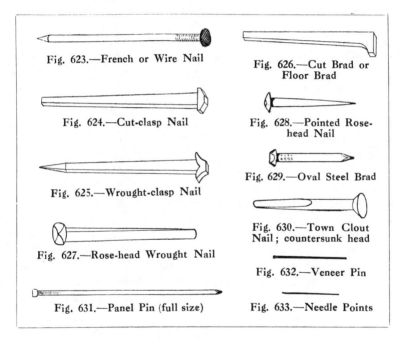

Fig. 623.—French or Wire Nail

Fig. 626.—Cut Brad or Floor Brad

Fig. 624.—Cut-clasp Nail

Fig. 628.—Pointed Rose-head Nail

Fig. 625.—Wrought-clasp Nail

Fig. 629.—Oval Steel Brad

Fig. 627.—Rose-head Wrought Nail

Fig. 630.—Town Clout Nail; countersunk head

Fig. 632.—Veneer Pin

Fig. 631.—Panel Pin (full size)

Fig. 633.—Needle Points

days, nails are manufactured in vast quantities by machinery instead of being hand-made, and consequently have a finer finish and more regular size and shape.

The common French nail (Fig. 623) is made of round wire which is pointed and the head made round and flat. The general smoothness of the nail and its flat head enable it to drive easily and to be withdrawn easily with pincers. The head is serrated or roughened to prevent the hammer slipping when driving, and the portion of the nail beneath is similarly treated to assist holding the nail in the wood. It is very strong and suitable for packing-case making and rough carpentry work where the points can be clenched, but for tight fixing these nails are not recommended. They are made from 1 in. to 6 in. or 7 in. in length.

The cut clasp nail (Fig. 624), being stamped from sheet-iron, is parallel in thickness and tapered in its width. The head is slightly thicker than the stem of the nail, inasmuch as it is hammered up after the nail has been stamped out. When driving this nail (and all other tapered flat nails) it should be so placed that the head does not cross the grain. The general rule is to place nails with the length of their heads in the same direction as the grain of the upper piece of wood. The sharp square edges and the flat rough surfaces give this nail a very tight fixing. From Fig. 622, which shows the position of the fibres when the nail is driven in, it will be seen that the fibres are likely to withstand any tendency to withdraw the nail, and when such a nail is inserted in hard wood it is almost impossible to draw it out again. A bradawl is sometimes needed if near the end of the wood, and the head, not being large, can be punched beneath the surface of the wood without difficulty. These nails are made in sizes from 1 in. to 4 in. or 5 in. long.

The wrought clasp nail (Fig. 625) is somewhat similar in shape to the foregoing. The head is a better shape for clasping the wood, and the nail has a better point, which allows of clenching. These nails are made up to 6 in. or 7 in. in length.

The joiner's cut brad (Fig. 626) somewhat resembles the cut clasp nails, but its head is smaller, projects only on one side, and is the same thickness as the stem, so that, when punched in, the nail holes in the finished work are small. It is used for light joinery work, matchboarding and flooring.

Rose-head wrought flat-pointed nails (Fig. 627), sometimes called board nails, are driven in across the grain so as to cut the fibres of the wood. The strong head and the flat point enable them to clench well, and they are largely used in wagon building and for fencing and rustic carpentry. The " patent " rose-head nail (Fig. 628) is of steel and is pointed.

The oval steel brad (Fig. 629) has been brought into general usage of recent years. Its thinness enables it to be driven without splitting the wood, and the head is comparatively small, and when punched in makes a very small hole. For this reason these nails are used in the best joinery work ; being made of steel, they are stiff and strong enough to be used for hardwood, in which cases a bradawl is sometimes required but only a small hole is necessary. These brads are first-rate for small work, and are much better

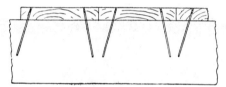

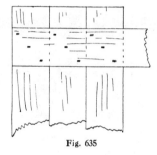

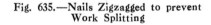

Fig. 634.—Nails Inserted on the Slant to give Dovetail Effect

Fig. 635.—Nails Zigzagged to prevent Work Splitting

Fig. 635

than the cut clasp nails in sizes of 1 in. and less. They are obtainable from $\frac{1}{2}$ in. to about $3\frac{1}{2}$ in. in length.

The town clout nail with countersunk head (Fig. 630) has a flat chisel-shaped point which is driven in across the grain of the wood. The nails are used for fixing ironwork to wood ; the many iron plates in connection with wheelwright's work are generally fixed with these nails. When wrapping heated iron plates around curved surfaces these nails are invaluable. For these purposes they are used from 1 in. to 3 in. in length.

Panel pins (Fig. 631), which are of steel and are used for panels and mouldings and the finer cabinet work, are somewhat like a boot rivet in appearance but of a slighter and much better finish. They are made from $\frac{3}{4}$ in. to 2 in. in length.

Veneer pins (Fig. 632), also of steel, are of a still finer

make, similar to panel pins, and vary from $\frac{3}{8}$ in. to $\frac{3}{4}$ in. in length.

Needle points (Fig. 633) are of hard steel and resemble needles without eyes; they are very handy in delicate work where the brad or pin head would be detrimental to the finished surface. No bradawl is required, as they are simply driven in and broken off without difficulty. They are largely used by picture-frame makers for fixing gilt mouldings.

Method of Inserting Nails.—The length of a nail should depend upon the thickness of the piece to be fixed. In places where the timbers beneath are large enough, the

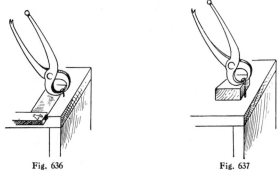

Fig. 636   Fig. 637

Figs. 636 and 637.—Blade of Square and Wooden Block used to Prevent Pincers Damaging Work

nail should be four times as long as the thickness of the piece to be fixed, there being one-fourth of the nail in the top piece and three-fourths in the underneath piece. Of course, there are many cases where this rule cannot apply. Fig. 634 is a diagram showing the positions of nails to obtain the greatest strength. Nails driven obliquely are more likely to keep in one plane; this is an important matter in small work or when fixing on to a narrower surface, such as the edge of a thin board beneath. The straightness of the nail is partly assisted by the fibres of the grain when driven in obliquely. Again, by this manner of inserting nails the piece is less likely to draw away from the board, as the nails really form a dovetail. When nailing boards together it is often necessary to place nails zigzag, as in Fig. 635, to prevent the pieces splitting. Such an arrangement also increases the strength of the joint. For clenching a nail, knocking over the point with a hammer is often thought good enough. The proper way of doing it, although this is not always possible, is to drive it nearly home and then turn the point well over on a drift pin or punch so as to bury the point in the wood. Then hold a heavy hammer or other weight against the nail at the back, and drive the nail until the point is buried flush with the wood.

Withdrawing Nails.—When driving nails in woodwork it sometimes happens that the nail runs to one side and its point is ultimately found to be projecting through one side of the work. If this has occurred, the exposed point can be knocked back with the hammer and nail-punch and the head grasped with the pincers. It is in with-

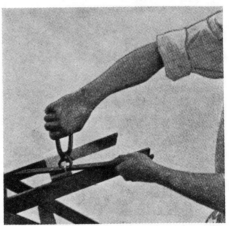

Fig. 638.—Withdrawing a Nail

drawing the nail with the pincers that the worker often seriously marks or bruises the surface of the wood, and to obviate this a good method to adopt is to place the blade of a try-square flat on the work and lever the pincers on it as shown in Fig. 636. If the nail is a long one, and the grip is not sufficiently tight to continue the levering motion lower down the shank, then replace the try square with an odd block of wood (Fig. 637), and lever on this until the nail comes out easily. A photograph showing an actual case in practice is presented by Fig. 638.

In cases where a nail is to be withdrawn and the head is so deeply embedded in the wood that a grip cannot be

P

obtained with the pincers, it can often be eased above the surface by the aid of an old chisel or screwdriver. The blade of the try-square is placed as near as possible to the head of the nail, and the point of the screwdriver is pushed under the head. Then by a slight twisting or prising motion the nail can be raised sufficiently to be gripped with the pincers without much injuring the surface of the wood. When a dent or bruise, such as from a hammer hit, etc., does occur, it can often be entirely obliterated by holding

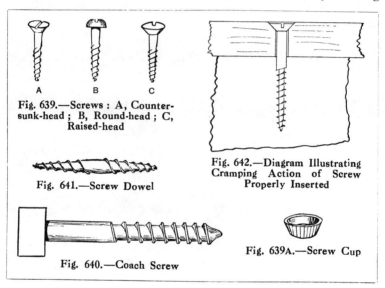

Fig. 639.—Screws : A, Counter-sunk-head ; B, Round-head ; C, Raised-head

Fig. 641.—Screw Dowel

Fig. 642.—Diagram Illustrating Cramping Action of Screw Properly Inserted

Fig. 639A.—Screw Cup

Fig. 640.—Coach Screw

a wad dipped in hot water over the mark until it is raised level, and afterwards rubbing down smooth with glass-paper.

Screws.—The screws used for woodwork are of three kinds, which differ chiefly in the shape of the heads—the countersunk head, the round head, and the square-headed coach screw. The countersunk head, shown at A (Fig. 639), is used for general work and also in cases where the head is required to be flush or below the surface, to allow for filling up for a finished surface. The round-head screws, as at B, are used where an ornamental finish is required, as in locks, etc. These two kinds of screws can be obtained from ¼ in. to 6 in. in length, and are graded in diameters for No. 1 up to No. 20, so that for a screw of a given length there is a good number of different thicknesses obtainable. Raised-head screws, c, are sometimes used for the sake of appearance. The coach screw (Fig. 640) is used for fixing ironwork to wood and is tightened with a spanner. It is a heavier type, and ranges from 2 in. to 8 in. long.

The proportion of the threaded part of a screw to the plain part gives an idea as to the length of screw required for fixing any particular job ; it is roughly three times the length of the plain portion of screw above. For screwing wood to wood, choose a screw whose length is from two and a half to three times the thickness of the top piece ; its diameter and size must be chosen with regard to the strength of the job and the amount of substance or thickness into which the screw penetrates.

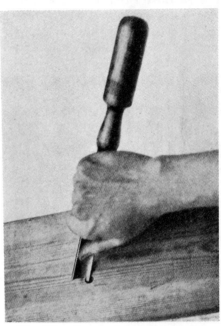

Fig. 643.—Countersinking Screw Hole with Gouge

When screwing iron plates to woodwork the foregoing rule does not apply, and judgment is necessary having regard to the strain that tends to separate the two materials. In many cases three-quarters or five-sixths of the length of the screw enters the wood. In the hinges of a door the proportion is even greater because of the thin plate of the hinge and because of the greater length of screw required to support the weight of the door.

Method of Inserting Screws.—When screwing one piece

of wood to another, first bore a hole with a spoon bit a trifle larger than the body of the screw, and then bore with a small spoon or pin bit a hole in the underneath piece less in depth and diameter than the threaded stem of the screw. The free fit of the body of the screw in the top piece allows the full cramping action to take place, and the smaller hole in the piece beneath gives the screw a chance to cut its own thread tightly (*see* Fig. 642). Russian tallow should be rubbed on the screws before driving to lubricate them and to ensure easy removal at any future time. The small hand drills with bevel gears, already referred to, are the most convenient tools for boring screw holes, as they save a lot of time, and their use is simplicity itself. All screw-heads should be driven in flush with the surface of the woodwork, for which purpose the

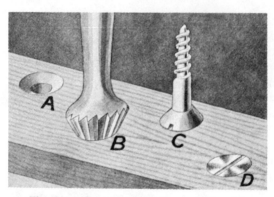

Fig. 644.—Countersinking Screw Hole with Rose-bit

hole generally needs to be chamfered, which work may be done in one of two or three ways. Either a chisel or a gouge may be employed, as in Fig. 643, always starting the cutting across the grain, or a rose-bit in a brace or hand-drill can be used, as in Fig. 644, in which illustration A is the countersunk hole, B the rose-head bit in use, C the screw, and D the head flush with the work. When a screw may require to be withdrawn from time to time, a cup or socket (Fig. 639A) may fit in the countersinking under the screw head. Dowel screws (Fig. 641) are used as dowels between two pieces of wooden rod, etc.

Withdrawing Rusted Screws. — If the end of a red-hot poker or iron bar be placed on the screw head for a minute or so, the expansion of the metal will probably break the rust contact and allow of the screw being withdrawn. Another method is to place a stout screwdriver in position in the nick of the screw and give a smart hammer blow (*see* Fig. 645), thus driving in the screw ever so slightly farther and breaking the rust contact as before.

Withdrawing Damaged Screws. —There are two or three ways of removing screws that have lost part of their heads and which project slightly from the work. One is to file the head so that it has two parallel faces, and then turn out the screw by means of a wrench, or, possibly, with a stout clock key, either turning the key with the fingers alone or with a wrench. Another method is to grip the head with a pair of pliers. In

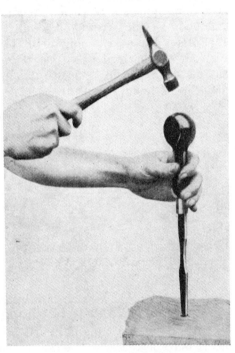

Fig. 645.—Starting Stubborn Screw with a Hammer Blow

the case of a stout screw, a new nick may sometimes be formed by cutting with file or hack-saw, but frequently the attempt to turn the screw with a screwdriver will simply cause a further fracture, there being insufficient metal to give the requisite strength. When the whole of the screw is embedded, and the head is too much damaged to allow of the screwdriver being used, there is seldom any alternative to boring it out ; or, in the case of a projecting screw, the damaged head may have to be hammered in or filed or sawn off, and a new screw inserted at the side of it. Old screws may be bored out by means of a shell bit, and the hole afterwards plugged.

Locking Screws in Place.—Screws can be secured against turning by filing a small notch in the head, and, after inserting, driving a fine pin through the notch into the wood ; or a small hole can be drilled at an angle through the head and body of the screw and a pin be inserted as before.

Bolts.—Bolts are made with heads of various shapes, and can be obtained in all lengths and diameters, the sizes ranging from 1 in. by $\frac{1}{4}$ in. to 12 in. by $\frac{3}{4}$ in. The common round-head bolt (Fig. 646), as generally used, has a more

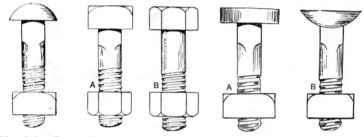

Fig. 646.—Cup-head or Round-head Bolt

Fig. 647.—Square-head and Hexagon-head Bolts

Fig. 648.—Cheese-head and Countersunk-head Bolts

ornamental appearance than other kinds ; the flat or cheese-head bolts A (Fig. 648) have but little projection to interfere with the surrounding parts of the work, and their heads may be recessed if desired ; these are generally used as pivot or hinge bolts in working joints, connecting rods, swivels, etc. Countersunk bolts B (Fig. 648) are used when any projection whatever above the surface of the work is unallowable, the head, like the common screw, being let in flush. There are two kinds of countersunk heads, for iron and wood respectively, those for wood being a trifle larger and flatter. The square part of a bolt beneath the head prevents rotation when screwing on the nut. All these bolts have square nuts. Bolts used for ironwork have square or hexagonal heads and have no square portion beneath the head, either square or hexagonal nuts being used (*see* B, Fig. 647); but square-head bolts, as at A, are also used in woodwork.

For fixing a bolt, bore the wood with a spoon bit for the smaller bolts and with a twist bit for the larger. Bore so as to drive moderately light. The thread should be oiled and the nut made to work freely before driving the bolt in, so as not to force the rotation of the bolt when screwing up. Washers are necessary beneath the nut when screwing against wood and the rounded corners of the nut should come next to the washer so as to facilitate a free turning movement. With hexagon nuts against iron surfaces the rounded corners are invariably turned outwards for convenience and appearance, this applying to bolts in machinery.

Glue.—Glue is made from hoofs and sinews of horses and oxen, these substances being boiled, and the glue purified and then cast into cakes of different thicknesses. There are two kinds of glue in general use by woodworkers, the dark " Scotch " and the light-coloured " French " glue,

Fig. 649.— Glue-pot

the former being made in thicker cakes than the latter. The best time to purchase glue is in the dry weather, as at that time good glue is crisp and bad qualities are soft. Another test of glue is to hold the cake up to the light, clearness denoting a good quality and cloudiness or patchiness inferior quality. By soaking a piece of glue in water for a day or two, good qualities will swell, but bad qualities will dissolve. Glue made from the sinews of old animals is much stronger than that made from young ones. For general work, a good plan is to use equal parts of " Scotch " and " French " glue, and for particular work in woods of light colour " French " glue only, to avoid a dark joint.

To prepare glue for use, it should be broken up and placed in the inner glue-pot, there being sufficient water to cover it. Let it soak for at least a day. Then nearly fill the glue kettle—the outer pot—with water, and boil steadily until the glue has thoroughly melted. Then remove the impurity from the surface and test its consistency. A good test is to allow the glue to run from the brush ; it should run in a steady stream and should make a slight rattling noise in the glue pot. If the glue is too thick or too thin the rattling noise cannot be heard. If the glue-pot is kept at boiling point, thinning with a small quantity of boiling water is necessary every time the glue is used, so as to make up for evaporation.

A strong glued joint is impossible unless the surfaces are perfectly straight and true. The glue must be hot and at its right consistency. A thin coat of glue, which is better than a thick one, should be obtained by rubbing the work together three or four times until the glue begins to set ; if the surfaces are wide the joint should also be cramped. When a good finish is required it is best to allow the glue that oozes out or any drops that may have been spilt to chill and then to scrape off while it is a jelly. With a sponge and hot water, wipe round the corners, etc.

The glue-pot is an essential, for, as already shown, glue must not be allowed to get hotter than boiling water. The glue-pot, being a water-bath, prevents this. Any capacity from $\frac{1}{8}$ pint to 8 pints is obtainable. A typical glue-pot having two vessels—the outer for the water and the inner for the glue—is shown by Fig. 649. An excellent glue brush for small jobs is a piece of cane with its end fibres loosened by hammering.

Fish glue, obtainable in tubes and bottles, is useful for small jobs, for which, also, Seccotine is reliable and can be recommended.

To waterproof glue prepared in the ordinary way, while it is hot add 1 part of bichromate of potash for every 2 parts of cake glue used ; thus prepared, the glue must be kept in the dark (say, in a stone jar with lid) until required, for it becomes insoluble on exposure to light.

For a good liquid glue, soak broken glue in strong acetic acid. When swollen, stand the vessel in hot water and add more acid until the desired consistency is attained.

Marine glue is best bought ready made ; it contains about 1 part of rubber and 20 of shellac, incorporated through the medium of 12 parts of coal-tar naphtha and evaporated to dryness. For use, it is warmed and applied thinly.

CHAPTER XVII

TRIMMING AND MITRE CUTTING

IT is convenient to deal with both ordinary trimming and mitre cutting and trimming in this chapter. An edge— either square or mitred—having been shaped with saw or chisel often requires to be " shot " true, and this work is done by hand with a plane and the assistance of a shooting-board or by machine. Hand machine trimmers, of which one of the very best patterns is Fox's, have been greatly developed during recent years, and they accommodate either square or mitred work, the latter being made possible

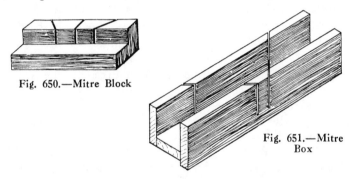

Fig. 650.—Mitre Block

Fig. 651.—Mitre Box

by the employment of adjustable fences. The wood having been sawn or otherwise worked to shape is put on the table of the machine, adjusted for position, and a stroke of the keen slant-edge blade, actuated by wheel or lever, trims the wrought surface of the end grain to a smooth finish, thus economising much time compared with the method of shooting with a plane. With a little practice, work can be shaped in a trimming machine by a series of " nibbles " to a convex line. Particulars will be given in this chapter of a home-made trimmer which will answer the needs of those who cannot afford one of the catalogued patterns.

233

Mitre Cutting. —Mitres are sawn in blocks or boxes (Figs. 650 and 651) which are used as in Figs. 652 and 653, the kerfs keeping the saw blade in the correct plane. In Fig. 651 the box is made with its front side deeper than the back one so that it may be easily held on the

Fig. 652.—Sawing Mitre in Mitre Block

edge of the bench; and the box shown in Fig. 653 has iron guides which can be adjusted to accommodate any thickness of saw. In the absence of a mitre block or box it is possible to make a bevel serve as a guide for the saw, the method of using it being shown in Fig. 654.

Shooting Boards.—Squared and mitred edges are shot true with a plane, the work being held on a shooting board, many patterns of which are in use, but all of which must provide for the work to be held in such a way that a plane, run alone in contact with a guide or fence, will remove a fine shaving from the work and correct any slight inaccuracy imparted in the preparatory processes.

For squared stuff, the shooting board may resemble

Fig. 653.—Sawing Mitre in Mitre Box

Figs. 655 and 656. In the first of these the top board is capable of sliding parallel with the front edge to accommodate different kinds of work. The board A in the second of these figures is to support the work, and can be, say, 11 in. by $\frac{7}{8}$ in. Board B is to support the plane, and should be wide enough for the side of the plane. The blocks c (see also the underneath view, Fig. 657) should be made of 3-in. by $2\frac{1}{4}$-in. stuff and be 1 ft. 6 in. to 2 ft. apart, the boards being screwed to them as shown. A shooting board made on this principle will keep the boards A and B flat, and their surfaces will remain parallel. An end board is screwed on A at right angles to the shooting edge to serve as a stop against which to press the work. Another pattern of shooting board is shown by Fig. 658 ; its feature is that while

Fig. 654.—Sawing Mitre, with Bevel as Guide for Saw

the plane moves horizontally, as usual, owing to the inclination of the board that supports the work, the plane makes a slanting or oblique cut, this having two advantages : the cut is cleaner, and the plane iron, being used at every part of its edge instead of at one part only, keeps its keenness for a longer period.

Shooting boards for mitred surfaces must, of course, have the stop or fence as a mitre with the shooting edge. The simplest form is that shown in Fig. 659, and the method of using it will be apparent from the photograph (Fig. 660), which shows a piece of moulding in course of being " shot."

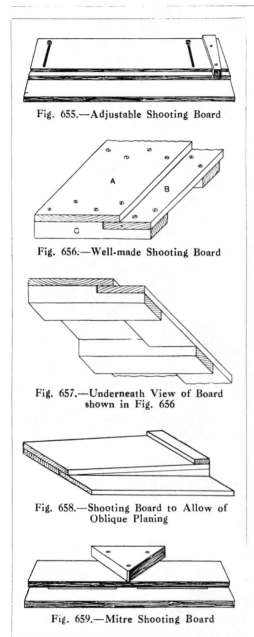

Fig. 655.—Adjustable Shooting Board

Fig. 656.—Well-made Shooting Board

Fig. 657.—Underneath View of Board shown in Fig. 656

Fig. 658.—Shooting Board to Allow of Oblique Planing

Fig. 659.—Mitre Shooting Board

The operation calls for a finely set plane and a very keen cutting edge, which must not be rounded.

Home-made Wood Trimmer.— Particulars will now be given of a home-made hand-power trimmer (Figs. 661 to 663), which will obviate the use of shooting board and plane on square, bevelled, or mitred work. This is certainly a machine which all woodworkers would find useful. The cutter is worked by a lever. The work is held against the fence plate, which is hinged at the front, and kept at the required angle by means of a bolt and flynut which are fixed at the back. The base A is of iron 1 ft. 6 in. long by 10 in. wide by $\frac{1}{4}$ in. thick. The uprights B are $1\frac{1}{4}$ in. by $\frac{3}{8}$ in. section, bent to the shape

shown in Fig. 662, and fixed at the base with rivets. The
guides in which the cutter works are made up as shown
in Fig. 664. The sides c are $\frac{7}{8}$ in. by $\frac{1}{4}$ in. in section, and
the centre piece D, which forms the groove, is $\frac{5}{8}$ in. by
$\frac{1}{4}$ in. in section, the whole being riveted together and fixed
to the uprights with $\frac{3}{8}$-in. bolts. The height over the
top and bottom guides is $7\frac{1}{2}$ in. The plate E, to which
the cutter is fixed, is $7\frac{1}{2}$ in. long at the top and $3\frac{1}{2}$ in.
long at the bottom, by $\frac{1}{4}$ in. thick, working in the groove
in the guide. The cutter G, a side view and section of
which is shown by Fig. 665, is of steel 3 in. wide by $\frac{1}{4}$ in.
thick, and is fixed to the plate E with three screws. The

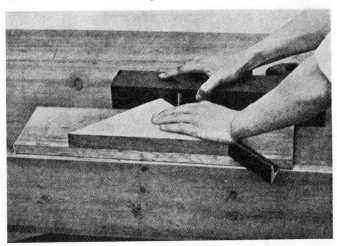

Fig. 660.—Shooting a Mitre

lever H is 1 ft. 5 in. long by $1\frac{1}{4}$ in. by $\frac{3}{8}$ in. in section, and
is fitted with a handle at the top 4 in. long. The spill J,
on which the lever works, is shown enlarged by Fig. 666.
It has a flap 4 in. long, which is fixed to the base with two
$\frac{3}{8}$-in. bolts. The spill K, which works through the lever,
and by means of which the cutter is worked, is fixed to the
cutter plate E with two $\frac{3}{8}$-in. bolts.

The baseboard L is of beech $1\frac{1}{8}$ in. thick, and is fixed to
the base with screws from underneath. The fence plate M
is $\frac{1}{4}$ in. thick cut to the shape shown in Fig. 662 ; it is riveted

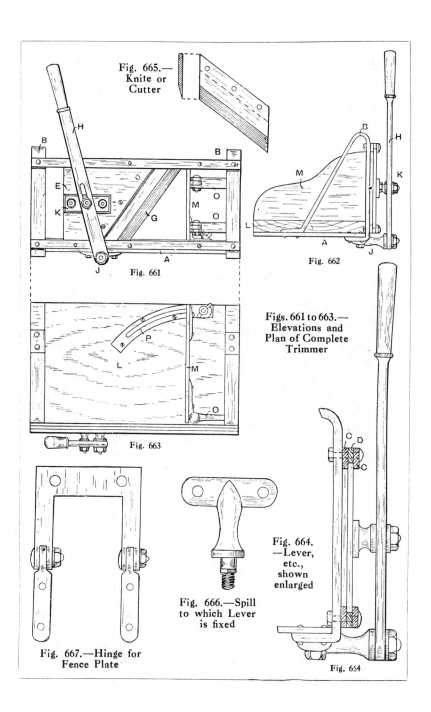

Fig. 665.—
Knite or
Cutter

Fig. 661

Fig. 662

Figs. 661 to 663.—
Elevations and
Plan of Complete
Trimmer

Fig. 663

Fig. 667.—Hinge for
Fence Plate

Fig. 666.—Spill
to which Lever
is fixed

Fig. 664.
—Lever,
etc.,
shown
enlarged

Fig. 654

to and works on the hinge shown enlarged by Fig. 667. The hinge o is fixed to the upright with two $\frac{3}{8}$-in. bolts; the flap on the upright is $1\frac{1}{4}$ in. by $\frac{3}{8}$ in., the ends being $\frac{7}{8}$ in. by $\frac{1}{2}$ in. The distance from the outside edge of the upright to the inside of the fence plate is $4\frac{1}{2}$ in. The fence plate is held at the desired angle by the bolt and flynut at the back. A slot is cut in the baseboard, and is protected on the top by an iron plate P, through which the bolt passes. The fence plate is attached to the bolt and flynut by means of a small corner plate fixed with rivets.

CHAPTER XVIII

Making Mouldings.—Designs for the best types of mouldings in use by the wood worker are given in Fig. 668. Instructions on making mouldings such as occur in jointing up work have already been given. The running of a moulding with a plane or number of planes is largely a matter of selecting the proper tool or tools, and seeing that these are in perfect order and held in correct relation to the work. French moulding and the Stanley universal planes should be used at a right angle with the edge to be worked, whereas English planes require to be tilted, there being an inclination line on the front to serve as a guide.

In running a moulding, the stuff must first be planed up—faced up truly and squared and gauged to width and thickness. On each end of the wood a true section of the required moulding must be marked. The usual procedure is next to chamfer off the waste wood, but it is better to plough a series of narrow grooves almost right down to the outline of the moulding so that they will form guides as to the depth of the various hollows, etc. The next proceeding should be to take off the surplus wood in the form of chamfers, after which a very little work with hollows and rounds will bring it to the section required.

In the past, the professional woodworker was called upon to use a great variety of moulding planes, but at the present time he depends more and more upon the product of the vertical spindle moulding machine, which has a power-driven spindle supporting a block in which is a number of steel cutters shaped to the contour of the moulding required. By means of a table and fence, a strip of wood can be guided along in contact with the cutters, which remove the waste and produce the moulding at great speed. The

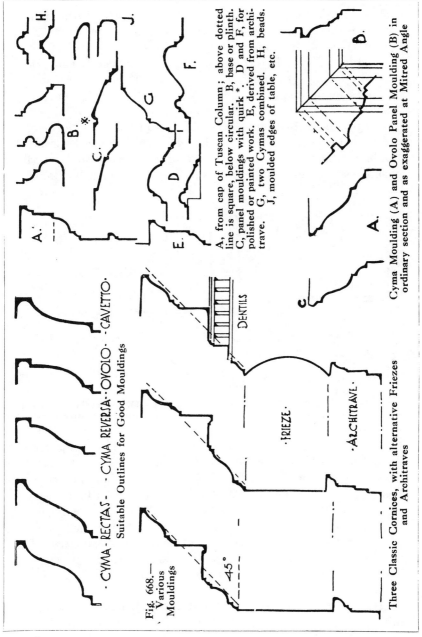

· CYMA · RECTAS · · CYMA REVERSA · OVOLO · · CAVETTO ·
Suitable Outlines for Good Mouldings

Fig. 668.—
Various
Mouldings

45°

A, from cap of Tuscan Column; above dotted line is square, below circular. B, base or plinth. C, panel mouldings with quirk *. D and F, for polished or painted work. E, derived from architrave. G, two Cymas combined. H, beads. J, moulded edges of table, etc.

DENTILS

FRIEZE.

ARCHITRAVE.

Three Classic Cornices, with alternative Friezes and Architraves

Cyma Moulding (A) and Ovolo Panel Moulding (B) in ordinary section and as exaggerated at Mitred Angle

Q

smaller professional and the amateur, to whom the purchase of such a machine is out of the question, have the alternative of the universal plane, which is a tool of remarkable utility. Before describing it, however, a common workshop dodge in making a slight bead may be referred to, and the method of obtaining the true shape of the cutting iron of a moulding plane explained.

Improvised Beading Tool.—For running a little bead on the edge of a piece of work, when the proper tools are not available, take a small block of hard wood and insert a short screw into it about ¾ in. from one edge, as shown

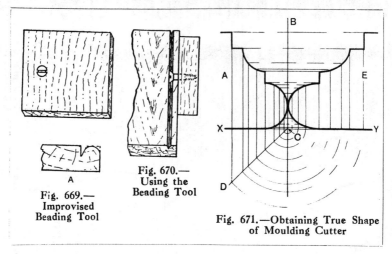

Fig. 669.—
Improvised
Beading Tool

A

Fig. 670.—
Using the
Beading Tool

Fig. 671.—Obtaining True Shape
of Moulding Cutter

in Fig. 669. Turn the screw until its head is projecting from the block a distance equal to the width of the bead desired, ¼ in. for a ¼-in. bead, etc. Then, using the screwhead as a cutter and the block as a fence, it will be an easy matter to cut a bead of sorts (*see* Fig. 670). This will only need rounding off a little on the outside edge and glasspapering to become quite a presentable bead (*see* A). Choose a screw having a clean-cut slot and sharp edges. The method is, of course, not to be compared with the use of the proper tools.

Determining Shape of Moulding Cutter.—In determining the true shape of the cutter of a moulding plane it must be remembered that the pitch—the angle at which the cutter is held in the plane—has the effect of reducing the depth of cut, and therefore if the cutter used were the exact counterpart of the moulding required, the latter would prove when finished to be shallower than intended. Assume the pitch to be 45°. Let A in Fig. 671 be the true shape of the section of the moulding to be worked. Draw x y, then draw B c at right angles to x y, and touching the

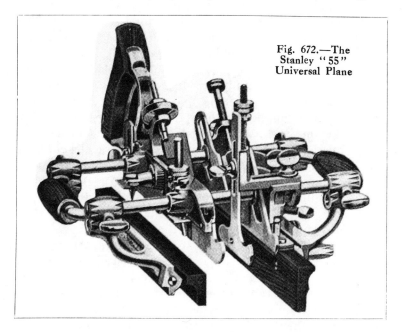

Fig. 672.—The Stanley " 55 " Universal Plane

greatest projection of the moulding. From c set out the line c d at 45° to x y. Taking any convenient points in the contour of the section, from these points draw vertical lines (ordinates) as shown, continuing them down to the pitch line c d. Now, with c as centre, draw the circular arcs from where the ordinates terminate on c d, making the arcs touch x y. Then from the points thus given raise vertical ordinates, and by projecting horizontally as shown by the dotted lines, a number of points in the oblique section that will correspond with those in the square section will be obtained. Through the points obtained, the oblique section can be drawn as shown at E, which is the shape of the cutting iron required.

THE STANLEY " 55 " UNIVERSAL PLANE

For the craftsman who wishes to do a variety of moulding, rebating, beading, matching, etc., there is one type of plane above all others which it will pay him to acquire. It is a " universal " plane of the Stanley make, the number " 55 " tool (Fig. 672) being the best for his purpose. This is a truly wonderful tool, being a plough, dado plane, rebate plane, fillister plane, beading, reeding, and fluting plane, slitting plane, and, of course, a moulding plane possessing almost limitless possibilities, since it will accommodate cutters of almost any shape and size. Fifty-two cutters (Fig. 673) are supplied with it, forty-one more (Fig. 674) are carried in stock, and special forms can be made from blanks by the worker himself. The plane is a nickel-plated tool 10 in. long, weighing $7\frac{3}{4}$ lb. Parts for repair and replacement are easily obtainable (*see* Fig. 675). Information on the handling and adjustment of the plane will now be given, and it should be understood that all the illustrations show the plane as it looks from the front.

To get the best results and to preserve the tool in good condition, note the following : (1) Always slacken the cutter bolt before adjusting the cutters. (2) When raising or lowering the adjustable runner on the sliding section, first loosen the thumb screws which fasten the sliding section to the arms, then slacken the thimble check nuts. Reverse these operations to tighten after the runner is correctly adjusted. (3) Keep the fences at right angles to the edge of the cutter or parallel with the runners. (4) In placing the fences on the arms, use the upper holes whenever possible, there being then more command over the tool. (5) Keep the cutters well sharpened, especially those used in working fancy mouldings.

The Stanley " 55 " Plane Described.—Fig. 676 is a diagrammatic view of the plane. The main stock A carries the cutter, cutter adjustment, and cutter bolt, slitting tool, depth gauge and handle, and provides a bearing for one side of the cutter. The sliding section B has an adjustable steel runner and gives a bearing for the other side of the cutter. It slides on arms H secured in the main stock. The adjustable runner can be raised or lowered so that cutters can be used having one side higher or lower than the side in the main stock.

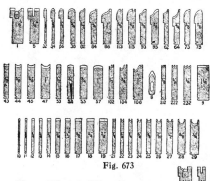

Auxiliary centre bottom c forms an additional bearing, and is used in connection with irregular shaped cutters, also as a depth gauge for the matching cutters. It can be adjusted for width or depth, and

Fig. 673

Figs. 673 and 674.—Cutters for Stanley Plane

when required should be attached to the sliding section B.

Fences D and E can be used on either side of the plane and the rosewood faces tilted to any desirable angle up

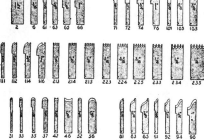

Fig. 674

to 45°. The face on fence D may be regulated by screw R for extra fine adjustment. Fence E is machined on the outside so that when reversed it gives an extended reach for centre beading wide boards. Arms H are used to carry the fences and sliding section at the position desired. Two sets of arms (one 8½ in. and one 4½ in. long) are provided with each plane. Cam-rest G can be fastened on either the front or back arm between the sliding section and the fence D, and acts as a rest when the fences are wide apart as in centre beading. When the auxiliary centre bottom is in use, the cam-rest provides additional support when

required, and should be placed on the rear arm. Gauges
F and J are fully explained later.

In Fig. 675 the separate parts of the plane are shown
as near their position in relation to the main stock as possible.
They are as follow, and may be ordered by the numbers
given :—

1, Cutters ; 16, main stock or bottom ; 23, cutter bolt,
with wing nut 24, clip and screw 25, adjusting screw 27,
and nut 28 ; 29, arm set screws ; 30, sliding section, with
thumb screw, 31 ; 32, thimble, with check nut, 33 ; 34,
adjustable bottom, with screw 37 ; 40, auxiliary centre
bottom ; 41, centre bottom adjusting nut ; 42, angle iron
and adjusting screws ; 43, angle iron thumb screw ; 50,
fence D ; 51, fence thumb screws ; 52, fence D, rosewood face ;
53, fence D casting with swivel ; 54, fence D adjusting screw ;
56, fence E, with rosewood face, 57 ; 60, long arms ; 61,
short arms ; 70, adjustable depth gauge, with nut, 71 ;
73, adjustable beading gauge ; 75, slitting cutter gauge,
with thumb screw, 76 ; 80, cam stop, with set screw, 81 ;
85, spurs with screws ; 86, rosewood face set screw ; 87,
cutter stop screw.

Of the cutters shown in Figs. 673 and 674, Nos. 1 and 2
are sash cutters, $1\frac{1}{2}$ in. ; 5 and 6, match cutters, $\frac{3}{16}$ in. and
$\frac{1}{4}$ in. ; 8, slitting cutter ; 9, fillister, $1\frac{1}{4}$ in. ; 10 to 19, plough
and dado cutters, $\frac{1}{8}$ in. to $\frac{7}{8}$ in. ; 21 to 29, beading cutters,
$\frac{1}{8}$ in. to $\frac{3}{4}$ in. ; 31 to 38, fluting cutters, $\frac{3}{16}$ in. to $\frac{3}{4}$ in. ; 42
to 47, hollows, $\frac{3}{8}$ in. to 1 in. ; 52 to 57, rounds, $\frac{3}{8}$ in. to 1 in. ;
61 to 66, quarter hollows, $\frac{3}{8}$ in. to 1 in. ; 71 to 76, quarter
rounds, $\frac{3}{8}$ in. to 1 in. ; 81 to 86, reverse ogees, $\frac{3}{8}$ in. to 1 in. ;
91 to 96, Roman ogees, $\frac{3}{8}$ in. to 1 in. ; 101 to 106, Grecian
ogees, $\frac{3}{8}$ in. to 1 in. ; 111 to 116, rounds with beads, $\frac{3}{8}$ in.
to 1 in. ; 212 to 215, 222 to 225, and 232 to 235, reeding
cutters with two beads, $\frac{1}{8}$ in., $\frac{3}{16}$ in., and $\frac{1}{4}$ in.

The Fences Described.—The fences are of metal, with
adjustable rosewood faces attached by screws to form the
bearing surfaces, and are used to guide the plane along the
work. Any slight variation from a right angle can be
readily overcome by loosening these screws and changing
the angle of the faces. The plane should stand at an exact

right angle to the edge of the work, as in Fig. 677. To ensure this the rosewood faces must be adjusted to come parallel with the *side* of the cutter. If the plane is tipped as shown in Fig. 678, the groove will work away from the fence as it goes deeper, and owing to the wood acting as a wedge between the cutter and the fence, the plane will bind. If tipped as shown in Fig. 679, the groove will work towards the fence as it goes deeper, thus forcing the fence away from the wood. The upper arm-holes in the

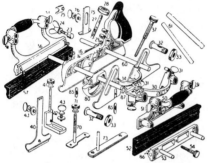

Fig. 675.—Parts of Stanley "55" Plane

fences allow the fences to slide under the cutter to regulate the width of cut required, as in rebating, while the lower holes

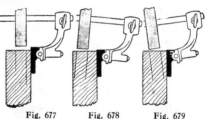

Fig. 677   Fig. 678   Fig. 679

Figs. 677 to 679.—Necessity for Holding Plane at Right Angle to Work

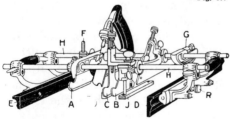

Fig. 676.—Diagram of Stanley "55" Plane

can be used when a narrow fence is needed; both fences should be used where possible, the tool being then kept true to the work with slight effort.

The Runners Described.—These are thin steel plates attached to the main stock and the sliding section, and form the bearings for the cutter.

For the purpose of illustrating their proper position when in use, a bottom view of these runners set to use cutters of various forms is shown (*see* Figs. 680 to 684),

A being the main stock, B the sliding section, and C the auxiliary centre bottom, the use of which will now be explained. When a square-edge cutter or beading cutter (Figs. 680 and 681) is used, both the main stock and sliding section runners are required. With the fluting cutter (Fig. 682) the main stock runner only is needed, the cutter being recessed on one side so that the runner will come to its highest point. In using a round cutter (Fig. 683) both main stock and sliding section runners are required, the sliding section being set to the centre of the cutter and its adjustable runner set to govern the thickness of the shaving to be removed. The auxiliary centre bottom is not required for the cutters shown in Figs. 680 to 683.

With an " ogee," or any cutter that has an irregular cutting edge, with one side extending below the other (Fig. 684), the auxiliary centre bottom should be used to form an additional support, it being readily adjusted sidewise by means of the angle iron to which it is attached, and for depth by the adjusting nut on its stem.

Where the bearing surface for the auxiliary centre bottom is $\frac{1}{4}$ in. or more in width, an additional support called a sole plate is furnished, to be attached to its bottom.

Cutters and Depth Gauges.—Near the upper end of each cutter a slot or hole is made to engage with a pin located near the end of the adjusting screw on the main stock. The proper way to set the cutter is as follows: First loosen cutter clamp K (Fig. 685), and place cutter in position with slot on pin L. Adjust by means of adjusting nut M, and tighten cutter clamp K; then bring up the sliding section and secure it as required. Where the cutter is to be used its full width, see that the side of the cutter extends beyond the runner only enough to give clearance (*see* Fig. 686). The channel in which the cutter rests in the main stock regulates this on the right-hand side. If too much clearance is given (*see* Fig. 687) through allowing the sides of the cutter to project too far beyond the sliding section runner B, the cutter will scrape the sides of the groove, making a rough, uneven cut, as well as causing the plane to work hard. The sides V (Fig. 688) of the cutter are given only a slight bevel for clearance only. Whenever possible, both depth gauges should be used (*see* Fig. 689), setting gauge F on main stock first and then gauge J on sliding section. Gauge F should always be clamped with the slotted screw P.

Holding the Plane.—As the tool is held in both hands (Fig. 690), the beginner tends to push as much with the left hand as with the right, thus drawing the plane over to the left away from the stock, making good work impossible. It should be pushed forward with the right hand only, the left hand being used to keep it

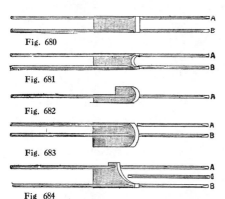

Fig. 680

Fig. 681

Fig. 682

Fig. 683

Fig 684

Figs. 680 to 684.—Various Cutters and their Correct Runners

steady and hold the fence up to the work. The palm of the left hand should rest on the fence handle, the thumb passing over and resting on the front arm, the fingers being against the lower part of the fence.

Space will now be devoted to explaining

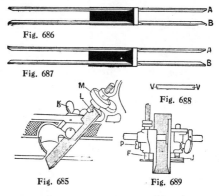

Fig. 686

Fig. 687

Fig. 688

Fig. 685

Fig. 689

Figs. 685 to 689.—Use of Depth Gauge, Amount of Clearance, etc.

how the plane is used in the production of rebates, grooves, chamfers, beads and mouldings.

Rebating. — Insert a cutter wider than the proposed rebate, and move sliding section B to about $\frac{1}{4}$ in. inside the outer edge of the rebate, so bringing as an extra support the sliding section inside the edge of the cutter. Attach fence D, putting it on the arms through the upper holes, so that it will slide under the cutter the required distance to give the width of rebate wanted (Fig. 691). Depth gauge F regulates the depth.

Dado Grooving.—As the plane has to work across the grain in making a dado, spurs are necessary in front of the sides of the cutter to score the wood and thus prevent the tearing of the stocks ; they are set in the sides of the main stock A and sliding section B. Loosen the screws securing them, so that spurs will drop into position (Fig. 692) with cutting edges extended beyond the runners fully the thick-

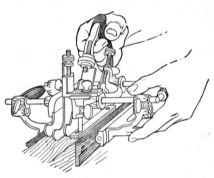

Fig. 690.—Holding the Stanley Plane

ness of shaving to be removed, and tighten screws. Insert a plough cutter as wide as the dado wanted, and move sliding section B up to cutter until spur is in line with its outer side. When so placed there will be no danger of the cutter tearing the side of the groove. Insert depth gauge J in sliding section as shown in Fig. 693, and set it to regulate the depth of dado. Nail a strip of wood (batten) on the board in which the dado is to be cut, for gauging its position. If batten is of uniform thickness and nails driven so as not to interfere, depth gauge F can also be used by allowing for the thickness of batten when setting the gauge for depth. The fences are not required and should be removed.

Ploughing.—When used as a plough, set the sliding section runner as already directed for setting cutters (*see* p. 248). It is possible to make a groove of any width by working it twice or more, one cut running into the other ; and in making such wide grooves the fence must first be set to work to the side of the groove farthest from the edge of the wood against which this fence is to bear (Fig. 694) ; otherwise it will be difficult to keep the fence up to the wood when running the second part of the groove. It is desirable to use a comparatively narrow cutter when making extra wide grooves, as otherwise the cutter tends to " run off " where there is only a narrow strip left to be taken from the side of the groove. Both of the depth gauges should be used.

Slitting.—For cutting strips from thin stuff a cutter is provided which will perform the work more rapidly than if a saw were used.

The slitting cutter is inserted in a slot on the right side of the main stock just forward of the handle (*see* Fig. 695). Depth gauge W is placed over the blade, and both cutter and gauge fastened by the thumb screw V. Fence D gauges the distance of the cut from the edge of the board. Thicker boards can be cut by first running the cutter partly through on one side, reversing the stock, and completing the cut on the other side.

Fig. 692

Fig. 691 Fig. 693

Figs. 691 to 693.—Rebating, Dado Grooving, etc.

Fig. 694 Fig. 695

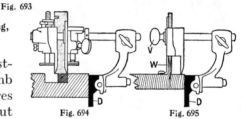

Figs. 694 and 695.—Ploughing and Slitting

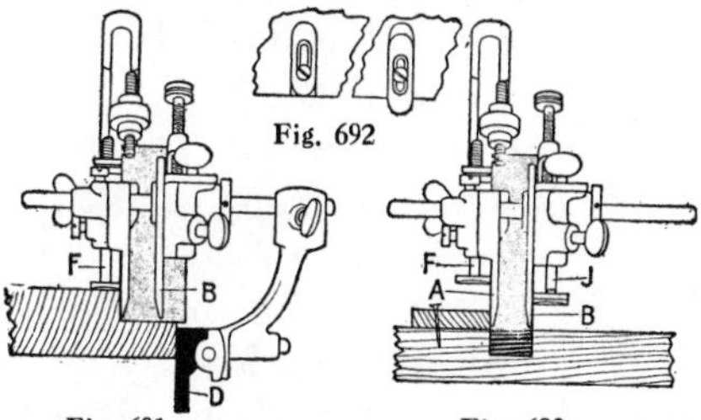

Matching and Sash Moulding.—To make a tongue on boards of any thickness from $\frac{3}{4}$ in., to $1\frac{1}{4}$ in., a tonguing tool or cutter is provided (*see* Fig. 696). The auxiliary centre bottom is used as a depth gauge, and the position of the tongue is regulated by fence D.

To make the groove, use the $\frac{1}{4}$-in. plough cutter. Fence D regulates the distance of groove from face of board and gauge F the depth (*see* Fig. 697). Double-tongued joints, as in Fig. 698, are easily worked by using plough cutters to make both members.

For sash moulding, the " ovolo " cutter carries its own depth gauge s, secured by a set screw on the gauge (Fig. 699).

The moulding can be worked on a strip of wood of the necessary width and thickness by cutting one side first, then reversing the strip and repeating the operation on the other side, the depth x of the rebate of the moulding being regulated by the fence D, and the width z by the gauge s on the cutter. The other portions of the moulding are determined by the shape of the cutter. An easier way is to work the moulding on the two sides of a board of suitable thickness, obtaining depth x by cutting off with a slitting cutter or saw.

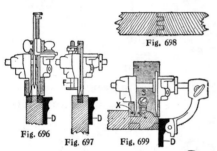

Fig. 698

Fig. 696

Fig. 697   Fig. 699

Figs. 696 to 699.—Matching and Sash Moulding

Beading.—Fig. 700 shows the plane with a beading cutter inserted, and the fence properly set for working an ordinary bead. To cut a bead on the

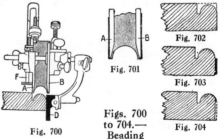

Fig. 701

Fig. 702

Fig. 703

Figs. 700 to 704.—Beading

Fig. 700

Fig. 704

edge of a board, bring up the sliding section B so that the bevel of the runner will allow the cutter to take off a shaving of the same thickness as that on the side in main stock A (*see* Fig. 701). This bevel will allow only the thinnest shaving possible to be taken off by the part of the cutter forming the quirk. The fence must be set so that it comes exactly to the inner point of the cutter, as shown in Fig. 700, thus bringing the outside face of the bead to the edge of the board. Set depth gauge F on the main stock so as to allow the bead to be worked down to the proper depth below the surface of the wood. It is advisable to finish beads and similar mouldings well below the surface of the wood, so that any subsequent cleaning off the surface will not change their form (*see* Fig. 702), the round gradually merging into the straight without a break. The first attempt may result in a bead as shown in Fig. 703, necessitating the planing off of the edge (*see* dark line) to form a perfect bead (here, the fence has not been brought up to the point of the cutter); or, worse still, as in Fig. 704, which cannot be made into a properly shaped bead (here, the fence has been set inside the point of the cutter).

Centre beading is shown in Fig. 705. It can be worked at any required distance up to 8 in. (even more, if specially long arms are obtained) from the edge of the board

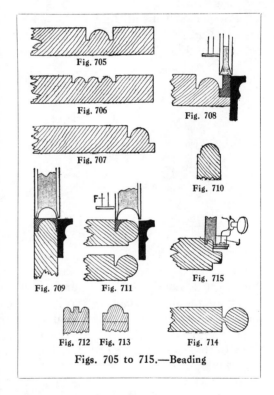

Fig. 705

Fig. 706

Fig. 708

Fig. 707

Fig. 710

F

Fig. 709   Fig. 711

Fig. 715

Fig. 712   Fig. 713   Fig. 714

Figs. 705 to 715.—Beading

by using the longer set of arms and reversing the fence. The cam rest is useful in preventing sagging when beading at any distance from the edge; it is placed on the front arm. Fig. 706 is a section of reeds worked in the same way as the bead in Fig. 705 by using the reeding cutters for small sizes, and by working a series of centre beads for larger sizes. The bead farthest from the edge against which the fence bears should be worked first, or there will be difficulty in working the succeeding beads so that they will properly connect with those first made.

The torus bead (Fig. 707) is easily worked by first forming the centre bead at the required distance from the edge of the board, and working the square or quirk with one of the narrow plough cutters the full width of the square (*see* Fig. 708).

For a return bead, first make a bead on the edge of the board (Fig. 709) so that a small quirk is left on the face side, as in Fig. 710. Finish by setting the plane with the

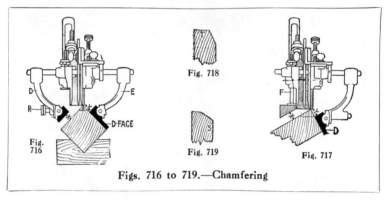

Fig. 718

Fig. 719

Fig. 716

Fig. 717

Figs. 716 to 719.—Chamfering

depth gauge F so adjusted as exactly to take off this superfluous quirk on the face side and no more (Fig. 711).

Small mouldings can be worked on the edges of boards and cut off to the thickness required (*see* Figs. 712 and 713). Similarly, round rods can be formed by working a bead from both sides of a board, cutting off and finishing as in Fig. 714.

In beading matched boards (Fig. 715) the ordinary side fence cannot be used as the tongue is not always of the same width. Instead use gauge J, placing it in the socket on the front of the sliding section. The adjustable bottom on this gauge can be moved under the sliding section runner, thus bringing the bead to the edge of the board, if no quirk is desired. In either case it gauges on the edge of the work, above the tongue.

Chamfers.—For working a chamfer on the edge of

square-section stuff (*see* Fig. 716) both of the fences are used, the wood faces being set at 45° with the cutter edge. In working chamfers, either plain or moulded, it is best to support the wood in notched blocks whenever possible, as this permits of the plane being held in a horizontal position. Where a number of right-angle chamfers of the same size are to be made it will be of advantage to change the rosewood faces on the fences, and to change the fences, putting D on the right-hand side of the plane and E on the left. This will bring the wide face on the bearing side and give the advantage of the fine adjustment R on the fence used as a gauge. Fig. 716 shows the plane assembled in this way.

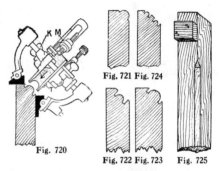

Fig. 721 Fig. 724

Fig. 720

Fig. 722 Fig. 723   Fig. 725

Figs. 720 to 725.—Forming Moulded and Stop Chamfers

The width of the cutter should be a little more than the width of the chamfer. Bring the auxiliary centre bottom near the centre of the cutter and set the sliding section so as to form a bearing for the first cut, locating it just inside the corner of the wood A. For width of chamfer, set the fence so that the distance x from the fence to the work will be the same as the distance y from the corner of the work to the finished chamfer.

For making a chamfer at an odd angle the fences are used as regularly assembled (Fig. 676). Set the rosewood face on fence D to the angle required for the bevel of the chamfer (Fig. 717). Work from the edge T of boards for chamfer as in Fig. 718, and from the side s for chamfer as in Fig. 719. While fence E can be used to gauge the width of chamfer, better results will be obtained by using depth gauge F, attaching a wood face of proper shape to its bottom, as shown in Fig. 717.

Moulded Chamfers or Edge Mouldings.—Arrange the plane as shown in Fig. 720, the two fences forming the bottom support and being in contact with the work at all times. Slightly loosen cutter clamp K, and draw back the cutter before starting the work.   As the work progresses, feed down the cutter by slightly turning the adjusting nut M between each shaving.   If the fence were used as a gauge, the cutter would move parallel with the face of the stock and the form of the moulding be entirely lost.   The cutter must be given an extra support on the sliding section to prevent its working to one side.   This is done by putting screw T (found in the main stock below the back handle) in the sliding section runner, bringing the head close up to the cutter.   The patterns of mouldings shown in Figs. 721 to 723 can be easily executed in this way at one working ; Fig. 724 is done in two.

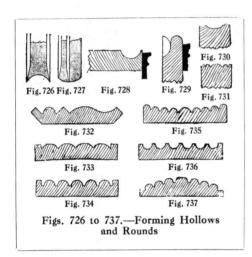

Fig. 726 Fig. 727   Fig. 728   Fig. 729   Fig. 730   Fig. 731
Fig. 732   Fig. 735   Fig. 733   Fig. 736   Fig. 734   Fig. 737

Figs. 726 to 737.—Forming Hollows and Rounds

Stop Chamfers. —For working these, nail stops on the work against which the runners will strike, thus governing the point where the chamfer is to begin and end (*see* Fig. 725).   Proceed as for moulded chamfers, using a straight cutter a little wider than the chamfer.

Hollows and Rounds.—In working convex mouldings or rounds, the main stock and sliding section runners should be at the extreme points of the cutter (Fig. 726), when they will gauge correctly the thickness of the shaving to be taken off.   In working concave mouldings or hollows, set the adjustable runner on the sliding section to form a bearing for the cutter at its lowest point, as in Fig. 727.

Thumb mouldings can be worked with the hollow and round cutters when curves having a rather large radius are desired; but curves of smaller radius can be better worked with the fluting and beading cutters. First cut the hollow on the face of the board (Fig. 728), and then form the round on the edge of the board (Fig. 729), using the auxiliary centre bottom in finishing.

The mouldings shown in Figs. 730 and 731 are worked with the hollow and round cutters and beading cutters. For such mouldings as Fig. 732 the depth gauges and fence can be readily set so as to bring the concave and convex parts of the moulding together. The mouldings shown in Figs. 733 and 734 are worked from both edges of the board, working the member farthest from the edge first. In Fig. 735 the face of the moulding must first be worked to the required curve, but not to a fine finish, and then the rounds worked as in Figs. 733 and 734, changing the wood face on the fence to the proper angle.

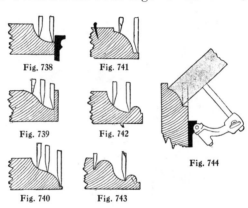

Fig. 738
Fig. 741
Fig. 739
Fig. 742
Fig. 740
Fig. 743
Fig. 744

Figs. 738 to 744.—Working Mouldings

Fig. 736 can be worked with a fluting cutter; Fig. 737 is simply a repetition of Fig. 735 in reverse order, worked in the same way.

Mouldings.—In working all mouldings, and particularly quarter mouldings (*see* Fig. 738), it is of the utmost importance that the fence be kept firmly against the work, since the cutter tends to force the fence away from the wood, as the runners come partly on the curve of the moulding. With reasonable care, and setting the cutter so that it only takes off a thin shaving, there will be no difficulty in forming perfect mouldings. By setting the fence so as to leave a narrow strip of wood between the fence and the cutter, as shown in the Roman ogee (Fig. 739), the plane

R

will be much more easily held up to the work. Having completed the moulding, the extra material can be removed with an ordinary plane.

Reverse ogees (Fig. 740) and quarter rounds (Fig. 741) having squares or quirks to deal with can be readily worked without leaving any extra material, as shown in Fig. 759.

In working the quarter hollow with bead (Fig. 742)

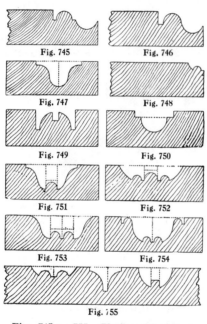

Fig. 745
Fig. 746
Fig. 747
Fig. 748
Fig. 749
Fig. 750
Fig. 751
Fig. 752
Fig. 753
Fig. 754
Fig. 755

Figs. 745 to 755.—Various Mouldings

and the Grecian ogee (Fig. 743), the sliding section should be brought to the inside of the bead, which serves to hold the fence up to the work. Quarter hollow and quarter round mouldings of practically any shape and size and to any angle may be made with the appropriate cutters and by setting the rosewood face of the fence to the angle desired (Fig. 744), but first the part shown by dotted lines must be rebated out and the fence set at exactly the right position to bring the cutter to the angle.

Combination Mouldings.—In working mouldings requiring two or more operations to complete, the fence and depth gauges must be accurately set, or the members will not work into one another, and the second operation will partly destroy the result of the first. Figs. 745 and 746 show sections of two slightly different mouldings, formed by a bead and fluting cutter in combination. Fig. 747 shows a deep moulding made by forming a Roman ogee from each edge of the wood, being careful to set the fence so that the two grooves exactly meet at the bottom. The small moulding (Fig. 748) is suitable for edges of doors and panelling in various kinds of cabinet work. It is made with one of the quarter rounds with bead, the depth gauge F (Fig. 676) being used to prevent the cutter from working down to its full extent. Fig. 749 is worked with a plough and beading cutter, making the groove first and finishing with the bead. Fig. 750 is worked with a wide plough cutter and a fluting cutter, the latter making the hollow groove first, in order that the edges of the groove will be sharp on the finished moulding. Fig. 751 shows a moulding similar to Fig. 747, but the ogees are divided by a bead. The ogees are worked from opposite sides, keeping them far enough apart to leave the width of the bead intact; then the extra stock remaining is reduced to the required depth with a plough cutter, and the bead formed in the usual way. Fig. 752 is worked the same as Fig. 751, using the quarter round with bead, but not working it to its full depth. Fig. 753 is worked the same as Fig. 751, first using the ogee from opposite sides, but far enough apart to leave room for the two beads which are to be made with a regular beading cutter. Fig. 754 is made with a Grecian ogee from both edges of the work, the cutter being worked to its full depth.

Three more sections of mouldings are shown in Fig. 755; the first from the left is made with the quarter round with bead, but the cutter is not carried down to its full depth. The middle one is formed by using the quarter hollow cutter in the same way. The one to the right is formed by the quarter round, the fence being set so that a small upstanding square is left at the bottom. If the square is first made to the proper height with a plough cutter, thus removing some of the waste stock, the working of the quarter rounds will be materially aided.

CHAPTER XIX

BEVELS FOR OBLIQUE-SIDED VESSELS

Face Bevels.—The determining of the angles to which to cut the splayed sides of a wash-tub, trough, knife-box, etc., is a matter of applied geometry. A typical case will be worked out in this chapter, and similar problems can then be solved in the same way. Some slight acquaintance with geometry is, of course, essential.

Fig. 756 shows the elevation and also the plan of a hopper, trough, etc. The thickness of the stuff is shown exaggerated. The plan is the view seen from above, and the elevation the view seen from the side. To simplify this expression, let the space below line x y represent the ground or floor of a room, and the space above represent the wall; then the line x y, or ground line, will represent the corner line of the room; that is, the line where the wainscot touches the floor. The reader should make this drawing to a large scale, and then fold the paper on line x y to a right angle to illustrate this. Next imagine just one side and end of the trough resting on the ground. When looking at the box from the side, consider it as being level with the eye; the view thus obtained would be shown on the wall; this is known as the elevation (Fig. 756). After the material has been prepared, the edges of the front and back members should first be planed to the angle A (Fig. 756). This should be transferred by placing the sliding bevel on the drawing as shown. To obtain the true shape of the pieces which will form the splayed ends, it is necessary to imagine them laid flat on the ground or flat against the wall; the thickness of the wood should be ignored. Supposing the outside surface of the end piece be folded on to the ground, the line c c acting as a hinge, then the elevation of this line is a point c′. Set the compasses to the width of the material being used, and, with c′ as centre, draw the curve traced by the surface when swung down. It is obvious that the plan will then show the true width of that surface on the ground, if the measurement is carried down to D D. The plan of the part of circle traced is a straight line, so that *d* has gone to D; join C to D, and obtain the required angle from the plan as shown.

In the construction of most articles with splayed sides, the front pieces are of the same splay as the end pieces,

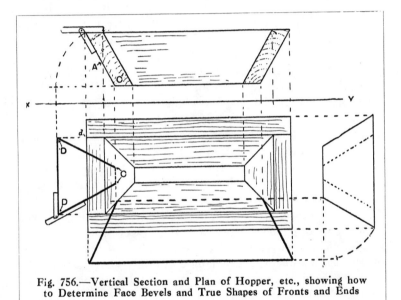

Fig. 756.—Vertical Section and Plan of Hopper, etc., showing how to Determine Face Bevels and True Shapes of Fronts and Ends

so that no more drawing is necessary; but should the front and back be splayed at a different angle from the ends, an end elevation should be drawn as shown on the right (as a matter of fact, the two splays are the same, but the principle holds good). For this the paper should be turned round and the new elevation drawn and the paper folded as before.

Fig. 756A shows a housing joint in an article with splayed sides; the bevels are obtained and the sides developed in exactly the same way as illustrated. The lines for the grooves being parallel to the ends are marked with the sliding bevel at the same angle.

The thick lines in the plan indicate the true shape of the end and front.

Another Method.—Fig. 757 shows in thin lines a section through a trough or other vessel of which all four sides have equal splay. The sides are assumed to be mitred together. The end pieces A, obviously, are shown in their true sections, but the side piece B, owing to its splay or obliquity, is not so shown. To determine at once the correct face angles of all four sides and the true shape of the inner face of the sides B, erect perpendiculars from the points c, and with either of those points as centre and with the depth of the material as radius, describe an arc D intersecting the perpendicular just drawn. Draw a horizontal line through the intersection, and raise perpendiculars from the point E to cut the horizontal line at the points H H. Then H C C H gives all the information required.

Edge Bevels.—Should the pieces be mitred (not housed) together, another bevel has yet to be determined ; that is, the bevel to which the mitred edges must be cut. One of the most graphic methods of determining this edge bevel is shown in Fig. 758. Draw a vertical section through the trough as shown, and continue the top surfaces of the end pieces to form the triangle A C B. The dotted line A B represents the outer edge of the side. From c drop a perpendicular c D, which, obviously, will bisect A B at E. Continue A F, and set off above A the distance A E, to give the point G. Join G c, and the required bevel is then given by A G c (*see* the thick black lines).

The following is the more usual method of obtaining the edge bevel of the mitred pieces. Fig. 759 is a plan of one corner of a mitred trough, and Fig. 759A is a sectional elevation, A being the front or back and B the end. The top edge of B is shown in the plan narrower than it actually is, owing to the fact that it is inclined ; and to get the required angle this edge must be brought level or horizontal, to do which set the compasses to the thickness of the stuff and with c as centre describe an arc D E. Continue the top (inner) edge of A until it cuts the arc at E, and from this point in the elevation drop a perpendicular to the plan. Here, again, continue the edge of piece A, but the outer edge, until it cuts the perpendicular at G. Then if C and G in the plan are connected, the required bevel will be as shown. The thick black angle indicates the bevel applied to the drawing for transference to the top edge of either front or end member.

The same principle is embodied in the following, which

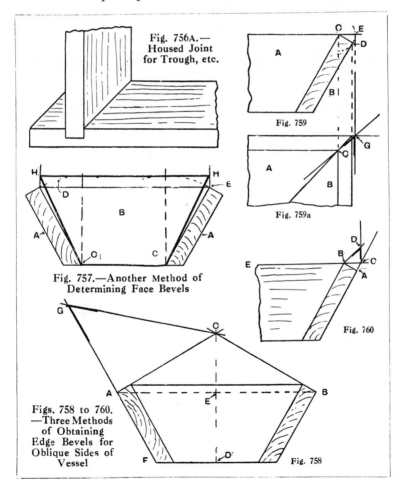

Fig. 756A.—Housed Joint for Trough, etc.

Fig. 759

Fig. 759a

Fig. 757.—Another Method of Determining Face Bevels

Fig. 760

Figs. 758 to 760.—Three Methods of Obtaining Edge Bevels for Oblique Sides of Vessel

Fig. 758

explains a still more simple method. Fig. 760 is a part section, as before. At A continue the sloping line of the side, and extend the top edge E B of the side to give the point C. Erect a line on C perpendicular to the base line, and above C set off the thickness of the stuff A B, so obtaining the point D. Join B to D, and B D C will then be the bevel required.

On pp. 202 to 205 will be found instructions on setting out oblique dovetail joints, which instructions embrace the lessons conveyed in this chapter.

CHAPTER XX

Carcase Making

Probably the two most important factors toward success in practical cabinetwork are the proper setting-out of the work and the planing up of the material. Planing up is the actual foundation of a job, and considering that faulty planing cannot be subsequently put right, it should rightly be accorded first place in the order of importance. It is assumed that the craftsman has prepared the full-size drawing of the job, and the next preliminary is the preparation of the cutting list. Many woodworkers, particularly amateurs, are apt to do without this very necessary and economical feature. It is unfortunately often dispensed with in regular commercial workshops. It should

Cutting List for a Small Pedestal Cupboard.

No.	For	Length	Width	Thick	Wood	Quan.	Notes
	Carcase—	ft. in.	in.	in.			
1	Ends	2 2	11¼	⅝	Mahogany	2	
2	Top	1 0½	10¾	⅝	American whitewood	1	¼-in. mahog. slip at front
3	Bottom	1 9½	10⅛	⅝	ditto	1	ditto
4	Back	2 2	13	½	ditto	1	
5	Drawer, right	1 1	2½	⅝	Mahogany	1	
6	Drawer runners	1 1	1½	⅝	American whitewood	1	1 length cuts 2
7	Dustboard	0 10½	8½	¼	ditto	1	
	Drawer—						
8	Front	1 0	3¾	⅝	Mahogany	1	Plain for veneering
9	Sides etc.	0 10½ etc.	3¾	⅜	Mahogany etc.	1	

show all the necessary cutting sizes of every piece of wood required to make the job, together with special notes that may be necessary with regard to special items, such as panels to be " well figured." A moulding length may be required to cut up to make several short lengths, in which case a marginal note is added, " 1 cuts 6 lengths," and so on. Reference to the cutting list on p. 265 shows a suitable arrangement of the columns, and it should be noted that a subdivision of the job, such as is indicated, facilitates reference and reduces the risk of missing essential items. The sample job taken for explanatory purposes is a small pedestal cupboard, the exterior being of mahogany and the interior of American whitewood.

It should be particularly noted in regard to the filling in of this list that " lengths " should always be shown in feet and inches, and " widths " in inches only. It sometimes happens that a piece is required wider than its length, and if both dimensions are shown in feet and inches, one may be nonplussed as to which way it should be marked out. If, however, the practice suggested is adhered to, this information is indicated. It will be seen that 2 ft. 6 in. × 2 ft. 9 in. leaves room for doubt ; but 2 ft. 6 in. × 33 in. being length and width respectively on the rule indicated above, shows that the grain is to run in the direction of the first measurement. Some surplus material must be allowed for planing and fitting ; $\frac{1}{2}$ in. in the length is the usual allowance, with $\frac{1}{4}$ in. added on the width. Part of the latter allowance goes for the saw cut, and the remainder for planing true to size and fitting.

The cutting list having been prepared, the next step is to " mark out " the timber. It is advisable to cut out all the timber for one job at one time, the pieces being identified later by chalk marks coinciding with the numbers on the cutting list. This entire " cutting out " at one time enables the timber to be more economically used, as small pieces can be marked out to fit in with larger pieces, and it also allows the timber to cast (wind or warp) and dry somewhat before starting the planing. If the cut pieces can be put on a dry shelf or rack in the workshop until

required for the actual planing and working, it will considerably minimise the risk of casting after planing and setting out.

The timber having been " marked out " and " cut out "
in the manner indicated, the next step to consider is the
planing. If the work is to be made in odd evenings or
occasional days only, certain parts only should be planed
up at one time, the remainder being allowed to dry more
thoroughly until actually required for working. In cases,
however, where the work is to be proceeded with day after
day until finished, it is more systematical to plane up all
the timber at one time. Should the work be extensive,
the part-by-part planing will be preferred, as the time
lost will be repaid by the improved condition of the wood
due to air drying. Too much stress cannot be laid on the
need for trueness or freedom from winding. Many woodworkers find it extremely difficult to make door frames
true and free from winding, which may nearly always be
accounted for by careless planing. In course of planing,
the rough surfaces should occasionally be tested in both
directions with a straightedge, and also with winding strips
(*see* p. 90). One of the strips should preferably be provided
with either white bone or ivory sights, and the wood tested
by placing one at each end. The top edges are then glanced
over, and if the sights are quite parallel to the nearest strip
the wood is free from winding. If, however, one sight is
higher than the other, some wood must be planed off the
high parts of the work and again tested. An alternative
test is to line one long edge with the eye against the other
edge, and the wood will be quite free from winding when
both lines appear quite parallel. A further test is to place
two pieces of wood together, such as, for example, two door
stiles. Should they not be quite true they will rock slightly
on the diagonals, which must be rectified by planing away
the high parts.

It will be found upon examination that nearly all " setting out " can be reduced to a few certain factors, such
as doors, stands, carcases, etc., all of which consist in the
main of dovetailed, tenoned, or mortised parts. The
framing of a table, for instance, is made with tenoned joints

to connect the rails to the legs, and if a drawer is introduced, then the top rail is dovetailed. Each job, so far as
its setting out is concerned, is simply a collection of joints,
and as much system as possible should therefore be introduced in order to economise time and to ensure accuracy.
If a particular piece of work has two door frames of equal
size, all the mortices should be set out at one time if possible,
and, similarly, all shoulder lines should be marked at once
so that all are exactly the same length.

To give a few concrete examples introducing principles
that can be readily applied to a large number of jobs will
enable these points to be better understood, for which
purpose the building of the chest of drawers shown in Fig.
761 will be described. This example will represent the practice of setting out in connection with ordinary carcase work,
whilst the table dealt with in the next chapter will serve
for the setting out of table work. All the timber having
been planed up true and free from winding, both the carcase ends are obtained and placed together with their hollow
sides inside. They are then screwed in the bench vice at
one end, the other being supported by means of a handscrew, as illustrated in Fig. 762, or by a peg if the bench
has a peg board (*see* p. 42). The total length is then ticked
off on the edge, and then marks are made to indicate the
positions of the drawer rails. A sharp striking knife is
then used against a small try-square to mark the length
lines across, the rail lines being squared across with a fine
pencil. The carcase ends may then be separated, and the
length lines squared across the ends with a striking knife.
The insides of the ends are then marked for the rails with
a striking knife, the lines running right across so that they
can be used as a guide for fixing the drawer runners. The
surplus material in the length should then be sawn off and
the end grains planed down to the knife-cut lines. They
are then gauged and planed to the finished width and
rebated along the back edge to receive the back. Greater
accuracy is obtained if both ends are sawn and planed
before they are separated, mechanics frequently planing
six or even eight at one time for this reason.

The rails and top and bottom are the next to be dealt with. All the shoulders must be exactly the same length, therefore the five pieces are put together as indicated in Fig. 763, and hand-screwed together at each end. The extreme lengths of rails, and the top and bottom, will vary, so the shoulder lines are struck right across first (*see* lines B B). The length of the dovetails is then marked on the two large pieces and the lines squared across as indicated at C C. The length of the stub tenon is usually less than that of the dovetails, as indicated by the lines D D struck across the rails only. The pieces may now be separated, and all the lines squared across both faces of each piece with a striking knife. The surplus wood is then sawn off

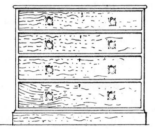

Fig. 761.—Front and End Elevations of Chest of Drawers

the rails, there being no necessity to plane the ends, whilst the carcase top and bottom have the surplus wood first sawn and then planed off. Gauge lines are then made on the end grains for the dovetails to coincide with the lines on the edges of top and bottom. The two large pieces are then gauged and planed to the finished width. A mortice gauge is then set to the width of the tenon indicated in the lines A A in Fig. 764. All the rails are then gauged from the face edges on the faces and ends, and corresponding marks are then made on the insides of the ends between the mortice lines. When all have been marked the gauge is extended to the second set of lines indicated by B B in Fig. 764 and the gauging process completed. All tenon lines should be cut on the outside of the lines and all mortices on the inside of the lines in order to ensure a close fit. A little practice soon enables one to judge accurately the exact amount to leave, but it should be borne in mind by beginners that it is far easier to ease joints a little than it is to tighten them up.

To set out the carcase dovetails a bevel should be set to an angle of 1 in 6, on the system illustrated by Fig. 538, p. 189, this giving the best angle for carcase dovetailing. The dovetails are then set out as indicated in Fig. 764A, the bevel being used to mark out the slopes in all cases. It will be seen that a small dovetail is introduced at the front, this being to prevent the ends curling away from the rails, as sometimes happens when a large dovetail is introduced which has smaller holding power. The top and bottom should then be handscrewed together and fixed in the vice, and both dovetails cut at one time, the pieces being next separated and one end fixed in the vice, as in Fig. 765. The carcase top is then placed as shown, one end being supported with a jack plane or anything handy, the shoulder line being exactly above the inside line of the end. The top piece is then pressed down firmly, and a dovetail saw is drawn through the saw cuts, thus marking the end grain. The pieces are then separated and the process repeated with the other ends. An end is then fixed in the vice as shown in the diagram (Fig. 766) for the purpose of sawing the sockets for the dovetails. The important thing to remember is that the saw lines should be left upon the wood when the sockets are cut in order to ensure a tight fit. The dovetail saw should be carefully started on the corner part and then worked across the end grain, keeping close to the marked line until the gauge line is reached. At the same time, the wood is cut down to the other gauge line marked A (Fig. 766), these cuts being at right angles to the end grain. When both ends have been cut in the manner described, the ends are placed on the bench as indicated in Fig. 767. The pieces are held firmly as indicated by means of a cross-piece or a holdfast, great care being exercised to ensure the ends bedding firmly down to the bench. A firmer chisel and mallet are then used to chop away as much as possible of the surplus

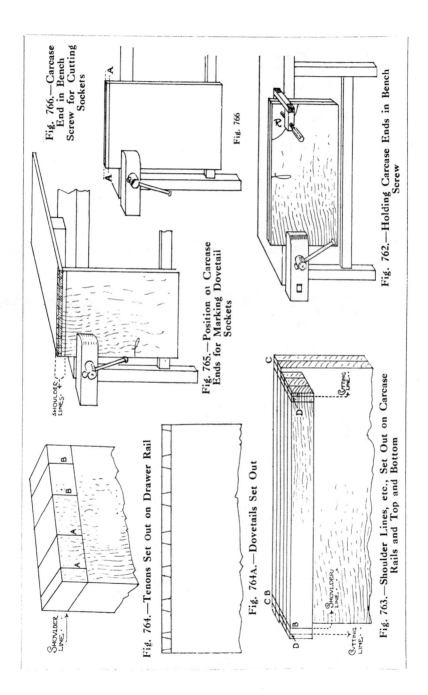

Fig. 766.—Carcase End in Bench Screw for Cutting Sockets

Fig. 766

Fig. 765.—Position of Carcase Ends for Marking Dovetail Sockets

Fig. 762.—Holding Carcase Ends in Bench Screw

SHOULDER LINES.

Fig. 764.—Tenons Set Out on Drawer Rail

Fig. 764A.—Dovetails Set Out

SHOULDER LINE.

SHOULDER LINE.

CUTTING LINE.

CUTTING LINE.

Fig. 763.—Shoulder Lines, etc., Set Out on Carcase Rails and Top and Bottom

socket wood, the last cut on the line being slightly inwards so that a close joint on the inside may be obtained when the dovetails are put together. The ends are then removed, and one fixed as in Fig. 766, when the corners can be finally cleaned out with small chisels.

The next step is to cut away the surplus wood between the dovetails on the carcase top and bottom. These pieces are fixed on the bench similarly to the ends. A first cut should be made as shown, midway between the end and the gauge line, and about half the thickness in depth. A final cut is then made exactly on the shoulder line with the chisel pointing slightly inwards as indicated in Fig. 767A. All the parts having been cut in this manner, the pieces are turned over and the process repeated. By this means a very blunt **V**-shape is formed in the bottoms between the actual dovetails which allows the pins to be inserted so that the wood fits quite closely against the shoulder lines. The shoulders on the outsides of the dovetails are made by sawing with a fine dovetail saw down to the dovetail.

To glue up a carcase such as is illustrated, the glue should be carefully prepared and made very hot, and of such a thickness that it runs easily off the brush when it is lifted from the glue-pot. All the parts, ends, carcase top and bottom, and rails are then got together, and the tenons of the latter warmed. The ends are then laid flat on the bench and the mortices glued with a small brush. All the sockets for the dovetails are then glued, this being followed up by gluing the dovetails of top and bottom. One end of the top and also the bottom should be driven home, and then the corresponding tenons are glued and driven in. The remaining end is then driven on to the drawer rails, this being followed up by driving down the remaining ends of the top and bottom. The carcase is then laid on its back in the bench as indicated in Fig. 768, and cramps are applied across the drawer rails until the shoulders are brought right up close. If the tenons are properly made it will not be necessary to leave the cramps on, but if the tenons are slack the cramps should be allowed to remain.

To test a carcase for squareness, it is best to measure

the diagonals indicated by the dotted lines in Fig. 768. These should be measured with a straightedge, one end being pointed to fit in the angle. A thin lath or even a length of dowelling serves quite well for the purpose, and if these are not long enough, two thin laths can be held together by the hands; or the wax line (p. 8) may be used. The great thing is to make the two diagonals measure exactly the same length, and this is done by pushing the carcase or by adjusting the cramps on the front. This method is even better than testing with a large square,

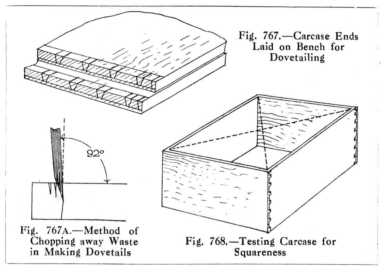

Fig. 767.—Carcase Ends Laid on Bench for Dovetailing

92°

Fig. 767A.—Method of Chopping away Waste in Making Dovetails

Fig. 768.—Testing Carcase for Squareness

as with the latter instrument, unless the sides are dead straight and true, the test is misleading. In the case of large carcases it is a good plan to nail a strip across at the back to keep the carcase square while the glue is drying.

Large carcase ends which cannot be placed in the bench vice have the sockets cut, and are then placed on the carcase top and bottom, a marking awl being employed to mark the pins which are cut outside the line.

The practice described in this chapter is that followed by the majority of professional workers, but the reader can please himself as to the method of making sockets from pins, etc., matters that have been discussed in earlier chapters.

s

CHAPTER XXI

Table Making

The object of this chapter is to deal thoroughly with the various methods employed in general table making, the reader having obtained by now an insight into systematic planing up, the preparation of a cutting list, and tests for planed work.

For the present purpose a simple table has been designed (*see* elevation, Fig. 769, and plan of under-railing, Fig. 770). It is intended for a writing table, but with slight adaptations could be varied for other purposes. It embodies the essential feature of table work in the connection of rails to legs, and the arrangement of rails to receive two drawers. The under railing also is usually found in table work. So far as the construction is concerned, it will be seen that washstands, dressing tables, draught or chess tables, card tables, and occasional tables embody almost identical constructions, all these having certain common features

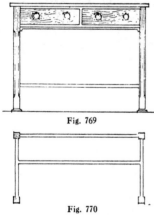

Fig. 769

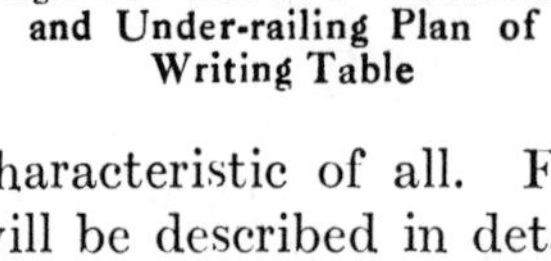

Fig. 770

Figs. 769 and 770.—Elevation and Under-railing Plan of Writing Table

characteristic of all. For this reason each particular part will be described in detail.

It being assumed that all the parts have been properly planed up, the first step in table construction will be to connect the end rails to the legs. Generally speaking, turning or tapering is done after the joints have been made. The four legs are therefore placed together as in Fig. 771 with the inside surfaces uppermost, and the marking for the mortises proceeded with. Two lines should first be struck right across the four legs to indicate the total length of the legs. The mortise lines are then struck across, these being indicated by those marked 2, 3, 4, and 5. The line No. 6 is then struck across, and indicates the finished width of the end rails. The lines marked 7 and 8 may then be struck across, these indicating the mortise lines for the end under the rails.

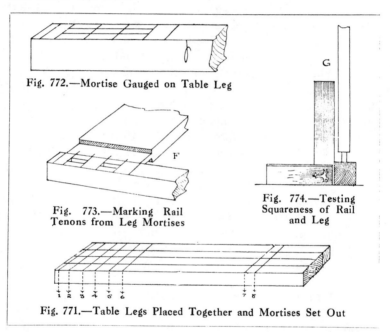

Fig. 772.—Mortise Gauged on Table Leg

Fig. 773.—Marking Rail Tenons from Leg Mortises

Fig. 774.—Testing Squareness of Rail and Leg

Fig. 771.—Table Legs Placed Together and Mortises Set Out

The next step is to mark the shoulder lines of the end rails and stretcher rails. Both sets of rails will in this case be exactly the same length, and should therefore be hand-screwed together, and then the shoulder lines marked across all four edges. They are then separated, and the lines returned across the front and back surfaces with a striking knife. A fairly deep cut should be made, as this facilitates cutting the shoulders with a dovetail saw. After the legs and rails have been marked as indicated, the mortises and tenons are marked out. The wide rails should be dealt with first, a mortise gauge having the pins set so that a mortise chisel one-third the thickness of the material just fits between the points (*see* p. 154). The head of the gauge is then adjusted so that the points come midway on the thickness of the wood. Each end is then carefully gauged on the three sides for the tenon on both of the rails, and then the gauge should be adjusted for the mortise marks on the legs. The rails usually set in $\frac{1}{8}$ in., and the mortise gauge is therefore knocked out a similar amount without altering the pins. Each leg is then gauged off the outside as indicated in Fig. 772. The tenons should then be marked on the under rails to form the joint indicated at 4 (Fig. 776). When cutting the tenons care should be taken to leave the gauge line on the wood, and the mortise lines should also be left in order to ensure tight joints. The shoulder lines of the tenons should then be cut carefully with a dovetail saw before proceeding to mark and cut the tenons to width as illustrated on the rail E (Fig. 776). Correctly to mark the tenons to width, the rail should be held in the position indicated in Fig. 773, and points coinciding with the mortise are then marked on the tenons with a pencil. Lines are then marked with a square to the shoulder line, and cuts made to the shoulder line. The outside waste pieces are then cut away with a dovetail saw, and the inside pieces by cutting from each side with a firmer chisel.

Next fit the rails into the legs. A leg should be fixed on the bench and the rail inserted as indicated in Fig. 774. Before it is driven right home, it should be tested with a square and fitted so that when the tenon is driven right in, the surface of the rail is quite parallel to the edge of the try-square as shown. Should the rail not rest quite true, the mortise should be eased slightly at the bottom, which causes the rail to incline towards or away from the try-square. Should the rails not be quite perpendicular, the table ends will wind and cause a great deal of trouble.

When the ends have been fitted in the manner described, the lower rails should be dealt with in like fashion. The ends are then tested carefully to ensure freedom from winding, and are then separated prior to chamfering and inlaying the legs, or otherwise treating them as required for turning or twisting. The latter part having been done, both ends should be glued together and cramped.

Figs. 775 and 776 show the construction of the table in detail.

To cramp the ends after gluing, one should be laid flat on the bench with the legs parallel to the front. A cramp is then applied across the wide rail, care being taken to keep it square with the work. Another cramp is then put across the bottom rail, this being followed up by testing the diagonals between the rails for squareness. If measured with a rule, the diagonals should measure— if the end is

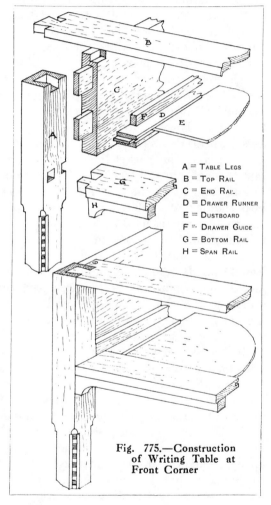

A = Table Legs
B = Top Rail
C = End Rail
D = Drawer Runner
E = Dustboard
F = Drawer Guide
G = Bottom Rail
H = Span Rail

Fig. 775.—Construction of Writing Table at Front Corner

square—exactly the same length. Should the diagonals not be the same length, the cramps should be adjusted to the left or right as required until they are equal. This part having been settled, it is necessary to ascertain if the faces of the legs lie in exactly the same plane. To test this, a straightedge should be placed across the legs, and if the faces are not exactly flat one with the other, they must be adjusted by raising or lowering the head or foot of the cramps. The end is then set aside to dry for about twelve hours before removing the cramps. The surplus lengths above the rails are then sawn off and planed down quite level with the rails.

The next thing to do is to set out the shoulder lines of the rails connecting the ends. All the shoulder lines should be marked at one time, and the rail B in Fig. 775 planed to length. The lap dovetail joint at each end is then made as shown at the top of Fig. 775, the dovetail being cut on the rail and the socket marked by drawing the dovetail saw through the " kerfs " on to the end grain of the leg. The bottom rail G in Fig. 775 is then tenoned and housed into the leg at each end as illustrated. In this example one tenon only is used with housing ; but if a thicker leg is employed, two tenons may be employed to advantage.

The back rail is next proceeded with (*see* c at the top of Fig. 776). It frequently happens that the mortises exactly meet, and when this is the case the tenons are roughly mitred in the mortises as indicated. In this case, however, the ends being glued before the back-rail mortises are cut, it would be quite good practice to butt the back-rail tenons on to the side tenons. The rail F (Fig. 776) should also be tenoned in, and the stretcher rail H is then slip-dovetailed between the ends. A small diagram shows the detail of the slip-dovetail, which forms a better tie joint between lower rail E and stretcher H than tenoning.

If the practice suggested has been followed, all the long rails will have been connected, and may be followed up by fixing the division marked 1 and 3 in Fig. 776. It will be seen that a clamp about $3\frac{1}{2}$ in. wide is made with a groove to receive the division marked 3. After the pieces have been glued together, the division should be planed carefully to thickness. It is then gauged to width to correspond with the width and squared at the front. Fig. 776 shows the connection, commonly called " pinned joints,"

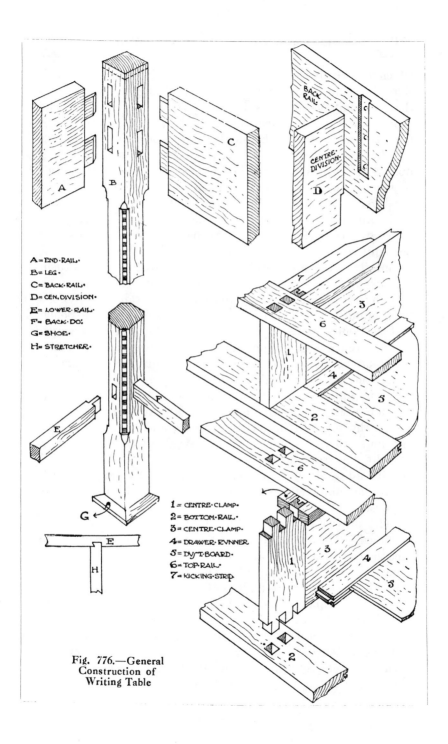

A = END·RAIL·
B = LEG·
C = BACK·RAIL·
D = CEN.DIVISION·
E = LOWER·RAIL·
F = BACK·DO:
G = SHOE·
H = STRETCHER·

1 = CENTRE·CLAMP·
2 = BOTTOM·RAIL·
3 = CENTRE·CLAMP·
4 = DRAWER·RUNNER·
5 = DUST·BOARD·
6 = TOP·RAIL·
7 = KICKING·STRIP·

Fig. 776.—General
Construction of
Writing Table

which are really tenons, the mortises being cut from each
side of the rail with the chisel pointed slightly inwards so
that a blunt **V-**shape is formed.   The back part of the
centre division is then shouldered and fitted into the
back rail as shown in the small centre diagram in Fig. 776.

The framing of the table is now almost ready for gluing
up.   A groove is worked on the inside of the bottom rail
to receive the dust-board, and then the inside surfaces of
the legs, both sides of the bottom rail, centre division and
back rail, as well as the lower rails, are scraped and glasspapered.   To glue the framing together four cramps will
be required.   The ends should be placed on the bench with
the mortises upwards, and glue inserted with a small brush.
The back, drawer, and both lower rails are then driven in
and the other end carefully placed on the rails, the tenons
being guided in.   The framing is then stood on the bench
and the four cramps applied, one on each of the lower rails,
and the remaining one on the bottom drawer rail.   To test
for squareness the best plan is to measure from corner to
corner on the front, and also at the top to ensure that the
table is square both in plan and elevation.   The centre
division is then carefully glued into the drawer rail before
gluing the top rail into the dovetails and over the centre
division.   It is a good plan to test along the top with a
straightedge from leg to leg at the front.   Should the rail
not be quite straight it can be made so by tapping with
a hammer above the top rail or under the bottom rail as
required.

The drawer runners 4 (Fig. 776) are the next pieces to
be fitted.   These are made with a groove on the inside to
receive the dustboard, and are stubbed as shown into the
groove of the drawer rail.   The dustboard and runners
would have to be inserted altogether in this table, the runners
being glued and hand-screwed.   Alternately the runners
and drawer rail are made without grooves, and then a thin
dust-board is screwed underneath the table to all the rails,
it being notched to fit over the legs.   In tables, however,
where drawers are placed one above the other, the dust-
boards are fitted as illustrated into grooved runners, and

are usually pushed in from the back before the back is screwed in. The framing can now be planed level on the top and front, scraped and glasspapered prior to screwing on the shoes G (Fig. 776).

The table top when squared up and moulded should be secured by secret screwing to the side and back rails ; or if a removable dust-board is introduced, it can be pocket-screwed through the side and back rails. In each case the fixing is completed by screwing in two or three places through the front rail from below.

CHAPTER XXII

Drawer Making

In a drawer of medium size, such as a table drawer 12 in. wide, 2 ft. back to front, and 4 in. deep, without ornament, there are eight pieces of wood, each of which has to be prepared in a different manner to get the best result. In Fig. 777, which is the side elevation of a drawer showing lap dovetails in front and common dovetails at the back, the arrow shows the direction of the grain of the wood. These pieces consist of the front, which should be cut out of 1-in. stuff, 12½ in. long and 4¼ in. wide ; the back, 12½ in. long, 3¼ in. wide, and ⅜ in. thick ; two sides, each 2 ft. long, 4¼ in. wide, and ⅜ in. thick ; two slips to hold the bottom, 2 ft. long (of the section shown in Fig. 780) ; and two blocks to keep the bottom and sides square to the front.

Large drawers have the bottom in the form of two panels and a muntin in the centre. Very small drawers have no side slips, the bottom being grooved into the sides.

Drawers with fancy-shaped fronts, or with a raised bead round the edge, or of irregular shape, are not so popular as they formerly were, possibly because they cost much more to make than a plain drawer, never run so well, and the fancy moulding is always coming off.

Perfectly dry wood should be used in drawer making, but this is seldom to be obtained. Therefore the material for the drawers of a piece of furniture should be the first part of the work to be sawn out, smoothed over with a plane, and put upright to dry while the other parts are being prepared and put together. To prevent distortion, or what is known in the workshop as casting, no two flat surfaces should be placed close together to dry, unless, as often happens, they have cast already. If this is so, place the hollow or concave sides together, and this may cause them to become straight in the course of two or three days. This treatment applies only when the wood is hollow from side to side across the grain. When crooked in its length or across its opposite corners (that is, winding), there is little or nothing to be done except to plane it straight, with consequent loss of thickness. Hence the necessity of great care in the selection of wood when purchasing.

It should be remembered that in drying, wood always curves inside out, that is, the side of the board that was next the centre of the tree becomes convex or rounding; and whenever practicable, the inside of the board should be placed on the outside of the work.

Having got the wood as dry as possible, it should be prepared as follows : Plane up the front straight and out of wind, note the direction of the grain, and put the face mark to the left ; this will be the bottom edge. In preparing work that is to be framed, such as the stiles and rails of a door, the face mark should be to the right to facilitate the final clean up. Shoot the face edge square and straight, remove the saw marks from the other edge, but do not reduce to width, and get to one thickness all over. Prepare the back in the same way.

The sides are prepared in pairs, the grain so arranged that it planes from the front to the back. (The arrow in Fig. 777 denotes the direction of the grain.) Plane to thickness and square at both ends to the proper length, 1 ft. $11\frac{1}{4}$ in., the front ends marked as shown in Fig. 777. If more than one drawer is being made at the same time, careful numbering is essential.

The front of the drawer is fitted into its opening at the bottom and the two ends, which must be kept square on the edges, as tight as it will go. The beginner should resist the temptation to bevel a little off the inside of the edges, otherwise a bad fit will result. With a pencil point gauge the finished width of the front and sides ; the dovetails will determine the width of the back. Clean up all on the inside, but do not glasspaper.

To mark for dovetailing, set a cutting gauge to $\frac{5}{8}$ in., and gauge the ends of the front from the inside and all round the front ends of the sides. The gauge should be tested frequently to make sure it does not move. Next set the gauge, or another one, a little less than the thickness of the sides, say $\frac{1}{32}$ in., and gauge the inside of the front from the ends and the outside and inside of the back, not the edges. Set the gauge the thickness of the back, and gauge the sides from the back end ; but not the edges. Then set the gauge $\frac{13}{16}$ in., and cut along the inside of the front from the bottom edge. This will prevent the plough from tearing the wood should the grain be crossed or curly. Plough the groove for the bottom to go in $\frac{5}{16}$ in. wide and $\frac{3}{8}$ in. deep.

To cut the dovetails, place the sides together in pairs in the bench screw, insides together, and divide out evenly, allowing for the little to be taken off the top edge, square across the ends with a pencil. The bevel may be about 10°. To ensure this, make a little template 3 in. long, 1 in. wide, and $\frac{1}{2}$ in. thick, as shown in Fig. 778, all perfectly square on the edges. Placed on the top of the ends, this will form a guide to the angle at which the saw is to be sloped. It can be turned round or upside down, as required, to cut the other parts. When the front ends are cut, turn the sides upside down, and cut the back ends as shown in Fig. 777. The bottom dovetail will be $\frac{13}{16}$ in. from the face edge, and the top dovetail $\frac{1}{4}$ in. from the top. It is better to stop a trifle short than to go on cutting beyond the mark.

To mark the front, place it in the bench screw, inside towards the bench ; lay the proper side on the top in the exact spot where it is to drop down when the dovetails are cut, the other end being supported by the jack plane placed sidewise on the bench. Put a weight on to keep it steady, and mark the position of the dovetails by placing the end of the saw in the cut and drawing it forward ; or it is better to get a very thin piece of steel and cut a few upright teeth in it without set. This is less likely to disturb the side when marking. A piece of broken band-saw or metalworker's hack-saw set in a handle, the set of the teeth being ground off, answers admirably.

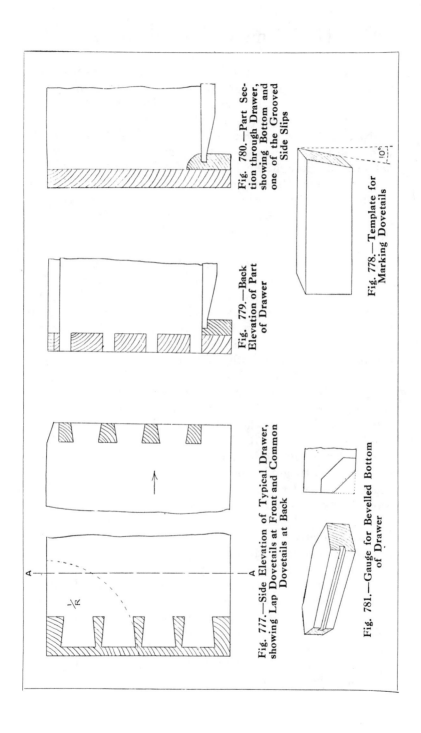

Fig. 777.—Side Elevation of Typical Drawer, showing Lap Dovetails at Front and Common Dovetails at Back

Fig. 781.—Gauge for Bevelled Bottom of Drawer

Fig. 779.—Back Elevation of Part of Drawer

Fig. 778.—Template for Marking Dovetails

Fig. 780.—Part Section through Drawer, showing Bottom and one of the Grooved Side Slips

As the sides are very much alike, some care is necessary to see that each piece is marked to go in its proper place. This is best ensured by numbering each part before beginning. The back is marked in the same way.

Next cut down the dovetails of the front, leaving the whole of the saw mark on the pins. As the dovetails do not extend through the front only, part can be sawn; the remainder must be cut out with a chisel. The back pins can be sawn right through. An expert keeps the saw perpendicular merely by practice; the beginner had better square down with a pencil, or use the square end of the template.

The next job is to chisel out the dovetails. A fret-saw will reduce this part of the work considerably. The most economical way is to saw out the dovetails of the back immediately they are marked, before removing from the bench screw. Do not attempt to cut quite up to the marks; leave a little for the chisel. The centre dovetails of the sides are removed with a fret-saw, and the corner pieces of the front end with a dovetail saw, finishing with a chisel.

Having removed as much as possible with the fret-saw, the quickest way of finishing the sides is to turn the left side of the body to the bench; hold the chisel with the left hand, with the left elbow on the side to keep it down. The mallet should be in the right hand, the fingers of which can be used to guide the chisel. Always have a piece of waste wood under the work to save the bench. Cut half-way through, inclining the chisel inwards to the slightest degree; turn the side over, and cut from the other side. To cut perfectly square right through would be better, but this is impossible to do by hand.

To chisel out the necessary part of the wood to form the dovetails in the front is very difficult for the beginner, as the saw cuts can only be carried half-way, and great care is required, particularly if the wood is " short " or cross-grained. The best tool to get into the corners is a nearly worn-out carver's chisel. Being short it is more under control, and being broader at the edge, enables it to get into the oblique angle.

Carpenters' chisels are often poor tools for very fine dovetailing ; they are too thick and very often soft. Carvers' chisels are much better ; but they will not stand rough usage. Some shops keep a $\frac{3}{8}$-in. carver's chisel ground out of the square, the same angle as the dovetail, both sides being bevelled to enable it to be used for either right hand or left hand.

Before trying together the various parts, take a little off the edges of the dovetails on the inside of the sides, not quite out to the back end, or it will show. See that the sides enter the back and front ; but do not drive home. They should fit just tight enough to require gentle tapping with a hammer. They will go in much easier with the glue, which, if hot enough, will act as a lubricant.

Considerable care is required to cut the dovetail pins the right size, and any error will now be apparent. If too tight they will split or bruise away the sides ; if too small they will not hold. One or two misfits may be rectified by paring away a little, or inserting a little " joiner " beside the pin ; but if the dovetails are not marked and cut correctly, no amount of botching will make a good fit.

If the inside of the drawer is planed clean it is better not to glasspaper it.

In gluing up, unless the room is very warm, the dovetails should be warmed, not made hot. Place the front upright in the bench screw, and with a small flat brush rapidly cover the dovetails with rather thick but very hot glue, then those of the side, and tap home gently with a hammer. With a wide drawer, place a piece of narrow wood on the side to send it home altogether, or the side may split. When apparently home, hit harder with the hammer, but do not bruise the side. The remaining three corners are best glued and driven home on the bench, completing the one side first, then the other end of the front, and lastly the side and back. Make sure that all the joints are close, and afterwards hammer just a little. This will spread out the wood softened with the glue, and ensure a close joint. Wash off with warm water all superfluous glue from the outside, and this will raise any bruises which may have been made with the hammer. Only a slight bead of glue should find its way out of the joint on the inside. This must be taken off with a chisel when nearly dry ; washing will discolour the wood. Set the drawer square, measuring from corner to corner, and leave for six hours or all night for the glue to harden.

The slips (*see* Figs. 779 and 780) are made by ploughing a board $\frac{3}{8}$ in. from the edge, rounding over and sawing off wide as shown. Planed flat and even on the back, they can be made to hold to the sides simply by warming and gluing the inside and pressing down with the hands ; but it is better to use weights or hand-screws if possible. The front end of the slip is squared off, and the back end is notched to run past the bottom. The bottom should be got to exact length and parallel, and the front edge made to fit the front edge of the carcase, allowing a little for the latter being wider at the back.

To bevel the bottom evenly to the proper thickness, take a piece of wood $1\frac{1}{4}$ in. thick, cut off a corner at an angle of 45°, plough the edge in the centre the same width and depth as the slip, and cut it off 2 in. or 3 in. wide (*see* Fig. 781). The bottom should be bevelled down until this gauge can be passed along its whole length easily without shake from end to end. Take off the sharp edge on the top of the bottom to enable it to enter without breaking away the plough groove. Then drive in the bottom.

The drawer is now ready to be fitted in. First see that the bottom is out of wind, then reduce the sides, trying one at a time until it will nearly enter. Next plane off the sides until the end grain of the back and front is reached, then a little more off the top edges until the drawer will enter, but very tightly. In theory the drawer ought to run either on the bottom or upside down ; but the opening is never quite rectangular, consequently gauging and squaring must not be depended on to ensure a good fit.

When the drawer fits into the carcase as tightly as it will go without injuring it, see that the front is set in evenly all round, and then fix the stops. It is usual to place these on the front rail for the front to hit against. A better plan is to put them at the back against the ends of the sides. There is then no strain on the dovetails.

Lastly, glue two or three little blocks underneath in the angle formed by the bottom and front. These will keep the whole firmly fixed. The drawer front may now be

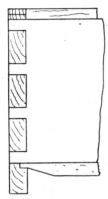

Fig. 782.—Bevelled Drawer-bottom Held in Grooves in Sides

Fig. 783.—Glued Block under Drawer-bottom

cleaned up for the polishing, after which the handles may be fixed on.

In common work the bottom of the drawer may enter a groove cut in the sides, as in Fig. 782, the slip shown in Fig. 783 being dispensed with; blocks, as in Fig. 783, may be glued on underneath when the bottom is not reduced in thickness.

T

CHAPTER XXIII

Doors and Gates

In the making of doors and gates, the lessons taught in earlier chapters may be applied. All the joints involved have already been described in detail, and it remains to explain simply the general principles of construction.

Ledged and Braced Doors.—The simplest possible form for a small door is that known as "ledged," consisting of a number of pieces of vertical boarding (usually matched or tongued together) nailed or screwed to horizontal battens or ledges. If nails are used, they are "clinched," that is, their points project at the back and are hammered over (*see* p. 225). For doors up to about 3 ft. in height two ledges fixed a few inches from the top and bottom of the boarding respectively (Figs. 784 and 785) will be sufficient, while for higher ones three ledges may be necessary. As the tendency for such a door is to twist a little after a time, unless made of very well-seasoned wood, and in any case to drop somewhat with its own weight on the side away from its hinges, it is desirable to add sloping "braces," as in Fig. 786, which considerably strengthen the construction. Braces can be bridled or merely notched into the ledges (*see* Chapter VIII.), and, to obviate to some extent the dropping tendency, they should invariably slope upwards from the edge on which the door is hinged.

While quite a usual form, the door shown in Fig. 786 is rather unsightly from the braced side, although it shows a perfectly regular face on the exterior. A more presentable form is shown in Fig. 787, and this can be developed into Fig. 788, the additional brace in this being either halved with the first one, or merely put on, as shown in two separate pieces butting against it in the centre. One possible method of making a ledged door more presentable is explained by Fig. 789, and consists simply of the alternating use of two

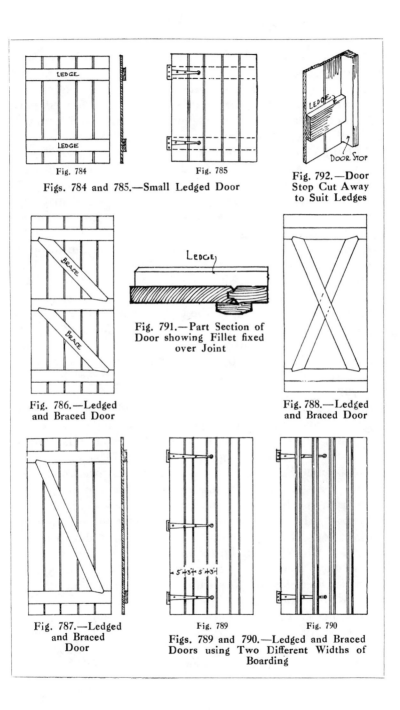

Fig. 784

Fig. 785

Figs. 784 and 785.—Small Ledged Door

Fig. 792.—Door Stop Cut Away to Suit Ledges

Fig. 786.—Ledged and Braced Door

Fig. 791.—Part Section of Door showing Fillet fixed over Joint

Fig. 788.—Ledged and Braced Door

Fig. 787.—Ledged and Braced Door

Fig. 789

Fig. 790

Figs. 789 and 790.—Ledged and Braced Doors using Two Different Widths of Boarding

contrasting widths of V-jointed boarding ; this can be
made to produce quite a good effect, as can also the arrangement shown by Fig. 790, and in detail cross section by
Fig. 791, in which rather wide boarding is employed and
the joints covered with thin, slightly chamfered and rounded
strips, about 1 in. wide, and taken over the " strap " hinges.
The fitting of hinges is dealt with in a later chapter.

An important point to consider is that of hanging, this
being effected by means of ordinary butt hinges fixed just
where the ends of the ledges come, or, more frequently, by
means of long T or " cross-garnet " hinges, also arranged
centrally with the ledges and capable of producing quite
a good effect (see Figs. 789 and 790). The inside of such
doors often does not matter as regards appearance, but
can be improved when desired by such means as those shown
in Figs. 786 and 788, and the ledges and braces give a
more finished appearance by the chamfering of their exposed
edges. When the ledged side of a door closes against a
rebate or continuous stop, either the ledges must be cut
short to miss the stop, etc., or the latter must be cut away
to suit the ledges, which will then fit into it as shown in
Fig. 792.

Panelled Doors.—With regard to small panelled doors
for cupboards and furniture generally, the combination of
tenon and grooving involved in simple framing is shown
in elementary form by Fig. 793, a detailed explanation of
which is unnecessary. For convenience in working, the
grooves for the panel should invariably be the same distance from the back and front faces of the framing as are
the tenons, the mortises or slots becoming in consequence
continuations of the grooves, with which they should agree
in width. The edge of the tenon at A should line with the
back of the groove at B. The joint shown will be adequate
for the smaller class of door with framing up to about $2\frac{1}{2}$ in.
by 1 in., but there are, of course, more involved varieties
of tenon better adapted to heavy work (see Chapter XI.).

One slight improvement upon the merely common-
place square finish round a panel will be found in Fig. 794,
and has the advantage of being easily executed. In it

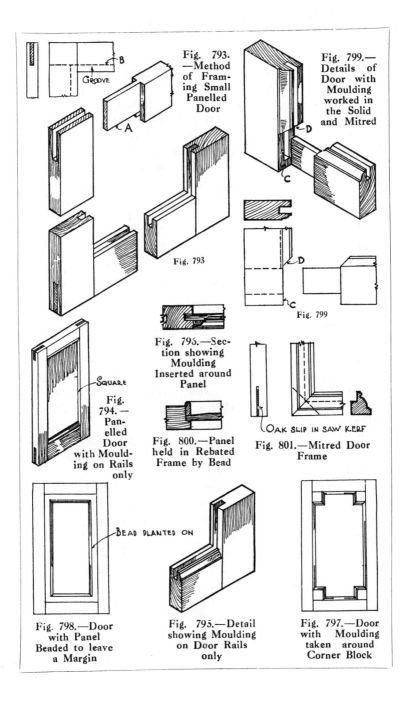

Fig. 793.—Method of Framing Small Panelled Door

B

GROOVE

A

Fig. 793

Fig. 799.—Details of Door with Moulding worked in the Solid and Mitred

D

C

D

C

Fig. 799

Fig. 795.—Section showing Moulding Inserted around Panel

SQUARE

Fig. 794.—Panelled Door with Moulding on Rails only

Fig. 800.—Panel held in Rebated Frame by Bead

OAK SLIP IN SAW KERF

Fig. 801.—Mitred Door Frame

BEAD PLANTED ON

Fig. 798.—Door with Panel Beaded to leave a Margin

Fig. 796.—Detail showing Moulding on Door Rails only

Fig. 797.—Door with Moulding taken around Corner Block

the top and bottom rails are simply moulded, the moulding butting against the square upright sides as in Fig. 795. A moulded panel can be obtained by means of a small moulding mitred round as in Fig. 796, but a more interesting effect is produced by taking it round small rectangular blocks fixed at the corners and finished off flush with the face of the framing, as in Fig. 797, the various joints being rendered as inconspicuous as possible. Another treatment, suitable whether a panel moulding has been applied or not, is the addition of a very small neat bead or moulding, mitred round the panel at a little distance from the edge of its exposed surface, as in Fig. 798. Panels should not be actually fixed in their grooves but left free to expand or contract slightly, and, in consequence, whenever possible any mouldings should be fixed to the framing and not to the panel.

When the framing is rather larger and more substance is available for the joints, the mortise should be kept away from the extreme ends of the rails, as at c (Fig. 799). This also shows how a joint should be set out in a case where a moulding actually worked on the solid edge of the framing has to be mitred right round. The moulding must be worked on the style and then cut away at the end, finishing with an angle of 45° as at d, thus preparing a face against which the rail can butt when treated in a corresponding manner as shown. As before, the mortise and tenon agree in thickness with the panel grooves.

A panel is sometimes secured in a rebated frame by means of a bead, as in Fig. 800, although this method is more often employed for glass. When the work is small, it is often necessary to slightly chamfer the panel as shown, in order to obtain sufficient fixing for the bead. If the bead be left projecting a little as indicated, it has quite a good appearance.

For small glazed doors to cabinets and the like, it is quite practicable to avoid tenoning completely, using instead a mitred angle-joint, strengthened with a piece of stout oak veneer glued in a saw-kerf as in Fig. 801 (*see also* pp. 172 to 174). This figure actually shows, not a plain

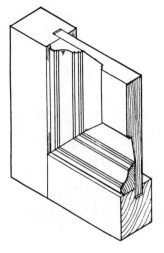

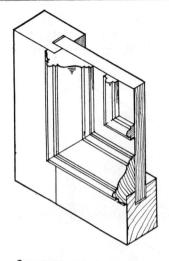

SECTION

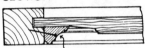

MOULDING FIXED TO FRAMING ONLY

Fig. 802.—Framing with
Planted Moulding and
Raised Panel

SECTION

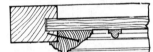

Fig. 803.—Framing with
Bolection Moulding, Bead
Planted on Panel

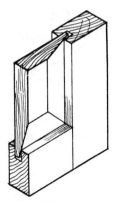

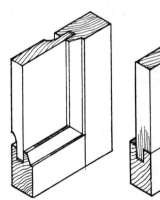

Fig. 804.—Square
Framing and
Chamfered Panel

Fig. 805.—Panels with Bead worked on
Framing and Panel respectively

piece of framing, but a length of rebated moulding of the picture-frame variety, which, if of suitable wood, is often excellent for such purposes.

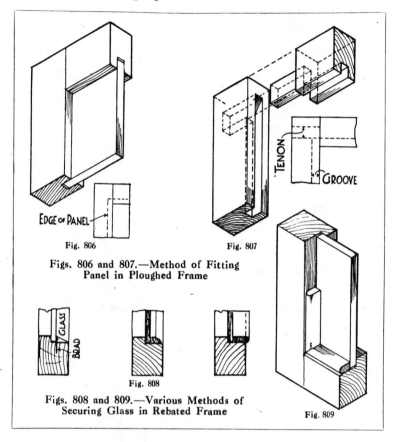

EDGE of PANEL

Fig. 806

Fig. 807

Figs. 806 and 807.—Method of Fitting Panel in Ploughed Frame

TENON

GROOVE

GLASS

BRAD

Fig. 808

Figs. 808 and 809.—Various Methods of Securing Glass in Rebated Frame

Fig. 809

Figs. 802 to 809 show some related details of door construction—tenoning of ploughed and moulded framings, the application of mouldings, and the fixing and securing of panels and glass.

CHAPTER XXIV

Curved Woodwork

In this chapter some examples of utilitarian and artistic curved woodwork will be considered, the simplest case that can be taken being a wooden ring as in a circular louvred ventilator, the rail of a circular table, or the rim of a cart wheel. These three articles serve different purposes and are differently constructed.

A Louvre Frame.—If the sawn-out pieces forming any wooden ring are too long and extend too far round the curve, the ends are weak because of the cross grain, as shown in Fig. 810. The frame for a louvre will require four pieces, and as the material is, say, 4 in. by 3 in., it is best to make a pattern out of thin wood about $\frac{1}{4}$ in. thick or of sheet metal. This pattern, if in wood, is struck out with compasses, a trammell, or with a strip of wood, and two nails, and is then bow-sawn $\frac{1}{8}$ in. away from the line and finished with a spokeshave, the ends of the pattern being cut off to the required length when the angle has been obtained with the sliding bevel as shown in Fig. 811. The bevel is set and tried reverse sides until the lines drawn coincide, this giving the radial line as desired. When a plank of the right thickness has been chosen, the pattern should be placed on it and scribed round. Advantage should be taken of any curvature of grain so as to partially coincide with the pattern.

In a commercial shop the pieces are sawn out of the plank with the band saw, $\frac{1}{16}$ in. away from the line to allow for finishing; should the work be done with a bow-saw of usual size, about $\frac{1}{8}$ in. must be allowed for finishing the curve. It is possible to adze the concave surface, but this is an operation of greater difficulty when the curve is of a smaller circle. The outside could be chopped round with an axe. A wheelwright carries out these operations with his hardwood felloes after they are sawn out, even if he has only $\frac{1}{8}$ in. to cut off. The direction in which to chop the grain with adze and axe is shown in Fig. 812.

In planing, after the face has been made true, the concave surface is finished to the line with a compass plane, and the outer or concave side finished with a smoothing plane. Adjustable planes for working concave and convex curves can be obtained, but are not essential. Many workmen would finish these surfaces with a large spokeshave, obtaining as good a curve in this way as with any other tool. Both of the surfaces are tested with a try-square, from the face side. Then with the pattern mark the ends, square the lines across, and saw them off. The four pieces are placed together for trial, and if the ends require easing this should be done with a finely-set smoothing plane, the stroke being mainly with the grain, in an outward direction from the centre of the ring ; but a circular motion of the plane is needed to preserve the flatness of such a small end-grained surface. It should then be tested with a try-square. On an earlier page it has been shown how to secure the pieces with hammer-headed keys, which are recessed into the frames to about three-quarters of the depth, care being taken to see that sufficient clearance is allowed at the ends so that the four small wedges draw up the joints tightly. When the grooves for the louvre boards have been cut and any necessary moulding worked on, the joints should be glued and the keys wedged in. When the glue is dry, the joints and the keys are smoothed off in the usual manner.

Rim of Circular Table.—Fig. 813 shows the rail or rim of a circular table built up of a series of pieces forming layers, which, when finished, is veneered on the outside. Take, for example, a rim 3 ft. in diameter, 4 in. wide and $\frac{7}{8}$ in. thick. This would be formed with a series of layers five or six in number, each being $\frac{5}{8}$ in. or $\frac{3}{4}$ in. thick, each layer to form a ring of five or six pieces. The joints of the pieces must not coincide with those in the layer above or below. Proceed to make a pattern to the shape and length required, and then mark out on a $\frac{3}{4}$-in. board, cut out with a bow-saw, and finish with a spokeshave. The

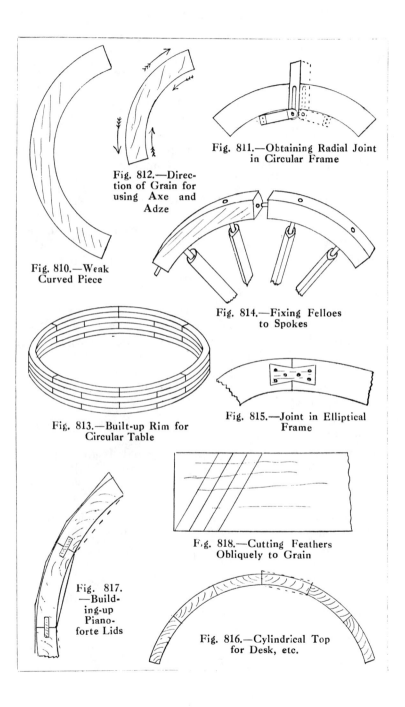

Fig. 811.—Obtaining Radial Joint
in Circular Frame

Fig. 812.—Direc-
tion of Grain for
using Axe and
Adze

Fig. 810.—Weak
Curved Piece

Fig. 814.—Fixing Felloes
to Spokes

Fig. 813.—Built-up Rim for
Circular Table

Fig. 815.—Joint in Elliptical
Frame

F,g. 818.—Cutting Feathers
Obliquely to Grain

Fig. 817.
—Build-
ing-up
Piano-
forte Lids

Fig. 816.—Cylindrical Top
for Desk, etc.

gluing up should be done on boarding on which are drawn the rings showing the plan of the rim, the boarding being small enough to allow the pieces to be cramped. Pieces forming the first ring are cut and fitted on the plan, the ends being cut to the pattern the bevel of which has been obtained by the method previously explained. It is not essential in this case that all the pieces should be the same thickness providing they are approximately the same length and are cut to fit the plan.

There are two methods of gluing the first ring. One is by chalking the board thoroughly all round so that the glued joint will more readily separate when the rim is finished. The other is by gluing paper on to the board on which the plan must be drawn, and then gluing the work to the paper. When the glue is dry, true the surface with a plane and fit the pieces on for the next ring in the same way. Then glue again, cramp the pieces down all round, using one or two brads or pins for the ends, if necessary. When dry, level off and repeat the process until the right depth is obtained. The rim is released from the board when finished, the inside is cleaned up with a compass plane and spokeshave, and the outside also rounded to a good surface ready for veneering.

Cart-wheel Rim.—The rim of a cart wheel is divided up into pieces known as felloes, each being long enough to receive two spokes. They are prepared from a pattern which is a part of a circle larger than the wheel, so as to make the rim higher at the joints. The joints are not fitted close, as in the other cases, but are made slightly V-shaped. The subsequent cramping-up is due to the contraction of the tyre. The felloes, after being shaped to pattern, are placed round the shoulders of the spokes of the wheel and the holes marked to receive the spoke ends. The felloes are joined to one another by means of dowels, and after the felloes have been shaped and chamfered, they are driven on the spokes simultaneously (*see* Fig. 814). Some kinds of carriage wheels have the rims in two semicircular pieces, but these are bent by steam, ash or hickory being generally used.

Elliptical Frame.—A ring of wood often takes the shape of an ellipse as in frames for looking-glasses, etc. This requires two or three patterns of different shapes. The method of fixing the joints is shown by Fig. 815. A piece of hardwood $\frac{1}{4}$ in. or $\frac{3}{8}$ in. thick, of double-dovetail shape, is recessed in at the back of the joint and glued and screwed in. After the joints have been cleared off, the mouldings are worked on by means of routers.

Cylindrical Work.—The shaping of wood to cylindrical form, as in desk tops, piano fronts, carriage panels, curved footboards, etc., is done in various ways. Boards bent by heat are used when they can be permanently secured by other framework or by iron fastenings. This method of bending is largely adopted in the carriage-building trades, where glued joints, such as are used in other constructions of curved boards, would soften and jar apart in the exposure to the weather and the vibration of the vehicle. Another method of bending a board, when only a slight curvature is required, is by heating the concave side and continually wetting the other side of the board. The heating is done by moving the board to and fro over a fire or forge. Advantage should be taken of bending the board in the direction of its natural tendency ; that is, the convex or outer side should be nearest the centre of the tree (*see* Figs. 854 and 973, pp. 319 and 381). If the planing is done before the bending, a good finished surface can be obtained with scraper and glasspaper.

The following describes the course adopted for making circular desk-tops and such-like articles which are generally veneered. First draw the end view of the boards full-size, as in Fig. 816, showing the width of the pieces of which it is made ; supposing the boarding is to finish $\frac{3}{4}$ in. thick, the width should be about 3 in., but if the curve is of smaller radius the pieces should be narrower. Hard wood should be used, mahogany being especially adaptable for such work.

The thickness of the board can be ascertained by drawing a line from the corners inside, and another line parallel to it and tangential to the outer curve, as shown by the dotted lines. If the curve is circular, the angle for the edges will be equal, and should be taken by the bevel from the drawing. Care is required in shooting the edges to the correct angles, and after testing with the bevel they should be tested on the drawing to make sure of obtaining the correct shape. The joints are rubbed when gluing, which should be done in two or three operations, giving the joint time to harden before being weighted by the extra piece. When ready for rounding off, the ends should be marked with a pattern obtained from the drawing. The inside curve should be worked with a " round " plane as wide as obtainable ; or, if many boards of this shape are to be made, an old jack plane might be rounded to fit the curve, and the cutting iron ground accordingly. A scraper could be ground to fit the curve for finishing before the glasspaper is used.

A stronger method of shaping by grooving and feather-.ing the joints is shown by Fig. 817. After shooting the edges, plane a tangential surface at right angles to the joint sufficiently near to allow for finishing. Then plough the grooves as indicated about $\frac{1}{2}$ in. or more in depth on each edge. Now cut off a number of feathers obliquely from a board the thickness of the grooves, as in Fig. 818. Cutting the tongues as feathers in this fashion allows the grain to cross the joint instead of running longitudinally with the joint, which would be a source of weakness. The feathers should be shot sufficiently narrow so as not to bind and prevent the joint being rubbed close when gluing. The finished piece of work, as in Fig. 819, is then ready for veneering.

Bending Boards by Saw-kerfing. — Saw-kerfing, a method of bending board, can be adopted in cases where no great strain or stress is likely, and where the adjacent fixings can give their support. Saw-kerfing on the concave side of a board for a convex or external finish requires care in making the cuts regular in depth and equidistant. Fig. 820 illustrates a method of approximating the distances apart of the saw cuts. A piece of wood, the same thickness as the board to be bent, is sawn nearly through or until it

is sufficiently flexible to close in (*see* A), and is then placed
to the centre of the curve required. Holding the strip
firmly at the centre, move the outer end round the circum-

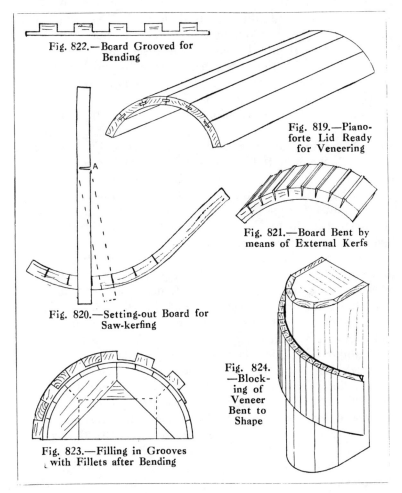

Fig. 822.—Board Grooved for
Bending

Fig. 819.—Piano-
forte Lid Ready
for Veneering

Fig. 821.—Board Bent by
means of External Kerfs

Fig. 820.—Setting-out Board for
Saw-kerfing

Fig. 824.
—Block-
ing of
Veneer
Bent to
Shape

Fig. 823.—Filling in Grooves
with Fillets after Bending

ference in such a way as to close the cut. The amount
by which the outer end of the strip moves (see the dotted
lines) gives the space between the cuts on the board. The
same saw must be used and the cuts made to the same
depth as in the test piece.

A method of bending by saw-kerfing the external or convex side of a board is shown in Fig. 821, some solidity being given to the work by gluing in V-pieces of wood, afterwards cleaning off the surface to shape. Another way—grooving and filleting—is done as in Fig. 822. The grooves are cut deep enough to allow the board to bend freely to the required shape, and pieces are then fitted in and glued. A fair job can be made by this method if the work is bent over a cylinder of wood built up to the curve required, as in Fig. 823.

Veneer Method of Bending.—Veneers can be bent over a built-up cylinder or other shape, and blocks or strips of wood fitted to the veneer and glued on as in Fig. 824, this method being adopted in making the concave well-hole of a staircase, in which instance the whole work is bound and strengthened by gluing canvas over the fillets or strips.

Figs. 825 to 828 show a method of reducing a board almost to the thickness of veneer and, by the aid of steam, bending it round a block of wood built up and made the required shape to give an external or convex curve. The lower risers of a staircase such as a bullnose, round end, or curtail step are good examples of such work. For a bullnose step three or four pieces of thick boarding to the depth of the step are cut out reverse ways of the grain, glued and screwed together (*see* Fig. 825). The board for the riser, about $\frac{7}{8}$ in. thick, is reduced by planing to $\frac{3}{16}$ in. thick in the portion to be bent. A splayed fillet of hard wood, to form a hook, is well secured by gluing and screwing as in Fig. 826. After the block has been fitted the portion of the board for bending is well steamed, folded round, and secured by folding wedges. Screws are then fixed through the block to the thicker portion of the board. This is shown with the end housed into the newel post (Fig. 827). The block for a round-end step is sometimes made of four parts dovetailed together, and rounded off with saw, smoothing plane, and file. The wedging and screwing are performed in the same manner as the bullnose step (Fig. 828).

Curved Work in Chair-making, etc.—The curved work in connection with furniture is chiefly of an artistic char-

acter rather than geometrical as in building construction.
It consists of work composed of a number of curves which
cannot always be set out geometrically, but are symmetrically constructed from a freehand design. Examples of
such work can be seen in the art of chair-making. There
should be no difficulty in preparing a pattern of any fancy

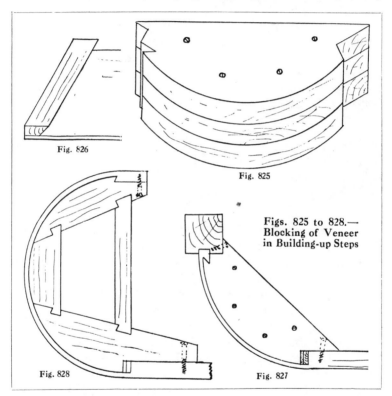

Fig. 826

Fig. 825

Figs. 825 to 828.—
Blocking of Veneer
in Building-up Steps

Fig. 828

Fig. 827

shape and making the required article, providing the piece
is of the same thickness as the plank from which it is made.
Should there be a double curvature on the piece to be made,
the worker should ascertain the width and thickness from
the drawing showing the two views of the article. In the
case of pieces forming the back of a chair, some will resemble
pieces like the circle on circle, or, to be more correct, circle
on cylinder, so that many pieces have to be cut of cylin-

U

drical form for such work and then the required circle or other pattern marked as in Figs. 829 and 830. The second curve or pattern is not always definitely marked on these cylindrical pieces until they have been approximately dressed to shape, fitted and joined up temporarily by dowelling. Then the pieces are dressed to shape before gluing up. The tools required for such work are the bow-saw, spokeshave, smoothing and compass planes, the firmer chisel for paring the small convex surfaces, the paring gouge for the small concave surfaces and the half-round file for finishing. Two or three routers may be wanted for grooves, beads, and mouldings.

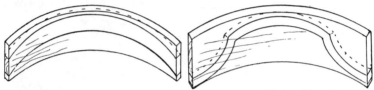

Figs. 829 and 830.—Making Second Curve in Work of Double
Curvature

Special curved work in relation to aeroplane construction is dealt with in the following chapter.

Other Methods of Heat Bending.—Most people are familiar with the method of bending a bamboo cane— that of holding one end in a staple or vice, applying the flame of a bunsen burner or spirit lamp (any sort of bottle with a loose-thread wick burning methylated spirit), and then gently but firmly bending the cane as required, and holding to shape until cool (*see* Fig. 831). Wood is readily bent by the aid of heat, but except in the case of bamboo, it is unusual to apply a naked flame, a much lower degree of heat being sufficient. Steam-heating is customary, but other methods of heating are efficient. J. H. Beebee, in an American publication, has given some information on the subject which is not generally known. He states : " It is often desirable to fit a piece of wood into a screwed metal socket. This can be accomplished by heating the metal to a little over the boiling point of water and screwing the wood piece into the metal while hot. Or, if it is impracticable, on account of size, to heat the metal, make a screw plate by cutting a thread in a small piece of metal, the size and thread corresponding to the hole into which the wood piece is to be inserted, and heating it to the required temperature, then running the wood with some pressure through the thread. The wood then can be screwed into the larger piece, where it will hold firmly. The process of heating wood without the aid of steam can be used to advantage in a number of ways; for instance, a hammer handle that is crooked can be straightened by careful heating without burning; also billiard cues, or almost anything of hard wood. The Indians at one time made their arrows from small hard wood twigs which were almost always crooked to start with; but after being dried they were

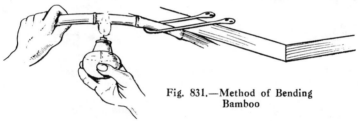

Fig. 831.—Method of Bending Bamboo

warmed over a fire and straightened. Another use for the application of heat is as follows: When it is desired to place a screw in a fragile piece of wood that is likely to split, if the screw is heated to a blue colour and turned into the wood while hot, there will be scarcely any danger of splitting. In this case, do not try to use oil or a lubricant of any kind, as the screw is sure to set before it is in place."

In large wood-bending works the " steaming chests " are connected direct with steam generating boilers. The chests are generally of cast-iron, and in them the wood is subjected to the softening effect of steam for a number of hours. As the rods are removed they are quickly pressed round suitably shaped moulds which will not allow of the rods shifting about, and at the same time enable cramps to be used to exert pressure until they are thoroughly dry.

In the absence of facilities for steaming the wood, a makeshift plan is to immerse the wood in sand, kept as hot as possible by frequent changes of boiling water, the receptacle being covered with bagging. But a quite small steaming apparatus can be rigged up without much trouble, as shown in Fig. 832. The steaming box A B is about 1 ft. 4 in. long by 3 in. square of ½-in. wood, the joints being securely screwed and packed with red-lead. The ends (Fig. 833) are left open to allow for long articles, but they must be tightly packed with clean white rags during the steaming operation. An ordinary 3-qt. kettle is used, and by tilting it as shown it will hold sufficient water to last for an hour and a half without refilling. It is tilted to allow the steam to escape more readily by the spout, as

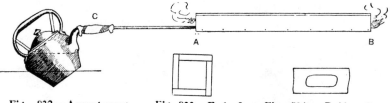

Fig. 832.—Arrangement for Steaming Small Work   Fig. 833.—End of Steaming Box   Fig. 834. — Rubber for making Lid Steam-tight

the lid should be securely closed and made steam-tight by opening out a portion of an old cycle inner tube, and cutting it as shown in Fig. 834; this is stretched round the edge of the lid, which is firmly wedged down with two sticks, fitted between the handle and the lid, as in Fig. 832. Steam is conveyed from the kettle to the box by a brass rod inserted into the mouth of the kettle, wrapped round with more cycle tubing at c, and securely tied with string. The portions of wood to be bent having been placed in the box, the tube is inserted and the ends are packed with rags. The kettle is filled with boiling water, fastened down, and set on a fire (preferably a gas or oil stove). One hour and a half is allowed for steaming small strips, which can then be bent and tied down or clamped to a mould or former, on which they should be left till cold.

CHAPTER XXV

AEROPLANE WOODWORK

THIS chapter is concerned with the adaptation of ordinary woodworking to the requirements of aviation. Vast numbers of woodworkers have passed into aeroplane factories, enormous interest in aeroplane work is likely to be taken in the future, and all craftsmen will probably wish to be given an insight into the methods and processes employed.

Naturally, machine work is utilised to the greatest possible extent, but the tools required include the ordinary trying, jack, and smoothing planes, chisels and gouges, tenon saw and dovetail saw. As most of the work has to be finished to a limit of $\frac{1}{64}$ in., or even very much less, an engineer's 12-in. steel rule is necessary. A rule marked with English measures on one side and metric on the other is the handiest. The hand-drill, with a chuck to take round-shank morse drills, is in constant use in some branches of the work. A set of spokeshaves, screwdrivers, and the usual oddments of a woodworker's kit almost complete the set, but, of course, different branches of work require different tools.

The woods mostly used are silver spruce, ash, hickory, American whitewood, mahogany, and pine. The greater part of the work is in spruce or ash, and three-ply is used for various purposes.

Wing Building—Figs. 835 to 837 show typical spars used in wing building. The first is an ordinary spindled spar ; the second, one of the hollow box variety, tongued together ; and the third a laminated spar, made of three layers glued together and then worked. In some cases the middle layer is of ash. Figs. 838 and 839 show sections of inter-plane struts. The first is worked in two halves, with a stiffening web of ash placed in the centre, the other being very similar in construction. Fig. 840 shows the arrange-

309

ment of a rib used in the construction of wings. The centre web of spruce is lightened out, and the flanges bradded to it. The leading edge is spindled to a hollow section, and the trailing edge a plain fillet. All work must be finished extremely accurately to size.

The building of a conventional wing is one of the principal operations in aeroplane work. Wings for biplanes are built up in halves, the lower wings abutting against the body, and the top two meeting, so that a complete machine requires four sections. A typical wing is composed of main spars, ribs, which are built up beforehand, as shown in Fig. 840, and threaded over the spars, the leading and trailing edges, and the longitudinal stringers. The latter are thin strips about $\frac{1}{2}$ in. by $\frac{1}{4}$ in., running parallel with the main spars. Their objective is to prevent the covering of the wing from bagging in between each rib. There is also the internal wire bracing.

The two spars, having first been set out, are laid on a bench, and the requisite number of ribs threaded on. These are then glued and bradded at the places marked on the spars, and the internal bracing wires, shown in Fig. 841, are then tightened by means of wire strainers (*see* Fig. 842), until the wing is absolutely square. This is a matter of some importance, as a wing not square will set up irregularities in flight. The leading edge is next applied, being screwed and glued to the nose formers and ribs. Great care must be taken to ensure this being quite straight when viewed from the front. The trailing edge is fixed in a similar way. In some machines this consists of a flattened steel tube. The stringers are then pushed through the slots in each rib, and glued and bradded. The point which requires the greatest attention is the continuity of the wing curve. This must be absolutely uniform the whole length of the wing, and a good plan is to use a pattern, cut out on the top and bottom to the correct wing curve. This can then be tried on as each rib is fixed to the spars. The wing having been passed, is varnished and covered.

Erecting Aeroplane Body.—The erection of the body of the aeroplane necessitates extreme accuracy and care.

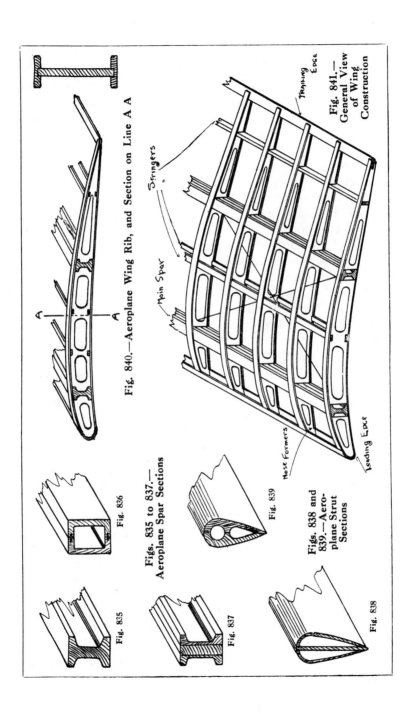

Fig. 840.—Aeroplane Wing Rib, and Section on Line A A

Fig. 841.—General View of Wing Construction

Figs. 835 to 837.—Aeroplane Spar Sections

Fig. 836

Fig. 835

Fig. 837

Figs. 838 and 839.—Aeroplane Strut Sections

Fig. 839

Fig. 838

Stringers

Main Spar

Nose Formers

Leading Edge

Trailing Edge

The names of the various parts may be seen from Fig. 843, which illustrates approximately the lay-out of a typical body.

With regard to the materials used, ash or hickory, and occasionally spruce, is used for the longerons, while spruce is nearly always used for the struts. The cross struts and longerons are prepared beforehand, so that it will be seen that the job is almost entirely one of erection. The main principle underlying its construction is that the longerons are not pierced by bolt holes. Accordingly, all joints are affected by steel clips of one sort or another, such a joint as a mortise-and-tenon being unknown. A characteristic joint is shown in detail by Fig. 844.

The longerons are first set out from a rod, the clips bolted in place, and the struts and wires inserted. It is usual to build up the sides of the body first, and connect up with the top and bottom struts. This completed, the next operation is what is called truing up, and there are one or two methods of accomplishing this. One method consists of marking out on the floor, or boards made for the purpose, the complete side elevation. The wires are then tightened and adjusted by means of the wire strainers, until it accurately corresponds with the marking out. A centre line is then marked on each top and bottom strut, and the operation of adjustment is continued until the marks are in alignment with a cord stretched from end to end.

The cross or sectional wires are tightened until the whole body is quite square. This may be verified by running a line from end to end at the point where the sectional wires cross, and any deviation from this will show inaccuracy somewhere. The whole body may be levelled up, and each strut tried with a plumb-bob. Too much care cannot be taken to ensure that the cross struts are trimmed to the correct bevels. The least difference will cause the struts to bow when the wires are in tension, necessitating the removal of the strut. It is absolutely essential that the stern post is kept quite upright. If this is at all out of plumb, the rudder, which is attached to it, will probably be the same, with bad results in flight. Fig. 845 shows the stern-post fitting.

The success of this job is due largely to the care with which the material is prepared beforehand.

When the fuselage is finished every wire is locked, this term being applied to the process of fixing each strainer with soft wire, as shown in Fig. 846. Its object is to prevent them unscrewing from the vibration of the engine, and consequently loosening the wire. The illustrations show just one practice. Different makers use different methods, although the fundamental principle is the same, and alterations and improvements are constantly being effected.

Making a Propeller.—The efficiency and almost the success of the aeroplane are largely dependent upon the precision with which the propeller is made. The material used is almost always wood, but the blades are often tipped or sheathed with metal. The woods most frequently used are walnut and mahogany. Boards about 1 in. thick are cut and planed, and are then glued together in the manner shown in Fig. 847, each board being stepped a little. These laminations may be about seven in number, and are sometimes arranged so that alternate layers are of a different colour, giving a pleasing effect. The reasons for making a laminated propeller as against one from the solid is, in the first place, the extra strength of the laminæ, as the grain is running straight through, whereas if solid wood is used, short grain must occur close to the boss. Secondly, there is the difficulty of obtaining wood sufficiently large and at the same time absolutely sound. The laminations being thoroughly dry, the resultant block is cut out roughly to shape, and superfluous portions worked away with the drawknife and spokeshave. Templates are used at certain points along each blade to ensure both sides being exactly the same. This is a fairly long operation, and demands a certain amount of skill. Even when taking every possible precaution, the propeller is invariably a little out of balance, this being made up with lead placed in the boss.

Making an 8-ft. Propeller.—The following deals with the building of a propeller for quite a small machine, one driven by a 50-h.p. engine keyed direct to the shaft. The propeller is 8 ft. in diameter, with a pitch of 4 ft. 6 in.

The " pitch " is the definition of the distance travelled forward during one complete revolution of the screw. It will be necessary to procure four pieces of material decided on, say mahogany, each 8 ft. long by 6 in. wide and 1⅛ in. thick, free of warp and blemish, and to bring them to a perfect surface. Take one plank, and after marking each end into 3-in. divisions, warm it evenly before the fire, together with the second strip ready for the glue. The object is to ensure perfect adhesion, the glue when applied boiling hot rapidly cooling unless precautions are taken. Lay the second strip on top to the right of the first, and repeat with the remaining two. When all are uniformly overlapping, strong cramps are affixed at equal distances of about 9 in., the length of the screw, and screwed tightly with a uniform distribution of pressure (*see* Fig. 848). The work is now laid by in a warm place for at least three days to dry.

When dry and the cramps removed, the work should be stringently overhauled in order to discover whether any flaw is apparent. If so, and the planks are not thoroughly joined together because of warping, etc., on no account endeavour to fill up the slit by means of fillets of wood or the like. It is absolutely imperative that the refractory strip be taken apart· and a perfect one substituted. No other resource is permissible in propeller construction, or, in fact, any other part of aeroplane building. When all is satisfactory in this respect, proceed to divide the newly " welded " beam into four quarters, as shown by the dotted lines in Fig. 849, where A represents the centre for the boring of the shaft hole, B the longitudinal line encircling the beam, c the central line at right angles thereto, and D a circle of 5-in. diameter to be drawn both top and bottom. For the sake of clearness the diagram is purposely shown as a perfect rectangular beam. The " welded " or glued strips should lay flat at right angles to the craftsman, the top strip thus projecting towards him. From this position, draw a straight line from the right to the left in the direction E to E intersecting the centre, and from the centre draw two curves on opposite sides of the centre to meet the design of the blade.

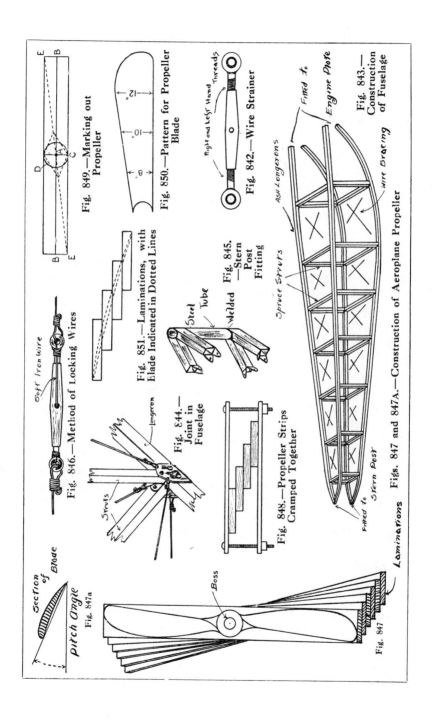

Fig. 849.—Marking out Propeller

Fig. 850.—Pattern for Propeller Blade

Fig. 842.—Wire Strainer

Right and left Hand Threads

Fig. 843.—Construction of Fuselage

Fitted to Engine Plate

Wire Bracing

Ash Longerons

Spruce Struts

Fig. 846.—Method of Locking Wires

Soft Iron Wire

Fig. 851.—Laminations, with Blade Indicated in Dotted Lines

Steel Tube

Fig. 845.—Stern Post Fitting

Welded

Fig. 844.—Joint in Fuselage

Longeron

Struts

Fig. 848.—Propeller Strips Cramped Together

Fitted to Stern Post

Laminations

Figs. 847 and 847A.—Construction of Aeroplane Propeller

Section of Blade

Pitch Angle

Fig. 847a

Boss

Fig. 847

The pattern of one blade should now be carefully cut out from stiff pattern paper or thin metal to the shape and dimensions given in Fig. 850, and should then be laid on and carefully marked off on the glued-up strips.

The structure must now be turned over, and the same procedure gone through on the opposite face. After this it should be placed parallel with the workman's eye, and the curve agreeing to the angle of incidence of the blades must now be marked at each tip. In Fig. 851 the design of the concavo-convex section is shown by dotted lines.

The propeller is now ready to be cut out with a saw to the correct design, after which it may be worked down to its rounded contour with a jack plane first, and finished off with a smoothing plane. Some constructors prefer to plane down roughly to the approximate helical curve, then mark off from the pattern and finish off. The centre hole is bored dead straight with the ordinary bit. The smaller holes each side average from two to six in number, and should not be bored unless the holes in the collar on the engine shaft are known.

Finish off with coarse and fine glasspaper, then suspend the propeller with strong twine through the centre of the shaft hole in order to note the balance. If one side is even slightly heavier than the opposite it will set up a " shivering " or clattering noise in rotation. Hence it must be accurately trued up, and any bias in this respect, in either blade, rectified or made good by loading as already stated. When all is properly faired up to suit the workman's tests, complete with french polish all over, so as to minimise skin friction when rotating at high velocities.

It will, of course, be understood that the above is a mere insight into the work and must not be taken as a literal statement of current practice. Aeroplane making is a progressive industry, every different factory has some particular methods peculiar to itself, and design develops at such a rate that both methods and materials have constantly to be altered to keep abreast of the times.

CHAPTER XXVI

Veneering and Inlaying

Veneering is the art or practice of covering furniture and fitments with a thin leaf or layer of a wood possessing a pleasing grain. Much has been written for and against it. Much of the cheap furniture produced in the factories, very badly built of soft, faulty material, and given the semblance of respectability simply by veneer, has naturally been condemned ; but there is plenty of really good veneered furniture in general use, and there is no reason why a veneer properly chosen and correctly applied should not be used as an effective form of finish for articles that have been constructed in a workmanlike manner of thoroughly sound material. In cutting veneers, advantage may be taken of the grain and medullary rays of the timber to produce some very beautiful figure effects, and such effects would be largely lost were veneering dispensed with, because wood of such beautiful figure would be too costly or too scarce to allow of its being used solid in furniture making ; and, in addition, such wood with its often curly grain would not be strong enough for use constructionally.

Kinds of Veneer.—Veneers are of two kinds — the thicker, known as saw-cut, from about five to fourteen to the inch, being cut from the log by means of a special type of circular saw, whilst that known as knife-cut, from about fourteen to sixteen to the inch, is produced by mounting a log in a special lathe in which is mounted a long, fixed cutting knife, and taking off a continuous cut as wide as the log is long and of a length depending on the cubic content of the log. Saw-cut veneer is dearer than the knife-cut, and is preferable for lasting work of any size. Owing to the pressure applied during the process of veneering, the glue which fixes the veneer to the ground (by " ground " is meant the constructional woodwork) is likely to be squeezed through a veneer of open grain and interfere later with the staining and polishing process. For this reason alone the thicker saw-cut veneer has an advantage over the knife-cut. The latter is laid much more easily, and, as already remarked, is cheaper. The hand or hammer process is possible only with the knife-cut variety. It is common to prevent the glue absorption of porous veneers by backing them with a mixture of glue-size and whiting, which can be coloured up, if desired, to the tone of the wood.

Cutting Veneer.—Veneer should be chosen for freedom from shakes and other flaws, due consideration being paid to the position it will occupy. For cutting it to size, a chisel should not be used, or probably the material will split or break up. Use instead the special saw shown in Fig. 852, guiding it by means of a steel straightedge. Failing this, the iron of the toothing plane referred to in a later paragraph may be used in the same way.

In knife-cut veneers, the right side will be known by tiny projections at the pores which correspond with the depressions on the wrong side. By laying the veneer with the projections uppermost, the surface can be brought to a good finish at a later stage by the scraper, fine glass-paper, etc.

The " Ground."—The preparation of the ground is of great importance. Of course, the ground will have been very carefully planed for thickness and for surface, and, although it will be hidden by the veneer, it should, as far as possible, be free from blemishes, particularly knots, shakes, and sap. Timber merchants sell what are known as panel boards for the special purpose of forming the foundation for veneering, these boards being cut right through the heart of the tree, or as close to it as possible (*see* Fig. 853). A board A (Fig. 854) cut farther from the heart has a natural tendency to become rounded (convex) on the heart side (*see* B), and this is counteracted by applying the veneer on that side, as indicated at C by the thick line which represents the veneer in section. One of the best foundations for veneering is made up of strips of wood as at A (Fig. 855), the heart side alternating top and bottom

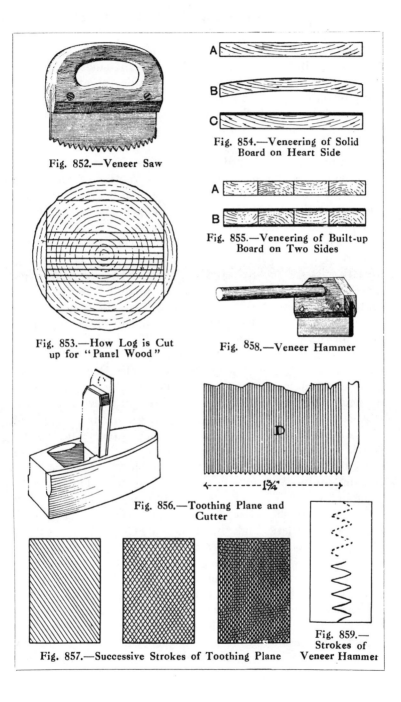

Fig. 852.—Veneer Saw

Fig. 854.—Veneering of Solid Board on Heart Side

Fig. 855.—Veneering of Built-up Board on Two Sides

Fig. 853.—How Log is Cut up for "Panel Wood"

Fig. 858.—Veneer Hammer

Fig. 856.—Toothing Plane and Cutter

Fig. 859.— Strokes of Veneer Hammer

Fig. 857.—Successive Strokes of Toothing Plane

so that one strip counteracts the warping tendency of the next one ; but to get the best effect on such a built-up ground it is advisable to veneer both sides as at B, so that the pull on one surface is balanced by the pull on the other. It should be noted that the veneer, while being applied, has to be damped, which has the effect of expanding it ; in the subsequent drying it contracts, and thus tends to cause the veneered board to go hollow on its surface. In the case of a single-piece board the contraction of the veneer simply balances the natural tendency of the wood in drying and contracting to go round on its face (that is, if the veneer is applied to the heart side).

To give the glue a good key, the surface of the ground is worked over with the toothing plane, in which (*see* Fig. 856) the iron is held at right angles to the work and has a series of close grooves formed in its front face (*see* D) so that, when sharpened, the cutter consists of a number of teeth. These teeth vary in fineness according to the purpose for which the plane is used. The toothing plane is employed also in finishing saw-cut veneers, being followed by scraper and glasspaper, and the teeth then require to be finer than when used for preparing the ground. The diagram (Fig. 857) shows the directions in which the toothing plane is successfully used, first and second diagonally and the third in the same direction as the grain. The ground is not yet ready for the reception of the veneer. Having dusted it, well rub into it with a brush some rather weak size made by mixing some glue from the glue-pot with some hot water. The size must not show as a coating when it is dry, and should it do so it must be roughened with the toothing plane and the dust wiped off. The sizing is of great importance, particularly when the work includes end grain, as without it the glue used in affixing the veneer is liable to sink into the grain and the lack of adhesive may give rise to blisters and other troubles.

Hand or Hammer Veneering.—In this process, although it is well for the work to dry under pressure, the knife-cut veneer is brought into close contact with the ground by the action of the veneering hammer (Fig. 858), which has a wooden head into which fits a metal blade. It is used by scraping the blade on the work, the hand gripping the wooden head and the lower part of the handle, the last-mentioned pointing away from the worker, as a rule. The blade may be of zinc, iron, or steel, with a rounded and polished edge so that it slips easily over the work and does not scratch or dig in. This hammer is also a convenient tool for testing the solidity of the work, a slight knock with its handle betraying a blister or other faulty place by the hollow sound.

A supply of veneer pins will be necessary, these being from $\frac{1}{4}$ in. to $\frac{3}{4}$ in. long and headless. The small ones are often driven right in below the surface and allowed to stay, and the longer ones are driven partly in and bent over, being afterwards withdrawn when no longer required.

The actual process of hand veneering is as follows : Press flat the pieces of knife-cut veneer and moisten the good side with a wet cloth. The work will need to be kept quite moist all through the process, but not sloppily wet. Coat the ground evenly with glue, and apply a little to the under-side of the veneer here and there. Without delay, place the veneer in position, and, if necessary, secure with a few pins only partly driven in. Then begin to expel air and surplus glue in the way already mentioned ; that is, press on the work with the polished edge of the veneering hammer, starting at the centre and proceeding in a zigzag direction towards the side (*see* Fig. 859). Work all over the veneer in this way, always starting at the centre, and when the whole is solid, place the work face downwards on the bench or floor, put a weight on it, and leave it to dry ; or, instead, cramp it in a press or by means of hand-screws. The veneered face of the work should not be exposed to the atmosphere when drying. If two pieces of work are being done at the same time, place them face to face, with a piece of newspaper between them to prevent sticking together should there be any glue on the faces, and then pile weights on them or put into the press or between screws.

Occasionally, blisters will occur. They are caused chiefly

v

by the presence of air between the veneer and the ground, and are best prevented by careful attention to detail. Should they persist in coming, keep the outside of the veneer moistened with size water instead of with clean water. They are remedied by slitting with a thin, keen knife, inserting a touch of glue, and then with the hammer rubbing out both air and surplus glue. Cover the place with a piece of paper and place under weights or in a press.

Slightly curved work can be hand-veneered in the same way as the above, but it will be desirable to use size water instead of clean water with which to keep the veneer moist.

Caul Veneering.—Cauls are strips, boards or blocks of wood (occasionally of metal) which are pressed into close contact with the veneered surface by handscrews, cramps, etc. Their use is essential when saw-cut veneers of any thickness are employed, as these are not amenable to the pressure of a veneering hammer. But not only do they transmit pressure, they also are a means of heating and melting the glue. Zinc holds the heat better than wood, but the latter is more convenient, is cheaper, and more extensively used. Zinc-faced wooden cauls are often used by professionals.

Let it be assumed that two panels, furniture ends, or anything similar, are to be veneered by the caul method. The back of the saw-cut veneer is rough enough to give the key to the glue, and the groundwork will be required to be prepared as before. Much will depend upon the readiness of all the accessories. The caul, which will be at least $\frac{3}{4}$ in. thick and large enough to overlap the work by an inch or so on all sides, must have been brought to a good heat over a fire, such as that made in the open with shavings and waste. A number of cross-bars (they will be used in pairs at intervals of about 7 in.) must be already to the hand, and the cramps or handscrews by which they will be cramped up should have the jaws just sufficiently open so that they may be slipped in place with the minimum of trouble. The cross-bars maybe, say, 3 in. wide and of any convenient thickness, say 2 in., and they are very slightly rounded on their undersides in the direction of their length.

Fig. 860 is a side view of one, 24 in. long, $2\frac{5}{16}$ in. thick in the centre, diminishing to 2 in. at the ends, and no greater roundness than that indicated by these dimensions is necessary. In the diagram the dimensions are correct, but the roundness is slightly accentuated in order that it may the more easily be seen.

While in hammer veneering the veneer is applied while

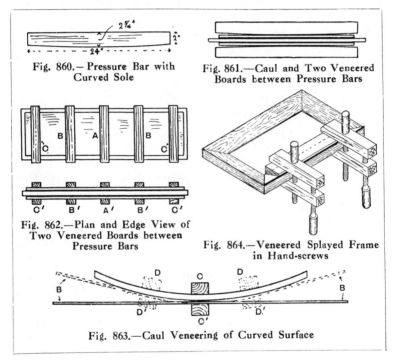

Fig. 860.— Pressure Bar with Curved Sole

Fig. 861.—Caul and Two Veneered Boards between Pressure Bars

Fig. 862.—Plan and Edge View of Two Veneered Boards between Pressure Bars

Fig. 864.—Veneered Splayed Frame in Hand-screws

Fig. 863.—Caul Veneering of Curved Surface

the glue is wet, in caul veneering, on the other hand, the wetness is allowed to disappear before the two are brought into contact. Both work and veneer are well coated and then left until the finger will not adhere to the glued surface. Should the veneer be applied before the glue reaches this condition, the two surfaces will seize immediately they come into contact and possibly before the veneer has been moved into its exact position. Put the first piece of work down on the bench, glued side uppermost, and place the veneer in position, holding it so with pins partly driven in. Then place a sheet or two of newspaper over the veneer and cover with the caul, which should have been raised to such a heat that the hand cannot comfortably bear it. Next comes more newspaper, and then the veneer, pinned in position on the second piece of work, which will therefore be face downwards. Place two cross-bars in position, one under and one over the work (*see* diagram, Fig. 861). In Fig. 862 A A′ are the first cross-bars to place in position. Tighten up the handscrews, and the curvature of the bar will cause the surplus glue to be squeezed out at the sides. Next add bars B B′ and then c c′, tightening up one by one, finally giving an extra turn to all the screws, and adding handscrews or cramps at the ends at the centres of the outer bars. In the arrangement shown by Fig. 862, five bars are indicated, but the actual number will depend upon the length of the work, the intervals between the bars being about 7 in. The work should be left cramped up in this way until the glue is hard, and should it be found that the paper has stuck to the veneer at any place it can easily be removed in the cleaning-up stage.

Curved Work with Cauls. — The operations for this will be exactly the same as just described for flat work, but the caul will be quite thin, say, $\frac{1}{4}$ in. or $\frac{3}{16}$ in. thick. In Fig. 863, A is a plan of the curved front of a drawer and B is the thin caul. c and c′ are bars about $\frac{3}{4}$ in. or 1 in. thick and $1\frac{1}{4}$ in. wide. The work is glued, allowed to chill, and in all other ways treated as already described. Handscrews are tightened across the bars c c′, then two pairs D D′ are applied one at each side of the first pair, and so on. Extra cramps can be applied at the edges if found desirable. It will be understood that Figs. 861 to 863 are mere diagrams, and not scale drawings.

To obviate the trouble and expense of making curved cauls, moulded work, etc., is sometimes veneered with the help of a " sandbag " which under pressure adapts itself to the shape of the work. A bag of strong calico is filled with silver sand, which has first been heated in an oven or on a sheet of iron over a fire or gas-stove ; the open end of the

bag is folded over two or three times and pinned, or it may
be rapidly sewn up. The work is prepared and carried
through as far as the application of the veneer in the manner
already described. It is covered with paper, the sandbag placed over it and pushed down with a stick into the
hollow places, turns, etc. Then come a number of pressure
bars so arranged that when the handscrews are applied the
sandbag is forced into contact with every part of the work.
Pressure is maintained for at least twelve hours. A safer
method is to place the sandbag in a long shallow box, the
veneer being on top of the bag instead of underneath it,
applying pressure to the work through the medium of a
stout board, very slightly shorter and narrower than the
box, which it can therefore enter under pressure.

Veneer Presses.—There is a considerable variety in the
forms of the presses used by veneerers. For a small, perfectly plain job, it would suffice to cover it with a true
smooth board and load with heavy weights, as already
explained, but this is an inconvenient and tiresome method
which could not be adopted for a large amount of work.
Simple cramps and handscrews are often made to serve;
see, for instance, Fig. 864, in which it will be noticed that
the caul is such a section that the parallel jaws of the handscrew can properly exert pressure on the work. Handscrews with adjustable jaws as illustrated on page 214
would be found useful for jobs of this sort. In the case of
curved moulding, a counterpart of it would require to be
made to serve as a caul, and the two may then be inserted
between the jaws of a number of handscrews. It will be
understood that in curved work generally the caul must
be a counterpart of the work itself, so that the two, work
and caul, make together a solid block, the top surface of
which is parallel with the bottom one.

The most convenient presses are screw-operated, as in
Figs. 865 and 866, the pressure-bar being of a rounded shape
so that the pressure is applied first at the middle of the
work. The amateur is not likely to go to the expense of
screw presses. Of course, for small work, he might adapt
a domestic press or a copying press to his requirements,

but they would be only makeshifts, and would be soon messed up with the glue. Still, a very large number of the veneering appliances in shop use are of the makeshift order. The arrangement shown in Fig. 867 has proved useful; it is simply a rough, strong box, without ends, strengthened with hoop-iron as indicated in the cross-section. Strips of wood are laid inside the box; the work, face upwards, is laid on these; and wide strips are brought into close contact with the work by means of the struts c, which are forced into position and moved gradually from the middle of the work towards the sides and then left until the glue is hard. Pins, and possibly handscrews, will be needed at the ends of the veneer. A wedge press can be made without difficulty, examples being shown in Figs. 868 and 869. The bars D are housed into ends E and secured by nails. There may be tiers of bars so that one press can accommodate two, three, or four pieces of work at once; in Fig. 868 the two pieces of work, placed face to face and separated by a piece of paper and covered with boards, have pressure exerted on them by the folding wedges c. In Fig. 869 there is a series of single presses at intervals of a foot or so along the veneered board w. Scores of other patterns of presses are in use.

Veneering Cylindrical Work.—An apparatus for rotating the veneered cylinder, shaft, etc., is required, and may consist of a board longer than the work, with two pieces of stuff attached at right angles and having dowels—like the centres of a lathe—to support the work. Holes to receive the dowels must be made in the work, and one of the dowels is removable to allow of the work being inserted. The glue is applied and allowed to chill. Then one edge of the veneer is pinned in place, and the work slowly rotated (anticlockwise, towards the worker) while the hands press the veneer into contact with the ground. Eventually, the veneer will be in contact with the whole of the cylinder, and the overlapping edges must be pinned down. Then a length of webbing is tacked on at one end of the cylinder, and the work rotated so as to wind the webbing tightly around it in a spiral direction, the end being tacked down. The work

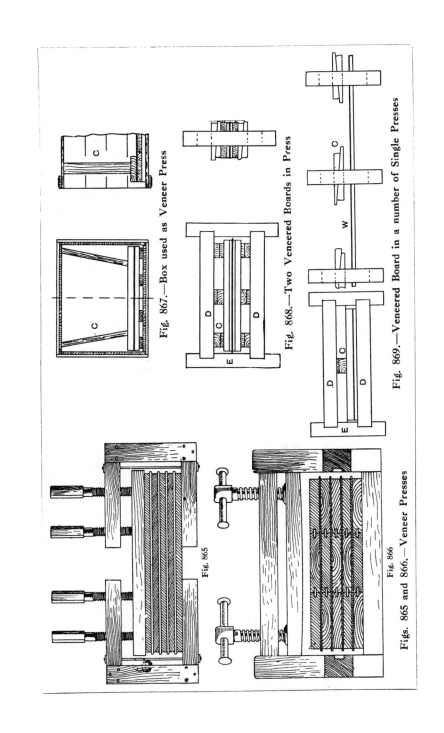

Fig. 867.—Box used as Veneer Press

Fig. 868.—Two Veneered Boards in Press

Fig. 869.—Veneered Board in a number of Single Presses

Fig. 865

Fig. 866

Figs. 865 and 866.—Veneer Presses

is next revolved over a fire so as to melt the glue, and the
webbing then thoroughly wetted, the contraction forcing
out some of the glue. Heating and wetting are repeated,
and the work allowed to dry, when the overlapping parts
of the veneer as well as the thickness beneath it are cut
through with a keen knife guided by a straightedge, and
the waste removed by wetting, heating, and slightly lifting
on edge.   Then a little glue is rubbed in and the joint pressed
close with a hammer. Finishing with scraper and glasspaper will render the joint almost imperceptible.

Veneer Inlaying.—The use of veneer is a means of obtaining some beautiful inlay effects. By one method, the design
is set out full size on paper, the pieces of veneer are cut
with the fretsaw to the shape required, fitted together to
form the design, and glued direct to the paper pattern,
glue being also worked into the joints between the veneers.
Another piece of paper is glued over the face of the veneer
design, and the whole is cramped between two pieces of
board until the glue is dry.   The paper at the back on which
the design was originally laid is stripped off, and the inlay
placed in position of the groundwork, next scribing round
the edges with a steel point.   The wood in the groundwork must next be cut away to receive the inlay, working
exactly to the scribed line. The cutting is accomplished
with chisels and gouges, and a router (Fig. 870) would also
be found most useful in removing the surplus wood. The
recess should be slightly undercut as in Fig. 871, and the
effect shown by Fig. 872 should be carefully avoided. The
inlay, paper upwards, is then glued in position, and cramped
until the glue is set, when the surface paper is cleaned off
by scraping and glasspapering.

Marquetry.—In this process two or more sheets of
veneer of different woods are glued together with the pattern
set out on the uppermost one and the design cut out with
a fretsaw, the sections then being separated and the design
rebuilt with certain of the woods interchanged in parts of
the design. Thus a draughtboard pattern could be formed
of two sheets, one of ebony or other dark wood and one of
holly. A simple marquetry pattern is shown in Figs. 873 and

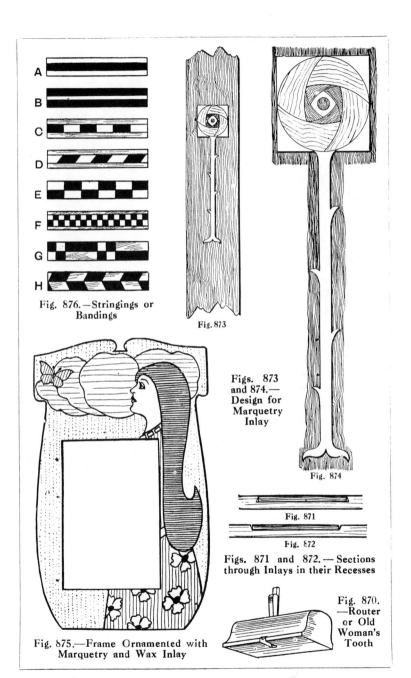

A

B

C

D

E

F

G

H

Fig. 876.—Stringings or Bandings

Fig. 873

Figs. 873 and 874.— Design for Marquetry Inlay

Fig. 874

Fig. 871

Fig. 872

Figs. 871 and 872. — Sections through Inlays in their Recesses

Fig. 870. —Router or Old Woman's Tooth

Fig. 875.—Frame Ornamented with Marquetry and Wax Inlay

874. The two sheets are glued together with a piece of paper between them. Indeed, several layers of veneer can be cut together if the design is in several woods, great accuracy of fitting being obtainable by this means. Fig. 875 gives a pattern in which the features could be executed in wax, by first ·incising them with a pointed tool and afterwards filling the depressions with sealing wax of the colour preferred, finishing the work with a keen scraper. All colours of sealing wax are obtainable. Brass, pewter, or other metals are sometimes incorporated in a marquetry design, in which case it is often called buhl work.

Stringings and Bandings.—These are geometrical-patterned bands of various widths, a series of single forms of which are given in Fig. 876 ; they are cut as thin as $\frac{1}{32}$ in., and are sold very cheaply. Their chief use is for bordering panels and for building up patterns, such as shown by Figs. 877 and 878. Straight bands, alternating light and dark, are made by gluing pieces together of the required thickness, to make the necessary width, as shown at A (Fig. 879), putting them under weights or screw-pressure between boards to harden thoroughly, and afterwards sawing into strips at right angles to the lines of the joints, the strips being finished with a smoothing plane. In example c (Fig. 876) narrow strips alternating light and dark are glued between a top and bottom layer c (Fig. 879) ; the edges of the strips in example D are planed to obtain the slope ; in example E (Fig. 876) the easiest method is to glue up a series of strips of square section, as shown at E (Fig. 879), and then saw down in the *width*, gluing together again with the upper board moved along one (*see* E'). This is one method of making draughtboards, a series of strips being glued as shown at J and then sawn across, each alternate strip being moved a space in gluing down to the foundation (*see* K). Examples F, G, H (Fig. 876) are produced similarly, one of the boards in the latter being turned round after sawing through, besides being moved along so as to obtain the slope of the lower portion of the pattern in the opposite direction to the other.

Innumerable geometrical patterns may be built up with

stringings, two simple ones being shown in Figs. 877 and 878. The first process in making is to set out the pattern on the wood with square and compasses, taking especial care that the angles at the joints are accurate. In both the patterns given all the mitres will be at an angle of 45°, so after having obtained the length of any particular portion, strike a line across the stringing with a set-square, and saw through

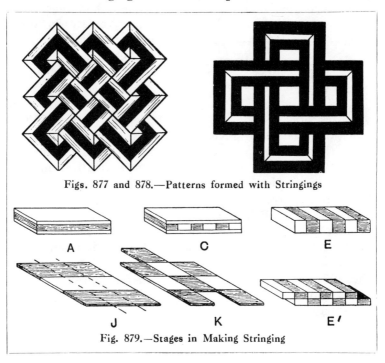

Figs. 877 and 878.—Patterns formed with Stringings

Fig. 879.—Stages in Making Stringing

with a small very fine backed saw specially sold for such work. After the outlines have been cut and fitted together on the pattern, the hollow to receive it needs to be cut out in the board. The scratch stock used in cutting narrow grooves for inlaying fine stringing is shown in Fig. 880. The tool is worked away from the operator, and, in the early strokes, it is important that it be kept at right angles to the side of the board, and that the guide is kept flush with the panel edge, as otherwise the blade will scratch the surface of the wood in wrong places, and so spoil it. When a channel is too wide to be cut in this manner, the best procedure is to use a cutting gauge with two blades to cut down the outside edges, and then chisel out the waste between, smoothing the ground with a router.

The companion work· " Furniture Making " contains a number of beautiful designs for inlaid drawer fronts, panels, etc., and also for stringings and bandings.

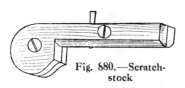

Fig. 880.—Scratch-stock

Colour Variety in Inlays. —Variety of colour in veneer inlays should, as far as possible, be obtained by using the naturally coloured woods. Sandal, purple, and the many varieties of rosewood supply a selection of reds. There is a tulip wood that gives a pink. Russian oak, amboyna, yew, thuya burrs, and various kinds of mahogany give browns. Plane tree wood, of a light-speckled brown, makes a fine combination with satinwood. American walnut gives brown of a purplish tinge, English walnut brown with black streaks, and French and Italian a brown of a colder tint. Snakewood is of a rich reddish brown. Satinwood gives bright yellows ; ebony and coromandel, the latter with dark brown stripes, gives blacks ; holly, white ; and sycamore, chestnut, and boxwood supply colours approximating to flesh colour. See also the exhaustive list of woods on later pages.

CHAPTER XXVII

A Few Varied Examples of Woodwork

WHILST there is no space in this book in which to give a wide range of examples which a reader who has mastered the earlier chapters could construct for himself, and whilst, as far as furniture is concerned, a companion volume, " Furniture Making," thoroughly covers the ground and gives many hundreds of drawings and working details, it has yet been thought desirable to find room in this and the following chapter for about a dozen different examples upon which the woodworker can try his 'prentice hand. They have been chosen for their simplicity, utility, and diversity.

Bookshelves for a Recess.—A simple way of fitting up a recess between fireplace and wall with shelving is shown in Fig. 881. Two 8-in. boards are placed flat against each wall, with shelves of the same material between, the latter having been carefully cut to make a tight fit and thus act as stretchers. The whole structure is easily portable, requires no nailing, and shelves can be readily added as the stock of books, etc., increases. Measurements will depend entirely upon individual requirements. The material should be selected, 8-in. by 1-in. deal boards, carefully planed up on both sides. The two side uprights have each a chamfered strip of $1\frac{1}{2}$-in. stuff screwed on across their inner faces at a distance below their top edges equal to the thickness of a shelf, as shown in Fig. 882 ; they should then be laid side by side and marked off for the positions of the shelves. The distance between shelves for ordinary books might be $9\frac{1}{2}$ in., but $11\frac{1}{2}$-in. at least should be allowed between the two top shelves to accommodate large volumes. Below, and close up to the marked position of each shelf, two peg holes should be bored with a centre-bit, as shown in Fig. 883 ; holes should be bored to take as many shelves

333

as the length of the sides will permit, irrespective of present requirements, so that additional shelves can be easily added as needed. The pegs are cut from round ½-in. dowel sticks, and should fit the holes tightly, go in the full thickness of the upright, project out about ¾ in., and have a shoulder

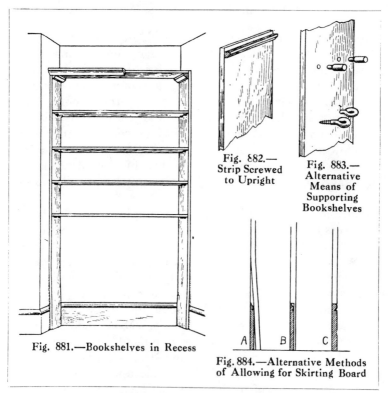

Fig. 882.—
Strip Screwed
to Upright

Fig. 883.—
Alternative
Means of
Supporting
Bookshelves

Fig. 881.—Bookshelves in Recess

Fig. 884.—Alternative Methods
of Allowing for Skirting Board

as shown in Fig. 883, though the latter is not essential. An alternative to the peg method of supporting the shelves is also shown, stout screw-eyes taking the place of the pegs ; but in this case care must be taken that the screw does not go right through the board or damage will be done to the wall. In cutting the shelves it is very important to see that they make a square and tight fit between the uprights, as the rigidity of the structure depends on their forcing the sides flat against the wall. The skirting of the

room can be allowed for by any of the methods indicated
in Fig. 884. Sometimes the " play " in the board will allow
the skirting to be disregarded, and the upright run down
to rest on the floor, as at A; or a piece can be cut out
of the thickness, as at B; or, if the skirting presents a
suitable ledge, the sides can rest on that, as at C. Finally,

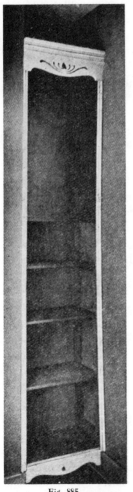 

Fig. 885   Fig. 886

Figs. 885 and 886.—Recess Shelving with Roller Blind

a piece of moulding can be screwed to the front edge of the topmost shelf, as partly shown in Fig. 1, and the whole either stained and varnished or painted or enamelled.

Recess Shelving with Roller Blind.—An alternative arrangement of bookshelves in a recess without permanent fixing is shown in the photographs (Figs. 885 and 886). The shelves may be completely covered in with a spring blind, which will keep out dust. The recess in which these shelves were fitted was 2 ft. 3 in. wide and 1 ft. deep, but the same details of construction will answer for any ordinary width of opening. If the room is not a lofty one, the cornice may go right up to the ceiling, but in many cases it would be better at about the same height as the picture rail. For the two side frameworks or racks that lie flat one against the walls, prepare four battens, each 3 in. wide by $\frac{3}{4}$ in. thick, and in length according to requirements. On one edge of each batten cut notches, as in Fig. 887, to within 10 in. of each end, for the reception of the bearers that support the shelves. To expedite the cutting and ensure the bearers being interchangeable, brad the four battens together and set out the notches 2 in. apart. Run a pencil line down each side $\frac{5}{8}$ in. from the edge, and make a series of saw-cuts to the line. Then pare down with the chisel from the top of one cut to the bottom of the next, taking care not to split off the succeeding piece. The battens should now be taken apart and both ends of each pair connected with pieces 6 in. wide by $\frac{3}{4}$ in. thick, dovetail-keyed to the battens as shown in Fig. 888, the effect being to make two long rectangular frames; and in order to receive a false top, a $\frac{1}{2}$-in. groove or housing should be cut horizontally $4\frac{1}{2}$ in. from the top end of each pair and the full width of the framing.

For fitting the spring blind, the racks should be temporarily fixed in position against the walls and the false top fitted in the groove. The blind runs down the front edges of the racks, and to allow a clearance for the ends of the roller the front of the top of the racks should be cut away and the metal seatings to receive the roller centres sunk to the required depth, as shown in Fig. 889. To form the groove on each side for the blind to work in, nail a $\frac{1}{2}$-in. by $\frac{1}{4}$-in. rounded fillet on the inside edge of the rack as at B in the section (Fig. 890), and to also a rebated length of moulding C on the front edge to cover the whole and to give a good appearance on the front.

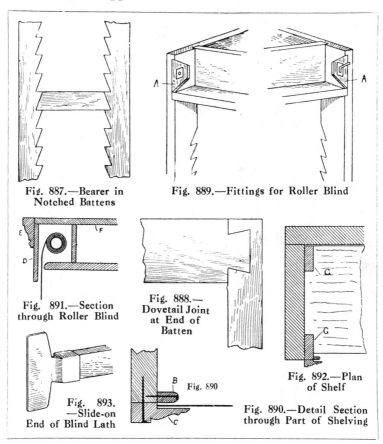

Fig. 887.—Bearer in Notched Battens

Fig. 889.—Fittings for Roller Blind

Fig. 891.—Section through Roller Blind

Fig. 888.—Dovetail Joint at End of Batten

Fig. 892.—Plan of Shelf

Fig. 893.—Slide-on End of Blind Lath

Fig. 890.—Detail Section through Part of Shelving

The cornice rests on the two side mouldings (*see* Fig. 885), and consists of a 6-in. by $\frac{3}{8}$-in. shaped and fretted face-board D with a 3-in. moulding E planted on $\frac{1}{2}$ in. above the top edge of D, thus forming a rebate in which the dust-board F is fixed (*see* the section, Fig. 891). The shelves are $\frac{5}{8}$-in. stuff, and the ends should be notched as at G (Fig.

W

892) to allow them to pass easily through the racks. The plinth is shaped from a 4-in. board, and is only temporarily hung on two blocks fixed to the skirting boards on each side to allow of cleaning beneath the shelves. To facilitate the easy running of the blind it should be fitted at the bottom edge with a wood lath, the projecting ends of which are provided with metal slides that run in the grooves at each side. These slides can be easily cut from a piece of sheet brass or tin and bent round the lath as in Fig. 893. Shop-window blind material will answer for the blind, the colour being chosen to harmonise with the wallpaper or furniture. The external woodwork may be polished, enamelled, etc.

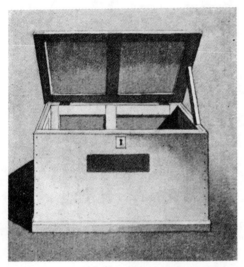

Fig. 894.—Clothes-box in Three-ply Wood

Clothes - box in Three-ply.—As an example to show the advantages that can be gained by the use of three-ply wood, a strong and useful light box (Fig. 894) is here described.

Make a skeleton frame of $2\frac{1}{2}$ in. wide by $\frac{3}{4}$ in. thick planed strips. The front and back are 2 ft. 10 in. long and 1 ft. 10 in. deep, the two ends being 1 ft. 10 in. square. Figs. 895 and 896 show the front and one end framed up respectively, the joints being halved together. The front top rail has a piece added where the lock is fitted, for strength. This is halved over the middle upright, as in Fig. 898, and nailed to the under side of the top rail. It is best to fit the lock before screwing the framework together. The middle rails of the ends receive the screws of the handles. When screwing the frames together put five $\frac{5}{8}$-in. screws in

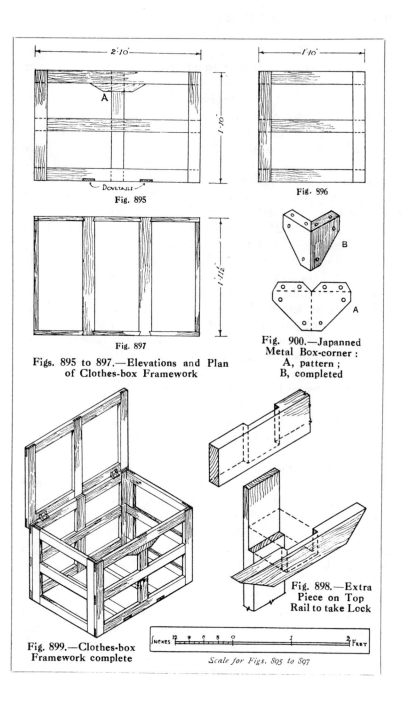

2'·10"

A

DOVETAILS

Fig. 895

1'·10"

1'·10"

Fig. 896

1'·11½"

Fig. 897

Figs. 895 to 897.—Elevations and Plan
of Clothes-box Framework

B

A

Fig. 900.—Japanned
Metal Box-corner :
A, pattern ;
B, completed

Fig. 898.—Extra
Piece on Top
Rail to take Lock

Fig. 899.—Clothes-box
Framework complete

INCHES 12 9 6 3 0 1 2 FEET

Scale for Figs. 895 to 897

each joint, making sure the joints fit tight. Nail the front and back frames on the framed ends with 2-in. oval wire nails. Then to receive the bottom get two rails 1 ft. 11½ in. long, and dovetail into the bottom rails at equal distances as shown in Fig. 897. Now cut a piece of three-ply for the bottom, 2 ft. 10 in. by 1 ft. 11½ in., and nail it on, using 1-in. fine wire nails. Nail well round the edges and to the rails. Then cut and nail the two ends, and finally the front and back, rubbing off all sharp edges with coarse glasspaper. Next frame a lid together to fit the top of the box, making it a little larger all round ; nail on the three-ply, fit a pair of 2½-in. steel butt hinges, and screw on the lock. The completed framework is shown by Fig. 899.

All that is now required is a chamfered strip 1½ in. by ½ in. round the bottom of the box, and if desired round the edges of the lid, two sides and front, and also two pieces nailed across the underside to take the rubbing off the three-ply bottom. Japanned box corners (Fig. 900) are a great improvement, and can be bought or made up from sheet metal. In driving home the nails a good appearance is obtained if they are placed at equal distances.

Lattice-framed Step-ladder.—Among the many kinds of steps in use for the house and shop the type shown by Fig. 901 is the lightest and cheapest to make ; in the case of the larger steps for shop use, the reduction in weight is an important matter. Less material is required ; but having a greater number of small pieces, there is, of course, more labour entailed in the making. The greater rigidity and strength is obtained by the triangular method of framing, which is carried out not only in the making of the three separate frames of which the steps are composed, but also in the method of connecting them with one another when stood ready for use. They fold together in compact form, and have the advantage that no hinges or ropes are necessary in the construction.

If deal is used, it must be of good quality ; birch is generally used for the larger sizes, although almost any kind of reliable wood could be used. The sizes of the material in width and thickness given in the illustrations are for a pair of steps about 5 ft. high, and of yellow deal. If hard-wood is used, the sizes should be slightly diminished for the same height of steps. These dimensions should only be slightly increased for steps of greater height.

An important practical point, when all the pieces are prepared for fixing, is the method of screw-ing. It will be noticed that most of the screws are fixed in suffi-ciently far enough away from the ends of the various pieces to avoid splitting. There is great strain on the screws when the steps are in use, so that the steps are designed to give sufficient strength to the screw fastenings. As already ex-

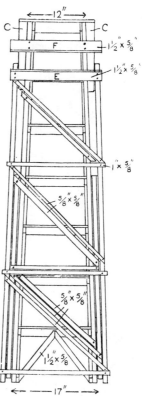

Fig. 902.—Back Elevation of Step-ladder Closed

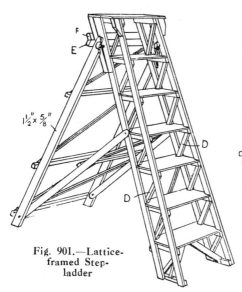

Fig. 901.—Lattice-framed Step-ladder

plained, a screw should fit freely in the piece of wood next to the screw head. This hole for the body of the screw should be bored with a shell-bit or spoon-bit and countersunk for the head. The hole in the piece beneath is bored with a gimlet, and should be small enough to allow the thread of the screw to cut its full depth. The screw then acts as a cramp which gets its pressure between the head and thread of the screw. When finally screwing together, the parts could be glued for extra rigidity, although this is not essential. All the screws are No. 10 in size and of 1-in., 1¼-in., and 1½-in. length.

Fig. 901 is a perspective view of the steps ready for use, and Fig. 902 is a view from the back when folded up. To make the height about 5 ft. when used, the pieces A should be 5 ft. 7½ in. long when they are cut off at the required angle, and placed as shown in Fig. 904. This is an angle of about 70°, and can be obtained by setting the bevel to a triangle as in Fig. 905, where the height is twice the length of the base. Set out the length into seven equal spaces of 9½ in., and mark lines with the bevel as shown. These pieces are 2¾ in. apart, measured at right angles as indicated. Now screw on fillets of 1-in. by ½-in. material B, with their upper edges coinciding with these lines, on the inner sides of pieces A, and cut off the ends after fixing as indicated. These seven fillets receive the treads, but another fillet is fixed on each frame to stiffen the lower ends. These fillets are also useful for bracing the lower tread.

The bottom part of the steps is 1 ft. 5 in. wide, and the top 12 in. Next prepare the material for the treads, which are 5¾ in. wide and ½ in. thick, and cut them off in length to the outside width of the steps. A good plan is to fit the bottom tread and the second tread at the top, cut to the shape shown in Fig. 903, and fasten into the fillets with two screws at each end. Then mark and cut off for the intermediate treads. The back edges of the treads are then planed level, and the corners in front finished off flush with a chisel. The top tread is longer, projecting over each side 1¼ in. ; it is left in its rectangular form and screwed into the fillets on the tops of the side rails. Two long fillets 1 ft. 5 in. long, of 1-in. material, are tapered off from 1¼ in. wide at the top down to ⅝ in. wide at the lower end ; these are screwed at the top on the back fillets as shown at c in Fig. 902. The back frame has a pair of catch plates that slide on these fillets when the steps are opened, so care must be taken to see that they are parallel on the outside. Two small blocks are also fitted and screwed in front of these on the front rails underneath the top tread. The small brace pieces D (Fig. 901) are ¾ in. by ½ in., and are fitted underneath the fillet B in front and on top of

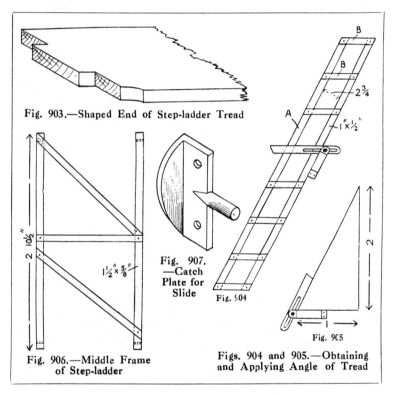

Fig. 903.—Shaped End of Step-ladder Tread

Fig. 907.—Catch Plate for Slide

Fig. 904.

Fig. 905.

Fig. 906.—Middle Frame of Step-ladder

Figs. 904 and 905.—Obtaining and Applying Angle of Tread

the tread at the back. Two struts are fitted underneath the bottom tread as shown.

Fig. 902 shows the back frame with the long sides of 1½-in. by ⅝-in. material placed edgewise; but the width cannot be obtained until the middle frame is riveted on to the side rails A 3 ft. from the foot of the steps. The side pieces or rails of the middle frame, as shown in Fig. 906, are first riveted on to the back frame at the lower end about 2 in. from the ground. The rivets require to be about

$\frac{5}{16}$ in. in diameter and washers should be used. It will be noticed that the rails of the middle frame do not touch the ground when the steps are closed together (*see* Fig. 902), and the back frame must not be longer than the steps at the bottom when closed together.

The bars and braces are fixed on to the back frame first. The top and bottom bars are of $1\frac{1}{2}$-in. by $\frac{5}{8}$-in. material, the top bar E being bevelled on the top edge and fixed with four screws, this being the bar that takes the thrust from the top bar F at the back of the steps. The middle bars are 1 in. by $\frac{5}{8}$ in. and the braces $\frac{5}{8}$ in. square. When these are

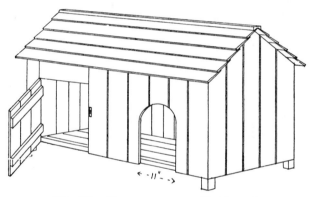

Fig. 908.—Two-compartment Dog-kennel

fixed, close the steps and fix the bars and braces on to the middle frame, sufficient to clear the other pieces already fixed. Two braces could also be fixed on the back of the steps for extra strength, and arranged in between as shown in Fig. 902. Fig. 907 shows the shape of the catch plates that are fixed on top of the frame so as to clip behind the taper fillets c. Finally, open the steps to the right distance and mark the top of the bar E. Then prepare the bar F to $1\frac{1}{2}$ in. by $\frac{5}{8}$ in., bevel it to fit, and fix with four screws.

Two - compartment Dog - kennel.—The kennel illustrated by Fig. 908 is different from the usual kind. It is warmer, having a second compartment when required, and is more convenient for cleaning purposes, because of the door constructed at the back end of the kennel. Felt is used inside the kennel underneath the roof boards for extra warmth.   Deal matching $\frac{3}{4}$ in. thick is the most suitable boarding to use.   The tongue-and-groove joints allow for any shrinkage or expansion of the boarding, and keep the kennel weather-tight from rain and draughts.   Matching having a V-joint should be chosen, and narrow battens

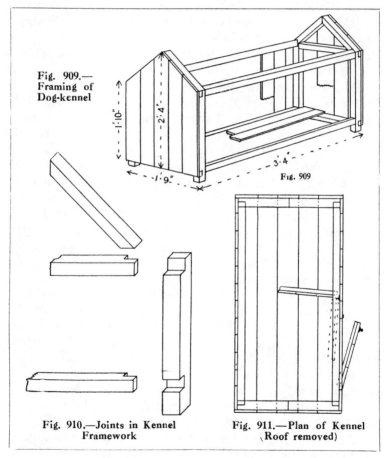

Fig. 909.—Framing of Dog-kennel

Fig. 909

Fig. 910.—Joints in Kennel Framework

Fig. 911.—Plan of Kennel (Roof removed)

of 5 in. or 7 in. wide are more suitable than the wider boards. When using boards for external purposes, they should be fixed so that the rain cannot penetrate in the joints, and if the matching is fixed horizontally, the tongue should be on the upper edge and the groove on the lower edge of the board ; but it is generally the better plan to arrange the boarding vertically as shown in Fig. 908. Feather-edge boards are, of course, an exception. These are always fixed horizontally, being made rainproof by one lapping over the other as shown for the roof of the kennel. All boards should be thoroughly dry for use, so as to prevent any undue shrinkage after the kennel is built. The floorboards should be arranged 2 in. or 3 in. above the ground, to prevent the dampness rising, and two or three slots should be made in the floor for drainage when cleaning.

Fig. 909 shows the skeleton framing of the kennel. The four corner posts are 2 in. square, and all the other pieces are $1\frac{1}{2}$ in. square. The joints are chiefly lapped as shown on the end frames, and the four long rails are secured with long screws through these joints on to the ends of the rails. The top pieces are simply splayed and nailed. Fig. 910 shows the method of making the joints before fixing together. Now fit and fasten with nails the back and the end boards, as indicated in Fig. 909, leaving the front open. Then fit in half of the front, and mark the entrance or doorway with the compasses and straight-edge. Take apart and cut to the shape with a bow-saw and spokeshave ; then refix.

The door is arranged to hinge on to a piece of match-boarding nailed on at the end of the kennel, and another piece 2 in. or 3 in. wide is fixed above the door and flush with the boarding. The door, which is made of matching fastened with battens as shown in Fig. 908, shuts against the bottom rail of the kennel, and is fastened with a button. The floorboards, which are $\frac{3}{4}$ in. thick, are then fixed length-wise, so that the ends can be nailed to the lower rails of the end frames (see Fig. 909).

The arrangement for a partial compartment is then made by hinging on a partition constructed the same as the door. It is fastened with butt hinges, and swings out of the way against the outer door when not required. A small bolt is fastened on so as to fix the partition to the floor when required. Fig. 911 shows the plan of the kennel before the roof is nailed on, with the partition as required, or swung back out of the way.

The feather-edge boarding for the top is cut so as to overhang 3 in. at each end. The lower boards, which over-hang about 2 in. at the front and back, are nailed on first, and the other boards overlap about 1 in. or more until the top is reached. Allow the two top boards to butt one on the other, and fasten with brads. A piece of wood is then

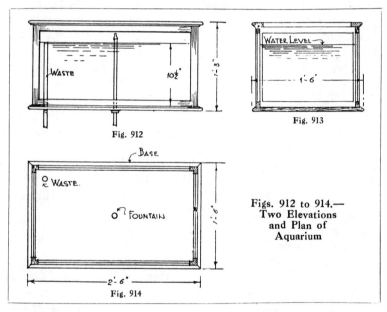

Fig. 912

Fig. 913

Figs. 912 to 914.—
Two Elevations
and Plan of
Aquarium

Fig. 914

rebated to fit, and nailed along the top. The kennel is then ready to receive two or three coats of paint.

Wood - framed Aquarium. — An easily constructed aquarium is shown by Figs. 912 to 914. One of the best woods to employ would be well-seasoned teak, which is pre-eminently damp-resisting, and also quite suitable for working to the small dimensions required for the frame. The bottom is $\frac{3}{4}$ in. thick, and in two or more widths tongued or dowelled together, moulded on the edge, and grooved on the upper face to receive the tongue of the bottom rail as shown in Fig. 916. The framing forming the sides is

composed of bars grooved for polished plate glass, and
mitred together as shown in Figs. 915 and 916. Each piece
of the top and bottom rails is tongued on the edge and
has tenons, $\frac{1}{2}$ in. by $\frac{1}{4}$ in. and as long as possible, mortised
into the stiles, as in Fig. 917. The glass should be cut
to the exact size and fitted and fixed in position, previous to the framing being glued up. After being glued
together, the whole should be allowed to stand for two
days until the glue is hard. The glass is then bedded in
with a composition of white-lead, red-lead, and gold-size
in about equal parts, which is an excellent aquarium
cement.

The sides and ends should then be fitted together, the
joints being painted with a thin coat of the composition
made more liquid by the addition of linseed oil. The whole
of the framed work can then be put together, the joints
tightened by means of brass screws, and the face cleaned
off level. When the tongues have been fitted to suit the
grooves in the bottom, the latter should be covered with
No. 14 gauge zinc, and a hole cut through the centre to
allow the tube which supplies the fountain to pass through.
A hole in an angle, through which the tube for the waste
passes, should also be formed.

The sides of the aquarium may now be secured to the
bottom. Well cover the zinc, groove and tongue with some
cement, and draw up the joint tight with screws from the
under side. The top rim (Fig. 916) is moulded on the outer
edge, slightly rounded on the inner edge, mitred at the
angles, and secured with round-headed screws to the top
rail. The outer faces can be blacked with stain and polished,
the inside faces being painted with bath enamel, or the
teak framework may be left in its natural colour and french-
polished.

The tubes for the fountain and waste pipe are secured
to the bottom with back nuts as in Fig. 918, the tubes being
threaded for the purpose. The fountain may be supplied
from an overhead cistern kept filled with river water. When
the metal parts, including the zinc bottom, have been fitted
and fixed they should be enamelled, and must, of course,

be allowed to stand until quite hard before the aquarium
is used.

A Wheelbarrow.—The greatest drawback to the ordinary
wheelbarrow is that more than half the weight of the load

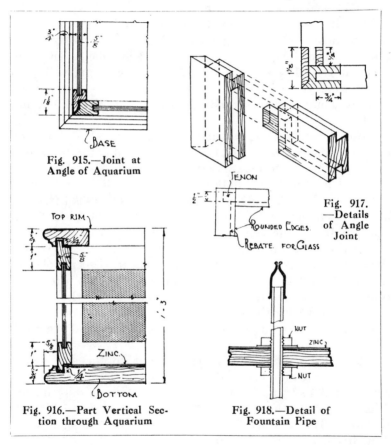

Fig. 915.—Joint at
Angle of Aquarium

Fig. 917.
—Details
of Angle
Joint

Fig. 916.—Part Vertical Section through Aquarium

Fig. 918.—Detail of
Fountain Pipe

and barrow are borne by the arms and shoulders of the
user. The wheelbarrow shown in side elevation by Fig. 919
is much easier to handle, and therefore very suitable for
female farm-workers and gardeners and amateurs generally,
the greater part of the load being carried over the wheel,
thus taking much of the weight off the arms. The barrow
is also shorter than an ordinary one, and narrow enough

to pass through a 2-ft. 6-in. doorway, this, together with the deep sides, being desirable features for stable use. Figs. 920 and 921 are back and front elevations respectively. Fig. 922 is a plan as seen from underneath, and Fig. 923 is a sectional elevation of the body.

The frame should be of oak or ash, and the panels and bottom boards of elm or good red deal. The two strines A are 4 ft. 1 in. long by $2\frac{3}{4}$ in. deep by 2 in. thick ; the two sloats B 1 ft. $10\frac{1}{2}$ in. and 1 ft. $7\frac{3}{4}$ in. long respectively by $2\frac{5}{8}$ in. wide by $1\frac{1}{8}$ in. thick ; two legs C 2 ft. $2\frac{1}{2}$ in. long by 2 in. by 2 in. ; and two standards D 1 ft. $8\frac{1}{2}$ in. long by $1\frac{1}{2}$ in. by $1\frac{3}{8}$ in.

The terms " strine " denoting the main side members or soles, and " sloat " or slot, also " sword " for the cross rails, are trade terms understood by wheelwrights, and are used by the large timber merchants.

The width of the bottom frame over the strines is 1 ft. 3 in. at the front, and 1 ft. 9 in. at the back of the hind sloat. The length on the centre line of the plan, from the front end of the strines to the front sloat, is 1 ft. $0\frac{3}{4}$ in. ; over the sloats 1 ft. $3\frac{1}{2}$ in. ; from the hind sloat to the end of the handles 1 ft. 8 in. The strines and sloats are let into each other $\frac{1}{4}$ in. so that the latter stand $\frac{5}{8}$ in. above the former to come level with the top of the bottom boards, which run crosswise between the sloats, the frame being fixed together with $\frac{5}{16}$-in. bolts.

The legs and standards are got out to the side splay obtained from Fig. 924, and is 5 in. in 1 ft. $5\frac{1}{2}$ in. The legs are tapered to $1\frac{3}{4}$ in. by $1\frac{3}{4}$ in. at the bottom, and $1\frac{3}{4}$ in. by $\frac{7}{8}$ in. at the top, the standards also tapering to $\frac{7}{8}$ in. thick at the top. The legs are fixed to the face of the strines with $\frac{3}{8}$-in. bolts, and the standards with $\frac{5}{16}$-in. bolts.

When setting out the side panels, the length of the various sections should be taken from the side line on the plan, and the height or width of the board from the side-splay line (Fig. 924). The panels are all $\frac{3}{4}$ in. thick, the back panel E, 11 in. wide, being housed $\frac{3}{16}$ in. into the side panels and nailed in position, being strengthened with corner plates at the top. The raised front is fixed to $1\frac{1}{8}$-in.

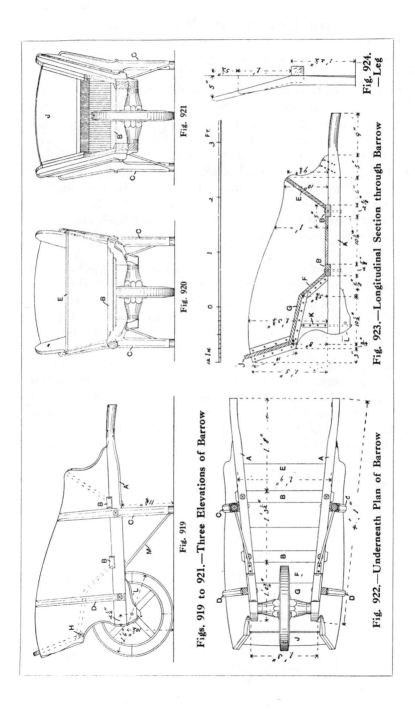

Fig. 921

Fig. 920

Fig. 919

Figs. 919 to 921.—Three Elevations of Barrow

Fig. 924.—Leg

Fig. 923.—Longitudinal Section through Barrow

Fig. 922.—Underneath Plan of Barrow

by $\frac{5}{8}$-in. fillets screwed to the side panels, the board F being
$\frac{5}{8}$ in. thick, and the other one G $\frac{3}{4}$ in. thick.   A $\frac{5}{16}$-in. long-
bolt H extends across the front of the body, underneath the
board G, embracing the side panels, to resist inside pressure.   The front panel J, 10$\frac{1}{2}$ in. wide, slides between fillets,
and can be taken out to facilitate tipping the load.   This
panel should be battened at the back to prevent its splitting.
At the front, a half-round strap-bolt K is fixed to the inner
side of the side panels with screws, the bolt taking the
front end of the strines and trunnion blocks.   The trunnion
blocks L are 10 in. by 2$\frac{1}{4}$ in. by 2 in., their back ends being
fixed with screws, and the trunnion holes lined with iron
tubing.

The legs are strengthened with stays M of $\frac{7}{16}$-in. round
iron, the lower end being welded to the hoop on the leg.

The wheel is best bought from a professional wheelwright.   It is 1 ft. 6 in. high " in the wood "—that is,
without the tyre ; nave, 1 ft. long by 3$\frac{1}{2}$ in. by 3$\frac{1}{2}$ in. ;   one
spoke, 3$\frac{1}{4}$ in. by 1$\frac{1}{4}$ in. ;   and the other one 1$\frac{1}{4}$ in. by 1$\frac{1}{4}$ in. ;
felloes, 2$\frac{1}{4}$ in. by 2$\frac{1}{4}$ in. ;   tyre, 1$\frac{3}{4}$ in. by $\frac{5}{16}$ in. ;   trunnions
of $\frac{5}{8}$-in. iron.   The wide spoke is mortised through the
centre of the nave and the square spoke at right angles,
the wide spoke being then dressed to 1$\frac{1}{4}$ in. in width at
the ends.   The tangs at the ends of the spokes should be
$\frac{7}{8}$ in. in diameter.

CHAPTER XXVIII

Some Outdoor Structures

Pigeon House and Aviary.—The pigeon house shown by Fig. 925 will accommodate about two dozen birds. The sizes and the dimensions of the several timbers are given in Figs. 926 to 930, the general framework being of 3-in. by 3-in. and 3-in. by 2-in. stuff. The larger sections should be employed for the sills A (Fig. 927) and angle-posts, the former being halved together and secured to stakes driven into the ground, while the latter are tenoned through the halved angles. The intermediate framing is all 3 in. by 2 in., and comprises two uprights on the front, B and C, with their 2-in. faces showing as at D in Fig. 929, a front head and rail E and F (Fig. 928), both set flat; two back uprights and a head, arranged as at G in Fig. 929, and H in Fig. 928, so that the boarding can be continued over them flush with the angle-posts; and back and side rails as at I and J in Figs. 926 and 928. All these should be halved where they cross as at K in Fig. 927, and either halved or preferably mortised and tenoned at their ends. Four sets of 2-in. by 2-in. rafters will complete the framing, two pairs, spaced $\frac{3}{4}$ in. back from the angle-posts, as at L in Fig. 927, to allow for the boarding of the ends, and the others as at M and N in Fig. 929. At the top they should be halved, as in Fig. 931, while the joint between an end rafter and the angle-post and head is explained by Fig. 932. In this the tenon of the head is " shouldered " or kept up from the bottom a little in order to avoid cutting away too much of the thin portion of the rafter. The intermediates can be merely splayed to fit the horizontal heads (Fig. 928).

Matched and V-jointed boarding, $\frac{3}{4}$ in. thick, will be suitable for the spaces between the posts and the rails. At each side of the trap the boarding is nailed to ledges and hung to the posts with cross-garnets, thus affording a convenient arrangement for cleaning out and also for access to the nests. The boarding for the roof and floor should be about ¾ in. thick, the former being felted in due course. Sufficient light can be admitted by a small opening filled in with ground glass or wire netting at each end as shown.

Fig. 925.—Pigeon House and Aviary

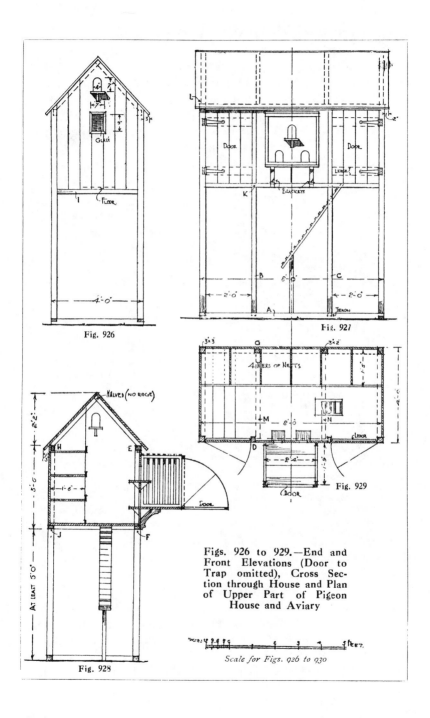

Fig. 926

Fig. 927

Fig. 929

Fig. 928

Figs. 926 to 929.—End and Front Elevations (Door to Trap omitted), Cross Section through House and Plan of Upper Part of Pigeon House and Aviary

Scale for Figs. 926 to 930

If desired, the lower part of the house can be enclosed with wire netting to form an aviary. In this case it will be necessary to provide an opening in the floor, and to fix a board, with strips nailed across, as shown in Figs. 927 and 928. The higher the loft is from the ground the better will be the protection against cats, etc.

The construction of the framework of the trap and of

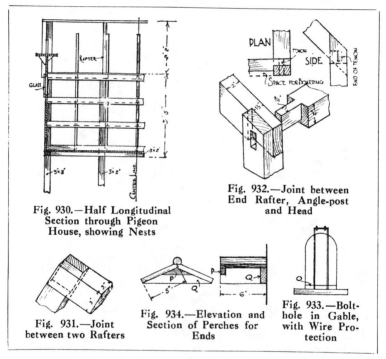

Fig. 930.—Half Longitudinal Section through Pigeon House, showing Nests

Fig. 932.—Joint between End Rafter, Angle-post and Head

Fig. 931.—Joint between two Rafters

Fig. 934.—Elevation and Section of Perches for Ends

Fig. 933.—Bolt-hole in Gable, with Wire Protection

the nests is clearly shown in Fig. 928, as are also the various inlets and small alighting boards. The trap has a boarded floor supported on two shaped brackets, and its sides and door can be of light stuff halved together and filled in with small laths as shown. Its door should be arranged to open out flat, as in Fig. 928, and can be worked with cords from the ground. The nests should be of ¾-in. boards, arranged as in Fig. 930, with three horizontal shelves, five sets of vertical divisions and strips along the front to retain the

nesting material.   Perches about 7 in. long should be fixed
to the boarding round the inside.   Fig. 933 shows an arrangement by which the birds can enter the loft by the top bolt-
holes in the gable-ends when the trap is closed.   A piece
of thick wire is bent and secured to the inside by means of
two staples, and butts against a small strip of wood o,
thus preventing the wires being pushed outwards.

Fig 934 shows the perches fixed on the inside ends of
the house.   Two pieces of board 5 in. long by 6 in. wide are
nailed together roof-like on a large and small triangular

Fig. 935.—Hut, Shed or Workshop

fillet (P and Q) ; then the top corner is planed slightly flat,
and a perch piece secured with two screws from underneath.   It can be fixed by nailing through the piece Q.
All that now remains to be done is to whitewash the inside
and to give the outside several coats of paint.

Hut, Shed or Workshop.—The small building shown
in Fig. 935 may be 10 ft. long by 8 ft. wide, by 6 ft. 6 in.
high to the top of the roof plate, and may be used as a
temporary or holiday dwelling for two persons.   The structure is portable, so that it may be taken to pieces and stored
during the winter season.   Figs. 936 to 939 explain the
method of construction.   The framework is shown in Figs.

940 to 943, while Figs. 944 and 945 are the chief sections, and Figs. 946 to 949 illustrate the details. The floor of the hut is of 1-in. tongued and grooved boarding, resting on 4-in. by 2-in. framing halved together (*see* Fig. 943 and A, Fig. 944). The side frames are built of 2-in. square posts, rails, and muntins, the sides as in Figs. 940 and 941; the ends as in Fig. 942. The door opening is obtained by omitting the rail at B, and the top corners are halved together as in Fig. 947. If desired, the sides may be braced with scantlings as at C in Fig. 941. This will be found necessary if the hut is to be placed in an exposed position where high winds are likely to be encountered. The outer boarding is of 5-in. by 1-in. wrought and rebated weather boarding D (Fig. 944). No inside boarding is shown, but the building will be more comfortable if it is lined with matched boarding, and the space between the two packed

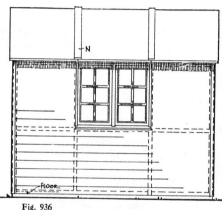

Fig. 936

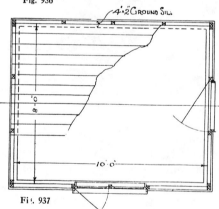

Fi*. 937

Figs. 936 and 937.—Front Elevation and Sectional Plan of Workshop

with slagwool. In the latter case the method of securing the framing by means of bolts as shown could not be adopted, but iron angle-plates and thumbscrews could be substituted.

The door is ledged and braced, and has a drip-board over, as at E in Fig. 939; rebates are formed for it by means of

small linings F (Fig. 945) projecting sufficiently to stop the
weather-boarding, similar fillets being likewise fixed at the
angles of the hut as at G. An oak threshold and fillet under
will be advisable, these being fixed to the bottom rail of
the end framing (*see* H, Fig. 949). The window is formed
of $1\frac{1}{4}$-in. casements, glazed with sheet glass to suit the
openings in Fig. 941. Rebates are formed with beads on
the inside as at J in Fig. 944 and 945, the former figure
showing a sloping board forming a sill fixed on a splayed
fillet K and finished with a rounded strip as at L. A stop
to the boarding is indicated at M. The gable ends contain

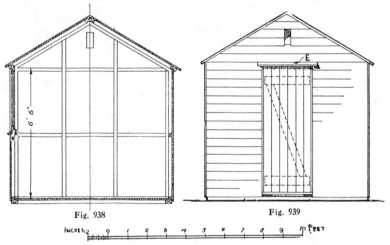

Fig. 938   Fig. 939

Figs. 938 and 939.—Cross Section through and Side Elevation of Workshop

a small hinged or sliding ventilator. The roof could be
formed with 2-in. by 2-in. rafters, 5-in. by $1\frac{1}{2}$-in. ridge,
4-in. by 2-in. bottom or eaves plate, and covered with 1-in.
tongued and grooved boarding fixed horizontally. It will,
however, be found more convenient for removal if the roof
be made in three sections, the joints being covered with
4-in. by 1-in. fillets as at N in Figs. 936 and 944. For this
arrangement six sections, as in Fig. 946, should be prepared,
the bottom rail being 4 in. by 2 in., the others 2 in. by 2 in.
and the top one splayed as at O in Fig. 944. The top of
the sides should be made up to the correct slope by means

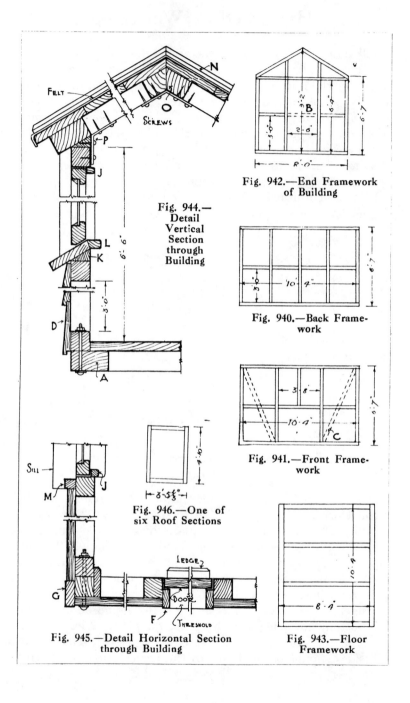

FELT

SCREWS

N

O

P

J

**Fig. 944.—
Detail
Vertical
Section
through
Building**

L

K

D

A

6′ 9″

3′ 0″

B

3′ 2″

3′ 4″

3′ 0″

2′ 0″

8′ 0″

6′ 7″

**Fig. 942.—End Framework
of Building**

3′ 0″

10′ 4″

6′ 7″

**Fig. 940.—Back Frame-
work**

3′ 8″

10′ 4″

6′ 7″

C

**Fig. 941.—Front Frame-
work**

S

J

M

3′ 0″

8′ 5⅜″

**Fig. 946.—One of
six Roof Sections**

LEDGE

G

DOOR

F

THRESHOLD

**Fig. 945.—Detail Horizontal Section
through Building**

10′ 9″

8′ 1″

**Fig. 943.—Floor
Framework**

of a triangular fillet as at P, and the roof sections secured in position by means of small iron angles screwed on as shown. The underside of the shed and the framing upon which it is fixed should be well tarred and a dry site chosen, failing which a base of bricks or ashes is desirable.

A Portable Span-roof Greenhouse.—The greenhouse shown by Fig. 950 should have a foundation of bricks or good gravel, etc. ; but as it requires no actual fastening to the ground in the form of concrete or mortar, it is without question a tenant's fixture. It has been designed in such a way that by the removal of a few screws the whole green-

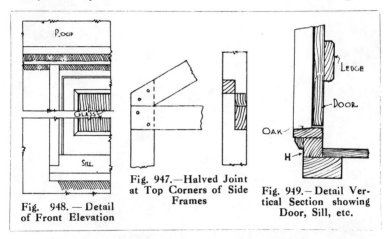

Fig. 948. — Detail of Front Elevation

Fig. 947.—Halved Joint at Top Corners of Side Frames

Fig. 949.—Detail Vertical Section showing Door, Sill, etc.

house can be separated into six main sections—two sides, two ends, and two roof-slopes. The working drawings, etc. (Figs. 951 to 963), where necessary are fully dimensioned, and the most suitable timber for the work would be good red deal. All the joints should be well painted before putting together, and the work involved can, if desired, be reduced by the purchase of the door ready made, and the matchboarding and sash or glazing bars ready worked.

The quantities of material required, apart from the door, are as follow : Boarding matched and V-jointed, 6 in. by $\frac{3}{4}$ in. or $\frac{5}{8}$ in., 54 ft. ; sash bars, $1\frac{1}{2}$ in. by $1\frac{1}{8}$ in., 115 ft. ; door frame, 3 in. by $2\frac{1}{4}$ in., 16 ft. ; sill F, 2 in. by 2 in., 30 ft. ;

stiles to sides G, and end rails to roof H, and side rails to skylight, $3\frac{1}{2}$ in. by $1\frac{1}{2}$ in., 43 ft. ; stiles to ends I, $2\frac{1}{2}$ in. by $1\frac{1}{2}$ in., 23 ft. ; bottom rails (above F), $4\frac{1}{2}$ in. by $1\frac{1}{2}$ in., 30 ft. ; top rails J and K, $2\frac{1}{2}$ in. by $1\frac{1}{2}$ in., 32 ft. ; muntins, etc., L, $2\frac{1}{2}$ in. by $1\frac{1}{2}$ in., 30 ft. ; bottom rails of roof and skylight, 4 in. by $\frac{7}{8}$ in., 22 ft. ; top rails of roof, $4\frac{1}{2}$ in. by $1\frac{1}{2}$ in., 22 ft. ; frame under skylight, 2 in. by $1\frac{1}{2}$ in., 4 ft. ; bottom rail M,

Fig. 950.—Portable Span-roof Greenhouse

4 in. by $1\frac{1}{2}$ in., 30 ft. ; door-stop, $1\frac{1}{2}$ in. by $\frac{1}{2}$ in., 15 ft. ; ridge, 5 in. by 1 in., 9 ft. 6 in.

The only special ironmongery requisite will be a casement stay for the skylight, and a simple rim-lock. At completion the whole work should be primed one coat before glazing, and have at least two coats of oil colour afterwards.

In view of the exhaustive nature of the illustrations and typical details given, it is not proposed to describe the work very fully. A suitable section of glazing bar is shown by

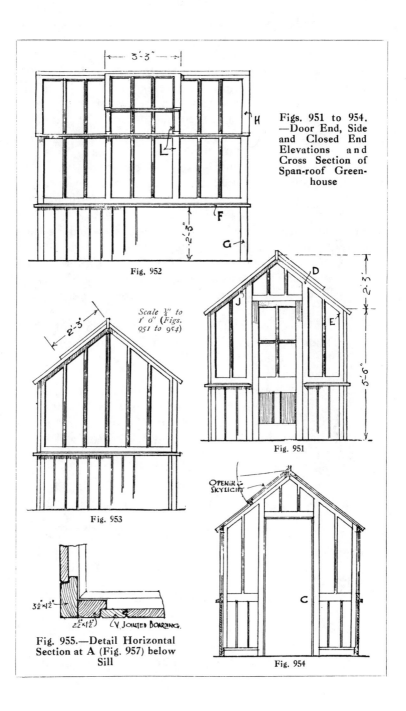

5'-3"

H

L

F

2'-3"

G

Fig. 952

Figs. 951 to 954.
—Door End, Side
and Closed End
Elevations and
Cross Section of
Span-roof Green-
house

Scale ¼" to
1' 0" (Figs.
951 to 954)

2'-3"

D

J

E

2'-3"

5'-6"

Fig. 951

Fig. 953

OPENING
SKYLIGHT

C

3½"×1½"

2½"×1½"

(V JOINTED BOARDING.

Fig. 955.—Detail Horizontal
Section at A (Fig. 957) below
Sill

Fig. 954

Fig. 963, and this will regulate the setting-out of the whole, as of course the rebates will apply throughout, and it will be most convenient to make the tenons coincide with the $\frac{1}{4}$-in. fillets between these and the chamfers. The skylight is explained by Figs. 958 and 959. In it the glass overlaps the greater portion of the lower rail (which is only $\frac{7}{8}$ in. thick), and is supported by means of small brads projecting slightly against the bottom edge ; this is the usual practice for cheap skylights and horticultural work, and affords no lodgment for damp. The outer framework is put together with shouldered tenons as shown in Fig. 959, and the bars are tenoned at the top and notched at their lower ends, as at N, the thin portion between the rebates being continued a little to suit the putty and afford better fixing. At O is a side view of the skylight showing the tenons (which can be wedged), and indicating the outlines of the top and bottom rails, and at P these rails appear in section, mortised and notched for the glazing bar, the ends of which are also seen, ready for insertion and cut to scribe over the chamfers on the rails. At the bottom ends they should be screwed or nailed from below.

The two roof-slopes are put together in just the same way as the skylight. Both have two wider bars, as at L in Fig. 952, to act as stiffeners, and in the one case to support the opening skylight. To suit this the top rail is cut down to $2\frac{1}{2}$ in. wide in the centre, and a $2\frac{1}{2}$-in. by $1\frac{1}{2}$-in. rail tenoned in position, as at Q and R in Fig. 958.

The construction of the end containing the door is explained by Figs. 954, 955, 956, 960, 961, and 962, the stiles I (Fig. 956) being rebated and chamfered for glass in the upper part, and rebated only below the sill to suit the boarding, as in Fig. 955. A rebated rail similar to that at S in Fig. 958 is tenoned between the stile and door frame as in Figs. 960 and 961, the former figure also showing at T the mode of fitting the upright glazing bars, and the latter the way in which the sill F (Fig. 958) is weathered and throated to throw off the rain. This sill is mitred round the whole greenhouse, and can be rounded where it stops next the door. The joints at the head of the fram-

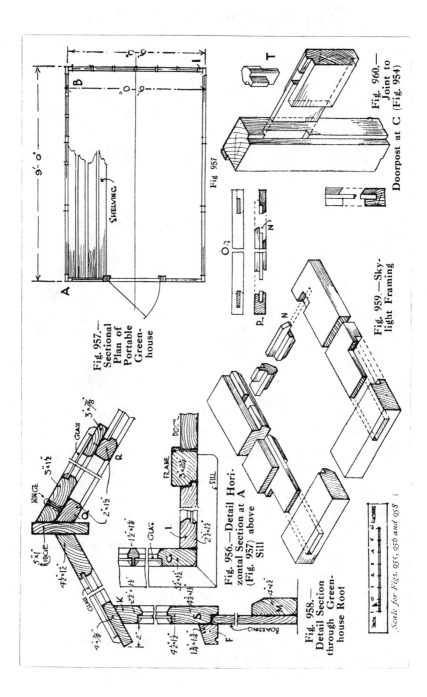

Fig. 957

Fig. 957.—Sectional Plan of Portable Greenhouse

SHELVING.

9' - 0"

6' - 0"

A

B

Fig. 960.— Joint to Doorpost at C (Fig. 954)

T

Fig. 959.—Skylight Framing

N

O.

P.

Fig. 956.—Detail Horizontal Section at A (Fig. 957) above Sill

GLASS

3" x 7/8"

HINGE

LEDGE

5" x 1"

4 1/2" x 1 1/2"

2 1/2" x 1 1/2"

3" x 1 1/2"

R

Q

GLASS

K

4" x 7/8"

2"

2 1/2" x 1 1/2"

1 1/2" x 1 1/2"

F

BOARDING

M

4" x 1 1/2"

S

4 1/2" x 1 1/2"

GLASS

L

1 1/2" x 1 1/2"

2 1/2" x 1 1/2"

2 1/2" x 1 1/2"

O

FRAME

DOOR

SILL

Fig. 958.—Detail Section through Greenhouse Roof

Scale for Figs. 955, 956 and 958

INCH

FEET

ing D and E (Fig. 951) are shown from the inside and also by plan and elevation in Fig. 962. That at the apex might be a simple halving, over which the ridge could be notched.

Both the sides and the other end should be framed up in a similar manner to that shown. The muntins at L in Fig. 952 are tenoned into the rail at sill level, not taken down to the ground as are the stiles, into which latter the

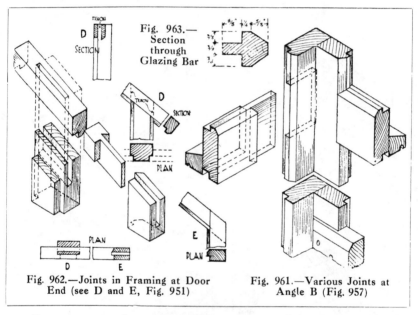

Fig. 963.—Section through Glazing Bar

Fig. 962.—Joints in Framing at Door End (see D and E, Fig. 951)

Fig. 961.—Various Joints at Angle B (Fig. 957)

rail tenons, as does also the top rail K (Fig. 958), which must be splayed off to suit the slope of the roof as shown.

Stability is given to the whole by the rail M (Fig. 958), which is mitred round the inside, taking the lower ends of the boarding, and is notched over the stiles, to which it should be screwed, as shown on the right of Fig. 961; it might suitably be a little heavier in section if convenient. Once the various units have been framed up they can readily be screwed together, and the interior fitted up with tiers of shelving composed of laths spaced about 1 in. apart and fixed on small standards or brackets.

CHAPTER XXIX

Wood Finishing

There is not much work that can be left in the rough with the marks of the hammer, saw, and plane upon it. Nearly all woodwork is finished with a coat, or several coats, of one of three things—polish, varnish, or paint. The paint or varnish finish demands a fair surface if it is to look its best, but in the case of work which has to be polished, a merely fair surface is not good enough, and the scraper and two or three grades of glasspaper have to be employed in succession to produce a perfectly smooth surface on which the polish can be applied with the best effect. The use of the scraper has already been fully dealt with (*see* pages 63 to 65).

What Glasspaper Is.—Glasspaper is a stout paper which has been coated with glue on which has then been sifted powdered glass, garnet, flint, etc. Sand was formerly employed and is now to a limited extent, but the cutting material used by the woodworker in "sandpaper" is generally glass. Various grades of fineness are obtainable the finest ordinary grade being No. 0 ; but there is a still finer one used by polishers, etc., known as "flour."

Glasspapering.—Tool marks on woodwork, except carpentry of a rough order, should be removed by glasspapering. The sharp points of glass or flint on the paper are so numerous that they have a scraping and levelling action on the wood, and although the glasspapering cannot improve the surface left from a really keen tool, it succeeds in removing the ridges caused by the successive strokes of a tool. Usually this first glasspapering is followed by the application of the varnish or other protective coat. Glasspaper should be used again after each coat of varnish or paint has dried before applying the succeeding coat ; but it is not used after the final coat. The fibres of the wood swell and rise when wetted, and when the surface has thoroughly dried again it feels rough in consequence. The glasspaper entirely removes this roughness, but gives the stained, varnished, or painted surface a slightly scratched and dulled appearance. As more coats are added the roughness on drying becomes less, and the final coat is not touched with the glasspaper. As the work proceeds finer glasspaper should be used. For removing tool marks it must be comparatively coarse. For smoothing the surface after two or three coats of varnish have been applied it should be very fine. In the latter case fresh glasspaper is never used, but pieces that have been worn considerably. If these do not happen to be at hand, two pieces may be rubbed face to face to remove their sharpness.

Glasspaper should almost always be used wrapped round a " rubber." The ordinary form of rubber (Fig. 964) is simply a rectangular block of wood, cork, or any other convenient material, measuring about 5 in. by $2\frac{1}{2}$ in. by $1\frac{1}{4}$ in. It keeps the glasspaper flat, and also affords a convenient means of holding and using it. It is used in the same way as a scrubbing brush, except that it is generally worked only in line with the grain of the wood. If used across the grain, the scratches made by the glasspaper are much more noticeable. When the attainment of a true surface is of more importance than appearance, as in patternmaking, the rubber is worked across the grain at first, but finally with the grain.

Fig. 965 shows a cylindrical rubber in use. Its movement would be both rotary and longitudinal, as indicated by the arrows. It might be the right diameter to fit the concavity, or in some cases the nearest one available of smaller diameter would be used to avoid making one specially. For small holes or semicircles a lead pencil, a piece of dowel rod, or the back of a paring gouge is often suitable.

For concave surfaces of large radius, a block of wood similar to an ordinary rubber may have one of its faces planed approximately to the sweep, as in Fig. 966. For convex surfaces special rubbers are seldom employed. In such cases an ordinary flat rubber may be used as in

Figs. 967 and 968 worked in the direction of the curve, to remove tool marks only. In a case like Fig. 967 it would only travel in the one direction indicated, to avoid returning against the grain. In both examples, after tool marks were removed and varnish applied, the glasspapering would

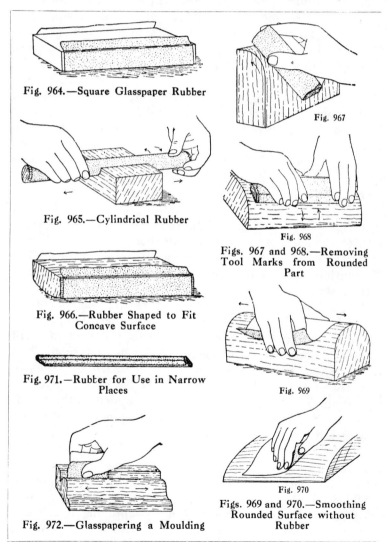

Fig. 964.—Square Glasspaper Rubber

Fig. 967

Fig. 965.—Cylindrical Rubber

Fig. 968

Figs. 967 and 968.—Removing Tool Marks from Rounded Part

Fig. 966.—Rubber Shaped to Fit Concave Surface

Fig. 971.—Rubber for Use in Narrow Places

Fig. 969

Fig. 970

Figs. 969 and 970.—Smoothing Rounded Surface without Rubber

Fig. 972.—Glasspapering a Moulding

Y

usually be performed without a rubber, as in Figs. 969 and 970, the movement generally following the grain.

For use in narrow places, a thin strip of wood (Fig. 971) may be used as a rubber ; or a chisel may be suitable. In other cases a piece of glasspaper folded and held between finger and thumb may be the best way of dealing with work. This method is shown in Fig. 972, where the glasspaper is being used for smoothing out a quirk in a moulding. The curved part of the moulding would also be done with a small piece of glasspaper held in the fingers and pressed to the contour.

Staining.—Inferior wood is often stained to imitate a more expensive variety. Modern stains are chiefly aniline dyes soluble either in methylated spirit or water ; an immense range of colours is available, but their permanency is questionable, and experienced wood finishers rely more upon natural stains, such as the following.

For *green* stains of varying shades, make two solutions :—
(*a*) Verdigris 1 oz., vinegar or dilute acetic acid 10 oz. ; (*b*) indigo 2 drm., vinegar or dilute acetic acid 15 oz. Heat both of the solutions before mixing them together, different proportions of the two producing different shades. The (*b*) solution darkens the shade ; 5 parts of (*a*) added to 1 part of (*b*) gives a very useful colour.

For a *blue* stain, place in a clean earthenware jar 4 oz. of sulphuric acid and add 1 oz. of the best indigo (well ground). Place the jar in a basin, as the contents will effervesce, and, if the earthenware jar is too small, boil over. When the effervescence has ceased, add such a quantity of the solution to distilled water as will give the desired shade of blue. This should be applied to the wood-work by means of a stiff brush. Keeping the solution greatly improves the colour.

A good *walnut* stain may be made by mixing together bichromate of potash 40 gr., vandyke brown 400 gr., carbonate of soda 200 gr., water up to 10 oz. The solution should be boiled, and can be applied hot or cold with a soft brush. *Oak* can be imitated by applying a solution of permanganate of potash. The quantity will depend on the shade ; 80 gr. of permanganate to 10 oz. of water is suitable.

A good *red* stain, which may be a little bright (but age will remedy that), may be obtained by boiling 1 oz. of logwood chips in 1 pt. (20 oz.) of water, to which must be added grain tin 30 gr. and dilute nitric acid 1 oz. See that the logwood is fresh, which is easily known by its bright red colour ; old wood is a dirty brown. The stain should be filtered and made hot before application.

For a *brown* stain, make a solution of catechu (cutch) ½ oz., carbonate of soda 120 gr., water 15 oz. ; boil, and then apply hot. When this is thoroughly dry, apply a solution of bichromate of potassium. The strength of the bichromate solution will regulate the depth of the colour.

The application of stain always results in raising the grain of the wood, the trouble being less with spirit stains than with the water stains, and light glasspapering when the stain is dry is therefore necessary. It is better to build up a good tone by several applications rather than by trying to get the effect by giving just one strong coat ; but remember that one coat must be dry before the next one is applied.

French Polishing.—In this kind of polishing a thin film of shellac is applied to the work and a lustrous polish obtained by subjecting the film to friction. Polish may be bought ready made, or the worker can prepare it for himself by dissolving about 6 oz. of shellac in 1 pint of methylated spirit, adding more of one of the ingredients, if necessary, to correct the consistency. For light polish, which is to be preferred for oak and all the lighter woods, use white or bleached shellac ; for the ordinary reddish polish, use orange shellac. Briefly, the process is to apply a good coat or body of the shellac by means of a pad (known as a rubber) of wadding wrapped in a clean soft rag, and then, when the work has become evenly coated, to continue the rubbing with a rubber in which the polish has been gradually displaced by methylated spirit.

The work will probably need to be surfaced by filling the grain with finely crushed whiting tinted to match the wood and made into a paint with turpentine ; it is rubbed in across the grain with a piece of rag. If the finest pumice powder is added to the whiting grain filler it will assist in producing a good surface. If the work has been stained it should be given a rub with linseed oil before using the grain filler, and the filler itself may be coloured up with the same stain. Most work is better for oiling before using the grain filler, as the oil assists in bringing up the figure of the wood. On reddish woods, such as mahogany, the linseed oil used should first be coloured with alkanet root. There are many other fillers used by polishers, but the above is all that the beginner need concern himself with, except that should he require to make good any damaged parts or to fill up nail holes, etc., he must have some hard stopping, which is a mixture of shellac, resin, beeswax, and colouring matter made up into sticks and used in much the same way as sealing wax. This hard stopping, which is known as beaumontage, can be melted into the holes and depressions by means of a hot iron, and should be well pressed in, cleaning off when cold with a chisel, knife, or scraper and with glasspaper.

In french polishing, the application of a coat of shellac is known as " bodying-up." First make a rubber by taking a piece of sheet wadding about 6 in. by 9 in., fold it across its width, and squeeze it in the hand until it becomes some-what of the shape of a pear, but keeping the skin of the wadding unbroken. Charge the rubber with polish by letting a little drip from the bottle on to the wadding, and then cover it with a piece of clean soft rag, taking care to avoid all creases on the working face. Twisting the rag on the upper side of the rubber will cause the polish to squeeze through.

To facilitate the working of the rubber over the work a spot or two of raw linseed oil should be applied to the face of the rubber. Use as little oil as will answer the pur-pose, inasmuch as, to get the best results, all the oil will have to be removed before the process is complete. Use as little polish as possible and apply it to the work by a continuous curved movement—a series of overlapping circles or figure eights—and do not cease the labour until it appears that the wood cannot absorb more polish. Then allow the work in its somewhat streaky condition to stand for at least a day, carefully protecting from dust. It is essential that the room be at a moderate temperature, as chills are fatal to the polish. Repeat the bodying-up, give another day's rest, repeat the process again, and, if necessary, give yet another coat, the object being to attain such a condition that the polish no longer appears to sink into the work. After each of these coats of shellac is dry, and before applying the next one, give it a very light rubbing indeed with a piece of fine worn glasspaper, or with wet felt on which some of the finest pumice powder has been sprinkled.

The work is now assumed to be covered with a good film of shellac, which will be only slightly lustrous. The next process is to submit the film to friction, by which means it can be made to assume a very high polish. For this purpose the same rubber is used as before, but the quantity of polish in it is gradually reduced, and at the same time methylated spirit is gradually introduced, so that by the time the " spiriting-out," as it is called, is complete, the rubber will contain almost wholly spirit. The rubber will need three or four coverings of rag to prevent a too rapid evaporation of the spirit, and, as it works dry after each recharging, the rags may be removed one by one. The danger is that the rubber may be made too wet, with the consequent risk that the body of shellac will be dissolved and actually washed off. This is a matter in which experience tells ; obviously, written instructions can only suggest the correct procedure and cannot actually teach the art. In spiriting-off no oil is used on the face of the rubber. If the condition of the rubber is satisfactory, and if the oil used has been kept down to a minimum, a fine gloss will soon be discerned ; continue the circular movement of the rubber, but towards the end of the process, when the polish is well in evidence, let the rubber work up and down the grain only, and not across it. Remember that a chilly room and the presence of dust are the polisher's chief enemies.

French polishing is a tedious process, and not so easy as it seems, and one or two quick and easy methods have been introduced to save some of the labour. For example, the bodying-up may be done by applying the french polish with a brush; and instead of the spiriting-out, which is the most difficult part of the process, it is possible to use what is known as glaze, which is a solution of 6 oz. or 8 oz. of gum benzoin in one pint of methylated spirit, there being other and more elaborate recipes. Glaze is applied with a rubber or brush; if the former, let it be fairly wet and give one or two strokes in the direction of the grain, and repeat if necessary once or twice when dry. If a brush is used, regard the glaze simply as a varnish.

Dulled french polish has an excellent effect. To obtain it, proceed as before described as far as the bodying-up. Allow the work to get hard, and then with a pad of felt saturated in oil, and dipped in pumice powder or the finest emery, rub the work lightly and evenly.

Wax Polishing.—Wax polish is a beautiful finish, which is frequently preferable to the lustrous french polish. It is obtained simply by applying beeswax dissolved in turpentine, the proportions not being of importance. It is rubbed on with a rag or stiff brush, and, after the work has been thinly and evenly coated with the wax, a polish is brought up by friction with another cloth or brush, repeating the rubbing at intervals.

Oil Polishing.—This is a laborious process, but is suitable for certain plain work. It produces simply a dull oiled surface, and plenty of time and plenty of friction are essential. It may require months of occasional rubbings to produce a passable effect. Some polishers use boiled linseed oil, and others raw linseed oil. In either case, the oil is rubbed well into the wood, which is then rubbed with another cloth, using plenty of friction, the rubbing being repeated many times until a dull polish appears. To maintain and improve this polish the rubbing at intervals must be repeated. This is an excellent way in which to finish mahogany and light oak, the oil having a remarkable effect in bringing up the tone and markings of the wood.

Varnishing.—Varnishes are of two chief kinds, oil and spirit. The former are made by dissolving certain hard gums in linseed oil by the aid of heat, and such work should not be done at home, as the chance of getting anything as good as shop-bought varnishes is remote, while the risk of fire is considerable. Good varnishes for interior use are "inside oak varnish" and "pale carriage varnish." Spirit varnishes can be either bought or made at home. They consist frequently of shellac with or without gum sandarach, gum benzoin, venice turpentine, etc., dissolved in methylated spirit. Spirit varnishes need to be applied quickly, as they are very quick-drying, and they do not give the high-class results that are obtainable with oil varnish. All that need to be said here with regard to the process of varnishing is : Use a well-worn brush of first-rate quality, perfectly clean and free from specks and loose hairs. Lay the dust before starting, and protect from dust while drying. Avoid a cold or damp atmosphere. For a really good result, rub down each coat when dry with a piece of felt moistened with water and sprinkled with pumice powder, washing off with clean cold water and allowing to dry thoroughly before applying the next coat. Leave the final coat untouched. On very " hungry " wood or on end grain the varnishing may be preceded by sizing so as to stop the suction. Varnish stain—a combined stain and varnish—often causes an amateur much worry, especially if applied over a coat of size ; it is best avoided.

Painting.—This is a very big subject in itself, and can only be briefly touched upon here. Ordinary oil paint often contains five things : (1) a base, consisting of white-lead, zinc-white or red-lead ; (2) a binder and vehicle, generally linseed oil ; (3) a thinner, generally turpentine ; (4) possibly a drier ; and (5) frequently a pigment in addition to the base. The base, itself a pigment, gives body to the paint and protects the surface treated ; the vehicle allows of the easy application of the base and gives a further protection ; the thinner makes the paint workable ; the drier assists the paint to " dry " (actually to oxidise, since the " drying " of oil paint does not mean evaporation) ; and the pigment imparts colour and frequently body as well. All materials, if the paint is made at home, should be bought from a reliable dealer, but paint making is not advised. Ready-made paint (not of the cheap oil-shop kind, but of the sort that is sold by decorators' supply houses in lever-lid tins) is an absolutely reliable material, and nothing so good can be made by an amateur. Interior woodwork is stopped with a mixture of 2 parts putty and 1 part of best white-lead stiffened, if necessary, with some dry whiting. Stopping is best used after the priming coat, which should consist largely of red-lead and contain 2 parts of oil to 1 part of turpentine. After the stopping the second coat of paint may be applied, this containing 5 parts of oil, 3 parts of turpentine, and enough white-lead to give the proper consistence ; for a cool colour a touch of lampblack and chrome yellow may be added. Apply thinly and well brush it out. For the third coat use equal parts of oil and turpentine ; and for the fourth and final coat use 2 parts of turpentine to 1 part of oil. In the final coat the base will be white lead as before, tinted with some other pigment as required. It is well to rub over each coat, except the last, when dry with some worn glasspaper.

Enamelling.—Interior woodwork is often finished in white enamel—a paint made of fine pigment with varnish as the chief vehicle. For enamelling, the work requires to be carefully prepared, and "filled" with a preparation—such as Alabastine—made by the makers of the enamel. To get a first-rate result, give at least three coats of the filler, and when dry rub down with worn glasspaper. Apply the enamel with a somewhat worn but perfectly clean varnish brush of good quality, and do not work the enamel much when brushing it on. Enamels can be obtained either "flat" or glossy (the filler or ground may be the same for both), and an excellent effect is obtained by finishing parts of a fitment glossy and other parts flat. Do not tamper with either varnish or enamel by attempting to thin it with oil, turpentine, etc.

CHAPTER XXX

Timber : Seasoning, Selection, Commercial Sizes and Varieties

Tree Growth. — The trees yielding timber for constructional purposes have a growth in the diameter of the trunk and branches by additional annual rings which develop beneath the bark. These rings are formed of two parts, the spring and autumn growth. The spring growth is the greater, and invariably the softer, more porous, and less defined part of the ring. In a cross section of a tree the spring growth will be seen to fill up the intervening space between these clearly marked rings of autumn growth. The continual expansion of the bark, to meet the needs of the growing tree, is provided for from the inside. The inner portion of the tree, known as the heart-wood, is harder and darker in colour than the outer wood (sapwood), due to the filling up and hardening of the inner rings of the tree. The proportion of the unripe sapwood should be at a minimum when the tree is ready for felling, because if the tree is felled prematurely the larger quantity of sapwood causes too much wastage. A tree allowed to grow too old is inferior in toughness and strength. The oak tree is mature for felling between eighty and a hundred years growth; ash, elm, and larch between sixty and a hundred years; the poplar between forty and fifty years. Spruce and pine trees are felled between seventy and a hundred years of age.

Sap ascends during spring and descends in the autumn, and the tree will therefore be at its driest period during the winter, which is the best time, in temperate climates, for felling. There is, however, always a large amount of sap remaining in the tree, which is of such a quantity that its weight is half as much as the timber itself; so that the tree in drying loses about one-third of its weight; but such a condition of dryness is seldom attained, and is only approached for the best cabinet work and joinery.

Drying or Seasoning Timber.—Wood that is sawn up and used in the sappy state will, as the sap evaporates, shrink considerably in width, though it will not be much affected in length. It will not only shrink, but the least strain in any direction, or the fact that some parts are able to dry faster than others, causes warping, the driest parts being in a more shrunken state than the others. This might not be very serious if uniform dryness eventually straightened the wood again, but once warping occurs it is usually permanent. If the wood is in a strained condition, which may occur by its own weight if improperly supported, it gradually accommodates itself to the stress and becomes permanently distorted—simple curvature in width or length, or a winding or twisted curvature. The shrinkage which occurs across the grain may result in the development of cracks. These evils are most pronounced if the wood is used in a sappy or unseasoned condition, but seasoned wood is capable of either losing or absorbing moisture, according to the state of the atmosphere, and of shrinking or swelling accordingly. Ordinary wood, as sold at timber yards, is seasoned, but it usually shrinks a little after it has been cut and used. The wood used by cabinet-makers has been more carefully seasoned and is drier and less liable to shrink. Warping can be prevented by forcibly keeping the wood flat and straight, first by proper storage and second by constructive methods which make warping impossible.

When drying or seasoning timber in the log shrinkage takes place circumferentially, the annual rings shorten, and if the timber is left whole too long many vee-shaped shakes will appear and spoil the timber. To prevent this the log is sawn into planks and stacked for drying in a partially enclosed shed, moderately accessible to the wind and sheltered from the sun and rain. The ground should be free from vegetation, a stony or asphalte floor best guarding against dampness. The ground must be flat, so that the planks or boards can be stacked straight and true to avoid permanent distortion. Strips of wood are inserted between the boards to allow of the circulation of air to facilitate drying ; these are placed as close as 3 in. apart for thin boards right throughout their length, the distance increasing according to the thickness of timber to be stacked.

Seasoning by this natural method takes from two to three years, or even more, for hard wood, and from one year to two years for pine, etc. There are methods (steam-heat, electrical, etc.) of artificially seasoning timber to save time and expense, but none gives better results than the natural method, in which the quality of strength and toughness is fully preserved.

Hard and Soft Woods.—Woods are divided into two classes—hard and soft. The first are the most numerous and the most expensive. The second are grown in the north of Europe and in Canada, and are used in Great Britain for all purposes where cheapness is a consideration ; they are of the pine or fir class, comparatively soft, and light in colour and in weight, and the cheaper kinds are commonly known as deal. Yellow pine is a superior variety, comparatively free from warping, shrinking, and knots. American whitewood has similar characteristics.

The distinction between hard and soft wood is a rather arbitrary one made by botanists, and has not much meaning to the woodworker. Some " hard " woods are as soft as, or even softer than, the nominally soft wood ; but generally hard wood is really harder, more durable and more difficult to work than soft, and it is often of better appearance. Often, too, a kind of hard wood is selected that has characteristics adapting it for the purpose required. Ash, for instance, is flexible, and suitable for implements and articles subject to shock and vibration. Greenheart and elm are durable under water, but no wood stands alternate wetness and dryness well. The most commonly used among hard woods are oak, mahogany, and walnut.

Conversion of Timber.—This is the sawing of the log into planks, deals, battens, etc., and is generally done before seasoning. The subsequent shrinkage is noticeable in the portions when cut as illustrated. Take, for instance, a log cut into planks and beams shown in Fig. 973. The middle piece a, when dry, will remain almost the same width and of the same thickness in the middle. The thickness of the edges will diminish a trifle as shown exaggerated at A. The piece b will take the shape of B. Owing to the shortening of the rings, this piece will shrink in its width more on the upper surface than the surface next to the heart of the tree, giving the plank a curved shape as shown. This also will be a trifle thinner at the edges than in the middle ; c and d, following the same action, are shown at C and D ; the shrinkage in width is more marked, but they keep more parallel in thickness. The tendency to distort with rect-angular-shaped piece is shown in E and F ; if the rectilinear shape is to be preserved they must be cut square with the tree, as in G and H.

If boards are required that will not warp or shrink in width they must be cut as shown at J (Fig. 974). This method is also pursued in cutting oak panelling to obtain the full-figured silver grain. It is an expensive method of converting timber, because it entails more waste, but most of the vee-pieces can be utilised for feather-edged tiling, laths, oak fencing, etc. A more economical method to approximate the above advantages is shown at K. For ordinary boarding, sometimes known as " quarter stuff," it is cut as at L. M is the best method of cutting thick " stuff." When cutting the log for beams or joists, or where strength is a more important matter than shrinkage, it has been proved the best to cut tangentially to the annual rings as at N in Fig. 975 ; this is stronger than when cut like P.

" Deals " are cut from the Scandinavian fir trees accord-ing to the size of the log, as shown in Figs. 976 and 977. A method of cutting pitch-pine and other timbers, for panel-ling tangentially to the rings, is shown in Fig. 978. The log, instead of being cut into halves or quarters, is first cut to a square balk, which is then gradually reduced as the boards are sawn off. The deciding factors as to the method of cutting up the log are its size, the amount of sapwood to cut off, and the presence of any particular defects—knots, shakes, or decay.

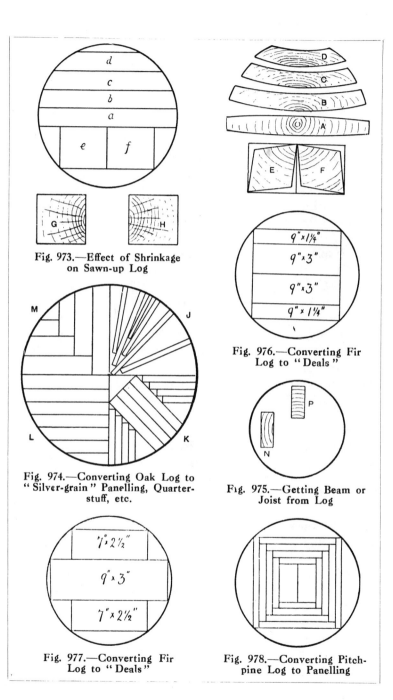

Fig. 973.—Effect of Shrinkage
on Sawn-up Log

Fig. 974.—Converting Oak Log to
"Silver-grain" Panelling, Quarter-
stuff, etc.

Fig. 976.—Converting Fir
Log to "Deals"

Fig. 975.—Getting Beam or
Joist from Log

Fig. 977.—Converting Fir
Log to "Deals"

Fig. 978.—Converting Pitch-
pine Log to Panelling

Commercial Sizes of Timbers.—The terms given to the various commercial sizes of timbers are as follow: A balk varies from 12 in. by 12 in. to 18 in. by 18 in. ; whole timbers from 9 in. by 9 in. to 15 in. by 15 in. ; half timbers from 9 in. by $4\frac{1}{2}$ in. to 18 in. by 9 in. ; scantling from 6 in. by 4 in. to 12 in. by 12 in. ; quartering from 2 in. by 2 in. to 6 in. by 6 in. ; planks from 11 in. to 18 in. wide and from 3 in. to 6 in. thick ; deals from 9 in. wide and from 2 in. to $4\frac{1}{2}$ in. thick ; battens from $4\frac{1}{2}$ in. to 7 in. wide and from $\frac{3}{4}$ in. to 3 in. thick ; strips and laths, say, 4 in. wide and $\frac{1}{2}$ in. to $1\frac{1}{2}$ in. thick. All these sizes are cross-sectional.

Pine and spruce timbers are sold by standard hundred, by the load, and by the square of 100 ft. super. The Petersburg standard is 120 pieces of 6 ft. by 11 in. by 3 in. ; the Christiana standard is 120 pieces of 11 ft. by 9 in. by $1\frac{1}{4}$ in. ; and the London standard is 120 pieces of 12 ft. by 9 in. by 3 in. Calculating the volume of timber in the Petersburg standard, which is the one in general use, gives 165 cub. ft., so that the 120 pieces are equal to a balk, 12 in. by 12 in., 165 ft. long. When buying timbers of other sizes this method of calculating is convenient. Supposing scantlings were bought, 9 in. by 4 in., it will be seen that this section of 36 sq. in. is one-fourth the area of the section of the balk, 12 in. by 12 in. ; therefore, to make the standard, the length would be four times as long as 165, which is 660 ft. A load is 50 cub. ft., so that $3\frac{3}{10}$ loads make a Petersburg standard.

Boarding is generally reckoned by the standard of 100 ft. super., so that the length of boarding required to make 100 sq. ft. varies inversely as its width, that is, the narrower the boarding the greater the length will be to give the standard area. This area is equal to 100 ft. of boarding 1 ft. wide, or if it were 6 in. wide these will be 200 ft. in length. Boarding, however, is generally sold in widths of 7 in., 9 in., and 11 in., which must be brought to the fraction of a foot so as to divide into the area of 100 sq. ft, For instance, 7 in. $= \frac{7}{12}$ ft., 9 in. $= \frac{9}{12}$ ft., 11 in. $= \frac{11}{12}$ ft. $100 \div \frac{7}{12} = 100 \times \frac{12}{7} = 171\frac{3}{7}$ ft., the length of boarding required 7 in. wide.

Mixed timber implies defective deals from the first quality mixed with seconds. Fir timber, sometimes imported as " hand masts," are the longest, soundest, and straightest trees when topped and barked, circumference from 24 in. to 72 in. " Spars and poles " have a circumference less than 24 in. at the base. " Inch masts " are those having a circumference of more than 72 in., and are generally dressed to an octagonal form. " Ends " are less than 8 ft. long. Scaffold and ladder poles are from young trees of larch and spruce, and average 33 ft. long. Rickers are about 22 ft. long and under $2\frac{1}{2}$ in. in diameter at the top end.

Buying Small Quantities.—During the last few years it has become easier to buy small amounts of wood of any sizes required for home use. A list of pieces required can be written out and taken to any of the retail timber dealers, who will saw and plane by machinery to exact sizes required, thus saving the purchaser much hard work. Or alternatively, there are always plenty of small pieces which can be selected for cutting at home as required, and so a great variety of thicknesses and sections are obtainable for a much smaller sum than formerly. Even in planks and boards and strips there is far more variety in size now than there used to be. In a small way, wood is sold by the square (superficial) foot or by the foot run. In the first case its thickness is either stated or the price is based on an inch of thickness, and becomes correspondingly less or more if it is less or more than an inch. This reckoning of 1 ft. square by 1 in. thick is the commonest. When sold by the foot run it is usually narrow and, its section being known, it is charged for at so much per foot of length.

Quality.—Good wood should look bright and have a fresh smell. It should be cut from the heart of a sound tree, be uniform in substance, straight in fibre, and free from large or dead knots. The surface should not be woolly or clog the saw, and it should also have a silky lustre when planed. Sound timber should be sonorous when struck ; a dull, heavy sound denotes decay within. The wood should not be waterlogged, softened, or discoloured by being floated.

Good timber should be free from the following defects :

Cup shakes, which occur between the annual rings in the spring wood, due to the inner portion of the tree shrinking from the outer portion. This often happens in the resinous pine and fir trees, but they are generally very small and not a serious defect.

Heart shakes, splits through the heart of the tree. They are often very small, but sometimes extend right across the tree. They are common with most timbers, but they can be largely prevented if not allowed to lie too long in the log.

Star shakes, splits radially from the centre of the tree, sometimes increasing in width to the outside. If the log is allowed to get into this state the timber is useless for planks, scantlings, etc.

Timber has other defects, primarily due to injury or some abnormal action to the growing tree, the fibres being upset or twisted in their length, etc. The rain may have penetrated a hole or hollow in the bark where a branch has been cut off, or some other cause may have started decay in parts. Even when the general defects are not visible, the experienced eye can detect the inferiority of the timber by the looseness of fibres, especially on the end grain, which can be verified by testing its lightness in weight.

Plywood, Compoboard, etc. — Besides the various natural woods there are more or less artificial products which for some purposes have advantages. Plywood consists of three or more layers of very thin wood glued together with grain crossing, so that it cannot split or shrink or warp, and is as strong in one direction as in another. Another advantage is that it is obtainable in large sheets or squares much wider than ordinary solid wood. It is used in comparatively large pieces such as for partitions, panels, drawer bottoms, and the bodies of most vehicles constructed of wood. It is too thin to be nailed up in box form without reinforcement at the corners (see, for example, the chest described on pp. 338 to 340). Often, therefore, the sheets of plywood fit with their edges in grooves in a substantial framework. Compoboard is an artificial product used for similar purposes.

Varieties of Wood. — The varieties of wood obtainable are more numerous than they used to be, wood now being imported which formerly never left the countries of origin. There used to be woodworkers who prided themselves on being able to tell the name of any kind of wood shown them. This was when the woods used were chiefly English with only a few well-known imported ones, and these men would have had their confidence shaken if they could have seen the hundreds of samples of different colonial woods in the Imperial Institute, many of which look practically alike, although they have different names. There is the further difficulty, also, in identifying a strange wood that different samples of the same wood may vary more from each other than from those of another variety. The long list of woods occupying the following pages has been very carefully prepared, and will be found of use to craftsmen handling or selecting imported woods and also to those readers who may happen to live in the countries of origin. An acknowledgment of the source of the information here given will be found in the " Editor's Preface."

LIST OF TIMBERS

ACACIA (see Locust).

ACAJOU (see Cedar, Cigar-box, and Mahogany).

ACLE. *Pithecolobium acle.* Source, Philippines. Dark brown, moderately hard; but little known in England.

ALDER. *Alnus glutinosa.* Europe, etc. Soft, fine grained. Used for household articles, turnery. Weight, 50-60 lb. per cub. ft.

ALDER, White. *Platylophus trifoliatus.* Cape Colony. Hard, tough, durable.

AMARANTHE (see Purple-heart).

AMBOYNA. *Pterocarpus indicus.* Moluccas, New Guinea, etc. Burrs, in slabs from 2 in. to 8 in. thick, and up to 9 ft. in diameter. Reddish brown to orange. Mottled and curled. Used for fancy work, etc. Weight, 39 lb. per cub. ft.

ANJAN. *Hardwickia binata.* India. Dark red, streaked. Hard, durable, strong. Used for building, cabinet work, etc.

APPLE. *Pyrus malus.* Europe and America. Dark brown, with red tint. Hard, brittle, and warps. Used for ornamental work, tool handles, etc. Weight, 50 lb. per cub. ft. BLACK APPLE

is *Sideroxylon australe*, of Australia; light coloured, veined.

ARBOR VITÆ (see Cedar, White).

ASH. (1) English Ash. *Fraxinus excelsior.* Britain, etc. Light brown, even grained. Hard, tough, but easily steam-bent. Used for handles, turnery, hoops, felloes. Weight, up to 50 lb. per cub. ft. Greatest in diameter, about 1 ft. 6 in. (2) Black or Cabinet Ash. *Fraxinus nigra.* Canada, etc. Dark. Inferior to white ash. " Burls " make valuable veneers. (3) Blue Ash. *Fraxinus quadrangulata.* America. Light coloured, hard, durable. Used for general purposes. (4) White or American Ash. *Fraxinus americana.* Eastern America. Light coloured (varies). Less elastic than English ash. Soft, easily worked. Used for carpentry, agricultural implements, cheap furniture.

BAMBOO. *Bambusa arundinacea*, etc. China, India, etc. Extensively used in countries of origin.

BASSWOOD. *Tilia americana.* America. Light coloured. Soft, durable if kept dry. Easily worked, even grained. In general domestic use. Weight, 28 lb. per cub. ft. Often confused with canary whitewood.

Z

BAY-WOOD (*see* Mahogany, Honduras).

BEECH. (1) European Beech. *Fagus sylvatica.* Temperate Europe. Yellow to reddish (best). Hard, strong and tough. Close grained. Used for handles, lasts, boot-trees, planes, piano wrest-boards, etc. Freshly felled beech may be reddened by steaming. Weight, 41 lb. to 56 lb. per cub. ft., usually 44 lb. (2) Red or American Beech. *Fagus ferruginea.* U.S.A. Inferior to European beech and used for same purposes. Weight, about 40 lb. per cub. ft.

BEEF WOOD. *Lophira alata, Rhopala montana,* etc. Africa, etc. Deep red. Used for furniture. Many Australian species are known as beef wood.

BIRCH. (1) European Birch. *Betula alba.* Temperate Europe. Yellowish or reddish white to light brown. Fairly hard, even grained, easily worked, difficult to split, liable to decay. Used for table legs, sabots, spoons, and many other domestic applications. Weight, 32 to 49 lb. per cub. ft. (2) Yellow, Grey, or Silver Birch. *Betula lutea.* N. America. Used for furniture and small hardware. Burrs used for mallets. (3) American Birch. *Betula lenta,* etc. Canada, etc. When seasoned sapwood is cream-white and heartwood pink to red; takes a satiny polish and exhibits " roll figure." One of the most durable birch woods. Used for furniture, etc. Weight, 38 to 48 lb. per cub. ft. (4) White, Paper or Canoe Birch. *Betula papyrifera.* Curly grain makes good veneers, but weak and perishable. Used chiefly for wood pulp.

BLACKWOOD. There are many woods of this name. (1) African Blackwood. *Dalbergia melanoxylon.* Tropical West Africa. Jet black or brownish-black. Used as substitute for ebony in turn-ing. (2) South African Blackwood. *Royena lucida.* S. Africa. Resembles ebony. Used for wagon building, etc., and suitable for general application. (3) Australian Blackwood. *Acacia melanoxylon.* Australia. Dark brown and well figured, with a ring of white sapwood. Hard, close grained, easily worked. Warps, takes good polish. Used for gun stocks, furniture, piano sounding-boards, and general purposes. (4) Indian Blackwood. *Dalbergia lati-folia.* India. Yellow to dark brownish-purple. Hard, tough, close and cross grained; difficult to work. Used for sleepers, agricultural implements, and in India, furniture. Weight, 46 to 66 lb. per cub. ft.

BLOODWOOD. *Eucalyptus corymbosa.* Australia. Reddish - brown, close grained, strong, durable. Used for rails, etc.

BOG-OAK. Found embedded in Irish bogs. Hard, almost black, close grained, takes high polish. Used for fancy cabinet work, inkstands, etc.

BOX. *Buxus sempervirens.* Europe, etc. Light coloured, yellowish. Hard, difficult to split, most even-grained wood known. Used for turnery, rules, inlays, fancy articles, etc. Bastard or

Australian Box is the name given to various species of Eucalyptus, their woods being of general usefulness.

BRAZIL WOOD. *Casalpina brasiliensis.* Brazil, etc. Dark red, heavy, takes high polish. Used for violin bows, turning, etc., and as a dye wood.

BRIER-ROOT. *Erica scoparia.* S. Europe and E. Africa. Mottled, dark brown, close grained. Used for tobacco pipes.

BUCKEYE. *Æsculus glabra,* etc. Ten-nessee, etc. Soft, white, easily worked. Used for splints, artificial limbs, and general purposes.

BULLET. *Mimusops globosa.* Guiana, etc. Dark red, heavy, strong, takes good polish. Liable to insect attacks.

CALAMANDER. *Diospyros quæsita,* etc. Ceylon. Red, hazel-brown or chocolate, beautifully marked with black stripes. Takes high polish; difficult to work. Now scarce, but occasionally used as veneer.

CAMPHOR-WOOD. *Cinnamomum cam-phora.* China, Japan, etc. Reddish, often prettily marked; coarse grained, easily worked, fragrant, durable, and insect-proof. Used for high-class furni-ture.

CANARY WHITEWOOD or AMERICAN WHITE-WOOD. *Liriodendron tulipifera* and *Magnolia accuminata.* U.S.A. Lemon-yellow to brownish, soft, close and straight grained, takes satiny polish, easily worked. Extensively used for general purposes. Weight, about 26 lb. per cub. ft. Two or three Australian woods are known as canary, but are here described under more distinctive names.

CATALPA. *Catalpa speciosa.* U.S.A. Brown, soft and coarse. Used for general purposes.

CEDAR. A name applied to a variety of woods that are brown, even grained and fragrant. A few out of a score or so are mentioned here. (1) Australian Cedar. *Cedrela australis.* New South Wales. Soft. Used for furniture and small cabinet work. (2) White Cedar. *Cupressus Lawsoniana,* etc. N. America. Hard, strong, durable. Used for boats, flooring, etc. (3) Cedar of Lebanon. *Cedrus Libani.* Asia and Europe. Pleasant odour, obnoxious to insects, brittle. Used extensively in ancient times; now used occasionally for carv-ings, cabinet work, etc. (4) Numidian or Atlas Cedar. *Cedrus atlantica.* N.W. Africa. Used for cabinet-making, etc. (5) Deodar Cedar. *Cedrus Deodara.* N.W. India. Used as a constructional timber. (6) Pencil or Red Cedar. *Juniperus Virginiana.* U.S.A. Rose-red. Formerly extensively used for great variety of purposes, now used exclusively for pencils. (7) Yellow, Canoe, or Western Red Cedar. *Thuya plicata* (otherwise known as *T. gigantia* or *T. Lobbi*). America. Used for shingles, internal fittings, furniture, etc.; the Indians of the North-West used it exclusively for their canoes. (8) Cigar-box Cedar, known also as the

West Indian, Cuba, Havana, Honduras, Jamaica or Mexican Cedar. *Cedrela odorata*. West Indies, etc. Softer than mahogany but somewhat resembling it, bitter, fragrant, peppery smell. Used for the best cigar boxes. Extremely useful. (9) White Cedar. *Cupressus thyoides*, *Thuya occidentalis*, etc. U.S.A. Used for building, fencing, and general purposes.

CHERRY. *Prunus Avium.* Europe. Moderately hard, yellowish brown, fine, even grained, not durable. Used for turnery, inlays, etc. (2) Wild Black, Rum, or American Cherry. *Prunus serotina*. U.S.A. Pink or reddish, moderately hard and durable. Used for furniture, etc. (3) Australian Cherry. *Exocarpus cupressiformis*. Australia. Hard, durable. Used for gun-stocks, axe-handles, spokes, turnery, etc. (4) Perfumed Cherry. *Prunus Mahaleb*. Austria. Red-brown or green-streaked, hard, fragrant. Used for walking-sticks, tobacco pipes.

CHESTNUT. (1) Chestnut or Spanish Chestnut. *Castanea vulgaris.* Europe, etc. Brown, resembling but softer than oak, and without broad pith-rays; coarse grained, fairly durable, takes a good polish, and takes glue well. Used for furniture. (2) American Chestnut. *Castanea dentata.* Eastern U.S.A. Similar in many respects to European chestnut. (3) Moreton Bay Chestnut. *Castanospermum australe.* N.W. Australia. Dark brown and streaked, somewhat resembling walnut. Used for gun-stocks, veneers, furniture, etc.

COCOBOLA. Species of Humiria. British Guiana. Deep orange, with black linear markings, hard, heavy, coarse grained. Used for inlays and turnery.

COCUS. Known also as American, Green, Jamaica or W. Indian Ebony. *Brya Ebenus*. Dark greenish-brown or purplish, fine grained, heavy. Used for flutes, inlays, etc.

COROMANDEL (*see* Calamander).

COTTON-WOOD (*see* Poplar).

COWDI PINE (*see* Kauri).

CUCUMBER (*see* Canary Whitewood).

CYPRESS. *Cupressus sempervirens.* Europe, Asia, etc. Reddish, fine grained, almost indestructible. Used in ancient times for mummy cases, statues, etc.

CYPRESS. Deciduous (known also by many other names). *Taxodium distichum.* Southern U.S.A. Resembles above cypress. Used for a great variety of purposes.

CYPRESS-PINE. *Frenela robusta*, F. *Endlicheri*, etc. Australia. Brown woods, sometimes with pinkish streaks and well figured, camphor-like smell, largely insect-proof, easily worked, takes good polish. Used for general purposes.

DAGAME, or DEGAME LANCEWOOD. *Calycophyllum candidissimum.* Cuba. Yellow, hard, very fine and close grained. Used as lancewood.

DEAL (*see* Pine and Spruce).

DEODAR (*see* Cedar, Deodar).

DOGWOOD. (1) Dogwood, Cornel, Cornelian wood or Boxwood. *Cornus florida*. N. America. Reddish-brown, hard, heavy, fine grained. Used for cogs, mallets, tool handles, etc. (2) Western Dogwood. *Cornus Nuttalli*. N. America. Nature and uses resemble those of dogwood above. (3) European Dogwood. *Cornus sanguinea* and *Rhamnus Frangula*. Europe and Asia. Pinkish, hard, used now chiefly for making gunpowder charcoal.

DOUGLASS FIR or OREGON PINE. *Pseudotsuga Douglasii.* Western North America. Reddish and yellowish white, with darker bands of autumn wood. Weight, about 38 lb. per cub. ft. Wood with 16 to 24 growth rings per inch is "yellow fir," with 12 to 16 rings per inch is "red fir." Former is light, soft, even, straight grained, and not liable to warp. Latter is uneven, weak, and more difficult to work. Both of them used for general purposes.

EBONY. *Diospyros, Maba, Euclea* and any member of *Ebenaceæ* family. India, Ceylon, Africa, Philippines, etc. Dark or black, hard. Used for boxes, inkstands, furniture, etc. Indian Ebony, *Diospyros melanoxylon,* is known as coromandel or "Godavery" ebony, reaches a good size, and sometimes has purple streaks. Ceylon Ebony is *D. Ebenum,* also of good size. There are innumerable other varieties.

ELDER. *Sambucus nigra.* Europe, Asia and America. Large pith; hardness variable. Used for turnery, shuttles, etc.

ELM. (1) English Elm. *Ulmus campestris.* Great Britain. Yellowish sapwood and dark brown heartwood. Hard and extremely durable. Used for general purposes and coffin making. Weight, about 44 lb. per cub. ft. It wears smooth and does not splinter, and is therefore used for chopping blocks, wheel naves, etc. Known as common or cork elm. Elm burrs yield fine veneers. (2) American Elm. Many species, including *Ulmus alata,* or cork-winged elm. Light brown, heavy, fine grained. South - Eastern American States. *U. fulva,* or red, moose, or slippery elm. Darker, coarser and larger than *U. alata.* Used for fencing and boat ribs. North-Eastern States and Canada. *U. americana,* or white or water elm. Large, light brown, coarse, subject to insect attack. Used for boat building and general purposes. Eastern States. *U. racemosa,* or rock or hickory elm. Hard, probably best American elm. Used for general purposes. Central States and Canada. (3) Scotch or Wych Elm. *Ulmus glabra.* Scotland, etc. Lighter coloured, softer and straighter than English. The old linen chests were often made of it. Flexible and tough. Used for boat building, chair making, etc.

FIR (*see* Douglas Fir, Pine, Spruce, etc.).

FUSTIC. Chiefly used as dye-wood, and of two kinds, "young" (*Rhus Cotinus*), and the "old" or large fustic (*Chlorophora tinctoria*). Brazil, etc. Second kind is canary-yellow, light, tough and hard. Used for spokes and bows. Both kinds used for inlays, etc.

GREENHEART. *Nectandra Rodiæi*. S. America, etc. Dark green or brownish, often nearly black at centre; fine and straight grained, hard, tough, durable, but liable to heart-shake. Weight, 60 lb. to 70 lb. per cub. ft. Used for shipbuilding, wharves, bridges, dock gates, etc.

GUM. (1) Black Gum. *Nyssa sylvatica*. Eastern U.S. Whitish, hard and tough; used for hubs and general work. (2) Blue Gum. *Eucalyptus globulus*. Native to Australia and Tasmania, but now growing in S. Africa, California, etc. Straw colour to grey or brown, with darker streaks; hard, heavy, fairly tough, strong and very durable; has a curled and twisted grain. Used for all general purposes. (3) Red Gum, known also as Flooded Gum, Yellow-jacket and Yarrah (not to be confounded with Jarrah). *Eucalyptus rostrata*. Victoria, Australia. Dark red, curly figure, very hard, difficult to work when dry, and takes high polish. Twists in seasoning, very durable and insect-proof. Used for paving, sleepers, house building. (4) Sweet Gum, known in America as Bilsted or Red Gum (not to be confounded with preceding wood). *Liquidambar styraciflua*. E. American States. Cream-white sapwood, reddish-brown, irregular heart, often with dark rings; fairly hard, close grained, tough, takes good polish, warps in drying unless first steamed. Not suited for paving, but used for that purpose under name of "Californian Red Gum." Gum in pores of wood susceptible to atmospheric change.

GURJUN or WOOD-OIL TREE. *Dipterocarpus turbinatus* and *alatus*. Native to India and Burma. Red, moderately hard. Used for general purposes and boat building.

HAWTHORN. *Cratægus Oxyacantha*. Europe, etc. Flesh-coloured, hard, heavy, and small; takes a good polish. Used for turnery, walking-sticks, etc.

HAZEL. *Corylus Avellana*. Europe and Asia. Reddish-white, soft and elastic; takes a good polish, and, being small, is used chiefly for barrel hoops, sticks, etc.

HEMLOCK. (1) Chinese Hemlock. *Tsuga chinensis*, etc. "Tich sha" or "Iron Fir." Used for roofing and general purposes. (2) Western Hemlock. *T. heterophylla*. Larger, heavier and harder, but weaker than Eastern Hemlock.

HEMLOCK SPRUCE, HEMLOCK, or EASTERN HEMLOCK. *Tsuga canadensis*. Northern America. Light reddish and lustreless; light, soft, stiff and brittle; shrinks and warps considerably in seasoning. Holds nails firmly. 3 to 6 ft. in diameter and 100 ft. high.

HICKORY. (1) *Hicoria glabra*, (2) *H. ovata*, (3) *H. alba* and (4) *H. laciniosa*. North America. White sapwood, nut-brown heart. Very heavy; 47 lb. to 52 lb. per cub. ft. Strong, tough, coarse, straight grained. Shrinks and splits in drying. Liable to insect attack. (1) is pig-nut or broom hickory, used for tool handles, etc. (2) is shell-bark or shag-bark, used for spokes. (3) is mocker-nut, having thick shell-bark; weighs less and colour darker than above. (4) is big or thick shell-bark, used for spokes, etc. The hickory woods are greatly used in carriage building, for barrel hoops, screws, etc., and resemble ash in general properties; not suited for building houses and boats.

HOLLY. *Ilex Aquifolium*. Europe and America. Hard and white (old trees liable to be brownish); very fine, close grain and hard. Excellent for turning. Shrinks and warps and becomes spotted in drying. Used for veneers, decorative and fancy work, etc. American holly is *I. opaca*.

HONEYSUCKLE-WOOD. In America, the plane tree, *Platanus occidentalis;* in New Zealand, the rewa-rewa (*see* separate heading); in Australia, various species of *Banksia*. Beautiful figure and take good polish.

HORNBEAM. *Carpinus Betulus*. Europe. Yellowish-white, hard, heavy, close grained and remarkably tough. Used for cogs, mallets, etc.

HORSE-CHESTNUT. *Æsculus Hippocastanum*. Asia, Europe and America. Light, soft, quick-growing. Used for general purposes, but weak and not durable.

HUON-PINE or MACQUARIE-PINE. *Dacrydium Franklinii*. Tasmania. Beautifully marked with dark, wavy lines and small knots. Tough, and the hardest of all pines; durable; scarce.

IRONWOOD. Many woods are so called, some of these being one kind of hickory (*H. minima*), hornbeam, various species of olive, two or three species of *Sideroxylon* (Greek word meaning iron-wood), the marblewood and wattle of Australia, etc.

JACK or ORANGE-WOOD. *Artocarpus integrifolia*. S. Asia, Ceylon, etc. Its second name suggests its colour. Fairly hard, coarse, crooked grain, brittle, and warps badly. Used as dye wood and for general purposes.

JARRAH. *Eucalyptus marginata*. S.W. Australia. Mahogany colour, sometimes mottled and curly grain. Very hard, close grained, smooth working, durable, of large size, difficult to burn; must be seasoned carefully to avoid warping and splitting. Used for a great variety of purposes, including boat building and paving. Probably S.W. Australia's most valuable timber.

JARUL (Bengal). *Lagerstræmia speciosa*, etc. Known by different names in different places. Reddish, large size, hard, heavy, durable. Used for heavy work.

JUNIPER. European junipers are

scarcely of value as timber, because of their small size; but *Juniperus excelsa* (Crimea) grows to 100 ft. high. Indian juniper (*J. macropoda*) is valuable. American juniper is pencil cedar.

KAMASSI, known also as Cape Boxwood, East London Boxwood and Knysna Boxwood. *Gonioma Kamassi.* S. Africa. Small, but hard, tough, heavy and close grained. Used for tools and cabinet work.

KARRI. *Eucalyptus diversicolor.* S.W. Australia. Reddish, slightly wavy or curled, hard and tough. Not so easily worked as jarrah; durable in water; of huge size. Used for general purposes, including paving.

KAURI PINE. *Agathis australis.* North Island, New Zealand. Wide sapwood is resinous; yellowish or brownish heart, straight, close grained, fairly hard, strong; works extremely well and is regarded as one of the best soft woods. Used for a great variety of purposes.

LABURNUM. *Cytisus Laburnum.* Europe. Yellow sapwood and brownish-green heart. Very hard, and used for turnery and inlaying.

LACEWOOD. American plane or buttonwood. *Platanus occidentalis.* Cut radially to show silver grain; honeysuckle wood.

LANCEWOOD. Guiana lancewood, yariyari, is *Duguetia quitarensis.* Yellowish, fine grained and used for fishingrods, carriage-shafts, bows and arrows, etc. Honduras lancewood, yaya, is *Guatteria virgata*, etc., and has much the same properties as the other.

LARCH. There are many varieties. (1) *Larix europœa.* Europe. Straight grained and tough; usually yellowishwhite or reddish-brown. Grows to 100 ft. in height. Used for ladders, scaffold poles, sleepers, etc. (2) *L. leptolepis.* Japan. Harder, heavier and more reddish in colour than the European. (3) *L. dahurica.* Manchuria and Siberia. Similar to the Japanese. (4) *L. Potaninii.* China. (5) *L. sibirica.* Western Siberia. Similar to the European. (6) *L. Griffithii.* Himalayas. Very soft and little used. (7) *L. occidentalis*, known also as Tamarack. Montana, Oregon and British Columbia. Red, heavy and hard. The largest of the many American larches; grows to 250 ft. in height and 4 to 8 ft. diameter. Used for fencing and sleepers. (8) *L. laricina*, known as American black larch. N.E. States. Straight, lighter and harder than European; resembles hard pine. Used largely for poles. There are several other varieties.

LETTERWOOD. *Brosimum Aubletii.* Known also as Leopard-wood. Guiana and Trinidad. A straight-grained, mottled-brown wood, heavy and hard, taking a good polish. The mottling appears in small patches, usually not more than 6 in., hence a difficulty in working larger areas. Used as a veneer, for inlays, and occasionally for walking-sticks.

LIGNUM VITÆ (Wood of Life). Of several varieties; all of the *Guaiacum* family. (1) *Guaiacum officinale.* American tropics, mainly Jamaica. A crossgrained, strong wood, very hard, difficult to split; dark green in colour at the heart. Grows from 20 to 40 ft., with a diameter of 12 in. to 24 in. Weight, from 60 lb. to 80 lb. per cub. ft. Contains about 25 per cent. of gum resin (*guaiacum*), by virtue of which it is often employed in pharmacy. Used for rulers, police truncheons, ships' blocks, rollers and machinery. (2) *G. sanctum.* Florida and the Bahamas. Similar to foregoing, but rarely below 25 ft. in height. (3) *G. arboreum.* Paraguay and Venezuela. Grows to about 70 ft. Brown in colour and not quite so hard and heavy as the other species. Australia and New Zealand produce a wood to which the name is given, but neither is the true specimen. That of New Zealand, the better known, is a species of *Metrosideros (Rata)*, while those of Australia are species of myrtle and acacia.

LINDEN or LIME. *Tilia cordata, T. platyphyllos* or *T. vulgaris.* N.W. Russia, district between Lower Dwina and the Niemen. Yellowish or reddishwhite, soft and close grained; liable to become worm-eaten and perish if not painted or varnished. Weight, 30 lb. per cub. ft. Used largely for carving, toys, small boxes and general fancy work. Resembles American basswood.

LOCUST. (A name often given to the Acacia of Great Britain.) (1) *Robinia pseudacacia.* S.E. United States. Yellowish-brown, with green and red streaks, hard, strong, and very durable. Weight, 46 lb. per cub. ft. Largely used for wheel-spokes, fence stakes and sleepers; shrinks considerably during seasoning. (2) Honey Locust, known as three-thorned acacia. *Gleditschia triacanthos.* U.S.A. A similar wood, lighter in weight. (3) *Hymenæ Courbaril.* Similar, but not true locust. Known also as Courbaril. West Indies. Hard and heavy, close and even grained. Reddish-brown, with darker streaks. Does not warp, and takes a good polish. Used for cabinet work, shipbuilding and engineering.

LOGWOOD. *Hæmatoxylon campechianum.* Central America. Very heavy, hard wood. Deep brownish-red, with sweet smell, something like violets. Imported in the form of logs, which are made into chips, moistened and exposed to the air, when they turn to a beetle-green colour. Used for making ink and dyes, not as a constructional timber.

MAHOGANY. Of several varieties, the names usually denoting their source. (1) Spanish or Cuban Mahogany (West Indian). *Swietenia Mahagoni.* Very heavy and hard; close and straight in grain, and takes a high polish. When newly cut is of a light reddish-brown, but rapidly darkens; has a variety of dark, mottled, dappled, wavy and other markings; very durable and practically non-inflammable. Grows to a huge size, and can be cut from 18 to 35 ft. long and squared to about 11 in. to 24 in. Weight, about 53 lb. per cub. ft. Used in bygone days as a substitute for oak in shipbuilding, and for costly furniture of the Chippendale and Sheraton type. Now used for good furniture (piano cases, dining-tables, etc.), and largely for veneering. (2) *S. macrophylla*, a similar variety from the same district, but lighter and softer. (3) St. Domingo Mahogany, also similar to the true Spanish, but smaller in growth and harder. The foregoing mahoganies are now rare. (4) Other mahoganies vary considerably, though mainly of the *Cedrela* family. Honduras, Tabasco, Panama, and a few others come from Central America. Honduras mahogany, called Baywood in the trade, is rarely figured, often of a brittle nature, and lighter than the Spanish. The logs yielded are from 25 ft. to 40 ft. in length and 12 in. to 24 in. square. Largely used by cabinet makers, mainly as a ground for veneers. (5) Guatemalan Mahogany, similar to and often sold as the Honduras product. (6) The Mexican is of larger growth, often squaring to 4 ft., and softer at the centre. (7) African Mahogany, of many varieties, mainly of the genera *Khaya*, *Trichilia* and *Entandrophræqma*, but related to the *Swietienia*. Tropical Africa, mainly West Coast. Rapidly becoming popular, but difficult to obtain because of the geography of the country. Imported in the form of logs, usually from 15 ft. to 20 ft. long and 20 in. to 30 in. square. Varies considerably in colour, usually from yellow to brown, with dark zones, sometimes a reddish-brown and well figured, the latter being in demand for veneers. Another African mahogany is the *Khaya senegalensis*. Gold Coast and French Ivory Coast. One of the most largely used of the mahoganies, having a cedar-like smell, and of fine quality. (8) East Indian Mahogany. *Soymida febrifuga*. Central and Southern India. Very closely related to the true (Spanish) mahogany, and known also as Coromandel redwood. A heavy, hard, cross-grained, dark blood-red wood, but brittle. Used largely for furniture and carving.

MANCONO. *Xanthostemon verdugonianus*. Philippines. Very hard, of crooked grain, and difficult to split. Of the same weight as and not unlike Lignum Vitæ, and a good substitute for it.

MANGO. *Mangifera indica*. The Tropics, mainly East Indies. Largely used in India for packing-cases and rough work, because of its cheapness. Porous, dull grey to light chocolate colour, holds nails well. When suitably treated it takes a high polish. Used as a veneering ground, for cart wheels, boats, etc.

MANZANITA. *Arctostaphylos pungens*. United States, mainly California. A heavy, fine grained wood of a reddish-purple hue, with lighter streaks. Used in turnery, for walking-sticks and veneering, the tree being a small one.

MAPLE. *Acer*. Of many species. (1) *Acer campestre*, the common, field or hedge maple, the only British species. A reddish-white or light brown wood, tough, hard, heavy and fine grained, with a satin lustre. Some specimens, known as " birdseye," are speckled or eyed on tangential sections, while others have dark pith-flecks. Used for turnery, cabinet work, veneering and charcoal making. (2) *A. platanoides*, Plane or Norway Maple. Europe, mainly Norway. Resembles sycamore. Hard, heavy, tough wood, easily worked; takes a high polish; largely used for certain kinds of work because of its well-marked pith rays. Used in turnery, for gunstocks, musical instruments, and wagon building. (3) *A. macrophyllum*. Oregon or Californian Maple, the name indicating its source. Moderately heavy, close grained, hard and strong, often with wavy grain of the " fiddle-back " pattern. Used largely for furniture, and locally for snow-shoe frames and rough work. (4) *A. barbatum*. Hard, Rock or Sugar Maple, the most useful of the American species. Eastern North America. Close grained, hard, tough, of a pale buff colour and satin-like lustre; takes a fine polish. Highly valued because of its characteristic " birdseye " and other fancy markings, which make it invaluable for veneers and panelling. Used largely as a substitute for oak, for building (frames and floors), and all kinds of interior work and furniture, also for wheel spokes, axles, and for fuel. (5) *A. saccharinum*, the Silver, White or Soft Maple. Softer, lighter in weight, and more red in colour than the Hard or Rock variety. Used for flooring, turnery and cheap furniture work. (6) *A. rubrum*, the Water, Swamp or Red-flowered Maple. Similar to the silver maple in substance; rarely seen in England. Used for turnery and chair making. There are numerous other varieties in America, but of little interest.

MARBLEWOOD, ANDAMAN. Known also as Zebra wood and figured ebony. *Diospyros Kurzii*. Hard, heavy, durable, of a black and grey colour, the colours appearing zebra-like in alternating layers. Used for furniture, handles, and walking-sticks.

MIRABOW. *Intsia bakeri*. Resembles Shoondul or Ipie (*I. bijuga*). Malayan region. Often called ironwood, because of its hardness and durability. Of fine and even grain, heavy, and of a reddish-brown colour, well figured; polishes well, when it closely resembles mahogany. Timbers about 35 ft. long and 18 to 30 in. in diameter. Used for cabinet work, and locally for posts and bridge building.

MOLAVE. *Vitex littoralis* and *V.*

pubescens. Malay Peninsula. Hard, heavy and close grained, colour varying from yellow, reddish-brown and olive-brown; resembling satinwood in figuring. Used for building and general purposes, often as a substitute for teak.
MORA. *Dimorphandra excelsa.* Guiana and Trinidad. Red or chestnut-brown in colour, and often with curled figures. Heavy, hard, tough and durable; straight grained, but subject to star shake. Used as a mahogany substitute and for ships' beams, from about 18 to 30 ft. long and about 12 to 20 in. square.
MULBERRY. (1) *Morus alba.* China and Europe. Yellowish-brown heartwood which becomes more reddish. Heavy, tough, flexible and lustrous. Used for furniture, veneers and inlay. (2) *M. indica.* India and Japan. Used for tea boxes and furniture. (3) *M. rubra.* United States. Similar to the European.
MYALL. (1) *Acacia pendula.* Often called violet wood, because of its pleasing fragrance. Australia. A species of wattle. Heavy, hard, cross grained; of a rich dark brown colour and nicely marked; polishes well, but loses its smell. Used largely for pipes, because of its resemblance to brier-root, and for general fancy work. (2) *A. homalophylla.* A similar Australian wood; has a raspberry-like smell. (3) *A. falcata,* known as the "bastard myall." Used mainly for whip stocks.
MYROBALAN. *Terminalia belerica.* India, Burma and Ceylon, where it is known as "behara," "thitsein," and "bula" respectively. Yellowish-grey, minus heart. Hard, quickly worm-eaten; often improved by saturating with water. Used for packing-cases and general work.
MYRTLE. Of several varieties. (1) *Backhousia myrtifolia.* N.E. Australia. Widely known as lancewood, also as grey or native myrtle. Hard, tough, durable and cross grained; light yellow in colour, with walnut-brown markings. (2) *Nothofagus Cunninghamii.* Evergreen beech, usually called myrtle. Tasmania. Australian myrtle is used mainly for turnery, tool handles, mallets, etc.
NAN-MU. *Machilus nanmu* and other species of the same genera, also *Lindera.* China. Close grained and durable; easily worked. Brownish and green in colour, with a fragrant smell. Usually met with in planks about 8 ft. long and 14 in. in width. Used mainly for building.
NETTLE-TREE. *Celtis australis.* Shores of Mediterranean and parts of Asia. Resembles satinwood when cut obliquely. Heavy, hard, strong and elastic. Yellowish-grey in colour, with dark streaks; takes a high polish. Used largely by the ancient Greeks for carving statues. Used mainly for turnery, tool handles, and occasionally for musical instruments and furniture.
OAK. Of the genus *Quercus,* of which

there are many varieties. Generally yellowish-brown to a decided brown in colour, with clearly marked pith rays. Heavy and hard, and of exceptional strength in proportion to weight; subject to star- and cup-shakes, and slight shrinking and warping while seasoning, but not afterwards. Splits readily, has a smooth surface, and polishes well. (1) British Oaks. *Q. Robur.* Europe and Asia, nearly as far as Arctic Circle. Of many varieties, three being the most important : (*a*) Pedunculate. *Q. Robur pedunculata.* Distinguished by long stalks to its acorns; the earliest of oaks, quick growing and dense; lighter in colour than other oaks, hence the French name for it, "chêne blanc." (*b*) Sessile-flowered. *Q. Robur sessiliflora.* Distinguished by long stalks to leaves, not to acorns; later than the former oak (*a*); greater lengths of clear stem and more red in colour; sometimes called chestnut oak, and by the French "chêne rouge." (*c*) Durmast. *Q. Robur intermedia* or *Q. R. pubescens.* Distinguished by short stalks to both leaves and acorns. Dark brown in colour. Practically impossible to tell one from the other when cut up and of British origin. (2) European Oaks vary more than the British. French Oak. Mainly *Pedunculata.* Normandy and Brittany. Like British variety, but usually of smaller growth; splits and shrinks less. Dantzig Oak. Mainly *Sessiliflora.* Poland, via the Vistula to Dantzig; also Odessa. Straight and clean in grain and minus knots; brown colour and often nicely figured, and called wainscot oak; met with in logs and planks. One of the most pliable of oaks, and often used for bending (after steaming); not so strong as the British variety. Riga Oak. Western Russia. Practically the same as the Dantzig variety. Shipped only in wainscot logs. Used largely for furniture and veneers. Adriatic or Serbian Oak is of a like nature. (3) American Oaks are numerous, but only the following are worthy of mention: White. *Q. alba.* E. United States and S.E. Canada. Heavy, tough, hard and close grained; reddish in colour. Quebec. Trade name for a serviceable oak of large growth; in great demand for building and general purposes; easily bent, free from knots, and often nicely figured. Met with in logs 25 to 50 ft. long and 11 to 28 in. square. Inferior to best European oaks. Burr Oak. *Q. macrocarpa.* Rich brown colour and slightly porous. Post Oak. *Q. minor.* Chestnut or Rock Oak, *Q. prinus,* and Basket or Cow Oak, *Q. michauxii,* are similar to the white oak; all heavy, hard, durable and of a rich brown colour. Red Oak. *Q. rubra.* Known also as Canadian Red or Black Oak. Heavy, hard and strong, light or reddish-brown in colour, with indistinct pith rays. Used largely for panelling and furniture. Other American oaks of a like character are the Texas Red or Spotted Oak, *Q. texana;* Scarlet Oak,

Q. coccinea; Willow Oak, *Q. Phellos;* Pin Oak, *Q. palustris;* and the Water or Punk Oak, *Q. aquatica.* There are numerous other specimens, China alone producing about sixty; others from Australia, Japan, India and Africa.

OLIVE. *Olea europœa.* Shores of Mediterranean. Light yellowish-brown colour; similar to boxwood in texture. Heavy, close and fine grained, without distinguishable pith rays, but having pleasing wavy dark lines and mottlings of irregular pattern; takes a good polish. Used mainly in turnery for fancy articles. The East Indian Olive, *O. cuspidata,* and many other species are similar to *europœa.*

ORANGE. *Citrus Aurantium.* Most of the tropical and sub-tropical countries. Small, light yellow, heavy, hard and close grained. Used for cabinet work, walking-sticks and general purposes. Black Orange and Congo Oak, used for some walking-sticks, is really a broom, *Cytisus scofarius,* from Algeria.

ORANGE, OSAGE. Known also as Bowwood or Bois-d'arc. *Toxylon pomiferum.* Arkansas and Texas. Of a brownish hue when cut transversely, but yellowish longitudinally; turns grey very gradually. Hard, flexible and durable in contact with soil. Used in bygone days for bows, hence the name above given. Used locally for sleepers, posts and general purposes.

ORHAM WOOD. A species of elm. Canada. Soft, coarse grained and not very durable. Largely imported for cheap furniture making.

PADOUK. Of many species, mainly *Pterocarpus macrocarpus, P. indicus, P. dalbergioides* and *P. echinatus.* India, China, Philippines, Fiji, Andaman Islands, etc., hence known also as Andaman redwood, Burmese rosewood, Philippine mahogany, etc. Colour varies, usually dark red or brick red, with very dark, almost black streaks, often prettily figured; fades a little on exposure to weather. Hard, heavier than mahogany, with a fragrant smell; durable and takes a fine polish. Some trees yield 60 ft. lengths. Takes about two years to season. Used for various purposes, according to country, but mainly for furniture, parquet floors, shop counters. Roots, often very handsomely figured, used for carved fancy articles. African padouk, *Pterocarpus crinaceous* and *P. angolensis,* is really rosewood, which *see.*

PAI'CHA. *Euonymus hamiltonianus.* China. Soft, close, fine grained wood, of a yellowish hue. Used for carving and largely for wooden printing type of large size.

PALISANDER. Of various species, some of the genus *Machœrium,* another *Dalbergia nigra.* Brazil. Known to some as Brazilian rosewood, because of a faint rose-like smell. Chocolate brown with black markings. Very heavy, hard and brittle. Best marked specimens come from the Bahia district in logs cut semi-circular and unsound

in centre. Other varieties, always in the form of complete logs, are more sound but not well figured. Used for cabinet work, piano cases and veneers.

PEAR. (1) *Pyrus communis.* Temperate climes. Light pinkish-brown. Fairly heavy, hard, close grained; no true heart; cuts in any direction and takes a high polish; very durable if kept dry. Used for cabinet work, turnery, textile printing blocks, and many other purposes. (2) *P. sinensis.* China. Similar to the British. Used for wood engraving and fancy work, the Chinese treating it with a yellow stain to imitate boxwood.

PERSIMMON, sometimes called Date Plum. *Diospyros virginiana.* United States. Broad creamy-white sapwood, sometimes as many as sixty rings, and brownish-black heart. Strong, tough and close grained; resembles hickory in substance, but finer in grain; takes a good polish. Grows tall, but rarely more than 24 in. in diameter. Weight, about 50 lb. per cub. ft. Used for cart shafts, plane stocks, shoemakers' lasts and general purposes.

PINE. *Pinus* strictly, but of many varieties and allied genera; known also as deal and fir. Pines generally are very stiff and strong in proportion to lightness, quick growing, durable, of good texture for working, and extensively used. There are hard and soft pines, the former being heavier and darker in colour—yellow to deep orange or brown—and showing a sharp contrast between sapwood and heart; soft pines range in colour from white to light red, and are lighter in weight. (1) Pine, or Northern Pine. *Pinus sylvestris.* N. Europe. The only British species is known as Scots Fir. Varies in quality according to climate; imported under such names as red deal, yellow deal, red wood or firs, according to place of origin—" Swedish," " Norway," " Baltic," etc. Used mainly for building, paving blocks, planks and general purposes. (2) Aleppo Pine. *P. halepensis.* Mediterranean, and introduced more recently into Australia. Fine grained, yellowish-white. Supposed to be the wood used for building Solomon's temple. Used locally for poles and general purposes, and for obtaining turpentine. (3) Austrian Pine. *P. nigra,* var. *austriaca.* Coarse grained, often very knotty. Used for building and for oil, etc. (4) Black Pine. *Prumnopitys spicata* and *Podocarpus ferruginea,* both of yew family, and called by the Maoris Matai and Miro respectively. New Zealand. Matai is of even grain, and smooth, strong, durable and easily worked; cinnamon-brown colour; grows to 80 ft. in height and 2 to 4 ft. in diameter. Weight, 35 to 49 lb. per cub. ft. Used by builders and millwrights and for general purposes. Miro is heavier, reddish-brown in colour, hard, and takes a good polish. Planes easily and often well figured. Used for cabinet work, piles, etc. Another "black pine" is *P. Jeffreyi*, of California and Oregon. Similar to and often confused with Western Yellow Pine, *P. ponderosa*. (*See also* Japanese Black Pine.) (5) Blue or Bhotan Pine. *P. excelsa*. Himalayas. Light red, close grained, compact, moderately hard, very resinous and durable. Used for planking and sleepers, and usually creosoted. (6) Canadian Red Pine. *P. resinosa*. Known to the trade as American red pine, in Nova Scotia as yellow pine, and in Canada as Norway pine. Hard, tough, elastic, very resinous and fine grained; colour ranging from straw yellow to pale reddish-tan, and with a silky lustre. Weight, 30 to 44 lb. per cub. ft.; reaches 100 ft. in height and 2 to 4 ft. in diameter. Used for flooring, boat building, etc., but rarely exported. (7) Carolina (Short Leaf) Pine. *P. echinata*. Eastern United States. Known at its source as yellow pine, in England as New York or Carolina pine. Coarse grained, hard, strong, durable, and easy to work; not unlike pitch or long-leaf pine; colour varies from golden ochre to yellow. Weight, 34 to 38 lb. per cub. ft. Used largely for house building, flooring and general purposes. (8) Celery-topped Pine or Tanekaka. *Phyllocladus trichomanoides*. New Zealand. Heavy, close and straight in grain, very strong and durable; yellowish-white in colour. Yields timbers 18 to 70 ft. long, squaring from 10 to 16 in. Used for building, sleepers, piles and shipbuilding. The Celery-topped or Adventure Bay Pine, *P. rhomboidalis*, of Tasmania, is similar, though smaller and more slender. (9) Cembra Pine. *P. Cembra*. Known also as Swiss stone pine or Siberian cedar. Kamtschatka to Urals, Alps and Carpathians. Resembles yellow or Weymouth pine. Cultivated mainly for its edible nuts. (10) Chile Pine. *Araucaria imbricata*. South America. Known in English gardens as the Monkey Puzzle. Takes a fine polish; yellowish in colour and often prettily veined. Reaches 100 ft. in height and 7 ft. in diameter. Used largely for masts. (11) Cluster Pine. *P. Pinaster*. Mediterranean. Coarse grained, very resinous and soft; of a reddish colour. Used for packing-cases, cheap carpentry, and in Welsh mines; also as raw material for lamp-black, charcoal and turpentine. (12) Corsican Pine. *P. nigra*, var. *Poiretiana*. Often called larch pine. Very resinous and durable; creamy-white when cut, but turns brownish-yellow. Almost of the same quality as Northern Pine. (13) Cuban Pine. *P. leterophylla*. Often classed with pitch pine, but coarser in grain and with wider sapwood. (14) Flexible Pine. *P. flexilis*. Eastern Rockies. Resembles sugar pine. Used for general purposes locally. (15) Fox Tail Pine. *P. Balfouriana*. California. Soft. Used for mine timbers. (16) Huon Pine. *Dacrydium Franklinii*.

(*See* Huon.) (17) Japanese Black Pine. *P. Thunbergii*. Western China (where it is known as Sung Shu), Japan (known there as O Matsu or Kuromatsu), and Corea. Close grained and resinous. Used for building and general purposes. (18) Japanese Red Pine, *P. densiflora*, known to the Japanese as Aka-Matson, is of similar quality. (19) Loblolly Pine. *P. Tœda*. Southern United States. Coarser in grain than long-leaf pine, often mistaken for it, but less durable, softer, and wider in annual rings; grows rapidly, easily felled and worked; very rich in resin and often used as fuel; sometimes called frankincense or torch pine, and yellow pine in some American markets. (20) Manchurian Pine. *P. manchurica*. Corea and Northern China. About 80 feet in height and 4 ft. in diameter. Reddish-white. Used for house and boat building, coffin making and general purposes. (21) Moreton Bay Pine. *A. cunninghami*. Queensland and New Guinea. Straight grained, hard and strong, works easily; light coloured, and, on account of small knots, often nicely figured; yields spars 80 to 100 ft. in length. Weight, 30 to 33 lb. per cub. ft. The principal soft pine in N.E. Australia, but inferior to European and American species. Used for general purposes. (22) New Zealand Red Pine. (*See* Rimu.) (23) New Zealand White Pine. *D. excelsum* and *D. ferrugineum*. Related to yew family; known to Maoris as Kahikatea. Resembles American white pine. White, even grain, soft and straight, but not durable; easily worked. Weight, 27 to 35 lb. per cub. ft. Yields timber 20 to 60 ft. long, squaring from 12 to 30 in. Used largely for building, furniture and general purposes; in Australasia for packing-cases and butter boxes. (24) Norfolk Island Pine. *Araucaria excelsa*. Excellent timber. Now scarce. (25) Oregon Pine. (*See* Douglas Fir.) (26) Pitch Pine. *P. palustris*. Known also as the Long-leaf, Southern or Georgia pine, and by names of ports (Darien, Savannah, etc.). Alabama, Georgia and South Carolina. The most valuable of American varieties. Imported in logs (20 to 45 ft. long and 11 to 18 in. square) and planks (3 to 5 in. thick and 10 to 15 in. wide). Tough, clean and straight in grain, varies in texture, takes a good polish, but often has cup and heart shakes, and difficult to work. Reddish in colour, the deeper red specimens—often called red pine—being considered the most durable. Closely resembles Northern pine, but heavier and more resinous. Used for sleepers, wainscoting, church and school fittings and general purposes, also for turpentine production. When nicely marked it is used for cabinet work. (27) Stone or Umbrella Pine. *P. Pinea*. Mediterranean. Small, light and moderately resinous; white in colour. (*See also*

Umbrella Pine.) (28) Sugar Pine. *P. Lambertiana.* California and Oregon. White and fragrant, light, soft, straight but coarse grained and easily worked. Often 300 ft. in height and 20 ft. diameter. Often called Western white pine. Used for carpentry and general purposes. (29) Umbrella Pine. *Sciadopitys verticillata.* Japan, where known as *Kôya-maki.* Belongs to cypress family. Straight grained and strong; nearly white to yellowish or reddish in colour. (*See also* Stone Pine.) (30) Western Yellow or Bull Pine. *P. ponderosa.* Western United States. Varies considerably in quality, but generally hard and brittle. Of great growth, often 300 ft. high and 15 ft. in diameter. Used for building, sleepers, mine timbers and general purposes. (31) Western White Pine. *P. monticola.* Pacific States, particularly Idaho. Similar to the sugar pine. Used for general purposes. (32) Westland or Silver Pine. *D. Westlandicum.* Called by Maoris Manao. Heavy, hard, tough and durable. Used for sleepers and piles. (33) Yellow or Weymouth Pine (English names); Pumpkin or White Pine (American names). *P. Strobus.* United States generally. Most important of the soft pines. Lord Weymouth planted it in England. Reaches 180 ft. in height and 6 to 8 ft. in diameter; often 100 ft. to lowest branch. Soft and compact, easily worked, almost free from resin, and takes a good polish; liable to shakes and not durable in contact with soil. Colour of heartwood varies from yellow to brown, always with a pinkish tinge. Weight, 20 to 30 lb. per cub. ft. Used for building and general purposes. Rapidly disappearing from some States because of its wide use.

PLANE. (1) *Platanus orientalis.* Levant. Resembles beech, but softer; apt to split and warp and become worm-eaten. Little used. (2) American or Western Plane. *P. occidentalis.* with Californian *P. racemosa.* Of better quality; known also as buttonwood; when cut radially as lacewood or honeysuckle wood. Sometimes wrongly called sycamore. Used for turnery, cabinet work, cooperage and general purposes.

PLUM. *Prunus domestica.* Heavy, hard, not very durable; heartwood deep brownish-red, not unlike mahogany. Used in turnery.

POON. Of many varieties. (Genus *Calophyllum.*) Poon is an Indian trade name of a wood known to Malays as Bintangor. *C. inophyllum.* Madagascar to Fiji. Known in Philippines as Pola Maria, the Penaga of Telugu, and Borneo mahogany. Reddish-brown, with a wavy figure. Fairly hard, coarse grained, strong and durable. Weight, 35 to 63 lb. per cub. ft. Grows to 80 ft. in height and 5 ft. in diameter. Used for sleepers in India; suitable for general purposes. *C. tomentosum* grows in Ceylon and

Queensland chiefly, and is similar to above. Used for tea chests and spars.

POPLAR. *Populus.* Of several varieties. Known in America as cottonwoods; vary but little. Soft and light in quality; hold nails well and without splitting; easily worked or turned. Colours vary, white, pale grey, yellowish or brown. Used for general carpentry, packing cases, etc., also for paper pulp and cellulose. (1) White Poplar. *P. alba.* Japan. Used for junk building, matches and carving. (2) Grey Poplar *P. canescens.* Europe. Superior to the white. (3) Balsam Poplar. *P. balsamifera* and *P. grandidentata.* America. (4) Black Italian, Canadian or Carolina Poplar. *P. deltoidea.* Exported to England as American cottonwood.

PORCUPINE WOOD. *Cocos nucifera.* The outside base stem of coco-nut palm, so named because of quill-like growths thereon. Very hard, strong and durable. Used for spear handles, walking-sticks, and as veneer for fancy articles.

PURPLE-HEART. Known also as Violet wood, Amaranthe or Paoroxa. Genera *Peltogyne* and *Copaifera.* Various species, of equal value and confused commercially. Brazil, Guiana and Trinidad. Very heavy, hard, strong, durable; easily worked; takes fine polish. Purple or brown in colour when cut; darkens rapidly. Yields timber 20 to 120 ft. long, squaring to 18 to 30 in. Used for furniture, building and general purposes, including fretwork.

QUASSIA. *Picræna excelsa.* Tropical America. Fine grained, light and soft; yellowish in colour. Used medicinally as a bitter tonic. Yields logs 6 to 10 ft. long and 6 to 10 in. in diameter. Used sometimes for drinking cups, the water taking its bitterness and tonic properties from the wood.

QUEEN-WOOD. (1) *Daviesia arborea.* N.E. Australia. Ornamental leguminous wood, close grained, hard, and takes a fine polish; has pinkish streaks. (2) *Piptadenia rigida.* Brazil. Similar, but reddish or dark brown, with black streaks. Known also as Angico. Both used for turnery.

RASPBERRY-JAM WOOD. *Acacia acuminata.* West Australia. Close grained and hard. Reddish-brown and smells of raspberry jam. Weight, 54 to 78 lb. per cub. ft. Used for furniture.

REDWOOD. A common name for many varieties, including Dantzig fir, *Pinus sylvestris;* Californian Redwood, *Sequoia sempervirens,* now best known as Sequoia (which *see*); Andaman Redwood or Padouk, *Pterocarpus;* Coromandel Redwood or Indian Redwood (East India Mahogany), *Soymida febrifuga.* (1) *Erythroxylon areolatum.* Jamaica. A handsome mahogany-like wood, known also as Ironwood, because of its hardness. (2) *Ochna arborea,* known also as Cape Plane, and to the Boers as Roodhout. Cape Colony. Hard, strong and durable.

Used for furniture and wagons. (3) *Eucalyptus piperita.* Known also as Blackbutt, Messmate, Peppermint and White Stringybark. One of the heaviest of the redwoods. E. Australia. Difficult to work, subject to shakes; durable. Used for rough building, posts, etc.

REWA-REWA. *Rymandra excelsa.* Known also as Honeysuckle wood. New Zealand. Large and heavy; will not stand exposure; becomes foxy if not properly seasoned. On a radial section a lustrous golden yellow with reddish-brown silver grain. Used for cabinet work and inlaying.

RIMU. *Dacrydium cupressinum.* Known also as New Zealand red Pine. New Zealand, very common. Straight and uniform in grain, strong, hard, not durable in contact with soil; works well and takes good polish. Chestnut-brown in centre, lighter at edges, with yellow or red streaks. Weight, 33 to 45 lb. per cub. ft. Yields timbers 20 to 80 ft. in length, squaring to 10 to 30 in. Resembles satin walnut, and the most promising of colonial woods. Used for furniture and general purposes.

ROBLE. Spanish for oak, but name carelessly used, mainly for Chilian beech, *Northofagus obliqua,* and Argentinian, *N. betuloides,* the latter a fine-grained, straight, handsome wood, not unlike American oak. Used largely for panels.

ROSEWOOD. Name given, often loosely, to many varieties of wood, best known of which is (1) the Brazilian *Dalbergia nigra;* three others of the same district are *Machærium scleroxylon, M. firmum,* and *M. legale,* all known as Jacaranda. Ruddy brown or dark chestnut colour, with black resinous streaks; smells of rose-water and takes a fine polish; often hollow or with heart shake. Weight, 53 to 65 lb. per cub. ft. Shipped in semi-circular logs 10 to 20 ft. long and about 14 in. diameter. Used for good cabinet work, piano cases, veneer, etc. Other varieties are a species of *Dalbergia* from Honduras and Nicaragua; *D. latifolia* and *D. sissoides,* East Indian or Bombay (*see* Blackwood). Rosewood of Burmese origin is Padouk. (2) African or Gambia Rosewood. *Pterocarpus erinaceus.* Known also as African Padouk. Hard, often with spongy centre; reddish-brown in colour, but quickly fades. Grows to 70 ft. in height and 5 ft. in diameter. (3) Seychelles Rosewood. *Thespesia populnea.* Hard and strong; dark red or claret colour, smells of roses, and resembles mahogany. Used for furniture, carriage building, gunstocks and general purposes. (4) Borneo Rosewood. Various species of genera *Melanorrhea* and *Swintonia.* Very hard and heavy, and having a poisonous gum; red with purple streaks. Used for furniture. (5) Australian rosewoods include some of the pencil cedars, myalls and bastard sandalwoods. *Synoum glandulosum,* of the north-east districts, is

the best known. Firm, easily worked, and takes a fine polish; deep red in colour and rose-scented. Used for furniture. (6) Canary Rosewood. Underground base and stem of several varieties of *Convolvulus,* smelling strongly of roses. Used for the preparation of perfume.

SABICU. *Lysiloma Sabicu.* West Indies. Hard, strong, close grained, elastic and durable; dark chestnut-brown, often with a curled figure; not unlike rosewood; takes a high polish. Little used.

SAFFRON-WOOD. *Elæodendron croceum.* South Africa. Heavy, hard, tough; reddish-brown in colour and grained like walnut. Used for furniture and general purposes.

SAL. *Shorea robusta.* Northern India. Brown, with dark lines. Coarse grained, hard, elastic and most durable; compares favourably with teak in strength; has an aromatic resin which protects it from termites. Used largely in India for bridges and general purposes.

SANDALWOOD. *Santalum album.* Southern India and Malaysia. Yellowish-brown, close grained, moderately hard, heavy and fragrant. Weight, 56 to 71 lb. per cub. ft. Used for carved and inlaid fancy articles, walking-sticks, etc.; also distilled for oil. There are several other varieties.

SANDERS, RED. (1) *Pterocarpus santalinus.* Tropical Asia. Fine grained, heavy and hard; takes a good polish; deep orange-red in colour, with lighter zones, turning to claret or black. Used for furniture, turnery, and for dye manufacture. (2) *Adenanthera pavonina,* sometimes called red sanders, also coral-wood, condori-wood and redwood. Close grained, very heavy, hard and durable; coral-red heartwood with darker stripes; may turn purple or dark brown on exposure. Used for furniture, building and dyes.

SAPPAN-WOOD. *Cæsalpinia Sappan.* East Indies. Known also as Brazilwood and Redwood. Fine grained, heavy, and polishes well. Orange-yellow or brownish-red in colour. Used chiefly for dyes, sometimes for cabinet work and inlaying.

SASSAFRAS. *Sassafras officinale.* North America. Light, soft, weak, but durable; dull orange-brown heartwood, with slight smell. Same name is common in many countries for certain species of *Lauraceæ* and *Monimiaceæ.*

SATIN WALNUT. (*See* Gum, Sweet.)

SATINÉ. (*See* Washaba.)

SATINWOOD. Of several varieties. (1) *Chloroxylon Swietenia.* India and Ceylon. Coarse grained, hard, heavy and durable; takes a good polish and with satin-like lustre; of light orange colour, often with beautiful curl. Used for general carpentry and furniture, the figured varieties being exported for cabinet work, coach panels, etc. (2) West Indian Satinwood. *Fagara flava.* Similar but unrelated. Bermuda,

Jamaica, etc. Known also as yellow-wood and by its Spanish name, Aceitillo. Close and even in grain, resembling box; of a yellow colour; smell resembles coco-nut oil. Used for the best furniture and cabinet work, brush backs, etc. (3) Australian Satin-wood, *Zanthoxylum brachyacanthum.* Known also as Thorny Yellow-wood, and similar to the above. (4) African Satinwood, genus *Cassia.* Southern Nigeria. Close grained, firm, and of a canary-yellow colour. Used for cabinet work.

SEQUOIA. *Sequoia sempervirens.* Cali-fornia. Known locally as Redwood. A valuable soft wood, close but short grained, light, brittle, not strong, but very durable in contact with soil. Maroon to terra-cotta or a deep brownish-red in colour, darkening on exposure. Wood practically the same as the Deciduous Cypress, *Taxodium distichum,* of the Mississippi. Grows to 350 ft. in height and often to 20 ft. in diameter. Used in America for car-pentry, furniture, sleepers, poles and general purposes; in England for cabinet drawers and blind wood.

SERVICE. *Sorbus domestica.* Central Europe. Very hard, fine grained, similar to pear; fawn coloured and often prettily figured. Used for cabinet work, turnery, etc., also engraving.

SHOONDUL. *Intsia bijuga.* Tropics from Madagascar to Sandwich Islands. Known by many different names. Valu-able, close grained, very hard, termite-proof and durable; dark reddish-brown in colour. Used locally for many pur-poses; in England for furniture.

SILK-COTTON. *Ceiba pentandra.* Tropics. Soft, white, and very light; rarely more than 18 lb. per cub. ft. Of large growth. Used for canoes, rafts, pack-ing-cases, toys, etc.

SIRIS, PINK. *Albizzia Julibrissin.* Tropics, Eastern Hemisphere. Legu-minous; of moderate size. Very heavy; takes a good polish; dark brown to black in colour and prettily mottled. Used for furniture, house and boat building.

SISSOO. *Dalbergia Sissoo.* Northern India. Close and even in grain, heavy, hard, strong and elastic; grows rapidly; seasons well without warping and splitting; durable. Colour varies from light brown to dark reddish-brown, with darker longitudinal lines; at times as beautiful as rosewoods. Met with in logs 10 to 15 ft. long. Used for furniture when nicely marked, also for general purposes; unrivalled for wagon wheels.

SNAKEWOOD. Crooked-grained Letter-wood, *Brosimum Aubletti.* Used for bellies of bows.

SNEEZEWOOD. *Pteroxylon utile.* South Africa. Very hard, extremely durable, and irregular in growth; little affected by moisture. Handsome, with a grain not unlike satinwood, and takes a fine polish; termite and teredo proof. Very

inflammable because of its gum-resin, dust of which causes sneezing. Weight, 65 to 67½ lb. per cub ft.; grows to 20 to 30 ft. high and 2 to 4 ft. in diameter. Used for carpentry and engineering work, furniture, agricul-tural implements and general purposes.

SPINDLE-TREE. *Euonymus europæus.* Great Britain. A hedgerow shrub. Fine grained, hard and tough, yellowish-white. Used for shoe pegs, spindles, etc. Poisonous.

SPRUCE. Many species, of the genus *Picea.* All closely similar, but varying in durability. Straight and even in grain, light, slightly resinous, fairly lustrous surface, easily worked, elastic and resonant, hence its value for musical instruments. Of whitish colour, with no distinct heart. The chief varieties are: (1) Common Spruce. *P. excelsa.* Europe, chiefly Norway. Young specimens are known as Christ-mas trees. Known as Baltic white-wood, white deal, Swiss pine or violin wood. Grows to 125 to 180 ft. in height and 3 to 6 ft. in diameter; Norway logs from 30 to 60 ft. long and 6 to 8 in. in diameter, imported with bark on. Weight, 28 to 32 lb. per cub. ft. Often has many small knots, and of a yellowish or reddish tinge. Quality varies according to locality, that from Petrograd being considered the best; White Sea product also very good. Used for general purposes. (2) Hima-layan Spruce. *P. Morinda.* Not durable. (3) Hōndo Spruce. *P. Hondo-ensis.* Japan. Fine grained, soft, light and glossy; yellowish-red in colour. (4) Red Spruce. *P. rubra.* S.E. Canada and E. United States. A valuable timber; reaches 80 to 100 ft. in height and 3 ft. diameter. Even grained, light, soft and fairly strong; pale buff in colour. Used mainly for general car-pentry. (5) Black Spruce. *P. nigra* or *P. mariana.* North America. Widely known as American, Canadian, New Brunswick, St. John's, or Double Spruce, or Spruce Deals. Best quality comes from St. John's and Quebec. Soft, light, elastic and compact; light buff or ruddy in colour, with a satin-like lustre. Weight, 28½ lb. per cub. ft. Very like Baltic spruce. Used for general purposes and pulp. (6) White Spruce. *P. alba.* Known also as single spruce. North America. Like black spruce in many respects, but inferior and yellowish-buff in colour; not strong. Used for inferior carpentry and paper pulp. (7) Sitka Spruce. *P. sitchensis.* North America, Alaska to California. Straight grained, soft, compact and strong; yellowish-brown tinged with red. Used for general purposes.

STINKWOOD. *Ocotea bullata.* South Africa. Known also as Cape Walnut or Cape Laurelwood. Very tough, almost as strong as teak, and durable; golden-brown in colour, often with walnut-like mottling, and occasionally

Varieties of Wood

iridescent. Used for furniture when well marked, and for general purposes.

STRINGY BARK. Various species of gum trees. (1) *Eucalyptus macrorrhyncha.* Known also as Ironbark. S.E. Australia and Tasmania. Close grained, hard, strong and durable; light brown in colour, tinged with deeper red-brown, and often figured with yellow and brown stripes; takes a good polish. Grows from 50 to 100 ft. in height and 2 to 4 ft. in diameter. Used for flooring, general carpentry and furniture. (2) *E. obliqua.* Known also as Tasmanian oak, and in Australia as Messmate. Tasmania. Rather coarse grain, straight, tough, very strong and durable; liable to shakes and gum veins. Colour varies from light to dark brown, with wavy figure near base.

SUMACH, STAGHORN, or VIRGINIAN. (1) *Rhus typhina.* Canada and N.E. United States. Soft, light and lustrous, of handsome appearance and fragrant; varies in colour from citron green to greenish gold-ochre, with darker zones. Used for inlaying and dyes. (2) Venetian Sumach, *R. cotinus.* Mediterranean, mainly Greece. Known also as young or Zante Fustic. Used as dye-wood.

SUNDRI. *Heritiera fomes.* India to Borneo. Brown; toughest of Indian woods, very hard, elastic, strong and durable. Yields timber 15 ft. long and 12 in. in diameter. Weight, 50 to 58 lb. per cub. ft. Used mainly for wheel spokes.

SYCAMORE. A British tree. *Acer pseudo-platanus,* but originally *Ficus Sykomorus,* the fig-mulberry of the Levant. Fine grained, tough, compact, easily worked and takes a good polish; requires careful seasoning, because of shrinkage. White in colour, but becomes yellowish or brown with age. Has a good fiddle mottle when cut radially, and in demand for violins. Grows to 60 ft. in height and 3 ft. in diameter. Weight, when properly seasoned, 29 lb. per cub. ft. Used for calico printing and washing-machine rollers, panels, bread platters, etc. Known as Plane in Scotland; in New England, Plane, *Platanus occidentalis,* is called Sycamore.

TALLOW-WOOD. *Eucalyptus microcorys.* E. Australia. Strong and durable, greasy when fresh cut, liable to shakes and often hollow; colour varies from yellow to yellowish-brown. Largely used for paving locally, also for ballroom floors, girders, etc., and by wheelwrights.

TAMARACK. (*See* Larch.)

TAMARIND. *Tamarindus indica.* E. and W. Indies. Large, heavy, very hard and difficult to work, durable, insect-proof, but often hollow. Yellowish-white, with irregular heart of purplish-brown blotches, resembling ebony or tulip-wood. Weight, 80 lb. per cub. ft. Used for turnery, mallets, pounders and mills.

TEAK. (1) *Tectona grandis,* and of the Verbena family. India. Varies in quality according to place of origin. Moderately hard, clean, straight and even in grain; often has heart-shake. Durable, and never changes in any climate when properly seasoned. Colour varies from light straw to brownish-red, darkening on exposure; fragrant when fresh cut, resembling rosewood. Some varieties from the Deccan district are beautifully marked, while those from Malabar are heavier, darker and stronger, but of smaller growth. Commonly grows to about 100 ft. in height and 8 ft. in diameter, logs from 23 to 50 ft. long, squaring from 10 to 30 in. Green timber heavier than water, hence custom of killing trees three years before felling, so as to lighten them. When seasoned smells like old shoe-leather. Teak is now cultivated under scientific principles. Used locally for bridge building, sleepers, etc.; in England for railway wagons, deck planks, backing armour plates and many other purposes. (2) Bastard Teak. *Pterocarpus Marsupium.* The Indian "Biji" and Cingalese "Gammala," one of the many timbers to which the name of teak is wrongly given. Heavy, hard and durable; takes a fine polish; heartwood yellowish-brown, with dark stripes. Expensive to work. Used for furniture, window frames, sleepers, etc.

TEWART. *Eucalyptus gomphocephala.* West Australia. Very strong and tough, hard, and twisted in grain; difficult to work. Used for dock gates, capstans, piles, etc.

THINGAN. *Hopea odorata.* India to Borneo. Yellowish, heavy and hard, easily worked and insect-proof; durable as teak. Used for building and sleepers.

TOTARA, or NEW ZEALAND YEW. *Podocarpus Totara.* New Zealand. Deep red. Fine and even in grain, fairly hard, straight and close; strong, teredo-proof, and very durable; does not warp or twist, and easily worked; the most valuable timber in the Dominion. Grows usually to 70 ft., but often to 120 ft. in height, and 6 to 12 ft. in diameter. Yields timber 20 ft., 45 ft., or longer, squaring 10 to 22 in. Weight, 28 to 37 lb. per cub. ft. Used for paving-blocks, sleepers, poles, etc.

TRUMPET-TREE *Cecropia peltata* and *C. palmata.* Jamaica, Brazil and Guiana respectively. Small, light and resonant.

TULIP-WOOD. *Physocalymma scaberrinum.* Brazil. Rose colour, nicely striped. Used for inlay and fancy turnery. Other tulip-woods, so-called, are *Harpullia pendula* and *Owenia venosa.* Queensland. Similar to the Brazilian. Close grained, hard, heavy, and takes a good polish. Yellow and black in colour.

UMZIMBIT. *Millettia Kaffra.* South Africa. Hard; heartwood dark reddish-brown, with yellowish-white, durable sapwood. Used for walking-sticks.

VIOLET-WOOD. The Myall of Australia and the Purple-heart of American Tropics. Former has violet-like fragrance. (*See* Myall.)

WALNUT. (1) *Juglans regia*. Europe. Fine and close in grain, rarely splits, durable. Heartwood usually dark brown, sometimes beautifully watered; takes a good polish; durable when kept dry. English-grown wood is pale, rather coarse, poorly figured, and often perishable; inferior to French. (2) Black Sea Walnut. Austria, Serbia, etc., of better quality; in waney logs 6 to 9 ft. long, squaring 10 to 18 in. (3) Italian Walnut; the best quality; in planks 10 to 16 in. wide and 4 to 9 in. thick. Average weight of all kinds, when dry, 46 to 47 lb. per cub. ft. Used largely for gun stocks and for many other purposes, according to quality. (4) American Walnut. *J. nigra*. Often called Black Walnut. United States. Larger than *J. regia*. Darker and more uniform in colour, dull, but more durable. Imported logs from 10 to 21 ft. long, squaring 15 to 50 in.; also planks and boards. Used for cabinet work, shop-fitting, veneering, gun stocks, etc. Now more popular than the European variety. (5) Grey or White Walnut. *J. cinerea*. Another American walnut, known locally as Butternut. Light and durable, but rarely exported. There are numerous other varieties.

WALNUT, SATIN. (*See* Gum, Sweet.)

WASHABA, or WASHIBA. *Ferolia guianensis*. Guiana. Red to red-brown, with yellow markings. Hard, solid, tough, elastic, takes fine polish. Used for cabinet work, fishing-rods, etc.

WATTLE. Australian *Acacia*, of many varieties. (1) *A. binervata*, sometimes called black wattle, also hickory. N.E. Australia. Used for axe handles and various purposes. (2) *A. mollissima* (called black wattle and sometimes silver wattle). S.E. Australia. Used mainly for cask-staves. (*See also* Myall.)

WHITEWOOD. (*See* Canary Whitewood and Spruce.)

WILLOW. Various species, genus *Salix*. (1) Crack, or Open-bark Willow. *S. fragilis*. America and Europe. Light, tough and elastic; salmon-coloured. Grows from 50 to 90 ft. in height, 4 to 7 ft. in diameter. Used for cricket bats. (2) White or Close-bark Willow. *S. alba*. N.W. India, N. Africa, Europe, etc. Smooth grained, soft, does not splinter, very durable, shrinks one-sixth in drying; heartwood has brownish tinge. Grows to size of *S. fragilis*. Weight, 24 to 35 lb. per cub. ft. Used for many purposes, mainly cricket bats.

YELLOW-WOOD. A name applied to many woods, but properly to the South African *Podocarpus*, *P. Thunbergii* and *P. elongata*. Pale yellow, close grained, soft, easily worked; liable to split and warp. Very tall, and from 2 to 5 ft. in diameter. Weight, 30 to 45 lb. per cub. ft. Used for building, furniture, flooring, etc.

YENDAIK, or YENDIKE. *Dalbergia cultrata*. Burma. Straight-grown, hard, tough, elastic and durable; full of shakes; does not crack or alter. Black in colour, with purple or light streaks. Weight, 64 lb. per cub. ft. Used for spokes, tool handles, carving, etc.

YEW. *Taxus baccata*. Great Britain, India. Reddish-brown, non-resinous, close grained, hard, tough, flexible, elastic, insect-proof, and most durable, especially in contact with soil. Resembles mahogany. Weight, 40 to 57 lb. per cub. ft. Used for chair-making, walking-sticks, turnery, etc. Known as German ebony when stained black. Japanese Yew, *T. cuspidata*, is used for furniture and pencils.

ZEBRA-WOOD. Of many varieties, all striped and streaked. (1) *Connarus guianensis*, known as Hyawaballi. British Guiana. Reddish-brown, heavy, hard, takes a good polish. (2) *Centrolobium robustum*, known as Araríba. Rio de Janeiro. A large leguminous wood. (3) *Guettarda speciosa*, a sea-coast teak, known as Ron-ron (Honduras) and Bua-bua (Fiji). Light reddish-yellow; resembles box. (4) *Diospyros Kurzii*, known as figured ebony or Andaman marblewood; grey and black streaks. Andaman Isles. (5) *Taxotrophis ilicifolia*, known as Cuiuscuius. Philippines. Greenish dark brown and almost black streaks, also scattered spots; of the mulberry family.

INDEX

399